ALSO BY ELENA BONNER

Alone Together

Mothers and Daughters

MOTHERS AND DAUGHTERS

ELENA BONNER

Translated by Antonina W. Bouis

 Alfred A. Knopf · New York · 1992

Copyright © 1992 by Efrem Yankelevich
Introduction copyright © 1992 by Antonina W. Bouis
All rights reserved under International
and Pan-American Copyright Conventions.
Published in the United States by
Alfred A. Knopf, Inc., New York, and
simultaneously in Canada by Random House
of Canada Limited, Toronto. Distributed
by Random House, Inc., New York.
Originally published in Russian as *Dochki—Materi* by
Chekhov Publishing Corporation, New York, in 1991.
Copyright © 1991 by Chekhov Publishing Corporation.

Library of Congress Cataloging-in-Publication Data
Bonner, Elena. [Dochki-materi. English]
Mothers and daughters / by Elena Bonner:
translated by Antonina W. Bouis.—1st ed.
p. cm.
"A Borzoi book"—T.p. verso.
ISBN 0-394-58761-8
1. Bonner, Elena, 1923–   . 2. Dissenters—
Soviet Union—Biography. 3. Women—Soviet Union—
Biography. I. Title.
DK275.B66A3   1991
947.084′092—dc20
[B]   91-19720 CIP

Manufactured in the United States of America

FIRST AMERICAN EDITION

List of Illustrations

Elka Dolenko, October 1937

Regina Etinger shortly before she died, 1982

The ninth grade of School No. 14, Leningrad, 1938–39

Tatyana Bonner with her grandchildren Natasha Bonner and Igor Alikhanov, 1938 or 1939

Natasha Bonner, Elena's cousin, after her evacuation from Leningrad under siege, 1944

Raisa Bonner, with her daughter Tanya, 1954

Seva Bagritsky, 1937

Seva Bagritsky, 1938

Igor Alikhanov, April 1938

Elena Bonner, 1940

Elena Bonner, 1940

Officers and noncoms of military-medical train No. 122, 1942

Seva Bagritsky, October 1941

Ruth Bonner with her son, Igor Alikhanov, February 1946

Elena Bonner, 1950

Tatyana Bonner, 1916

Ruth Bonner, with her great-granddaughter Sasha (Alexandra), summer 1984

Elena Bonner with her first grandson, Motya (Matvei), March 1974

Translator's Introduction

The woman the world came to know as Andrei Sakharov's courageous partner in the struggle for human rights in the Soviet Union arrived in that world as the child of fervent Communists. Born in 1923, six years after the Revolution, Elena Bonner grew up with the Soviet state. The regime's experiments in public education were first tried out on Lusia, as she was known, and her classmates. The curriculum changed from year to year, as did the number of years of compulsory education, and even the location of her school.

A sense of uncertainty and instability was present in her home, too. Her parents wanted to create a new world, and her mother, Ruth, had very strong ideas about family life. Ruth Bonner rejected all such "petit bourgeois" appurtenances as matching dishes and flatware, Christmas trees, and, most painfully for her daughter, hugs and kisses. For much of Elena's childhood, Ruth was away doing Party work. Her Armenian husband, Elena's stepfather, Gevork Alikhanov, was a high-placed executive in the Comintern, the Communist International. The family enjoyed the benefits and privileges of his rank, and were, in fact, part of the new Soviet elite. They lived in special housing set up for Comintern families (a former hotel in Moscow) with, among others, Tito and La Pasionaria. They had access to dachas (vacation homes) and special shops. But Lusia's parents were for the most part too busy to take advantage of these privileges, and too busy, even, to take care of their children. Lusia and her younger brother, Igor, affectionately called Egorka, were brought up by housekeepers and nannies supervised by Ruth's mother, Tanya.

Tanya, or Batanya, had been part of the prerevolutionary bourgeoisie and had nothing but scorn for the new order. As the strongest presence in Lusia's childhood, her grandmother

Batanya was a powerful counterweight to Soviet "reality." She introduced Lusia to great (and officially shunned) literature, to the theater and music (with the tickets that were Party perks but that Elena's parents had no time to use), and to the very outlook and values that were then being forcibly eradicated by the Communists.

Through the eyes of a privileged child, we see the great experiment from the inside: the ever-changing educational system attempting to mold the New Man, the communal approach to life even at the top, and internationally renowned Communists dropping by for tea or a quick chess game. As Elena approaches adolescence (meanwhile surviving several almost fatal illnesses), she begins to question and doubt. Confused by the general acceptance of the mass arrests of Stalin's purges, she watches family friends vanish one by one. Gradually, even her parents become anxious as their Comintern residence hotel begins to turn into a kind of ghost town. The book ends in 1937, the most horrible year of the Stalin purges, with all the men in Elena's life—father, uncles, grandfather, friends—gone, swallowed up in the maw of the Great Terror. Her mother was arrested a few days after her father.

This book portrays a turbulent and chaotic era in Soviet history. Bonner's perceptions of the world around her are neatly captured, too: the growing child was caught up in the clash between the beliefs of her devoutly Communist parents and the strongly opposing views of Batanya and her friends. Bonner spent her childhood trying to get love and attention from her remote mother, who had in her turn a troubled relationship with her mother. Batanya openly despised Ruth's ideals and friends. Ruth merely disregarded Elena's.

As a child, Elena was stubborn and determined—traits that remain part of her character today. Another of her best-known characteristics was and is honesty. And she demands as much honesty of herself as she does of others.

She writes about her childhood from the child's point of view. Small things, a favorite toy pitcher, crossing a scary bridge, play an enormous part in the child's life. Tantrums and jealousies, hates and loves, are related frankly. Bonner captures the beauty and confusion of her sexual awakening and of her first love. Even though *Mothers and Daughters* covers only her first fourteen years, there are flashforwards to Bonner's life in the army, the birth of her children, and her life with Sakharov. But most of all, this is a book about her mother and her grandmother. Three generations of strong women, each representative of a different Russia: prerevolutionary, Communist, and dissident—and each living according to her ideals and loving her family in her own way.

Antonina W. Bouis

Prologue

My mother died and created an emptiness so awful I thought my heart would burst. I kept wanting to talk to her, to explain, to ask, to remember. Suddenly, I realized that I missed my past life. That prompted me to take up a sheet of paper, white as snow, on the day of Mama's funeral. The day of her death, the cemetery, the wake.

I began writing a letter to my children. What I knew of Mama's family, what I had heard, what I remembered. At first remembering was difficult. It was like making my way to the road through a felled forest. There were names of people and places I could not recall. They surfaced at night, almost in my sleep. When I woke up, I made a discovery—the memory has to be awakened. Writing grew easier then. I had been handed a ball of string. I took one end and pulled. The string kept coming and coming.

Sitting down at the typewriter, I never knew where I would be led. That was my second discovery—reminiscence is not knowing what lies ahead. It is inextricably tied to every day I have lived, to my "today" and, if I have one, my "tomorrow."

And now the manuscript lies before me. Thick. It has its own life, as any manuscript to which a writer has put a period. I fear the reader will find it hard following me.

I had not planned to write this book. I had not even known that there would be a book.

If you ask me, "Did this happen?" I will reply, "No."

If you ask me, "Is this true?" I will say, "Of course."

Mothers and Daughters

1

I go over Mama's last days, afraid to forget anything. I feel I didn't tell you everything, that I overlooked something important. But what?

On Wednesday, December 23, 1987, Mama got up in the morning, as usual around ten. Andrei had already left. (I don't remember what he had to do that morning.) Mama had coffee and a piece of a bun with honey. Then she went to the bathroom and I heard her coughing very badly. I went in: she was sitting on a stool and told me that her heart was acting up. I brought her some nitroglycerine. She took a deep breath and a few minutes later was able to come to the kitchen with my help. She said she had no pain but her heart seemed to be stopping. I made her lie down on the couch in the kitchen, but she didn't feel comfortable in that position. She sat up again, and I propped her up with cushions. Her pulse was weak and uneven. Her lips and nails were blue and her hands were cold. I filled all our hot-water bottles and put some at her feet, on a footstool, and by her hands. I gave her some heart medicine and said that I thought I should call emergency. She gave a weak, guilty smile and asked, "Think so?"

The emergency crew arrived about twenty minutes later. By then Mama had drunk a few sips of very strong coffee, and she was lying on the kitchen couch again. Her lips and nails were no longer deep blue, but their color was still not normal. She was clearly better by the time the doctor arrived, but her blood pressure was low. She was given a shot of Korglukon and something else, to raise her blood pressure—I think it was Mezaton. The doctor heard wheezing in her lungs, but when I told him she had been taking Erythromycin for the last three days, he did not prescribe anything else.

The minute Mama felt ill, the fear in my heart crystallized into a single thought: *I won't be able to pull her out of it this time, I won't.* As the doctor was leaving, my friend Belka dropped by. We had arranged the day before for Belka to go to the hospital to start checking Mama in for yet another stay. I confided my fears to her. Mama seemed to be better after the doctor left and so I moved her to her own room, where she took a nap.

Another friend, Galya, and her dog, Pele, came, and Belka returned from the clinic. We had lunch and Mama ate a bit, too, though not in the kitchen. She wanted to, but I wouldn't let her. And then we watched TV—a movie everyone had been waiting for, *Big Worlds,* a condensed history of the country with an attempt to discuss things not mentioned before: collectivization, the famine in the Ukraine, the purges of 1937, and a list of military commanders and the statistics on how many of them had been repressed by the regime. We brought the TV into her room so Mama could watch with us. And as usual, whenever her thoughts returned to that time (or something returned her to them), she grew agitated. She began speaking excitedly to Galya. I asked Belka to go for some oxygen—I wanted to have some on hand just in case. Andrei came back. We had an ordinary evening. Mama felt pretty much as usual, but I decided to sleep in her room.

She slept well, very quietly, a good night's sleep. On Thursday morning she breakfasted in the kitchen, but spent most of the day lying down. The local visiting physician came to see her. She found that the wheezing had diminished but prescribed another antibiotic besides Erythromycin as well as a heart medication. Mama played records—Mozart's Fortieth and once again, for the umpteenth time, Tarkovsky's poetry. She had no particular desire to come to the kitchen during the day, but she sat in an armchair when she listened to the music. Toward evening my friend Masha came, just when Mama was eating in bed. And then another friend, Lena, dropped by. I set the table and asked Mama whether she wanted tea with lemon or milk. She was talking with Masha, and replied that she had no intention of having tea in bed.

Mama was coming to the kitchen and, though Masha tried to help, she put on her robe by herself and joined us.

It was the day after the Academy elections, and Andrei recounted everything that had happened at the general meeting, while we stormily expressed our reactions. Mama too. And she smoked, though I noticed that while she lit two cigarettes, she gave up on each after only two or three drags. At eleven I asked Masha and Lena to leave because Andrei and I had something to type up. Mama got ready for bed herself. I put a mustard plaster on her, and Andrei and I got to work in the kitchen. When I came in later, Mama was lying there with the covers off and without the plaster. I began scolding her and she scolded back almost cheerfully. I turned out her light and went back to the kitchen. Andrei was looking for his glasses, saying that Masha had taken them away by mistake, and I chided him and said he was always losing things himself. About fifteen minutes later I again looked in on Mama. She wasn't asleep. When I asked her how she was feeling, she replied, "You go sleep in your own room. I feel fine. What's Andrei looking for now?"

"He insists that Masha swiped his glasses."

"He just stuck them away somewhere."

I went back to the kitchen but looked in on her in another ten minutes. She was still awake. I asked if she wanted some Valokordin or Zunoktin. She said she was drifting off. I bent over to fix her blanket, which was drooping off the bed, and kissed her. She said, "Why are you tucking me in all the time? I'm not a baby, you know." There was a hint of a smile in her voice.

And so that day passed. And yesterday's fear had not stirred in me. Nothing made me sense that these were the last words Mama would ever say to me, that this was to be Mama's last night. When I came in a half-hour later, she was sleeping quietly on her right side and her breathing was soft and even. I instantly fell into a quiet sleep myself. I got up twice in the night to check on her. She was asleep.

In the morning Andrei came up from our downstairs apartment around ten. Mama had not yet awakened, and I had coffee in the kitchen. She was still not awake when I looked in twenty minutes later. That didn't worry me either, since she had gotten to sleep late. I made some oatmeal for her and came back to the bedroom, raised the curtains, turned to her, and said, "Mama, get up, it's eleven o'clock." She opened her eyes (or did I just imagine it?) and lowered her lids immediately. I took her hand. It was warm but lifeless, no resistance to my movement. The other hand was the same. And her legs. But her pulse was steady, without jumps and with good pressure. I took her head in my hands and I felt some resistance, some life in her neck. I ran to Andrei in the kitchen and said that Mama must have had a major stroke that paralyzed her on both sides. He called for an ambulance. The doctor arrived fairly quickly and confirmed what I had said. She offered to take Mama to the hospital.

"What for? Can you help her?"

"No, but I must make the offer."

"No, let her stay home."

They gave her an injection, I don't remember of what. There's little I remember about that day at all, except for Mama. Another doctor came, from Mama's clinic, who insisted on hospitalization and kept saying, "What do you need with someone this sick at home, why deal with this at home, there's nothing that can be done anyway."

Talking with her was unpleasant and difficult. I was afraid I'd lose my temper and so Andrei dealt with her. He told her that Mama had lived with us and would do so to the very end. She lay quietly, her head turned slightly to the window, and then she smiled. I called Andrei. He stood next to me and looked at her. What was Mama seeing, what was she feeling? Whom was she greeting with this radiant, light smile? As I studied her face, I thought that she had finally forgotten all the grim and unbearably difficult things that had been her lot. Perhaps she had returned to her childhood. And she no longer experienced that tragic life, but perhaps another one instead that sounded like Mozart's Fortieth Symphony, which she had played just the night before. The smile gradually left her face and for the hours remaining to her it was calm, quiet, at peace. As if to say, I've done everything and now I can rest.

That evening a doctor from the Academy came. He said it was now a question of her heart and she could last anywhere from several hours to several days. My cousin Zorya came, and we gave Mama honey water—I spoon-fed her while Zorya held her chin. Then I lay down next to Mama, with my head on her pillow (she had a whole mountain of them). I said that I would spend the night that way, and I patted her hand. I thought that Mama's hand trembled when I touched it. Did Mama hear me, could she sense my presence? Around ten sweat broke out on her forehead—tiny, tiny shining beads. Zorya wiped them off. Mama's face was still calm and her breathing even—no signs of the slightest pain or suffering. And suddenly Mama opened her eyes. They looked right into mine. And she saw me. And she shut her eyes. And then there were two or three sharp, gasping breaths. And nothing more!

All the words I ever read about an easy death could be repeated here. They would all apply. And it would all be wrong. Probably every death, like every life, is unique. I have been with dying people many times. (They say, "One has seen death," but that's incorrect, because you don't see the death of anyone, even a stranger. You experience it and in those instants he is no longer a stranger.) But never before had death been so removed from suffering, so calm and so peaceful.

Mama was always making sarcastic comments about me as a doctor, but at the same time she was absolutely convinced that I could always help her and always spare her suffering. Nonetheless, I was afraid that a time would come when she would suffer and I would be unable to do anything but be with her. Providence spared her from suffering. And spared me the torment of being useless. Mama was the first person in my family to die in my sight and in my arms. Where and how did my father die? Or how did my first love, Seva, die in the village Myasnoi Bor? Or my grandmother Batanya in the siege of Leningrad? Or my brother Egorka in distant Bombay?

. . .

Mama had ceased to exist but she was still here, in her room, on her bed; her hands were warm, and her hair smelled of her, of Mama. Then the people who were to take her away arrived. They said they needed a sheet and asked us to leave the room. When we came back, there was a stretcher on the floor by the bed and on it a small white bundle. I suddenly realized how small Mama had become. That bundle! And only a thin sheet! My question burst out, "May I give you a blanket?" One of them looked at me strangely and said, "Not necessary." Andrei wanted to go with them. "Not necessary" again. For some reason we were afraid of those men. We were bewildered and confused. They quickly picked up the stretcher—the burden was light—and went down the stairs.

After Zorya left, we started calling the other side of the earth to find my children, Tanya and Alyosha. Earlier that day our friend Ed Kline had phoned from New York, and I told him what had happened to Mama in the night. But I hadn't thought the end would be so near and I had asked him not to spoil the children's holiday vacation. Now we reached Ed again, and soon Alyosha called. What a Christmas! Later someone told me that saints die at Christmas. I don't know. Maybe.

Mama's soul had flown away. The body was left and we had to bury it. The children flew in to Moscow. Their faces were black, eyes sunken. In the morning the coffin arrived. Mama's face was still peaceful but her hair looked strange, not like her at all. There were many flowers and the air was filled with the scent of earth and greenery. All our friends and all the family. Mama would have liked it. The coffin stood open. And I kept thinking that she was cold.

At the cemetery the fir trees were covered in white and the snow fell softly, gently. It didn't even seem cold there. Andrei said quietly, "You loved me and I loved you." I was stunned—it was the first time he had ever used the familiar "you" to my mother. Tanya began reading, "Blessed is he who visited this earth in its fateful moments . . ." Alyosha kept adjusting something on

Mama. Then . . . then . . . A hill of greenery and flowers. And the snow, falling.

Mamochka! At home everyone was so good and so calm. I kept thinking what you said about not liking Jewish funerals because everyone scattered from the cemetery and was no longer with the person they had seen off. You would have been happy, because everyone was together and in your house. When Egorka was buried, I remember you said to me at the cemetery, "If it's possible for it to be good at a cemetery, this is the place." And I kept thinking that if you could have seen your own funeral, you would have also said, "If it's possible to have a good funeral, then mine is the one."

2

That which man does not notice
Days of evil portents
As his mother gradually ages

Sei-Senagon (966–1017)

Forty days passed, during which time traditionally the possessions of the deceased are not touched. I entered Mama's room, and it was as if I were seeing it for the first time. Some furniture. A bed. A table that Galya had brought when we were preparing the room for Mama's return from America. A chest from Yuri Fyodorov, who was sentenced to fifteen years. Above it a mirror, a gift from Sara Yulyevna. Customs wouldn't let it through when she was going to America. Two small clothing cupboards that Tanya and I purchased with my fee for a book I put together. A Singer sewing machine. In order to buy it, when Mama came back from the camps, I sold my only war trophy, a Leica camera. And in the corner by the window a secretaire, which had belonged to Efrem, Tanya's husband. Its shelves held books that were considered Mama's property, and not family books. And in the lower drawers there were papers, photographs, and letters. You could almost call them an archive. Oh, it's not a great inheritance my mother left. It's sad and a bit funny. And it makes me want to cry.

I opened Mama's dress cupboard. The almost intangible, endlessly familiar smell. Alive. She had worn that blouse so recently. Another—her favorite, so old, almost the same age as Tanya. And the knitted dress that Belka had hemmed for her. (I remembered being hurt that Mama hadn't asked me to do it.) I would give away the clothing—sweaters, robes, underwear. I sat down on the floor by the secretaire. But as soon as I took out the photographs and letters, I understood that I was not up to reading and going through Mama's papers. The time had not yet come. And suddenly I understood I had not been prepared for Mama leaving so soon. I had expected her to be with us a long time. With Andrei and me.

And then I fell acutely ill. I had awakened in a healthy state, but by two in the afternoon, I felt I was dying. My heart either slowed down or hammered uncontrollably. I couldn't stand up. Or even sit. Then I had chills. A fever of 104 degrees Fahrenheit. An unbearable pain in my leg. It was red and swollen from the ankle to the hip. I couldn't move it or touch it. An infection. A few days later I felt better, but the course of the disease lasted two weeks.

I lay ill in Mama's room, and that brought me closer to her somehow. It was cozy being almost in her place. And for the first time since she died I dreamed about her. She was sitting at the table in her red sweater over a very dressy white blouse, just the way she had been right before her illness. I was across the table from her, and we were holding hands. Or rather, I was holding her left hand in mine and kissing her. This had never happened in my life; we simply would never have imagined or permitted ourselves such behavior—after all, our relationship had never made that possible. And lately, in the last months, I had often wanted to show some physical expression of my love for her, but that "Forbidden" sign was always there. I was afraid of scaring her, afraid that my actions would make her wary, worry that things were bad and that I was concerned for her health. And so I behaved like a stone block. But in the dream it was so easy—to kiss her hand, to weep—it was all permissible. And the strange thing is that in the morning after that dream, I felt the radiance of having been with her.

The memories began with that dream. Mama and Papa, Grandmother, their family. I remembered that I knew little about my mother's family and even less about her father's family. I knew little, and my children knew almost nothing. I wanted to tell them at least what I remembered. I ended up with a strange letter—a family tree. Crooked. A lot about my mother's mother's family, and almost nothing about her father's family, and just blanks on my father's side.

It was a boring letter. Now that I know this manuscript has become a book, I don't think reading all of it is necessary. But I can't discard it, because this book began with it. In 1990.

THE LETTER

I want to write to you so much, my dear ones, but my heart is so heavy and mute that it is very hard. Maybe partly because I have not quite recovered from my illness. But more because Andrei and I can't get used to the emptiness in the house, to the fact that Mama is not in the room where I am sitting now. In the morning I come in and immediately my eyes go to the place where her bed used to be. And then I tell myself—don't look there. Don't. Do something useful. Best of all, something that involves Mama. Maybe this letter is just that?

I remember my maternal great-grandmother very well. Her maiden name was Samsonovich. Her name was Elena Lazarevna, but we children called her Baba Elya. She was short, plump, but not fat. I remember her as being neatly dressed in dark clothing, with a warm shawl over her shoulders. Her smooth hair was pulled back into a knot. She had cataracts, and could see almost nothing. When someone came into the room, she asked, "Who is it?" She would travel from Irkutsk, where she lived with one of her daughters, to stay with us for a few days and then go to

Leningrad to be with another daughter. When she visited us, it seemed that the life of the house revolved about her. It was always, "Grandmother needs to be bathed today," or "Grandmother's having company today," or "We're having pike-perch for lunch today, so we have to get some whitefish for Grandmother."

When she was being bathed, my little brother, Egorka, once asked to be let into the bathroom so that he could see the tail. "What tail?" my mother demanded. He explained, "I was descended from you, you came from Batanya [our grandmother], and she came from Baba Elya, and so Baba Elya must have been descended from the apes."

In those days Egorka and I were not particularly concerned with the presence or affairs of the adults and lived our own very noisy lives, filling our rooms (we each had our own in those days) and the whole apartment, spacious for the times, with innumerable guests. When Baba Elya was there, we were quieter and did not invite our friends over. Maybe we were embarrassed by her extreme age, or maybe the presence of a person who seemed so old to us constrained us. How old could she have been? I think no more than eighty.

Then we would see her off to the train station. I remember taking carriages, and in later years, a car, which was quite an event in those days. The last time she came to visit was in 1937. She died soon after.

What do I know about my great-grandmother? She had been married twice. Her first husband was Matvei Rubinshtein. I have a vague recollection of someone saying that he had been a cantor in a synagogue and a very gifted musician. I remember his looks (from his picture) very well. The large painting (the size of half my desk) depicted a young man, elegantly dressed, with beautiful hair. He had an oval face, nicely shaped, with light eyes and a small nose. No sidelocks or anything else identifiably Jewish. A calm face, with a sense of inner dignity, and somehow transnational, I suppose. In all the photographs of my maternal grandmother Batanya I see a resemblance to him not only in facial features but in character.

Baba Elya had four children by her first husband: Tatyana (my grandmother), Sofia, Moisey, and Alexander. I give the names they used after the revolution, but I know that Alexander, when his birth was registered at the synagogue, was called Isaiah. Moisey is a Jewish name of course, but I don't know if there were other names for Tatyana and Sofia.

My grandmother Tatyana Matveyevna Bonner (née Rubinshtein, 1879–1942) was the eldest child of Great-grandmother Elena Lazarevna by her first marriage. A few snatches of conversation from her brothers gave me the impression that she did not get along with her stepfather. I know that Moisey (Mosya), her brother, had got into a fight defending her against him and left the house for good. He was then in his last year at the Gymnasium and took a job as a tutor in some merchant's house in order to finish school.

At seventeen Grandmother married a twenty-year-old nephew of her stepfather, Grigorii Rafailovich Bonner. Uncle Mosya said that "Grisha was a man, hot, bold, and irrational" and that he was "madly in love." Batanya (my grandmother) married him to get out of her stepfather's house. Uncle Mosya seemed to disapprove of the marriage, even though he always treated his older sister with profound respect and even awe. I always noticed the same attitude toward her from all our relatives.

A year later, in 1898, Grandmother had her first child, Matvei, a son. It was a difficult birth and she had puerperal fever afterward. Everyone expected her to die. Since she could not nurse the baby, the newborn was taken to Irkutsk, to my great-grandmother Baba Elya, who had just given birth to her youngest daughter, Aunt Lyuba. She nursed her daughter and her grandson at the same time. There is a photograph of my grandmother with very short hair, almost like a boy. That was after the fever. In 1900 she had a daughter, Ruf, my mother. And in 1902, a second daughter, Anna (Anya). Grandmother told me that she had wanted to call her Yudif. But her husband's uncle, who had gone to the synagogue to register her, forgot the name and agreed to the rabbi's suggestion.

When they got married, my grandfather was a partner in his

uncle's company. They purchased large herds of cattle in Manchuria and eastern Mongolia and brought them to Russia for sale. Judging from what Grandmother told me, this was a risky business, not only because there was the danger of losing money but physical danger as well, since Grandfather, as the youngest partner, accompanied the cattle herders in the difficult and sometimes dangerous climatic conditions of Eastern Siberia. In 1902 or 1903 Grandfather formed his own company and the family moved from Cheremkhovo to Chita, in Siberia. At first things went well. For one expedition in 1905 he took out a big loan and bought a bigger herd than usual. Most of the cattle were lost in a horrible storm. A few days after coming home, Grandfather shot himself. My mother saw it by accident. She had been playing on the balcony that ran around the outside of the house and just happened to peek into her father's study at that moment. Mama said that it was one of the most horrible memories of her life.

Grandmother was left with three children and no money. She went to work for the Samsonovich brothers (Baba Elya's family), who had a trading company. Later she learned accounting on her own and began moving up in her job. Then she worked for the famous merchant Vtorov, the owner of a gold mine. Having the absolute trust of her employers, in the last two years before the First World War she traveled to Germany, where she made wholesale purchases for both firms. After the Revolution she worked as chief accountant at the Hotel Select, built in the teens and owned before nationalization by the Samsonovich company. It had five or six stories, and was at the time the only multistory building in Chita. Later, in Leningrad, she became senior product comptroller at the Baltic shipping customs office.

I always called her Batanya, a contraction of Babushka Tanya, or Baba Tanya. My version of her name was picked up by all the nephews and grandchildren. She was an astonishingly beautiful woman. Of medium height and weight, just slightly plump, with light chestnut hair and gorgeous gray eyes. She had a graceful neck, a small mouth, and a lovely oval face. I was always impressed by the combination of her beauty and her calm and imperious manner. Everyone respected her, and in some people I noticed a shade of fear in dealing with her. My friends were always afraid of her. She was never physically cuddly with us, except when we were very little; in fact she was rather severe with her grandchildren. But for all that, there was never any distrust or injustice in her treatment of us.

I always wondered why she didn't remarry, having been widowed at such a young age. Perhaps her husband's suicide created a psychological barrier for her. But I don't think she felt a woman's loneliness all those years. When I was older and our blood ties were strengthened by family tragedy, I often wanted to have a frank talk with her, to get confirmation from her of my intuitive understanding. But she always rebuffed me and lectured me. She spoke with no respect of women who made the events of their personal life the knowledge of many. She liked to say, "You can't turn everything into a bazaar." I once asked her how she would react to a husband's infidelity. I was then still well under marriageable age, and the question was of the abstract-literary type. Batanya said, "There are two possibilities. One is not to know; the other, to leave. Both are hard, but there can be nothing in between."

Batanya had her tight circle of friends, with whom she was frank and communicative. But outside that circle and her family she was very reserved, even dry. She read a lot, but stubbornly refused to read contemporary literature. Western literature ended with Ibsen, Russian with Chekhov and Andreyev, and poetry with Blok. I had become a rabid Akhmatova fan and tried to impose my taste on her, but I'm not sure I succeeded. She loved the opera. When Glinka's opera *A Life for the Tsar* was reinstituted (Batanya never called it *Ivan Susanin*),* she took it as a personal triumph. No matter how poorly we lived before the war, she managed to attend the opera or the philharmonic once or twice a season with her best friend, Irina Semyonovna Dreksler. She didn't go to the movies, and I think that was on principle.

*Glinka's opera (1836) was restaged in 1939 on Stalin's orders, with a revised libretto and new title *Ivan Susanin,* to make it more "acceptable."

One time only, my aunt Raya and I talked her into accompanying us to *The Big Waltz*. Batanya's reaction was mostly negative: It was sweet, light, empty. Well, the music was all right.

Without a single music lesson, she could work out any melody on any instrument—piano, guitar, balalaika. Her favorite was the mandolin. Egorka and I were astounded once in the summer of 1938 when she picked up our landlord's accordion—we were living in a village beyond the Batetskaya Station in the Pskov region—and began to play it. I remember that one of the songs she did was "I remember, I was young then . . ."

Batanya's whole life was difficult and full of hard work. Soon after her mother was widowed, Batanya took on the household chores and the child care of her sister and two brothers. Then the stepfather came into the family. Batanya was not allowed the least bit of education. She was self-taught in everything, even reading, with her only teacher being her brother Moisey. He was not only a brilliant student himself but found time to help his sisters as much as he could and supervise his younger brother's studies at the Gymnasium, too. Her early widowhood meant taking jobs to support her family and to educate her three children. She also became responsible financially for her dead husband's two younger sisters.

Grandmother's three children, the two sons of her sister, Sofia, and her late husband's two sisters all grew up in Grandmother's house. Being head of such a household and working must have been hard. But I think the dominant character trait of my grandmother was a sense of duty.

The whole routine was repeated, but in even direr circumstances, when my parents and my uncle Matvei were arrested and his wife was exiled. Grandmother took on the work and the responsibility of three grandchildren. I was the eldest. My brother, Egorka, was ten, and my cousin Natasha, two. Two years after her arrest we started getting letters from Mama in camp. Then we were allowed to send her parcels. Batanya began to hope that she would see her daughter again. The sentence her son got—ten years without right to correspondence—gave her no hope of seeing him. All of Batanya's efforts were directed at saving us and bringing us up. When the war came, instead of staying with her, I foolishly ended up in the army. She sent Egorka into evacuation with his school. Natasha stayed with her in besieged Leningrad. "Write to your mother; worry about Egorka." That phrase was in all her wartime letters to me. Also this: "If I save Natasha, you can erect a monument to me!" Natasha is alive, and a mother and grandmother herself.

But I still haven't erected a monument to my grandmother. She died in Leningrad on May 10, 1942. Aunt Lyuba, her stepsister, our Lyubanya, washed her and sewed the body into a shroud made out of a red silk bedspread, the last decent thing left after exchanging all she had for bread during the blockade of Leningrad. And she pinned on a note: "Whoever takes this last clothing from the body will be damned." Then she accompanied the corpse to the place where all the dead from Gogol Street were brought. Many years ago I read a book of poetry by Vladimir Kornilov. There was the line: ". . . and it seemed that in our years there were no mothers. There were only grandmothers. . . ." Grandmothers there were!

Mama's older brother, Matvei, finished the Gymnasium in Chita in 1916. He was not subject to the draft into the tsar's army. Later, when the governments kept changing in Siberia and the Far East—Semyonov, Kolchak, the Reds, and then someone else—Grandmother kept him from being drafted into any of the armies, using her old ties and the fact that she had helped many political exiles who were now numbered among the new bosses. It always seemed to me that my mother got involved in Bolshevism because her mother was not watching her—when she was living in Moscow with Uncle Mosya to finish up the Gymnasium. Matvei and Anna, who stayed with Grandmother, were kept clear of "romantic" temptations. In the upper grades, Matvei had ties to a Jewish Social Democratic organization (I think it was called the Bund). After Soviet power came to Chita, he worked in the regional committee of the trade unions. Then he moved to Sretensk to work, and got married. It was only when Grandmother managed to get him and his wife registered to live in Leningrad that Matvei began studying at the Wood and Timber Academy. He worked as an engineer and then as chief engineer at a factory making wooden toys. When, in the 1930s, the Christmas tree was revived in the Soviet Union as the New Year's tree, Matvei's factory was among the first to produce tree ornaments. Among his friends from the Gymnasium was the brother of one of the principal NKVD chiefs of Leningrad, Maior (or Meier) Litvin. Perhaps it was because of this friendship, or the fact that Egorka and I moved in with Grandmother in Leningrad after Papa was arrested, that the NKVD began to focus on him. Matvei was arrested on October 29, 1937. But he had been fired before that, after a meeting at the factory at which he was accused of taking in children of an enemy of the people. On December 31, 1937, his wife, Kaleria Stepanovna Skurlatova, was exiled to Central Asia. Matvei got ten years without right of correspondence. A friend of Matvei's from the Academy, Andrei, who had no family, was arrested at the same time as Matvei; we don't know Andrei's sentence. The Litvin brothers were also arrested and, as far as I know, both perished. One had decided other people's fates, the other, like my uncle, had been nothing more than a member of the Russian non-Party intelligentsia.

I have tried to recall everything I can about the relatives on Mama's maternal side. I know a lot less about her father's side. I will tell you later about three of them—Lazar Rafailovich Bonner, Mother's father's brother, his wife, Fedosya Evseyevna (née Goltsman), and their daughter, Raisa, our favorite Aunt Rainka.

I have little information about the family of my stepfather, Gevork Sarkisovich Alikhanov. I do know they didn't realize that I wasn't his own daughter. He asked Mama never to tell them.

I knew only one person from the family of my real father, Levon Sarkisovich Kocharov (Kocharyan), and that was his mother, my grandmother Gertselia Andreyevna Tonunts. I don't remember my grandfather or my grandmother's sister, Elena, who nursed me when I was an infant. Before the Revolution they lived in Shusha in Nagorno-Karabakh, but they fled to Turkestan when Armenians were being killed during the civil war.

That's the end of the family tree.

Why did I write this letter to you, my dear daughter and son? To remember. So that I don't forget. So that you know. And because with the years comes the need to know where you came from.

3

It's a good thing I didn't start out thinking I would write a book, or I would have been worried about how "today" bursts into the past.

In late November 1988 the phone rings. Long rings mean long distance. It's a call from Yerevan. Nothing strange. I've been on the phone day and night with people in Yerevan. In Kirovobad, women and children were besieged in a church. I had a telegram on my kitchen table from the priest—a cry for help. There was a flood of refugees. Going in both directions now—from Azerbaijan into destroyed Armenia and the rest of the Soviet Union and from Armenia into Azerbaijan. And there were victims. Also on both sides now. There had been no violence on the part of the Armenians for nine months, even after the horror of their slaughter at Sumgait. Now their patience had burst. I had been calling the United States, France, someone here in Moscow. I was prepared quite literally to beat my head against the wall in my frustration to get something done, something fair.

A woman was calling. She said she was my cousin. At first I didn't understand. I thought it was a mistake, not a call for me. But it was! The journalist Zori Balayan had published an article on Academician Sakharov which mentioned that I was the daughter of the first secretary of the Central Committee of Armenia, Gevork Alikhanov. She read it and went to see Balayan, but he was out of town. Then she visited Silva Kaputikyan. Amazing—she went to my only Armenian woman friend. Silva gave her my number.

Her name was Ruzana. She was the daughter of Father's sister, in whose family he had grown up. After their father died, their mother lived with Father's sister. And now I remembered Aunt Aikanush. She had come to visit us in Moscow. She had two sons and a daughter, a girl older than me. She had shown us their photographs. And I remembered her husband. He had the same name as my father, and Papa called him Uncle Gevork. He had visited us a few times.

After the conversation with Ruzana I had a strange ambivalent feeling—happiness, but also fear that a firm memory might be shattered.

We met later. In December. The twenty-fifth. Seventeen days after the earthquake. Andrei and I had been to Baku, Stepanakert, and Yerevan. We had seen Armenian and Azerbaijani refugees. We had met with officials, academicians, and writers. And we had returned from the disaster area only two hours earlier.

We had walked on the gray ground, scattered with houses, roofs, chunks of concrete, and brick. And children's jackets in all colors. And schoolbags—red, blue, yellow. The wind ruffled the pages of textbooks and notebooks and flapped laundry that had miraculously remained on a torn clothesline. Like ghosts from a previous life, people wandered around, with black unblinking eyes, with black sunken cheeks. This was the world "after." Snow started to fall. It felt as if it would cover not only this ground, but these people, everyone. Not just Armenians, but the Azerbaijanis, and us, everyone, near and far. The whole world.

The helicopter shuddered like a person who was cold and afraid. But one had to do what had to be done. And slowly it rose. The snowflakes beneath it, each living its own life, began to turn into a solid blanket through which our lone helicopter broke. Opposite us sat a little boy, as still as a statue, staring with round eyes at the open hand of a fellow passenger. It held a red apple. And the voice cajoled the boy, "Armenak, take it." What I heard was, "Armenia, take it." "Armenia."

When we got back to our hotel, I was chilled and I took a hot shower. And I thought, "God, they don't have water there." I pulled on warm socks. And again, "All the clothing and food sent there is being grabbed up by the strong and the ones who are near the distribution points. What about the weak ones and the ones far away?" My chills wouldn't stop. They were coming from inside me.

And then Ruzana arrived with her husband and son. The boy was tall and handsome. He looked like my father in his youth. Everyone was uncomfortable. We could feel their respect for Andrei. It raised a barrier for us and probably for them, too. Ruzana took out photographs. The first was of Egorka and me in the summer of 1928. The second, of Papa as a student. Then Ruzana's parents. Her brothers, one of whom had lived with us in Leningrad for a while. Papa's mother, Grandmother Shushanik, in an ancient Armenian costume. I looked at the pictures, which I had never seen, at Papa's young face, and my chills gradually went away. Ruzana began talking about the past. She did not remember my father, who had left Tiflis* when she was four. But she told me what she had heard from her grandmother, her mother and father.

Gevork Gabrielovich Kazaryan, the husband of Papa's sister, was a wealthy man, and he supported Papa's education. Papa's sister was involved in all his political doings, which had begun back in school. He and his friends would gather at Kazkaryan's house and use it as a hiding place for all kinds of illegal things. Once, when he was sitting on the couch in the living room, Gevork Gabrielovich said to Aikanush and Papa, "The only thing I ask is that you not bring any firearms into the house." He did not suspect that there were rifles hidden in the couch on which he was sitting. After the Revolution Papa helped him get a job at some institution.

Gevork Gabrielovich visited us in Moscow for the last time in 1937. He was having problems at work and apparently thought Papa could help him. Ruzana did not say whether he did or not,

---

*Tbilisi, the capital of the Georgian SSR, was called by its Russian name, Tiflis, until 1936.

but her father had not been repressed. When he came back from Moscow, he told them that "Ruf is very sad and worried about Gevork," because Papa had spoken out against Beria at a meeting. He had said, "For what deeds has he been put on our backs?" Apparently this was a reference to Beria becoming secretary of Georgia's Central Committee.

Soon after that Aikanush stopped getting money from Papa and the monthly certificate for Grandmother Shushanik, which allowed the family to buy food and goods at a special Party store in Tbilisi. They wrote to the Moscow address several times, but there was no reply. Grandmother Shushanik went to see Kabulov's mother, whom she had known since Papa was a young man. Kabulov (then in the Georgian NKVD) had been one of the young men who had gathered at Kazaryan's house before the revolution. Kabulov's mother screamed at Grandmother and told her never to show her face there again.

Their last attempt to find out about Papa and our family was made in early 1938. Gevork Gabrielovich traveled to Moscow and went to the Luxe Hotel. He was told that neither Alikhanov nor his wife lived there. "They're gone!"

He knew what that meant. He asked, "What about the children?"

"Gone, too."

"Where?"

"We don't know. Somewhere."

That "somewhere" stunned the old man and he repeated the story many times. Ruzana was seventeen by then and she remembered her father's attempts to find us very well.

When it was time for rehabilitation, some people (from the Party committee, I think) came to Grandmother Shushanik and asked her to apply for a personal pension, but she chased them out. She said that they couldn't return her son, and that she didn't want their pension. Thank God, she wasn't out on the street, but living with her daughter's family. Grandmother Shushanik died in Tbilisi in the late fifties. Ruzana and her family moved to Yerevan. Both she and her husband were engineers, and are retired now. They had two children and four grandchildren.

Ruzana's story did not disturb my memories at all. I only felt pain that Mama had not lived to hear it.

We had dinner at the hotel restaurant. I told them that it was the anniversary of Mama's death. Friends had gathered at home on Chkalov Street. And it was Christmas! Someone brought and lit candles at the table. Outside the huge restaurant windows the snow fell and fell. The tanks on the square—and there were tanks in Baku, and in Stepanakert, and in Spitak—were turning into huge snowbanks. Ruzana and Sergei had to hurry home. There was a curfew.

4

You were born and probably
Somewhere a bright star burst
You did not know whether or not
You would have a happy life. . . .

    Vsevolod Bagritsky (1922–42)

I was born on February 15, 1923, in the old city of Merv, in my grandparents' house on the banks of the Murgab River in Turkmenia. It was already spring, and the pink apricot and peach blossoms of their garden, which sloped down to the river, were reflected in the water. The blossoms were very lush that year and Grandmother Gertselia Andreyevna said that it was a good omen. Grandfather sent a telegram to my other grandmother, Batanya, in far-off Chita: GIRL BORN STOP SO BEAUTIFUL STOP. "Everything passes" . . . but the telegram, yellow and crumpling, has survived. Now the city where I was born is called Mary, Turkmenian SSR.

I do not remember the city of Merv. Or the year we lived in Moscow, in 1923–24. Time began for me in Chita.

We lived as a big family there in the house of Moisey Leontyevich Keleiman, the husband of Grandmother's sister, Sofia. Moisey Leontyevich, Nyutochka, a relative of his, my grand-mother, Mama, Papa, Mama's brother, Matvei, and I were the permanent residents. But there were always guests, too, relatives and friends. There was a cook, and a nanny for me. I always considered Grandmother to be the head of the family. I had been convinced for the longest time that it was her house and not Moisey Leontyevich's. Like everyone else in the family, I used his name and patronymic, even though he was like a grandfather to me. I knew that he would always be on my side in any conflict with the world of grownups.

When he finally decided to leave Russia—we were living in Leningrad by then—I felt very unhappy that he had received permission. I kept hearing all the conversations of the adults about the hassles of leaving. I was against his departure. His first granddaughter was born in Paris. Perhaps his attachment to me was reflected in the fact that she was called Lusia, as I was as a child.

I remember the yard and the house—a dark log house with big windows, very long on the street side, but half-hidden from the yard side by a tall fence. It stood on an intersection with a bakery on the corner. The front door faced the street, but we always entered from the yard. The porch led through an entryway to a big kitchen. Next to it was a room which we called "the dark room," in which the cook and nanny lived. All the rooms opened on the hall stretching from the kitchen. Four rooms had windows looking onto the street—my parents' room, Matvei's, Nyu-tochka's, and the very large one belonging to Moisey Leon-tyevich. Three opened on the yard—Batanya's, which I shared, the "passage room," and the dining room. The passage room was for guests. There was an entryway at the very end of the hall, but no one entered there and it was used to hold trunks and coats. At the kitchen end of the corridor was a large white door. It was boarded up with two rough planks and covered with a thick green curtain. Later, when we were living in Leningrad I learned that beyond that door was the other half of the house, which had been "taken away."

My highchair stood next to Batanya's seat at the dining room table, and Moisey Leontyevich always was opposite me. The overhead lamp had a shade trimmed with gold-beaded fringe. All I have left from the house in Chita are a trunk and a necklace (my daughter Tanya has it) that we made from the lampshade's beads.

My sharpest memory, and perhaps my earliest one, is of the lampshade swaying. Moisey Leontyevich picked me up in his arms and we all ran out onto the street. I remember the word "earthquake," the smell of Moisey Leontyevich's fur coat, which someone had tossed over us, and the dark, starry sky. I think it was the first time that I saw stars.

There is a family legend that I often ran away from home in Chita and would be found in town on the way to or at the house of Batanya's brother Uncle Sanya and his wife, Aunt Ronya. Their house was the most beautiful place in my early childhood. And they had music. The very concept of music and all the emotions connected with it came from Uncle Sanya. I don't recall whether or not there was an instrument in the house where we lived. But I remember the upright piano in the big room of Uncle Sanya's house not only for its chocolate brown sheen, but for its feel and even its taste, because I used to lick it secretly. It stood against the wall between two tall windows (maybe they only seemed so then?), with rustling lace curtains (it was always summer, it seems), and there were two large Chinese vases on either side. They were ornamented with ladies with umbrellas, high hairdos, and kimonos tied with broad ribbons and big bows. I thought Aunt Ronya was one of those ladies, and not only because she had a kimono. I had already seen many women in kimonos and in blue jackets tied with laces, and small wooden platform shoes, since there were many Chinese in town. But everything Aunt Ronya had was beautiful, and that was not the case on the street. Moreover, she had music. I did not use that word to describe what I heard in the yard or elsewhere, or the songs of my nanny. I used it only for what Uncle Sanya played. And I remember very well that when the music played, I did not want to see people. I would go behind the black silk drape in the right corner of the room and I would look at its bizarre gray trees and white birds flying somewhere embroidered on it. The birds and the music were inextricably linked. Now I think of Aunt Ronya and Uncle Sanya's house as my first concert hall and first museum.

Is it there that I began to like listening to music when I was alone? In my school years it was radio—a black dish or earphones. Then long-playing records. I wonder if that term is used anymore. Later the radio. And I used to like attending concerts alone. It was only with Andrei that I wanted to listen to music with someone else.

I also used to run away to the billiards room of the hotel where Batanya worked. Papa, Matvei, and Papa's friend Lyova Alin were often there. Papa or Matvei would pick me up and I could see the table from my high vantage point. When it was their turn to take up the cue, they handed me over. But once Papa set me down on the table. For some reason that green expanse frightened me, and I was mad at Papa. It was the first hurt I can remember.

In the summer Batanya took me to the resort at Darasun, beyond Lake Baikal, developed by Grigorii (Grisha) Mikhailovich Berlinsky, the husband of Batanya's sister Beti. He was also the chief physician there. We traveled by a horse-drawn vehicle, though I don't remember whether it was a wagon or a carriage. It was dark, and the rain poured. Trees swayed on either side of the rutted road, which I found very scary; it must have been the first time I was outside in bad weather. That night and that trip have remained in my memory ever since. Darasun is of legendary beauty, but I don't really remember it at all. I fell in love with a doll there. The owner, Nusya, daughter of Aunt Beti and Uncle Grisha, did not let me touch it. But whenever she was away Aunt Beti would permit me to hold her and even mother her. Of course it was a "goodwill" gesture, but my will was fettered by my perception that Aunt Beti was also afraid of Nusya. For the longest time my attitude toward Aunt Beti was colored by that childhood feeling, and it did not change until the last decade of her life.

I had complete and total trust in Uncle Grisha. He was a

surgeon, had served in the front lines throughout the war, and worked in Moscow at a pediatric trauma hospital. And since it's a small world, as we all know, when Andrei came into our house, it turned out that Uncle Grisha had treated his elder daughter, Tatyana.

5

In early 1926 our Chita household began falling apart. Matvei left for work somewhere near Vladivostok. Mama and Papa moved to Leningrad. Now I know that Papa had worked in Leningrad even before that, in 1922–24. He ended up in Chita in a sort of exile after some major disagreements with Grigori Zinoviev. So this was a desirable return for him, made possible by the fact that Sergei Kirov had become secretary of the Leningrad Committee after the 14th Party Congress.*

Soon after they left, Batanya started getting ready to take me to Leningrad. The idea was that Batanya would visit her younger daughter, Anya, in Moscow, deliver me to Leningrad, and come back to Chita. It was strange listening to the adults discuss this. Batanya, not Mama, was the center of my life, the peak, the most important person, and I could not imagine life without her. It was the same when I was later told that my cousin Zorya was born and that Batanya now had another granddaughter. I had the sense that this was wrong: my grandmother should not have other grandchildren, only me. It looked as if I had been brought up as a typical "only child."

Batanya and I did not travel alone from Chita. Uncle Sanya was with us, and his presence created a sense of comfort and

*Grigori Yevseyevich Zinoviev (1883–1936) was a Communist leader who conspired with Kamenev and Trotsky against Stalin. Accused of complicity in the 1934 murder of Sergei Kirov, he confessed in a "show trial" and was executed. Sergei Mironovich Kirov (1886–1934) was a Soviet political leader and Party boss of Leningrad. His assassination on Stalin's orders was used as the pretext for starting the purges of the Great Terror.

tranquillity on the train. Batanya's other brother, Uncle Mosya, accompanied us as far as Irkutsk, and that is my first memory of him. He convinced Batanya to let me take along a doll and also gave me a toy train, with a locomotive and cars that attached behind it. I don't know how long it was in those days from Chita to Moscow, something like eleven or twelve days, but in my memory it is a big piece of my life, with a certain order that I liked, special games in the carriage and in the corridor, and with memorable food—my first impression that food could be tasty comes from that trip. I remember walks along the platforms with Uncle Sanya when we stopped, the smell of smoke in the air, and being brought out all bundled up in Verkhneudinsk [Ulan-Ude] and Irkutsk (we went through both at night) to meet relatives, and lots of gifts and delicacies that they brought us. I think that my love of trains—climbing aboard and going somewhere far, far away— started then. I don't remember Moscow at all, even though Batanya and I stayed there for two or three weeks. I can't even remember where. In Leningrad Mama and Papa lived in the Astoria Hotel, but then it was often called the Leningrad House of Soviets. There were no soviets (councils) in the building, but many Party and Soviet workers of Leningrad lived there.

I loved that hotel. It seemed incredibly beautiful to me—tall windows, roomy lobbies, a revolving door, gray granite facade, and an elevator with mirrors, so you could see yourself from all sides. It was not on a street but on a square. I had never seen such a big open space.

My knowledge of Leningrad began there, and ever since I have, contrary to the usual view, considered St. Isaac's Square the center of the city. Even visually, if you go to the top of St. Isaac's, to the round balcony above the big cupola (lots of tourists used to do that in the past, and I did it myself as a child, a teenager, and a young woman many times, the first time with my father when I was three), you seem to hover at an incredible height (few people had flown in a plane in those days, and I didn't until the war) in the very center of the city spreading out below in ever-widening circles.

Mama and Papa lived on the Astoria's third floor in a room

whose windows opened onto the square and the cathedral. I loved that grand monument from first sight, and my Leningrad life, except for the last years, when I lived on Fontanka, always took place near it. Sometimes I think that a building can influence character and even fate. From a window it seemed I could always see it. In school my desk was near a window and the teacher would often say, "Bonner, stop staring at St. Isaac's."

The room where Batanya and I lived faced the inner courtyard. It was a strange courtyard without trees, almost completely filled with small buildings, where people were always loading and unloading things, and no matter how hard I looked at the Astoria from the outside, I could never find an entrance to the courtyard. Even today I don't know where it is.

I think that most of my parents' friends lived in the Astoria in those days, and I freely roamed the floors and spacious corridors of the hotel, visiting by myself. As far back as I can remember, I always counted them as my friends, too.

The Astoria had a kindergarten, primarily for the children who lived there, and I attended it. I have the feeling that before the Astoria I had almost nothing to do with children and knew only adults. My first interaction with my peers involved my crush on a little boy. When our teacher said that it was his last day with us and that he was moving, I hid in the room where we washed up and where our towels were kept (each child's hanging under a picture), burrowed in them, and wept, my face swollen, my nose wet. I didn't want to tell either the teacher or Batanya, who came for me, what was wrong, and they decided that someone had hurt me. I remember my grief to this day, but I forgot my hero's name quickly.

Another thing about the Astoria is that it was there I first saw and heard a radio. Papa's friend Sergei Kalantarov had brought one back from abroad. Grandmother and her aunt Anna Pavlovna used to go to his room and listen to it.

Right next to the Astoria was another hotel, the Angleterre, where some of the kids in our kindergarten lived, and it was from them I first heard the name Esenin. Initially I thought it was a given name, Eseni, and didn't understand. Then at home, it would come up often in the grownups' conversation. I began to understand that something very bad had happened and that people were sad and disapproving, even afraid. This must have been the first time I heard about death. I didn't realize that Esenin was a poet and that he had committed suicide, but a few years later I made the connection with another event also involving the square and St. Isaac's directly. But more about that later.

We did not stay long at the Astoria, as we soon moved to a different neighborhood, on the Petrograd side of the city, to another house with historic significance, 26–28 Kirov Prospect. Back then it was called Red Dawns Street. I thought the house looked like the Astoria, but not as beautiful. Like the Astoria, it was home to many Leningrad Party leaders.

One resident was Sergei Kirov, boss of the city, a fact that I understood even at my age, if only because a car picked him up and drove him home, and I didn't remember any other cars at our house. The doorwoman (later to be known as the elevator woman) hushed the children playing near the entrance as soon as the car pulled into the courtyard encircled by a pretty wrought-iron fence. Kirov and his wife had a personal relationship with my parents, so he would single me out from the other children with a brief word or pat on the head. That gave me a sense (age doesn't matter) of my eliteness. Once Kirov gave me a ride in his car in front of all the kids, and I was with him at the square during a parade. It was some not very important holiday, perhaps Children's Week or Children's Day. I later saw a photograph of me next to him, but we didn't save a copy. And I never found it among the official photo archives of Kirov.

All I remember of that apartment is that one of our two rooms was unusually big. My parents' friend Pavel Bronich (a future director of the Nikolayevsky Shipbuilding Plant, he died in the thirties, like all of Papa's friends) brought back a present for me from America, where he had worked. It was a folding roller-coaster game (just the right size for the room) which we called "American Hills." The adults played with it more than I did!

I also recall this house because it was in its courtyard that I lost my green pitcher. Probably every child has a "green pitcher"—a favorite toy loved for no particular reason and from as far back as you can remember. I carried it in my pocket from Chita and always went outside with it. Depending on the season, I filled it with sand or snow or utilized it to scoop water out of puddles. At home I sneaked drinks of tap water in it. And I always used it to hold flowers in my dollhouses.

I was allowed to play outside in the courtyard, but I would slip past the gate and stroll along the fence, studying its curlicued design from the outside instead of the inside. This gave me a sense of freedom. At first I permitted myself to walk only as far as the fence went, and when it ended, I would turn back. Gradually distance called me farther and farther. I would walk to the end of the block on both sides and eventually, around the corner. Once I discovered that if I kept going, turning corners along the houses, I would come back to our house, but from the other side. That gave me such a lift that I kept circling, as if under a spell. And wherever there was a fence or palings, I ran my pitcher across them, and then put it back in my pocket. Suddenly it wasn't in my pocket. I couldn't believe it and practically stripped to make sure it wasn't on me. But it was gone. I went back, checking every crack in the sidewalk, behind all the fences and doorways of my route. But I couldn't find it.

Later, as a district doctor, I walked all around house number 26–28 and my old route—it wasn't my district, but I often filled in for the local physician. And I would always look for my pitcher. Even now, if I happen to pass by, I can't help recalling my pitcher. I catch myself peering into holes, into cracks in houses and fences, still searching for it.

I didn't spot the pitcher, but they found me wandering around the street after dark. First I was punished for going out of bounds, then everyone felt sorry for me and I think all our relatives and friends gave me pitchers. But they weren't *the* pitcher. I had lots of toys, some of them fine and expensive and beloved, but there was none with which I had such a spiritual tie. I'm surprised that it wasn't a doll or stuffed animal, simply a green metal pitcher.

It seemed I saw the Neva River for the first time only when we moved to the Petrograd side. Various visits to friends, to the theater, and to other places involved crossing the river. No doubt that's why I had the false impression that house 26–28 on Red Dawns Street was much closer to the Neva than the Astoria.

We did not live long there, soon returning to the area around St. Isaac's—first to Malaya Morskaya Street and then to 18 Gogol Street. Another historic house. It was called the Grand Hotel and when we moved there it was being converted into an apartment house. Once upon a time (looking a bit different) it had belonged to Count Benkendorf, chief of the gendarmerie. The editor Faddei Bulgarin had rented an apartment there and been visited by the writer Alexander Griboyedov. Perhaps Pushkin had dropped in there once, too? In the 1870s the count's descendants turned the house into a hotel.

A beautiful, four-paneled door of dark oak for the main entrance, with a visor of matte glass and a narrow metal strip along the edge. A second door just like it. A roomy vestibule, with a large, full-length mirror on the left. That mirror reflected a large part of my life—as a little girl, teenager, young woman. I always cast a glance in that mirror as I was leaving the house, for a final check and touch-up—not concerning lipstick, powder puff, or comb, but just to have a different look at myself before going out. It was like the person in the wings who lets you out onto the stage. Then two staircases, to the right and to the left, three floors on the left, two on the right, and beyond the stairs in the back an oak partition, behind which on the left was a fireplace with a handsome marble mantelpiece and deep in the back a high glass door leading to the yard. They said that in the past there had been a pastry shop and tables with umbrellas in the yard. When I was a teenager there were two big maple trees and some lilac bushes outside and children played and volleyballs flew back and forth. After the war the lilacs were gone. Only one sickly maple remained.

Up the left staircase to the third floor—that's where I lived as a little girl, that's where Egorka would be born, that's where I would leave from for Moscow and return to after the tragedy of 1937 as if reborn, that's where I would depart and then return after the war, that's where Mama would come back from the camps in Karaganda, and that's where my daughter, Tanya, would be born. Both in time and in terms of everything connected to it, this was my home, the way Andrei's and my apartment on Chkalov Street is my home. All the rest have been simply temporary places to live.

The broad marble staircase in the early years was covered with a red carpet. At that time a doorman sat by the fireplace. Later he vanished, and so did the runner, leaving only the brass rings under each step that used to hold the runner in place. There were four flights of stairs leading to our third (top) floor. Between the first and second and between the third and fourth flights, enormous Venetian windows, twice as tall as a person, looked down into the courtyard. They were beautiful—matte glass in the center with a design, and colored glass around the periphery, flowers and leaves. The sills were broad and made of snow-white marble.

The banisters were of dark wood—wide, shining with polish, with smooth curves on the turns (they were perfect for sliding)— and rested on intricately carved wooden balusters. I'm describing the staircase in such detail not only out of love for its beauty but because between 1938 and 1940 that staircase became my first workplace.

For half salary as cleaning woman I swept it daily, washed it once a week (and twice a year I washed two of these huge windows). The task wasn't particularly hard in those years and didn't take up much time. I loved my stairs. The windowsill between the second and third floors was my favorite spot in the building. It heard so many heartfelt talks, secrets, and poems. Especially in the spring, when the window was open and the maple, so alive, rustled its dark green leaves against the pearly gray Leningrad sky.

But that was later.

In the spring of 1927 we moved into an apartment entered by a simple wooden door at the end of the hotel hallway, to the right of the stairs. We had seven or eight rooms, a generous bathroom (which lost its original function several years later when turned into a storeroom), and a very large kitchen, recently converted from a hotel room. The hallway was unbelievably long—Grandmother called it Nevsky Prospect (as she also insisted on calling the street which had been renamed in that period 25 October Street). The hallway floor was stone—we called it marble. Many years later I realized how convenient it was to wash. One wall was blank and the other opened into all the rooms, including the kitchen, with a door leading to the back stairs and the courtyard.

In early 1950, when the police came to arrest my mother a second time (they used to call it the "second run"), she was off visiting Aunt Lyuba. Her cousin Robert Bonner, who was staying with us while on a business trip from Omsk, went down those stairs and left the house to warn Mama. He helped her leave that very night for Moscow.

6

All the windows in the apartment faced the courtyard. When we moved in, the roof of the opposite wing of our building sparkled silver, like a candy wrapper, and above it, quite close, rose the big cupola of St. Isaac's filling half the sky. The roof changed its color many times afterward, sometimes turning bright red, or brick, or dirty brown, but St. Isaac's remained as pure and sparkling as life itself.

I think I got lost the day after we moved. The tendency to get lost appeared early in me, almost simultaneously with the ability to walk. My grandmother and parents and their friends had many stories on this theme. The first time I got lost was at the Novodevichy monastery when I was with Grandmother Gertselia— Mama had lived with her briefly, when I was brought from Turkmenia. As I've said, I disappeared many times in Chita.

My proclivity for evading adults and wandering around on my own outraged Mama. Much later, when Egorka was missing in Moscow and we learned that he had spent the day in the freezing cold at the entrance of the People's Commissariat of Defense (it may have been called something else then) in order to see Marshals Budenny and Voroshilov,* she said angrily, "He picked that up from her." Yet it hadn't been my fault at all and I had been just as upset as the adults when Egorka disappeared.

That particular day Mama took me to a store. I needed shoes, and they had to be tried on. I was rarely taken to stores, because I would demand everything I saw, and have a fit until I got it. This was a very big store, later called The House of Leningrad Trade. To this day I visualize it as big as it had seemed to me then. They sold flowers on the first floor, and I begged until I got a flower in a pot, either primula or a geranium—to possess such an object was almost a criminal offense in my mother's strict communist "anti-bourgeois" world. I think her fear of a public scene worked for me; otherwise I would no more have seen a "pretty flower for the window" than my own ears. Then we shopped for shoes. Later Mama left me with the flowerpot and the shoebox by the railing over the store's main floor and told me to wait. I stayed put until I got tired of waiting, and then left. I don't remember how I returned to the new apartment, but apparently I did so without great difficulty. I never had any trouble finding a place once I'd been there—be it in a foreign country, in a city or village, or in the woods.

I couldn't reach the doorbell, so I put the old shoes and the flowerpot by the door and went out for a walk in my new shoes. I walked around St. Isaac's, met the lions that guarded the school I would later attend, and continued toward the Bronze Horseman and the Neva River. The statue left me cold, but the Neva up close astounded me. It was something different—not the same river I had crossed in a trolley or horse carriage and once in a car. Up close it seemed enormous and endless. I went down to the water and, crouching, I rinsed my hands in it. But the waves splashed the step on which I was standing and it started to rain, ordinary warm, summery rain. I'm surprised I remember it so

*Semyon Mikhailovich Budenny (1883–1973), a military commander, led the Red cavalry in the Russian Civil War and was made a marshal of the Soviet Union in 1935. Kliment Yefremovich Voroshilov (1881–1969), a military commander and politician, co-founder with Dzerzhinsky of the Soviet secret police, was made a marshal of the Soviet Union in 1935.

clearly, but it struck me all of a sudden, like love, and that love has just grown stronger throughout my life—I love the spring rain, and that descent to the Neva from Decembrist Square is my favorite, with the square, divided into two by St. Isaac's yet in my opinion united by the cathedral, the school building, and the park in front of it.

I took off my shoes and walked home in the rain barefoot, happy that I had seen so many nice things, had come to love them, and wasn't ruining my shoes. But at home a storm awaited me, the worst of my life to date. The doorman, holding me painfully by the arm, dragged me to the third floor and our corridor. My flower, the empty shoebox, and my old shoes were on the dining room table. Mama was teary-eyed and in a wet dress (I was dripping, too). I realized that she had been out looking for me in the rain. Her dress hugged her big belly. I had noticed earlier that it was big, but now I saw that it was unusually big (Egorka was born three months later). Batanya yelled at Mama in front of me. She said she couldn't be trusted with one child and what did she need with a second when she kept losing this one (me). Mama shouted at me—why did I leave the store, why did I abandon the flower by the door and go out again, and why, oh why, did I take off my shoes and walk around barefoot in the rain.

Papa and Bronich came in, also wet, just back from looking for me. Everyone was dripping water on the floor. I saw that the floor was unlike the ones in every other house I had lived in, sort of like oilcloth, brown with a red pattern (I heard the word "linoleum" much later), and puddles were forming where we stood. Without meaning anything by it, I began splashing my feet in my puddle. Then Mama began shouting, "She's crazy, gallivanting about without her shoes." The word "gallivanting" was new to me then, but ever since it would always be used for me. No matter where I might be—at school, at work, taking the children for a walk—if someone were to ask about me, Mama's standard answer was "Gallivanting about somewhere." I never did get to explain why I had taken off my shoes, which was because they were new and I hadn't wanted to get them wet.

The way we initially lived in that big apartment was like this: the first two rooms from the entry were small and adjoining, with a single exit onto the corridor, and they were for Papa and Mama. Then came the door to the back stairs, then the kitchen, and beyond it the dining room and Batanya's room, which had two doors—one to the corridor and one to the dining room. Then two small rooms in which Bronich and Papa's nephew Suren lived originally. The next was a large room. Moisey Leontyevich stayed there before he left for France and then some friends of Papa's moved in. Later Egorka took this room with his nanny. Then Mama's cousin Raya, who had come from Irkutsk for her medical internship, and her friend with the strange name Pisetka (though that might have been a nickname). Pisetka was related somehow to Kirov's wife and to the wife of Agasi Khandzhyan, Papa's good friend (I think the two were sisters—Pisetka was either their younger sister or niece). They visited us often, and Agasi even more frequently—he lived around the corner at the Astoria. I would go over there by myself to see different friends of Papa's. The very last room down the hall was for me and my nanny, and it was called the nursery. Papa's nephew soon married and moved into his wife's place. The room was then taken by Papa's friend Tsolak Amatuni and his wife, Asya, who had a big belly just like Mama; I already knew that she and Mama would soon have babies.

When our Egorka and Asya's Andrusha were born, I liked Andrusha better, because Egorka was scrawny and kept crying all the time, while Andrusha was as cute as a kewpie doll. Asya had no milk, and Mama fed Andrusha. She had been forced to stop feeding Egorka, since he had developed an allergy to mother's milk. Then a famous doctor brought a fat woman to our house and she moved in with Egorka. She rarely let me in to see my brother. But the room with Andrusha was always open; I could shake a rattle over him and even watch when he was being bathed. No wonder Andrusha felt more like a brother to me than Egorka.

Tsolak and Asya and their son soon moved out. I was sorry they didn't leave Andrusha behind and even tried to persuade Asya several times to let him stay.

The small room next to Batanya was occupied for a while (it seemed like a very long time to me) by Comrade A. When the other adults couldn't see, he would walk around with his trousers unbuttoned and everything that should have been covered was revealed. I realized that he was doing it on purpose and that it was shameful, but I couldn't find the strength to tell my grandmother or mother about it. I don't know whether they knew of his pathological problem. I was terrified of him. Every time I ran into him in the corridor or the kitchen, I felt spasms that were almost like the dry heaves. I began locking my door when I was alone in my room. The adults yelled at me for that. I think they must have suspected me of some terrible secret vice. It was only after Comrade A. left that I began to feel free in my own house.

That summer, before my brother was born on August 27, 1927, I lived at the dacha in Martyshkino. This is the first dacha town I can remember. I lived there with my one-year-old cousin Zorya, a boy whose name I don't recall, and Shurochka, a girl two or three years older than me, the niece of Papa's friend Misha Merkuryev. We were in the charge of my nanny Nura and Alya, Misha's wife and Mama's friend. She was the only woman in their group who did not work and was always taking care of someone's kids. I don't remember the Baltic Sea at Martyshkino, but the forest was everywhere. It started right at the house. We had to cross it to reach the station to meet Mama, we went through it to go to the other dacha settlement and its market, and we spent all day playing in it. Our house was the last one and stood almost in the woods. It was new, still unfinished, and piles of aromatic wood shavings lay around it. I kept trying to go off in the woods alone, but I rarely managed, because Shurochka—at Alya's request—never took her eyes off me. Whenever I tried to slip away, she told on me. I must say that my bad relations with her formed that summer, even though I loved Alya both as a child and as an adult. Her calling, tending children, later extended to my own. She babysat for Tanya, and when she and Misha were retired, they spent a summer taking care of Alyosha in the village of Yukky.

Mama didn't come out to the dacha after mid-August; it was

too close to Egorka's birth. One evening while Papa was at a meeting and Batanya at a friend's house, she fell asleep and dreamed that the dacha was burning. She woke up worried and despite the late hour went out to the dacha. Walking through the woods, she could see the flames from afar and as she ran closer she realized it was the unfinished half of the house burning, still unoccupied, and that our half was quiet—everyone was asleep. Mama woke up Alya and the nanny. The children were carried out, the neighbors called. They started putting out the fire, but the house was severely damaged, including our half, so that our stay at the dacha was cut short.

In the morning Mama with the rest of us appeared on Malya Morskaya Street, having arrived by early train. There was panic at home, since Papa and his friends who were living with us had spent the night looking for Mama at all the hospitals and maternity homes. Who could have imagined that she was at Martyshkino, rescuing us. Two or three days later Mama had Egorka.

Mama always told this story as an example of how strong her intuition was; she claimed that she was a "witch" (our family expression, not at all derogatory, for someone with mystical qualities).

7

In those years Batanya worked at the Leningrad customs office. It was in talking to her that I first heard the word "spets" [from "specialist"]. I didn't know if that was good or bad. I thought that Mama seemed to use it rather ironically, perhaps in revenge for not being "head" of our household, as Batanya was. Her salary was higher than my parents' at their "Party maximum." I don't know if we had special food parcels or other privileges. At any rate, Papa, who was then secretary of the Volodarsky District Party Committee, traveled to work like everyone else by tramway from the corner on Nevsky Prospect, and did not have a private car and driver. He achieved that status only in 1933 or 1934, in Moscow when he was in the Comintern.

At that time my parents spent their evenings and nights writing brochures, which they said were on "questions of Party construction." For a long while I thought the Party built houses. The first brochure Papa wrote was for his friend Misha, who had either lost or stolen Party money (not his own). There was a lot of discussion about it at our house, and Batanya hurriedly borrowed from wealthy friends of hers, "formers"*—Aunt Anna Pavlovna, whose surname I don't remember (it might have been Pinkesevich); from the dentist Hanna Zazovskaya; and from a distant relative whom everybody called "The Pharmacist" behind his back (maybe he really was one?). And so Papa wrote a brochure in order to pay back the money.

Batanya's friends and acquaintances rarely came to our building, where only she and the children were not Party members. But I often went with her to call on them. I saw that they lived differently—they had different dishes, different furniture. (At our house Batanya was the only one with normal furniture and a few nice things. Her armoire—no beauty—still stands in Andrei's room as a relic and her armchairs and cot are at Tanya's in Newton, Massachusetts.) They talked about everything differently. I felt (this impression definitely came from Papa and Mama) that they were a different sort of people—what I couldn't tell was whether they were worse or better. I always perceived Papa's and Mama's friends as my own kind and Batanya's as strangers. In essence, I already belonged to the Party. Three or four years later Egorka "belonged" too. Once Batanya put him in the corner for some prank. And he said, "You can't boss me around; you're not a Party member." Batanya raised her glasses to her forehead, to get a better look at him, and said musingly, "It looks as if now you'll not only stand in the corner but get a spanking for those words."

The constant crowds of people in our big apartment, the

*"Formers" was the term used by Bolsheviks for people who had held high social positions in pre-Revolutionary Russia.

steady stream of visitors staying a few days or a long time, annoyed Batanya. She kept commenting that no amount of money would be enough to maintain that "caravansary," that "madhouse" (as she called our apartment).

Papa frequently invited people to dinner. Batanya asked him to give her fair warning, but he "never had time." And there was always some "comrade in town on business" spending the night. Once Papa mentioned someone's name and said the "comrade was coming tomorrow." Mama replied, "That eunuch?" It was a new word for me, but I remembered it because Mama saw that I was listening and blushed. The comrade was big and fat and he said nothing at dinner. But when he thanked Batanya, his voice was very high-pitched, falsetto-like. That evening Batanya said to Mama, "That Malenkov of yours is exceptionally unsimpatico." That was another new word, so I said, "That's because he's a eunuch." I was scolded by Batanya for "picking up all sorts of nasty words goodness knows where." I knew where, but I didn't tell on Mama.

Batanya also used to say that Nura, my nanny, was "gold," because she didn't abandon us and go work for some "decent" family, and that keeping a "royal" nanny was madness.

Egorka's fat nanny truly was royal—she had received special training in Switzerland and had worked in the tsar's palace before the Revolution. She had not nursed the children of royal and semiroyal blood herself, but had supervised the other nannies, something like a foreman, and was very proud of her past. When she went to the kitchen to cook something for Egorka, she struck fear in everyone, even Batanya I think, and when she took Egorka outside—to sit in the courtyard—my nanny brought out the chair for her. I sensed that she despised everyone in our household. The only person she addressed with a modicum of respect was Batanya. She also let my grandmother into Egorka's room at any time. Mama didn't have that honor too often, and I think that Papa never saw Egorka in that period. That nanny cleaned the room herself; she let Nura in only to light the stove and she left a pail with Egorka's diapers outside the door in the hallway for Nura. Nura said that the window was always open and that "that educated one" was going to kill Egorka with the cold: "He'll be deceased, he will," she repeated, and I thought it had something to do with ceasing to cry and wondered why she was so sad about something so good.

We parted with the "royal" nanny when Egorka was eight or nine months old, and he was so round, rosy, and cute that I would have given up all my treasures for him. He was moved into our "nursery" with Nura and me, and he became my main toy. Without the "royal" he was allowed to sit on the floor, and he would crawl—actually I would haul him over the high doorsill— into the hallways, and the whole apartment, especially the kitchen, became our free domain. Nura adored Egorka, so she seemed to consider my feelings for him perfectly natural. She simply couldn't understand anyone who didn't delight in him. Batanya was condescending toward my fussing with him. Mama, as it seemed to me then, was indifferent to us both, or at least managed to hide her feelings well. In their milieu being a "crazy mother" must have been considered nonsense.

The doorsill of our nursery became the point at which I began to understand that Egorka wasn't exactly a doll. Once as I was dragging him across, I stumbled and he fell, smashing his lips and cracking one of his front bottom teeth. The blood flowed wildly, and I was terrified. Somebody stopped the bleeding, and Egorka stopped crying. They didn't even yell at me, but I couldn't calm down and worried for a long time that he would die. The fear was intensified by two horrible events that had preceded this simple incident.

I had been walking alone near St. Isaac's. With two unfamiliar girls, I was digging in a pile of sand used for construction, left on the strip of grass between the front and right portals of the cathedral. Suddenly—it's always suddenly, but there's really no other word for it here—we heard a whistling from above, a movement of air, and a thud right in front of us of something big and heavy falling, and a crunch, and then our sandhill moved and slid, and I fell, and when I got up I saw that there was something strange but resembling a person lying in front of me. It was dark and unmoving. The mother of one of the girls ran over, and then other people, lots of people, and they kept saying, "She's dead; she killed herself." Then I was far away from there, on the steps, and didn't see anything else. The body was taken away in a carrier, the kind workmen use to carry sand, people were still standing around talking, and I heard: A woman had gone upstairs on the tour with a group and then stayed behind when they were going down. She got out on the portal balcony, climbed over the barrier, and jumped.

Carefully walking around the indentation in the sand where "it" had lain, I picked up my pail, failed to find my shovel, and went home. Batanya and Nura could tell something had happened to me, though I didn't say anything. But when we sat down at the table I threw up. Batanya took me to her room and started to take my temperature, and I told her that I wasn't sick, that I had seen death. "What death, what are you making up now?" Batanya scolded me. I told her everything, and she believed me right away. That calmed me down and I fell asleep unexpectedly.

I was awakened by Mama's voice, who was telling Batanya about this incident in the dining room. She had already learned that it had been a young woman, and she began talking about Esenin and mentioned Eseninism, while Batanya argued with her. And it all fell into place for me: the story I had heard long ago in kindergarten from the Angleterre Hotel children and "Eseni" and what I had just seen and the word "suicide." Then Batanya said to Mama, "Quiet, Lusia's in there; she saw the whole thing," and Mama said, "How awful," and there was horror in her voice, and I could sense even in the next room that she was afraid—and not simply afraid, but afraid for me.

The next day at kindergarten (to which I had returned after we moved back from Red Dawns Street to St. Isaac's—turn the corner, pass the Angleterre, and there's the Astoria) everyone was talking about that woman, but I was too embarrassed to tell anyone I had seen it. Why I thought it was shameful, I still don't know.

I couldn't begin to add up the number of times I passed that spot, each time thinking of the indentation in the sand and the shapeless something that had lain in it.

At the end of the hallway, beyond the nursery door, stood a chest, and often there were piles of clothing, coats and such, on top of it. I was afraid of this sight and begged people to leave the light on at that end of the corridor, but I was too embarrassed again, as at kindergarten, to explain that the things piled up on the chest reminded me of what had lain crumpled at the base of St. Isaac's.

Ten years later Papa read me Esenin's last lines (they were more or less banned at the time, and so it was rather strange to hear them from him) and he was surprised that I already knew them. But by then we read poetry to each other a lot; Papa was not a puritan in poetry (I mean a Party puritan).

The other horrible incident took place in our building. There was a family with a girl my age and a boy of two who lived on the third floor, in a room near the front entrance, with the window opening on the street. I often played with them in the courtyard and in their apartment. In the spring of 1928, when people were washing their windows and removing the winter frames, the boy fell out of the window during that flurry of spring cleaning and was killed. The family moved away soon afterward. I didn't see the boy's body. But when I passed their windows, I tried to project where he would have fallen. The sidewalks were paved with large stone slabs, and I was certain that I could see bloodstains on one of them. It was so hard to understand: how could it be, the boy I had known so well had existed and now he was gone. At the age of fifteen I read *The Life of Klim Samgin.* And I thought that Gorky must have been reading my mind when he wrote, "had the boy existed; maybe the boy never had existed?"

I have a terrible fear of open windows. Not for myself. The fear is of the combination "windows and children." And it didn't just appear when I became a mother, it has been with me ever since I was five.

8

Earlier I wrote that I didn't know of any privileges that my parents had in those years except for our large apartment, but I just remembered another one—a steady supply of passes to all the theaters in the city. I don't know how Mama and Papa "paid" for that privilege. I don't think they ever cared much for the theater. But every Sunday Batanya and I went to a matinee at the Maryinsky or the Mikhailovsky theater. By the time I was five I had heard everything in the opera repertoire more than once and had seen all the ballets. This might have been a rather early age, but maybe the earlier the better, because I was never bored, even at the opera. Though the productions were lavish, when I talked about them in kindergarten and to Nura, I managed to make them even more elaborate in costume, decor, and plot. I particularly enjoyed *Sadko* and *The Snow Maiden,* but no matter what was playing, the going-to-the-theater event itself was always a festive one. Batanya, who looked lovely in a beautiful blue dress with a shiny inset, and I, wearing a black velvet dress with a white lace collar and a huge white bow in my hair. I liked the way we looked; I liked the box in which we sat; I liked the candy and apples that Batanya gave me during intermission (we never went to the buffet). I learned that theaters had buffets only when I went with Papa.

Often after the theater Batanya and I went to visit her friends, in some fancy place where my velvet dress would not elicit Papa's smile and "Ooh, what a beauty," but rather would be taken seriously—that is, not mentioned. Later, when I began reading—almost all Russian operas and ballets are based on literature—I first thought that the literary works were incorrect. It was different in the opera. It took some time for me to learn which came first.

In those years I was known in the family as "crybaby," "chicken," "gossip," and "liar." I took offense at all those appellations and especially with Mama, because I was sure that she had decided to call me these names and did it more frequently than the others.

I cried most in front of my mother because I knew that she would call me a crybaby anyway, and I did it with little hope for pity, knowing really that tears would not work. Actually, I sort of played at being a crybaby. I don't know if I cried more than other children of that age and I don't really remember crying so much until later, when I learned to read and cried over books. The children's story *Fyodor's Grief* made me so sorry for Fyodor and the dishes he broke that I bawled. I was embarrassed by this and found myself a corner to read behind Grandmother's big armchair, where I thought no one could see me. There were fairy tales with orphans and a wicked stepmother or the song Nura liked to sing about the girl whose mother died and the new wife said to the father, "send her to the orphanage, or kill her, but do it fast, and if you don't I'll leave you and live happier alone."

The image of the stepmother often transformed itself into Mama, and shedding copious tears I imagined that she was my stepmother and watched her closely for signs that it was true. The only thing that didn't fit was that stepmothers were supposed to be ugly, and Mama was more beautiful than any of our women friends. She had long wavy hair which she pulled into a bun or braided. I couldn't decide which I liked better and I envied the hair and the fact that everyone saw Mama's beauty and admired her (I could see that even then). Mama persistently and frequently told me that I was ugly; it was all I could do to keep from screaming and crying and having hysterics—sometimes I couldn't stop myself. "You're ugly" were words Mama said to me repeatedly before she was arrested. When I was little I believed it and suffered terribly. Ugliness seemed a terrible thing: "ugly," "cruel," and "bad" were like synonyms. Everyone I loved I thought beautiful—Nura, Egorka, Papa, Batanya, all of my parents' friends. Especially Bronich. In the evenings he sang, "on that marvelous rock sat a bird with the face of a maiden." I thought he sang better than an Indian guest artist at the Maryinsky Theater. And of course, Mama was beautiful—she was the one with "the face of a maiden." The only ugly person in my life then was Comrade A., the man with the open fly.

As a teenager I began to think of myself as beautiful. I stopped believing what Mama said about my being ugly and a lot of other things at the same time. When Lion Feuchtwanger's book *The Ugly Duchess* was published in Russia, I was twelve years old. Mama started calling me that. I found the novel on her shelf, read it, and was outraged, and even said a lot of harsh and nasty things to her about it. But then in the summer of 1936 I looked in the mirror and decided that I was very pretty, so pretty that it took my breath away with an incredible feeling of joy and happiness and some other feeling I didn't know, filling my entire being. I can recall that moment to this day, and I've never experienced another one like it.

I could easily imagine my mother as my stepmother, but I never thought of Papa as an evil stepfather. I was only two when my first nanny, Tonya, told me that Papa, my Alikhanov, wasn't my papa at all. I remembered that forever. Just as I remembered the slender, elegant, and handsome man with a mustache who limped and walked with a cane, who showed up at our house in Chita embarrassed and somehow afraid of me. I would sneak looks at his picture in Batanya's album (he was seated and I was standing next to him with a basket in my hands). But at the same time I rejected it somehow. It was and it wasn't. And in the final analysis, it wasn't. Certainly Alikhanov was no stepfather.

I wasn't a coward, but if someone was looking I was too embarrassed to walk along a log, or even railroad tracks, to climb a tree or swing high on swings, to go too far into the woods, or read a poem aloud—I didn't like to show off, which is natural in children. I was afraid that I would fail, yet I would repeat the actions alone over and over, mastering myself, and often this mastering without an audience was truly dangerous. Perhaps my running away in the city or into the woods was part of it.

"Gossip" was a word that was applied to me early because I had the habit (not intentionally mean) of telling people what I had heard about them from others. As Batanya used to say, "Lusia's blabbed again." I was playing with the son of the Party secretary of one of Leningrad's districts, who lived in our building. Something went wrong in our game. The boy's father (his name was Pylayev, and we children used the adult form of address, surnames only—I even called Papa "Alikhanov" from time to time) tried to explain something to us, but I cut him off. "You keep quiet; Alikhanov says that you're a total idiot." That started a major Party squabble.

Hearing Mama say to Papa that Batanya was going to borrow money from her aunt, "that old landowner Anna Pavlovna," I remembered to shout down the whole corridor when she came to visit (which was very rare) that "the old landowner has come to borrow money!" (getting it backwards). Once I saw Bronich offering Mama money, probably to cover expenses, and Mama, red and embarrassed, pushing his hand away. I told Batanya about it immediately. Then I heard Batanya scold Mama and tell her that in the past people had a simple attitude toward money and knew that if they lived together they shared expenses, even though they weren't planning to do away with money, and that Mama had all the wrong ideas, and that was because she didn't want to think about the household and yet Batanya wouldn't live forever. Here I sided with Mama. First of all, because it was nonsense that Batanya wouldn't live forever. Secondly, because everyone knew that Mama shouldn't have to think about the household; she had plenty to think about in the Vyborg District Party Committee. The feeling that Mama shouldn't think about the household lasted a long time.

Sometimes my "blabbing" had a funny side. Once, Villi Brodsky came to visit Papa. I showed up and said, "Why are you here? Go away. Everybody says they want to get rid of you."

"What do you mean?" he asked.

"Just go away. I was outside with Nura, and everybody was walking around shouting 'Get rid of Brodsky.'"

Papa and Villi laughed and said, "Get rid of Trotsky."

Tatyana Bonner's father, Matvei Rubinshtein. 1870s.

Elena Bonner's grandparents, Grigorii (?–1905) and Tatyana Bonner, shortly after their wedding. 1896.

Tatyana Bonner's grandfather with her cousin Mikhail Rubinshtein, the future violinist at the Bolshoi Theatre (shown here in the uniform of a "cantonist," a child cadet conscript). On Mikhail's grave at Novodevichy cemetery two musical notes, "mi" and "fa," stand for his name. Circa 1883.

Tatyana Bonner as a child with her grandmother Anna Rubinshtein (?–1891). 1885.

Grigorii Bonner's father, Rafail—the so-called "soldier of Tsar Nicholas I."

Zisla (Aunt Zina) Bronshtein, who was once a political prisoner: in youth (below) and in 1936, at the dacha in Kratovo (right).

Elena Rubinshtein, Tatyana Bonner's mother. Irkutsk, ca. 1912.

Tatyana Bonner (left) with her sister, Sofia. Chita, 1898.

Tatyana Bonner's brother Moisey Rubinshtein with her husband, Grigorii Bonner. Irkutsk, May 4, 1899.

Ruth Bonner as a child. Chita, ca. 1909.

Tatyana Bonner with her children. Left to right: Anna, Matvei, Ruth. Chita, 1916.

Moisey Rubinshtein. Moscow, 1911.

Tatyana Bonner's brother Alexander (Isai) Rubinshtein, before leaving for the front. Moscow, February 18, 1915. (The inscription reads: "Think of your brother.")

Elena at two. Chita, 1925.

Elena Bonner's father, Levon Kocharov (Kocharyan). 1923.

Elena with her grandmother Gertselia Kocharov (Kocharyan), née Tonunts. Leningrad, 1937.

Gevork Alikhanov (left) with his nephew Armenak Kazaryan. Tiflis, 1908.

Gevork Alikhanov. Tiflis, 1914 or 1915. (The photo was taken by the secret police for the file on the case of the students of Nersesyan, the Armenian seminary in Tiflis, and is now in the archives of the Museum of the Revolution in Yerevan.)

Gevork Alikhanov (standing
at center) with his family.
Left to right: *his brother-in-
law Gevork Kazaryan, his
mother, Shushanik Ali-
khanyan, his sister Aikanush.
Tiflis, ca. 1915.*

Gevork Alikhanov. Tiflis,
1918.

Elena Bonner stands next to her grandmother Tatyana Bonner on the front steps of their house in Chita. *1926*.

Standing: *Alexander Rubinshtein (left), Matvei Bonner;* sitting: *Tatyana Bonner (left), Elena Rubinshtein, Moisey Keleiman. Chita, 1926*.

Matvei Bonner with his wife, Kaleria Skurlatova. Sretensk, 1926.

"Trotsky?" I was embarrassed and angry at Villi over my mistake. Later I learned who Trotsky was and even found out that though all of Mama's and Papa's friends said, "Get rid of Trotsky," Batanya did not agree. She knew Trotsky and had brought him books in Moscow once upon a time. Years later I learned that in the early twenties, when Batanya had worked at the Kremlin library, she had picked out books for Trotsky.

I must say that I still don't understand how at the age of four or five I managed to see and hear everything that the adults were doing in our house, especially since there was a nursery where I was constantly being sent. One thing I never saw or heard was my parents arguing. I never even heard an irritated voice or noticed any tension. To this day I don't know if there ever was anything like it in their relations.

I was a terrible liar (am I still?). I was constantly driven to make up something about the books that were read to me and later read myself; about the things I saw in the theater, on the street, at people's houses; about what happened at kindergarten, what I had heard. Every time I tried to stop myself yet couldn't, just as I couldn't explain why I had done it when I was caught. I would swear never to lie again, though I knew that I would, and, most importantly, I knew that lying didn't bother me and I didn't consider it a flaw. So I never cried when I was scolded for lying. It was a ritual—I lie, they scold, they scold, I lie. With the years, and with great effort, I learned to control myself, but not completely, and, realizing that this is an incurable flaw, I am astounded to encounter people like Andrei who are completely free of it. In my childhood I can say only of Batanya that she didn't have it, and I'm not sure about Papa. I almost never lied to Batanya.

In the spring of 1928 my kindergarten shut down and the Astoria stopped being a building where many of our friends lived. It was turned back into an ordinary hotel. I began going to a play group on Millionnaya Street (later Khalturin Street) at the home of the Otsupovs, not very close friends of my parents. They had a daughter, a girl my age, and a few other children were brought there. I didn't like the house. It wasn't as cozy and friendly as the homes of Batanya's friends and it was as familiar and simple as the homes of my parents' comrades. The house was an imitation of my parents', and I sensed this acutely. We were taken for walks in the summer gardens, and because I didn't like anything about the Otsupovs' house or the play group, I didn't like the park either. I always wanted to go to Alexandrovsky Park or to St. Isaac's. I hated Millionnaya Street; it seemed too flat and was always empty—no people, no carriages, nothing. It was only in recent years that I came to understand its incomparable loveliness, that it was older than my Gogol Street, but back then I hated it and was glad when the group ended and it was time to move to the dacha.

After Gorky, Andrei and I stayed a few times on that street. Once with Tanya and her children. But most often just the two of us. The tall windows of the Academy of Sciences hotel with their low, broad marble sills reminded me of my childhood home. When we would be coming back on a translucent, ghostly spring night, we could see the wind moving the light curtains from afar. And it seemed that it was my childhood returning and bidding me farewell. Once, as we were walking from Mars Field, floating in a lilac haze a man came out of an alley from the Moika River and turned toward Dvortsovaya. Swift. Light. In a black cape. Bareheaded. He seemed to fly past us and vanished into the entryway of the house across from ours. We exchanged a look and I whispered, "Pushkin." Andrei rushed forward and pulled at the door. It was shut. Locked. As usual. That house had long caused strange suspicions in us. It was a white and green two-story building. A portal with columns. And doors which no one ever entered. And now, we saw someone go in. Shades of the past.

At the massive gates of our hotel, Andrei looked back and said a bit uncomfortably, in an attempt to break the tension, "Pushkin lyagushkin [the frog]." "At it again?" I said indignantly, because he had said that once long ago as we passed Pushkin's monument in Moscow. Then I had promised to turn him in to Lydia Korneyevna Chukovskaya and spoil her exalted love for him (Andrei, not Pushkin).

As for my childhood dislike of Millionnaya? It was replaced by our joint love (Andrei's and mine) for the street with such an uncharming name and such charming ghosts.

9

The summer of 1928 was probably the best of my entire child-hood. We lived in a new log house, which stood almost at the river, the last in a line going down the right side along the railroad from the Sestroretsk Station. The station after that, Beloostrov, was already "abroad," in Finland. You could take the train to Leningrad through it, going through the "abroad," since it was a circle line. It was a single-track line, at least between Sestroretsk and Beloostrov.

The house was surrounded by fir trees and did not have a fence. The firs went almost all the way from the front of the house to the tracks. Between the firs and the ties there was a narrow swathe of tall grass, filled with swaying daisies, bluebells, and tall pinks. On a sunny day the aroma was so thick that it was more than warm air streaming above the tracks—it was the essence of grass and flowers. I loved lying in that fragrant grass face up, watching the fir crowns waving and the white clouds floating way above my head. My eyes would tire and the clouds would turn pink. I would be half mesmerized by their movement and the sway of the firs. To the right of the house the firs went so close to the steep sandy cliff of the riverbank that their twisted roots, like fat snakes, hung in the air over the water. You could crawl from one outcropping of the cliff to another along them, and you could sit on them and, holding on, lower yourself toward the shimmering water. The water was not silvery white, like the bay, but darker, with a golden glint, and it did not give off any sounds. On the other side was a cemetery, and sometimes I saw people there, but there were never any on our side. From the bank I could see the railroad bridge and easily count the cars on the occasional trains—long freight trains and short suburban ones, with only three or four cars hauled by a steam engine. If you followed the river to the bridge, you could tell from underneath that it wasn't solid, but made of planks, and you could see the cross beams and ties that held the tracks. But you had to shut your eyes when a train passed, to keep out the dust and small pieces of coal. Sometimes people crossed the bridge on foot, carefully walking from tie to tie and holding onto the railing. A person's shadow would glide slowly along the water under the bridge. This water wasn't still, as elsewhere on the Sestra; it moved and bubbled. It was very scary to watch a person on the bridge, yet I desperately wanted to walk from tie to tie myself.

One time I decided to do it. I don't recall how I got across or how I walked through the cemetery by myself, but I remember coming back to the bridge and realizing that I didn't have the strength to force myself to make the return trip. I don't know how long I spent by the bridge. I was afraid not only of the crossing, but that it was going to get dark soon. I went down to the water, washed up, got my feet wet, dried my sandals, and returned to the bridge. In that time several people had crossed over the bridge. Each time, I wanted to ask them to help me cross, but I didn't dare. At last, I won the struggle and went by myself. I can't describe how terrified I was. That must be why I forgot the first trip, because the fear of the second crossing eclipsed it. Once I was on the other side, I looked back and saw my berry basket. I must have crossed over holding on with only one hand to the railing and carrying the basket in the other. But I didn't remember that either.

When I got back to the dacha, Nura bawled me out for wandering around unfed and dirty when it was almost time to go meet Batanya's train, and that she would get into trouble for not taking care of the children. Without any fuss I washed up, ate, dressed, and went to the station, enjoying Nura's praise for doing everything so fast.

The next day I made my way to the bridge again and saw that my basket was still on the other side. I felt sorry; the basket was no longer new and therefore I was used to it. It was my own. That must have been the decisive factor in my going over the bridge again, still afraid, but without the terror of the day before. After a while those trips became quite ordinary. And I would return with a basket full of wild cemetery strawberries. Everyone praised me. Batanya said that no one but I could ever pick such nice berries and it was amazing since there were so little of them around. I never mentioned how I obtained them, though.

In late July 1937 I spent a few days with Anya, Mama's sister, and her husband, Lyova, at the dacha in Udelnaya. Seva, the boy I loved, came to visit, and we went off deep into the woods. It was the happiest walk of our lives. And the most tragic days of our country. Papa had been arrested, Seva's mother, Lida, would be arrested in a few days. Our world was collapsing. And the whole world around us.

I began making a bouquet of strawberry flowers for Lida, and Seva recited Tsvetayeva's poetry, ". . . nothing is bigger or sweeter than cemetery berries . . ." And I told him about the bridge, the cemetery, and the wild strawberries. I had never told anyone about it before; it was all somehow too intimate. Ever since then that bridge and that basket always come to mind like a lucky charm whenever I have to overcome something terrible and difficult.

We lived at the dacha with Nura, and Batanya came out every evening after work. Mama and Papa were there only during the first few weeks and then they went south for a vacation. I was happy that there were no other children besides Egorka and that we didn't have to take obligatory walks with the others. Nura demanded little of me: to eat well, wash up, and clean my feet at bedtime. The rest of the time, except for the hour that I had to stay with Egorka on a spread blanket on the grass or in the hammock while she went shopping, I was free and I sensed it acutely.

Batanya's train had to be met in the evening. This was enjoyable because I went to the station alone. There was something festive about these meetings. Perhaps because I spent all day in my underpants but got washed up and put on a dress for the train. They sold ice cream at the station. The ice cream of our childhood was a scoop between two vanilla wafers imprinted with either VALYA or KOLYA, which were the first two words I read on my own. Music would be playing at the station restaurant and at the Kursaal. Good-looking, well-dressed people strolled along the platform. I liked guessing which car Batanya would be in and then the slow walk home with her along the sand path near the houses. She would wear a light mohair coat and light straw hat and carry a long umbrella. She would breathe deeply, inhaling the fresh air, and say that it was wonderful at the dacha and stifling in the city. When I later read Tolstoy and his *"comme il faut,"* I always pictured Batanya in that coat and hat and with the umbrella-cane in her hand.

On Sundays (I don't remember if people worked a five- or six-day week then) Batanya and I and the usual guests (they came with boxes of chocolates, fruit, or watermelon—my parents' friends were capable of bringing a watermelon or a sack, but never a box, of candy) went to the bay. Dinner was always late on that day, so we would take a picnic lunch with us. Under the fir trees, where the sandy beach began, we spread blankets and towels. The food and bottles of soda pop were spread out on a tablecloth (always and everywhere, Batanya had a tablecloth). I was allowed to wade in the water and swim as much as I wanted. But it wasn't interesting to bathe in the bay, I didn't have the thrill I did swimming secretly in the Sestra River, expecting to be grabbed up by the "water monster" or the "whirlpool." Nura went on and on about them (I thought they were both living creatures), apparently believing that fear of them would be enough to keep me out of the river. But I went swimming and lied to her constantly, saying I merely waded in the river. Sometimes the adults swam in the bay, too, but I never saw Batanya swimming (or undressed at all).

At the beach, if I walked along the shore for a while I would reach a striped hut with an armed soldier standing outside. He spoke with the children and grownups who came over, never shot his rifle, and looked just like a tin soldier in a tall helmet. Not far down the beach beyond him was another sentry hut, with another patrolling soldier, but we weren't allowed to go there, because that was "foreign territory."

Sometimes instead of having a picnic in the woods we went to the restaurant near the train station. I always knew which it would be, by what Batanya wore: her blue-gray cotton picnic dress or her white silk dress with white embroidery at the neck, sleeves, and hem. I later saw the same outfit on Mama and her cousin Raya (was it the same dress, recut to suit one after the other?).

Going up the stairs to the restaurant, I would inhale deeply. It smelled delicious—something roasting, something baking—and it always made me hungry.

The following winter I once heard my father reading poetry aloud to himself—he often did, always readily answering my questions about what he was reading and repeating some of the lines for me. He was reciting: "In the evenings the heated air above the restaurants is wild and noisy, and the vernal and noxious spirit rules the drunken cries . . ." The only thing I got out of that was "noxious spirit," so I told him that was the spirit of roasting and baking at the restaurant in Sestroretsk. He did not agree and explained it differently. I don't remember how, but he read the whole poem for me several times and named the poet, Alexander Blok. I remembered the poet and the lines. It was the first poem by Blok I ever learned.

In the evenings we sat on the veranda, lit by a kerosene lamp. Nura wrote letters. She was always writing letters, first to her village and later, when we lived in Moscow, to somewhere "in exile." Batanya usually sewed, and I was supposed to read aloud. Back in the city the previous winter Batanya had started teaching me to read. That summer I crossed the barrier that separates knowing the letters and knowing how to form words from the desire to read. By the end of our dacha season I was spending less time wandering in the woods and along the river. Once I had mastered Chukovsky* and other children's books of poetry (I liked only rhymes then), Batanya brought a big heavy book bound in red and gold (the Marks edition) of Zhukovsky† and would read to me aloud from it several times. The book enchanted me, and mastering the old orthography was easily done. I began to read. "Svetlana," "Nal and Damayanti," "The Forest

*Kornei Ivanovich Chukovsky (1882–1969), writer and translator, whose children's classics in verse include *The Crocodile* and *Doctor Ai-bolit*.
†Vassily Andreyevich Zhukovsky (1783–1852), poet known as "the Balladeer"; "Ludmilla" (1808) was followed by another 38 ballads. His ballads, elegies, and epics were wildly popular.

King," "Lerchatka"—I read Zhukovsky until I got drunk on him, until I dreamed Zhukovsky every night. I read to Batanya in the evenings and to Nura in the daytime, I read from the book and I repeated it by heart on my walks. Why had Batanya brought Zhukovsky? She had the Marks editions of Pushkin in green, Nekrasov in blue, Gogol in dark green, Lermontov in light blue, and Nikitin in light blue. Zhukovsky may have been a random choice, but the combination of poetry and fairy-tale plot was just right for my age. I have always felt poetry to be the highest form of art.

I don't think there was a single rainy day that summer of 1928, only brief summer storms, which I adored. I always found hilarious Nura's fear of thunder and lightning. She shut all the windows and doors, chasing us away from them, and sometimes even made us lie down on the floor. Next she raced around setting up buckets, the trough, and our tub (zinc with high sides) under the corners of the roof, and then she sat with us, muttering something—I knew she was praying. In the evening after a storm we had bath time in the rainwater heated up on the stove. Nura washed Egorka first, then me "until my hair squeaked," and then herself. It was hot in the kitchen, but Nura wouldn't let us leave, so I sat and watched her wash. Whenever I see Plastov's famous painting *Spring*, with the little girl sitting on a bench and a young woman with loose hair kneeling and tying the girl's kerchief, I think of our Nura.

That incredible summer ended, and with it the best dacha time I ever had, and it had seemed long the way things can be long only in childhood.

10

The next autumn I wasn't sent to kindergarten or play group. I was a "homey." The day with Nura, when Batanya and my parents were at work, was not structured in any way except for lunchtime. I was allowed to go outside alone and do what I wanted the rest of the time. All I craved was reading. I don't know any other period in my life when I read as much. Just before New Year's my parents began packing for Moscow, where they were going to study; they were to take "Marxism Courses." A few days before they left I got sick, I don't remember with what. Using illness as an excuse, I got a Christmas tree out of them. Mama had resisted a long time and Papa too. He said it was bourgeois and "atavistic." He even explained atavism to me. But I demanded, cried, and whined. I don't remember ever having a Christmas tree before or where I got the idea that children should have one. I knew full well how "anti-Party" my desire was, but that merely increased my longing. And they gave in. In the corner at the foot of my bed a tree was set up. Nura decorated it, Egorka "helped," and Mama pretended not to see it whenever she came into the room. My parents left when I was on the mend, but the tree remained.

In the middle of February, Mama came for my birthday from Moscow and two or three days later Nura, Egorka, and I went to Moscow with her. On that early winter morning, almost in total darkness, exhausted after the train ride, we drove up in a carriage to a building that seemed uglier than any we had ever lived in. It was a vague brownish gray color and the best adjective for it was "dilapidated." The unmarked (almost secret) door from the street led to a staircase that was narrower and darker than our back stairs in Leningrad. There was a dormitory on the second floor, and we moved into it.

The doors of the rooms opened onto a wide and large entry *cum* hallway. At the end was a spacious kitchen with lots of tables along the walls and in the middle, and from the kitchen a door led to a room with several sinks along one wall and five toilet stalls along the other. The door to our rooms was near the entrance to the dormitory and very far from the bathroom. This, however, was not supposed to worry me since Mama and Nura immediately relegated me back to a chamberpot. We had three rooms which seemed to have been carved out of one big room. The hallway led into a narrow long room, one window wide, which became the dining room; to the right a door led into another narrow room for my parents, and to the left was the "nursery," rather large and strangely shaped, like a quarter-circle. The rounded part of the room had three large windows and a door to a balcony which circled it, facing the street on one side and the boulevard on the other. There was a monument on the boulevard, shaped like a big bell. It was called the Shipka. Neither the name nor its appearance was appropriate for a monument, as far as I was concerned. In Leningrad "monument" referred to either the fearsome flying Bronze Horseman or the other one, also with a horse, which I called the tsar's and which I could see from the windows of the Astoria.

Trolleys ran on the boulevard and the street, called Maroseika. The name sounded awfully shabby after Leningrad's street names. I didn't know the word "provincial" back then, but if I had, I'm sure I would have used it. All around were streets named Pokrovka, Solyanka, Myasnitskaya, Ilyinka, while back in Leningrad we had Nevsky (even if some called it 25 October), Tavrichesky, Morskaya, Admiralteiskaya, Dvortsovaya. And, most important, everything was narrow and crooked; there was no space, no vistas; you couldn't see far at all.

Judging from my first impressions of Moscow, I was already infected with the snobbery characteristic of Leningraders. Later I came to love Moscow and became a Muscovite, but back then I was a Leningrader.

Beneath our balcony was the entrance to a drugstore. "The

house with the drugstore" is how I described it to myself, and I felt a little sad, because in Leningrad we had lived in the Grand Hotel. On the first day in Moscow I got lost in a funny and humiliating way. I thought that everyone, even Mama, respected me for always knowing the way, and I respected myself for it too. They let me go outside on the boulevard by myself, because Mama and Nura were unpacking and I was in the way.

I stayed out for a little bit (the boulevard was boring and so was the street) and went home. It looked very easy. I could see the balcony overhead; it was "home" already. I walked past the drugstore, but I couldn't find the front door. There were many unsightly, undifferentiated doors. I would try one after the other, but it was always wrong. Behind one door was a small kiosk with a sign, "Keys Made"; another led to a staircase, but our dormitory was not on the second floor. The third was all wrong too. I shuttled back and forth from the drugstore along two or three houses from the end of the block, where there was a little church (certainly not St. Isaac's!), feeling hurt and frustrated. I could see the balcony and couldn't figure out how to get there. Suddenly I noticed a door opening, so unlike a door that I hadn't even seen it the several times I had walked past. A man I had glimpsed earlier that morning in our dormitory came out. He walked by me and I slipped into the door in a hurry, afraid to lose it again.

When I came home, Mama said, "You didn't get lost! I can't get used to that front door, I can never find it." I wanted to confess that I hadn't found it right off, either, but something stopped me. I settled for, "There is no front door; there's nothing but back doors here."* My father liked the line and he began using it when he was in a foul mood or not feeling well—"Nothing but back doors here." It became a family expression for something bad happening.

We rarely saw Mama and Papa. They left in the morning before we woke up and often returned after we were asleep. I don't even remember them having days off, because there were no Sunday lunches with meat pie on a pink tablecloth. In fact an

*In Russian the word *chorny*, or "black," is used for back entrance.

oilcloth appeared instead of the tablecloth. I don't think either of them ever ate at home. If Papa did return early, he sat down "to study." I was allowed to settle at the side of his desk with my book, but he was taciturn, didn't hear my questions, and in general was not interested in Egorka or me. He still drank his tea as before, from a glass in a holder, but not as in Leningrad, where he used to drink it in our large dining room, standing by the table with one leg on the crossbar of a chair, telling us all a story and laughing. Now he still drank it standing up, but in his room, silently, nose in a book or in his notes. His handwriting was small, with rounded letters, and very clear. I don't remember any of my other relatives with such neat penmanship. The pages he wrote always looked neat and even the crossed-out material looked nice, because the line was thin and straight—as if done with a ruler.

After Mama returned from the camps, we found Papa's blue "dress-up" double-breasted suit in Batanya's trunk. While cleaning it before Mama started taking it apart to sew my "dress-up" double-breasted suit, I found a note in the back pocket of the trousers, obviously written during a meeting. To whom? Where? When? Why didn't it get to the recipient? How did it get back to Papa? Mama didn't know. She took it from me silently and put it away. It was the last thing written by my father that I ever saw. The piece of paper, like a meteorite from distant burned-out worlds, had flown into my post-war life.

There were a lot of children in the dormitory. They attended the kindergarten in the building. A few days after our arrival I was sent there, too. The school at the Astoria had had several airy rooms, nothing was dirty, there were lots of toys, and the children were always clean and neatly dressed. Here things were cramped, with dim, gray light, because the kindergarten was on the first floor and the windows were on ground level opening into a small dark courtyard. The oilcloths on the tables where we ate were sticky. I constantly felt that stickiness on my hands, but I didn't want to wash them because the towel (just one for everybody instead of a personal one) that hung by the sink was always wet. The toilet was a real trial for me. It was filthy and it stank. I think the only thing I brought out of that experience was my lifelong dislike of public bathrooms and the habit of "holding." Much later, when I would return home from somewhere and head straight for the bathroom, our last cleaning lady would say to my receding back, "Don't go, don't go, and when you do, it's a flood."

We went for walks to the Shipka, but we weren't allowed to go down the boulevard. We could circle around it and swing on the chains (until the teacher chased us away). I don't remember any of the children or anything else about that kindergarten, not even what we did there or how they kept us busy. I don't think we did anything. It didn't last long. I got sick. For a long time. I had the measles, German measles, and mumps, a very bad case, all in a row. I liked being sick, because it brought Mama back into the house. She either didn't go to work then or returned very early, and it felt as if she were with me all the time.

I was moved into my parents' room. The overhead light was wrapped in newspaper and the lamp on Papa's desk was covered with a flowered blue scarf. At first it hurt to look at it even that way, but later I spent a lot of time staring at it, imagining that I had drawn those incredibly beautiful flowers, which gave light and color, sometimes pink, or yellow, or green, and the waves reached me, and I could float in the color and light as if in the bay, and they were warm, and when they were cold they gave me chills. I was covered with Mama's blanket: that was the custom whenever I was sick right up until 1937. The blanket was quilted, very light, filled not with cotton batting but camel's hair, and it radiated heat like an oven, instead of merely protecting you from the cold. It was iridescent, golden, orange-yellow-pink-green, and all those colors together were called Bukhara silk. That year Mama always wore something dark and grim; there was nothing bright in the house either, and only that Bukhara silk glowed. It was joy to lie under Mama's blanket, but it was allowed only when I was sick. Also allowed were crankiness, don't wannas, crying, and mean words aimed without reason at Nura or Mama.

Once during the mumps Mama put a compress on my neck, sat down wearily at the foot of the bed, and said, "Just think what a weakling she is. She's always throwing up, or has a cold, or now with the measles, German measles, and mumps all in a row. Egorka is a golden child—he's never sick at all and he hasn't even caught any of this from her. Amazing! After all, she could have infected him with all this nastiness." She said it calmly, not berating me, and not to me but to Papa who was "studying" in the room. But I blew up. I tore off the compress and shouted at Mama. I told her she was the reason I got sick, because she wouldn't hire a "royal nanny" for me who knew how to nurture healthy children. She did that only for "her Egorka." She didn't care if I died, and so I would die, just to show her; I'd die, I would. Mama jumped up from the bed and ran out of the room with the words, "I could just kill her." And I started bawling. Then, at that moment, I was certain that she was the "mean stepmother" and she would kill me or give me to an orphanage, where it would be worse even than in our kindergarten, just terrible.

I cried so hard that I got hysterical, but Mama wouldn't come. Papa spent a long time soothing me and then picked me up and walked me up and down the room. I'd forgotten what it felt like when he carried me home from a party when I was very little, but now, so big and tall—as everyone said—I liked it. He walked around the room and when we moved under the newspaper around the bulb, it swayed. I was crying "on purpose" by then. I reached up and pulled the newspaper; it tore off. Papa said, "There, that's all," and put me into bed. He smoothed the blanket very badly—I liked being tucked in, and he simply laid it on top of me—and said, "You're a big girl now, and to keep from dying you have to eat well, by yourself without coaxing. And now go to sleep." (I ate poorly, which made Nura nag me, while Egorka ate well.) For some reason I felt very calm, and I fell asleep right away, not waiting in case my parents had an interesting conversation to overhear while I pretended to be asleep.

The next day I was returned to the nursery, although I was allowed to be ill under the Bukhara blanket in the daytime. But I slept under my own at night. Egorka didn't catch anything from me that time or from any other of my many diseases. He really was a "golden child" in that sense.

Finally that long and boring winter ended and there was talk that we would go to Leningrad and from there to the dacha. They had rented a house once more in Sestroretsk. I thought about the dark and golden Sestra River, the bridge, the cemetery, the firs, and the meadow below them. I froze with joy thinking about my return. I wasn't in the least worried about the separation from my parents or that Batanya would be strict, with her "get in the corner" and sometimes even rather painful slaps.

11

My cousin Zorya went to the dacha with us. I don't remember if her parents, Lyova and Anya, were with us. In Moscow, at the Marxism Courses dormitory, we would have rarely seen them, if at all, and I don't recall seeing them before this summer.

Batanya didn't come to the dacha. She was sick and staying in Essentuki, a spa with mineral waters.

This summer Sestroretsk turned out to be different. We lived on an ordinary suburban street, from which you couldn't tell where the railroad and the forest were. And there was no river. The house had a small lawn in front of a glassed-in veranda. With a lilac and some other bushes. Behind the house was a garden, but that wasn't "our half." You could take the street to the station, and it was the same—they still sold ice cream in waffles—but there were no concerts in the evening and the restaurant had closed. When we went to the station to meet people, I would go over to the building where the restaurant had been the past summer and try to get a sniff of the former "noxious spirit" smell, but the air that came through the cracks in the shutters and boarded-up veranda was damp and unpleasant. And the "restaurant house" was old and beginning to look like our house in Moscow, dilapidated. The people at the station were grumpy and dumpy, and always under umbrellas. That summer, I don't think there was a single sunny day; it was always pouring.

The boss at the dacha was Sarra, the sister of Zorya's father, Lyova. And there were four children staying there: Egorka, Zorya, Maika (Sarra's daughter), and I. Nura was always in the kitchen. In the evenings and on his days off Sarra's husband, Misha, helped his wife handle us. It must have been difficult because of the rain, which made us all cranky—tired of waiting for it to stop and of having to play on the veranda. We never went into the woods and I didn't have a single opportunity to slip out the gate, much less find the woods. Every day we went for a walk in our coats and boots in the strip of pines along the beach, or we found our way along the wet sand to the border hut and back. But even the trip to the border guard was boring now, because it was the same thing every day, and always in the rain. Sometimes we were allowed to swim—also dull, because Misha stood onshore with his watch in his hands and said almost immediately, "That's it, five minutes are up." We had to get out before we could even reach the spot where the water was more than knee-deep. My aunt Anya (and I think her husband, Lyova) came to the dacha for their vacation. Then there were more adults than children, but not enough warm coats to go around and so only those adults who could bundle up accompanied us on the long beach walks.

Egorka and I came to love Sarra, who was very kind and merry, despite the weather. She and Misha liked "bringing up children properly," that's what I called it to myself. They never punished us, never even shouted, but we had to do everything on a schedule, eat everything on our plates, endlessly wash our hands, and say "please" and "thank you" all the time. Egorka tried so hard to be as good as the other kids (he was the youngest) that he actually once said, "Sarra, please, it's raining." That became another family joke, like my "There's nothing but back doors," and meant overzealousness in any undertaking.

In August, Mama came from Moscow "on vacation." She visited the dacha almost every day from Leningrad, but she didn't spend the night, going back to the city, where Papa was "on vacation" too. He didn't visit the dacha.

I think that Papa was embarrassed and at the same time bored by the company of Mama's relatives. He was always taciturn around them, never laughing, and in general tried to avoid them. Their relationship wasn't hostile; they just never developed one.

Later, when we lived in a very large place in Moscow, Mama's relatives were always passing through and staying with us, and when Batanya visited she had "her" guests almost every evening. If he came home when they were there, Papa would say hello almost soundlessly and go to his room. Then he would call me in and say, "Bring me some tea and something tasty."

"What?"

"What do they have?"

I would list everything on the table, trying not to forget anything, and he would pick. I would go to the dining room, pour his tea, fill a plate with everything he wanted and more and bring it to him. I could see Batanya compress her lips and look angry, and the guests at the table look uncomfortable. But I didn't care. Just as I knew that I would wander anywhere I chose whether they beat me or cut me to pieces, Papa could have his tea wherever he wanted. I would bring him the tea and he would give me a conspiratorial smile and say with a sigh, "The father didn't believe his son that there was love in the world . . ." or "The mother told her son, don't go with thieves, you'll be sent to hard labor, wearing shackles. . . ."

Even now, as I write those lines, I weep. "You'll be sent to hard labor, wearing shackles. . . ." It's as if he knew.

Batanya was privately outraged. And out loud. Once after her guests left, as we were getting ready for bed (when she came to Moscow, she slept in my room), she said, "A savage, a real savage, an Asian. And you bring him tea! You'd think he was your father!" I shouted wildly at her, jumped up and picked up a book with which to strike her, but I didn't. We glared at each other in silence (at eleven I was already a bit taller than she), then we turned away and silently got into our beds. Batanya never again said "He's here" or "He's left" in my presence, she always called him "Papa" or "your father."

There were exceptions among Mama's relatives—the ones Papa treated warmly, with whom he was at ease and always friendly. The most important one was Matvei, Mama's older brother. They had become friends back in Chita and to the end Matvei's visits (though they became infrequent) were as much of a pleasure for Papa as the arrival of Agasi, Bronich, Shura Breitman, or any of his other close friends. Papa and Matvei played chess, went off to shoot billiards, and talked late into the night, when Papa would explode with loud, contagious laughter. I think that if Papa had had a brother he would have treated him like Matvei. Papa also had familial relations with Mama's cousin Raisa, perhaps because in the Leningrad years when Papa was with us, we lived as a single family. Of Mama's older relatives, Papa liked Uncle Sanya, Aunt Ronya, and her mother.

Mama had brought pencils and paints to the dacha and showed us three girls how to draw, while Sarra taught us to sing. I was the least talented in both. Sarra wouldn't say so (I saw for myself), but Mama kept repeating, "You are so useless," as if I couldn't see for myself that I couldn't draw even some stupid flower. That summer my teeth ached all the time and my nose dripped. Mama decided to safety-pin a hankie to my dress, so that I wouldn't lose it. I would unpin it and bury it in the sand, even though not having it was bad—my nose was always wet. But I did it out of spite. I think that I hated everyone that summer and kept trying to do mean things. The only place I calmed down was in the small kitchen and storeroom where Nura cooked, washed dishes, and slept. But it was very crowded there. As soon as Nura saw that I was better, she would chase me out. And Sarra didn't think it was the "right place for children."

My teeth got worse and Mama took me to the resort dentist, who would pull a tooth each time. I screamed with convulsions, not so much out of pain as fear. On the way home, after the extraction, I would make a point of spitting every few steps, not into my hankie but on the ground, my spittle mixed with blood, and say to my mother, "Don't you see that I'm gushing blood?" I liked the word "gushing" and I thought that it would surely overcome Mama's heartlessness. But Mama said curtly, "I don't see," and we would walk on. She wouldn't even hold my hand.

That summer I believed Mama when she said I was ugly. All my anger derived from the feeling that Sestroretsk wasn't the same; it was aimed at the rain, at the people around me, my teeth, my cold. The sense that I was "useless" had done its work on me. I have documentary proof. There's a photograph of all the people at the dacha except Mama and with Batanya, taken when we came back to the city. It has adults and three pretty children— Egorka, Zorya, and Maika. And me—a stringbean of a girl, with bangs and an angry, sharp face. My lips are tight, and I'm looking at the lens as if I'm about to burst into tears or break the camera.

Before our stay at the dacha was over, Mama took me to the ear, nose, and throat man at the clinic, who said I needed an operation. Mama took me to the city. I was happy to be back in our rooms with the warmth that I missed at the dacha, and I was glad to see Batanya. That evening Mama bathed me, which was new, since I had always been bathed by the nannies. When she was combing my hair after the shampoo, Mama suddenly said in a light and cheerful tone, "Your hair is amazingly beautiful the way it falls, Lusia. When you grow up you won't have to do anything with it, and that makes life much simpler." Her voice, the words, and her tone, which was filled with love and pleasure, were unexpected and novel. It was also new that Mama sang while she washed me: "I wash my hands and run to his studio, throwing on my shawl." I remembered that song, "Bricks," from Chita, where I first had heard Mama singing it, but she hadn't sung it since; in fact, she had almost stopped singing.

The next morning I was taken for surgery. The doctor removed polyps and my tonsils. It's impossible to describe how I screamed through the whole thing. *My Tanya screamed the same way if they had to take a blood sample from her finger, fill a tooth, or something like that. I realized how my parents must have felt when Tanya had her tonsils removed and the doctor, taking off her gloves, said, "God forbid I ever see that girl again. I don't know what I'll do to her."*

Papa carried me out of the doctor's office and we went home by car even though home was close by. The operation had been done somewhere on Nevsky, almost across the street from Gostiny Dvor, at the office of a private doctor. At home, it was like before: lunch on a pink tablecloth and friends around the table:

our friends Alya and Misha Merkuryev, cousin Raya, and someone else. They gave me ice cream, which I ate lying down on the couch. Everyone else was at the table eating Batanya's pies, my parents laughing while telling them how I had screamed, but my feelings weren't hurt.

Because it was almost the end of summer, I didn't go back to the dacha.

12

In town everything had changed, and our house was different. We didn't go back to our nursery. The parents of Mama's cousin Raya, from Irkutsk, had moved in there. In the dining room and the room where Papa's friend Tsolak Amatuni, his wife, Asya, and their baby, Andrusha, had once lived, now were living the parents and sister of the writer Yuri Lebedinsky. He had visited Papa occasionally, but I had never seen his family before. Some other stranger moved into the room where Bronich and Comrade A. had lived. Nura, Egorka, and I were in our parents' two small rooms, and Batanya in hers.

Our apartment had turned into a communal flat, but there were no other children for the first few years—all the neighbors were childless. The neighbors changed with kaleidoscopic speed—people were always coming and going, switching rooms, and soon the only ones left of the people Papa had brought in were Raya and her parents. Raya lived with us from 1927 on and was like "real family" for Egorka and me; we were surprised when people told us that she was a cousin. Raya's father, Lazar Rafailovich Bonner, the brother of Mama's father (I don't know who was the older brother), was like a grandfather to us. We called him "Deda" and loved him dearly, especially when we became Leningraders again after 1937.

I don't know what Deda did before the Revolution, but he had no profession, working as a night watchman at a warehouse. The family treated him slightly mockingly and considered him a drunkard. I don't think people used the word "alcoholic" in those days. Coming back from his shift, Deda would have half a pint of vodka and in the evening, finishing it off, he would spend time with us, attentively listening to our stories about the yard, school, and other important events in our lives. I read poetry to him (for lack of other listeners). I think that passing time with him was particularly important for Egorka, since after the arrests of 1937 there were no other men in our lives—only grandmothers, aunts, and even more distant (but female) relatives.

Deda had a big crate under his bed with nails, awls, and other tools. I had never seen a hammer up close except at shop class in school before we moved to Leningrad in 1937, but at that point I fell in love with tools and (with Deda's help) quickly became a recognized repairman for all the neighbors' plugs, fuses, Primus and kerosene stoves, and other such items, which were much more in use then than now. These items, though expensive by the standards of the day, kept breaking. I also repaired and made shelves, doors, and benches for people. The love of doing things with my hands remains to this day, but I don't have the strength for it. Egorka also learned from Deda to work with his hands.

Deda was among the first of our relatives to die in the Leningrad blockade. His wife, Baba Fenya, lacked his kindliness. She was a tight, if not greedy, woman who managed to get everything into her own hands and make a personal profit out of every life situation. Before the Revolution, she had rented out furnished rooms with board in Irkutsk. Many former exiles passed through her apartment, people who were not allowed to return to Central Russia, and in my childhood she stubbornly gathered affidavits from them and got herself a personal pension from the state, even though her activity before and after the Revolution had consisted only in letting furnished rooms. As my grandmother used to say (not kindly, but accurately, I supposed), "Fedosya first took advantage of them and then got affidavits from them."

When we were still in Moscow, Baba Fenya would come for congresses of MOPR, the International Organization to Aid Revolutionaries, and I would accompany her to very fancy meetings at the Hall of Columns, where Zemlyachka* appeared, and then we would go to dinner at her house. The meetings were memorable because they destroyed my concept of the MOPR people. They were all so respectable, so well dressed and well fed, and even though they recalled their sufferings in the prisons and cells of foreign lands, their faces and words and manner of speaking did not jibe with the emaciated face behind bars on the MOPR button I wore in those days. And the dinner! I had never seen such *zakuski* (hors d'oeuvres) in my life, even with the extra food my parents got. I got my first taste of pineapple there, and they had enormous boxes of chocolates. The rows of shaped chocolates were wrapped in shiny paper, red, gold, or green. Before this, I had only seen silver foil and like my peers called it "gold." Once I was given a box to take home. I think that dinner was the culmination of Baba Fenya's search for affidavits and when she got the most important one, from Zemlyachka, she got her personal pension. And what was the fate of those who signed those papers for her?

I haven't written kindly about her. Yet she was good to us in her own fashion. She tolerated me, since her daughter Raya loved me, and she loved Egorka, buying him things that she could get through special means. She got him his first suit with long trousers. (He had came to Leningrad after Papa's arrest in short pants.) She was also very influential in our building management. She even succeeded in getting us a second room (almost impossible in those days). And it was her efforts that kept my room free while I was away at war, meaning that people from destroyed buildings did not move in. Otherwise once I returned I would have had to sue to get my room back, as many others had to.

In my last years at school my dream was to learn to dance properly, and Baba Fenya paid for dance lessons, with the stipulation that she could come to graduation. She left very pleased. Not only had we learned the foxtrot and tango but also the then popular Ukrainian ballroom dance the Moldavaneska, the pas

*Rozaliya Samoilovna Zemlyachka (1876–1947), Communist Party member from 1896, People's Commissar, led the Bolsheviks' armed struggle in the Crimea.

d'Espagne, the pas-de-quatre, and, even more important, the polonaise and mazurka.

Baba Fenya lived through the blockade, but grew very ill in late 1948. She spent a long time in the therapy ward at our institute, where she died in 1949. While she was there, I visited her every day, fed her, and did everything one is supposed to do in these cases; however, my attitude toward her and even toward her suffering was cold and lacking in inner sympathy. Deep in my heart I was ashamed of my hardness. If I can put it this way, I was angry that I hadn't done any of the things I was doing for Baba Fenya for my own grandmother. I felt it very strongly at the funeral in Smolensk Cemetery, where Batanya was buried in one of the group graves. I thought of her and of Papa, who might be alive or not, and if not, whether I would ever learn where his grave was, and of my beloved Seva, whose grave was never found. I wept so hard that Mama and Raya got worried, especially since I was pregnant with Tanya at the time. I later managed to explain to Mama somehow, but I couldn't tell Raya—after all, Baba Fenya was her mother.

Baba Fenya celebrated two holidays in a major way, with many guests and numerous delicious dishes—her birthday and Raya's birthday. I simply don't remember the birthdays of her son, Yevsey, or of Deda. Apparently, they weren't celebrated. Strangely (this still surprises me somehow), my Tanya was born in 1950, a few months after Baba Fenya's death, on her birthday, March 24.

13

In September 1929 Papa and Mama went off to Moscow to the Marxism Courses again. We stayed on. Before they left they did a lot of shopping and one time brought me a small globe and a big map of the world, consisting of six sections. Each section was so big that the entire map could be unfolded only in the kitchen. Papa spread it out and gave me my first geography lesson. It was interesting and very simple. Before he left, we assembled the map two more times in the kitchen. Then I found I could also unfold any two sections on the floor of our room. I never brought it out to the kitchen. Although the neighbors felt that the kitchen belonged to everyone equally, they still treated Papa with a certain fear. Thus he could spread the map out there. After all, at different times and for different reasons, he had let them move into his apartment, and then registered them, with it only then becoming their living space.

I loved the map and the globe as much as the books. Egorka liked it when I laid out the map. He crawled on it and repeated after me: America, Australia, Tasmania, Borneo. Soon he learned to find them and other places by remembering their location and shape, since he still couldn't read and was only beginning to play with letter blocks. He learned to read much earlier than I did—he could do so by the time he was four, while I only started reading when I was five and a half.

There was nothing striking or memorable for me in that winter of 1929–30. The house simply became less festive. I don't remember a single dinner party when the table was set with the "party" pink tablecloth and there were many guests. Batanya was tired in the evenings, but she prepared me for school almost every night. I had to write (I hated that) and solve math problems, which was more interesting; by spring Batanya had taken me through fractions and percents. I didn't get to that stage in school until fourth grade, and so up to fifth grade I never had the sense of learning anything; it was just repeating what Batanya had taught me. Everything I did with her I remembered for life. In the daytime Nura and I didn't go out a lot. She was spending considerable time "getting" things and being "in line."

At the beginning of winter, Mama came for a few days and we learned that now she and Papa weren't going to be living at the Marxism Courses but in the Central Asia Bureau, which was far away, in the city of Tashkent. After Mama left, we started getting letters frequently, and even more often we received packages with nuts, dried fruits, and other sweets. They were given only to me and Egorka, which was strange. Before, everybody ate everything. Batanya would say, "There's a letter from Mama; she sends regards." Egorka would ask, "Is it in a big box?" He got words mixed up then and couldn't tell "letter," "package," and "regards" apart.

I had stopped loving him so passionately by then, because he bothered me. All I wanted to do was read my own books— Zhukovsky over and over, or Pushkin or Gogol, or the books that Batanya gave me. He wanted me to read kiddie stuff, like *Moidodyr*, to him. Batanya's books were not always children's "classics," but they were in opposition to what my parents gave me. Batanya managed to get *Little Women* and *Little Men, Little Lord Fauntleroy*, and *Lady Jane*. After that came Sir Walter Scott and Dickens. I choked on my tears reading about little Paul and Florence, picturing Egorka and myself in their place. Batanya also let me rummage through the old copies of *Solntse Rossii* magazine, which were in a crate behind the trunk at the very end of the corridor. I read everything in them, from recipes for skin lotion to lists of "the bravely fallen officers and lower ranks." Mama told Papa that I was reading "damn-all," but she didn't dare say anything to Batanya. This was their battlefield and Batanya was clearly winning, for even Pushkin in those days (before his bicentennial) was being "thrown from the ship of modernity."

This is how it was with reading. Before I could read, Batanya, Matvei, Moisey Leontyevich, Bronich, and Raya read to me. Later in Moscow Uncle Sanya and Lyova and I read big (real) books to one another. But I don't remember Mama or Papa ever reading aloud to Egorka or me. Mama made up for it with a vengeance later, reading to Tanya and Alyosha and their children, her great-grandchildren.

Papa read only poetry, not from a book but by heart, and basically only when I read to him. He took liberties in poetry. What he read never corresponded with the official Party line. He read the Symbolists a lot. It was from him I first heard Blok, Bryusov, Balmont, Sologub, and Gumilyov. He loved to read Lermontov, more rarely Pushkin and Nekrasov; he read Esenin and even Nadson and Hippius. But I never heard Baratynsky, Tyutchev, Fet, Akhmatova, Mandelstam, or Pasternak from him.

After my twelfth birthday, Papa used to give me fifty rubles (a privilege) in Moscow so could I get books at the Akademkniga bookstore at 99 Tverskaya Street, not far from the building that was later moved aside to make room for the structure which now houses a cocktail hall and gourmet food store. Among other books, I bought the brown volume in the small "academic" format of Tyutchev. Reading it together, I got the impression that it was as new for Papa as it was for me. *The day after Papa's arrest I took that book and the big-format Faust from his desk, and I kept them all the years in Leningrad. They disappeared (stealing books isn't considered theft in our country!) after Tanya was born. I later saw the Faust at Lyova's house but was too embarrassed to ask for it. Recently, after Mama's death, I asked Zorya about it, but she couldn't find it at their house.*

Papa also knew the Georgian epic *The Knight in the Tiger Skin* by heart both in Russian and in Georgian. It was only then that I discovered that he knew Georgian as well as he did Armenian. After all, he had grown up in Tbilisi, the capital of Georgia, and not in Armenia. He read Armenian poets in Armenian, and I knew the names Narekatsi, Isaakyan, and Charents. The previous winter, perhaps under the influence of the Armenian poets he read, I had decided to study Armenian. My first language had been Armenian, not Russian, but by the age of twelve all I had retained was *kyz-mata, djan,* and *akhchik.* To Papa, Mama was always Rufa-djan; he never called her anything else. *Kyz-mata akhchik* or just plain *akhchik* was what he called me, and Egorka was always Egorka-*djan.* Papa started teaching me Armenian as you would an adult—with the alphabet and reading lessons. But because this was just before his arrest, I didn't get much of a feel for the language, and I soon forgot even the alphabet.

A new word appeared in our life, "order," which was given somewhere, and Batanya got one. It allowed her to buy a bolt of blue-gray flannel, with a design of red tractors and green pines. It's amazing how indelible that design is in my memory. The fabric was spread out on the table. Batanya used pieces of newspaper to make a pattern for a robe for herself, a suit for Egorka, and a dress for me. She and Nura sewed on a foot-pedal machine, which they dragged out from the storeroom, and Batanya said, "If they keep this up, we'll all be walking around naked soon." By the way she stressed the "they," I could tell that she didn't like "them." Yet I already knew that my parents were in the "they" category. There was a confusing conflict in this for me, for I know Batanya loved my mother. I'm still not sure about my father.

Shortly after this I heard that Egorka and Nura and I would be sent to the Central Asia Bureau, and Batanya started collecting silver coins, because "they don't like paper money in Asia." We put the coins in a black lacquer box, which I still have, though the key is lost, and there was so much change in there that it was hard to lift.

But we ended up not going. Instead Mama and Papa came home. I heard Batanya scolding them. She said that Uncle Mosya had been exiled and that Uncle Vitya (Prokhorov) had been arrested and that it was "worse than hitting on decent people for money." Furthermore "thank God Moisey Leontyevich has already moved away," and they weren't going to change things for the better, they were just going to "break their own necks." Papa was silent throughout. I couldn't hear what Mama was saying, but suddenly Batanya shouted, "And you can take your offspring with you." I guessed that we were the "offspring," and I was scared. I realized that I was afraid of going to the Central Asia Bureau; but Mama and Papa left without us.

Nura's eyes were swollen with tears, and then she went away somewhere, only to come back with her sister, Tanya. She was almost old, dry, and ugly, perhaps even mean, but she treated Egorka and me kindly, calling us "Nura's take-ins," which I couldn't understand then nor do now. At first she slept with Nura. In the evenings they talked a lot with Batanya about something and sometimes they both wept. Then Batanya went to see Misha Merkuryev several times, and Alya came to our house, and I heard Tanya tell her, "Nura won't do badly; she can read, and look at her—a queen." It didn't sound friendly the way she said it, even though Nura was just the way I pictured the third sister in a fairy tale, the one "who bore the tsar a big strong son." All these whispered conversations, tears, and then Batanya's visits came to an end. She returned one day, very pleased, and told Tanya something. Nura and Tanya laughed and cried, and Tanya kept repeating to Batanya, "I'll pray for you all my life, I swear I will." Then Tanya became a "houseworker" (a new word for maid) at Baba Fenya's.

When Egorka and I returned to Leningrad as "strange orphans" of 1937, Tanya treated us very well, even though all the other neighbors in the communal apartment thought she was a witch. She gave us (especially Egorka) extra food on the sly from Baba Fenya and always presented us with clothing for Easter and our birthdays. She would come to help me in the cellar laundry room, where I washed at night. Sometimes she cleaned the staircase for me, saying, "Go for a walk; your suitors are waiting by the door." She was referring to the twin brothers Fima and Yasha Fuchs, who often waited for me by the door. She lived in the storeroom at the end of the corridor, behind the "scary trunk," and stayed there until her death during the Leningrad siege in February 1942.

Just before New Year's I would start saving money for Mardi Gras week. The festivities took place all around St. Isaac's. There were shows, both puppet and human, there was accordion music, and a merry-go-round; and vendors sold colorful lollipops called "roosters on a stick," sunflower seeds, big candy canes, and other delicious things that made Batanya say, "how incredibly vile." And of course, they sold blini, the traditional pre-Lenten treat. But that was the least interesting possibility. Batanya made blini for that week and so did Baba Fenya, and we always went to visit Irina Semyonovna, Batanya's best friend, "for blini."

Their relationship began in Chita. I realized that she was a "former," too, but not a "lady." Unlike Batanya's other's friends, she did not have beautiful furniture or dishes and she lived far beyond the Finland Station in a small wooden house that resembled a two-story barracks. Everything around the house was ugly, and outside the "real Leningrad." But I loved Irina Semyonovna as well as going to her house, even though I never got gifts, chocolates, or candies. She reminded me of Uncle Mosya, Batanya's brother, when the two of them talked after tea. I didn't know then what the resemblance was, but later I understood that they both belonged to the intelligentsia.

Batanya and Irina Semyonovna were friends to the end of their days. Visiting her after 1937 I understood that she, her daughter, grandchildren, her sisters, and her nieces were living a harder and poorer life, but so were we then. In the beginning of the war she and her daughter and two small grandchildren moved to a village near Pskov (she invited Batanya to wait out the war there, too, but for some reason Batanya didn't go). They were deported from there by the Germans. The daughter and her children were gassed by the Germans. Irina Semyonovna survived the torture and beatings from the Germans in the prison in Mitava, was liberated by the Soviet Army, and then landed in prison again as a Soviet spy, like many of the people who had been under German occupation. She died in 1947. Now one of the nieces who survived the blockade of Leningrad and had worked all her life at the Hermitage Museum is living in the United States with her son. I don't know if there are any relatives left "beyond the Finland Station" of Irina Semyonovna Dreksler (nee Shokhor-Trotsky).

What I liked about the festivities was that they sold party favors, rubber balls, Chinese lanterns, and paper fans. That's what I collected money for. I sometimes got money from Batanya, Deda, and Raya, but most of all from Moisey Leontyevich before he moved to France. I would also "innocently" mention my saving up to everyone who came to our house, and that almost made it a done deal—I got what I wanted. Batanya would scold me for my "horrible manners," but since she didn't scold in front of guests, I risked only a lecture later on my manners and on begging, and continued to inform people of my savings.

I started saving that winter too. But in February, before my birthday (which was always celebrated no matter who was gone or visiting, exiled, arrested, or sick), Nura and Tanya came back from church, which they attended regularly though not frequently (I knew when they were going because Nura would put on a white scarf instead of her usual hat) and said that there would be no Mardi Gras. I was surprised, since I understood about calendars and wondered how you could just get rid of a week. I was right, of course—the week remained. The authorities had simply "banned" the holiday.

I counted my money, spread out on the bed, and felt sorry that it wasn't needed anymore. When I began to cry, Batanya said, "Well, you can thank your mommy and daddy for this." She almost never used the words "mommy" and "daddy"; no one did. For Batanya those words were as filled with dislike as the often-used "they." *I heard "daddy" and "mommy" once more after they were arrested, but about that later.* I don't know who angered me more—Batanya or my parents—but I recall gathering my money and when no one was watching throwing it in the kitchen garbage can.

That evening, when Egorka was asleep, Batanya was writing in a big bookkeeping ledger—she often wrote in books that she brought home from the customs office while counting up on her abacus. An angry Nura entered the room. Looking at me, but addressing Batanya, she said, "Just look at this, Tatyana Matveyevna. Our young lady is throwing money away," and held up a pitcher with my coins. "I had to scrape them, and myself, clean after pulling them out of the garbage. What a thing to do—throwing money in there."

Batanya pushed her glasses up on her forehead and looked at me in a way that made me think: she's going to hit me now. She was the only one who ever slapped me hard; no one else ever did. I didn't take offense since every beating was just, and my actions called for it. And at least she never scolded for long. Batanya didn't get up, didn't say, "Go to the corner." She simply shouted, "Well, why don't you say something?" I said nothing, and after a brief pause she said irritably, even angrily, and with a new shade of intonation that was almost approval, "Armenian character!" And then she turned to Nura and said calmly and rather indifferently, "Put it somewhere." From then on, "Armenian character" became both the highest measure of punishment and at the same time an acknowledgment of my right to do something as I saw fit.

There were never any more Mardi Gras weeks.

The summer of 1930 was as boring as the previous one. We stayed in Tarkhovka, in a large dacha, a two-storied house with three or four families on every floor, as "responsible" Party workers of Leningrad. Each family had a room (some had two) with a little veranda, and shared a kitchen on each floor—a communal dacha, in effect. There was no fence, just bushes, and brownish, trampled grass. Many children lived at the dacha—some of whom I had known for a long time, from kindergarten at the Astoria or from play group on Millionnaya Street at the Otsupov house. The Otsupov daughter was there, too. Though I interacted with the kids outside, played tag and hide-and-seek and jumprope, none of it really touched me. I felt no closeness with the others—I don't even remember their names.

Only a week and half or so of the summer was really good, when my parents came and we went somewhere: to town, to the puppet theater, to visit friends. I remember that the adults played volleyball in the evenings, and the best players were Papa and Bronich, who had also come to Leningrad from his town of Nikolayev. Another memory from Tarkhovka was my first boat ride. Bronich took us for rides every day he was there (I don't know if Papa ever rowed a boat in his life—I don't remember seeing him in a boat), leading Egorka to announce that he would become a sailor. No one took it seriously, the adults joking condescendingly the way they do when children try to think seriously about their future. A few hours later Egorka fell down the stairs— we lived on the second floor. He was bawling. And Papa, soothing him, said, "Come on, Egorka-*djan,* you're a sailor, don't cry." They bought Egor a sailor's hat. Almost all the children then wore sailor's hats and suits, but Egorka and I hadn't had any until then.

My parents left very quickly. Batanya was in Essentuki, like the previous summer, and the summer and the dacha had passed by the time she returned. Mama came on another trip from the Central Asia Bureau and moved us from the dacha.

I remember the move because it was the first time I rode in a truck. Nura and Egorka sat up in the cab with the driver, and

Mama and I reclined on a mattress in the back. I was worried that the strong wind would blow over the whole truck and us with it and all our belongings, but I loved the experience.

That September I went to school. They placed me in grade "zero" (kindergarten) because of my age. Mama took me one morning; they were leaving that night. Naturally, when I got back that first day everyone asked me about school. I said that nothing had happened there at all except lots of silliness. We didn't write, or read; they showed us the bathroom and assigned seats. I was far in the back, almost at the end of the row, because I was tall. Then we had to go out to the hall several times when the bell rang. Then everyone ran down the stairs and pushed so hard that I almost fell. Mama grew angry with my story and said that I was lying. Batanya, also upset, said, "Could she be making things up again?" But that time I wasn't lying or inventing things. I went to kindergarten for another two or three weeks. It seemed absolutely useless to me, since we didn't hold a pen or even a pencil in all that time, and there were no notebooks, or books, just a teacher talking and sometimes drawing on the board.

One time she began explaining what po-et-ry was and read some lines "for little ones." Then she asked who could recite a po-em by heart. Several hands went up and two or three girls recited and then a boy said that he knew one too but it was sung, not recited, and before anyone gave him permission he sang a song. Everyone laughed, even though it was a sad song and I liked it when Nura sang it.

When it was my turn I began reciting "Svetlana." I probably recited only three or four lines, but the teacher's face grew more and more stern. "Enough," she said. "Don't recite that."

"There's a lot more," I said weakly.

But she said, "I know. Don't."

I thought she just didn't like Zhukovsky, but she asked even more severely, "What, do you know how to read, too?"

I realized I was in trouble, but didn't know why. I said, "Yes."

"Read." She handed me a newspaper. I didn't like newspapers then, but I started reading—it didn't seem to matter what. After two or three sentences, she took the paper away and said, "Sit down."

I sat. Then she said, "Stand up." I stood.

"Where do you live?"

I told her. "Who are your parents?"

"What?" I didn't answer right away, because I thought she must be one of the "former" ones and that's why she was yelling at me. (Actually, she wasn't yelling, she was just angry.) Then I said, "Party workers."

"What?" Now she was sort of yelling.

"Par-ty-work-ers." I spoke loudly and challengingly.

"Sit down." I sat.

I said nothing to Batanya about this when I got home, just in case. And then, that evening, the doorbell rang. Nura came into our room (she usually answered the front door) and said, "Tatyana Matveyevna, someone's here about Lusia." I was there, and the fact that she called me Lusia instead of her usual Luska (which came from the Armenian "Lusik") worried me. "The teacher," she went on, "has come to find something out."

Batanya gave me a look, and then the teacher appeared. She was terribly embarrassed, didn't want to come in, and Batanya had to persuade her to enter and sit down. I thought she was there to complain about me, because I knew I had been impolite to her, but instead she began praising me for being so literate. "Zero class is not the place for her," she said. She couldn't do anything about it herself and asked Batanya for a favor: to go to the school to have me promoted.

She took a long time leaving. Batanya suggested, "Would you like to stay for tea?"

"No, no, thank you," she said, and left at last.

Batanya saw her to the door and when she came back, she said, "I don't understand why she's so scared. What is she afraid of?"

She gave me a searching look. I told her everything that had happened, and then she said, "You should say 'office workers.' "

"But they're Party workers; you're an office worker."

"Really? Is that what you think?" And then, as if she were

mocking me, she repeated, "Party workers. Party workers!" Then, after a pause, she spoke more calmly, "Don't scare people; say 'office workers.' And you shouldn't be reciting Zhukovsky wherever you go."

The next day our doorman, who let me sit by the fireplace in the lobby with him in winter—since I brought him Papa's cigarettes (he always said "to taste," even though it was always the same Kazbeks as usual)—said, "Well, why did the teacher come yesterday, to scold you, right? I told her that your father, Alikhanov, used to be a big boss here and now he's in Moscow, even bigger."

"But he wasn't a boss, he was secretary of the Regional Committee."

"And you don't think that's a boss?"

"Of course not."

"Oh, you're so smart, and yet you don't understand—that's being a big boss, and don't worry, she won't dare scold you."

A few days after the call an unfamiliar teacher came into our classroom and took me away to the first grade. I don't remember about that class or what we studied there, because after a few days I got such a terrible headache that I told the teacher. She sent me home. I managed to ring the doorbell, throw up, and pass out. The next day I saw Mama next to me and realized that I was very ill. It turned out to be scarlet fever; they took me to the hospital, where I spent over two months. All kinds of complications set in.

Mama's cousin Raya visited me in the hospital. She worked there "moonlighting" and every evening she spent time with me, feeding me, reading to me, and putting me to bed. No one came to see the other children—we weren't allowed to have visitors. Parents only got as far as the windows to look at their children. When I started getting out of bed, I saw Batanya through the window. Mama wasn't there.

14

Once Raya brought a visitor, a man incongruously bundled in a doctor's coat. I recognized him right away, even though he now had no mustache or cane and almost no limp. She left us alone. We both felt embarrassed. I sensed that by speaking to him, I was betraying Papa. But what could I do? Be silent? Throw him out? I felt sorry for him. He brought me toys, an extravagant doll, and something else. So we talked about the doll and her dress. I felt a total fool and to make things easier for myself pretended to be very little. That was disgusting and tiresome. I was glad to see Raya, who came to get him. When Raya returned, I wanted to tell her not to bring him to see me anymore, but I couldn't. We both knew it had been wrong, but we didn't speak of it, as if it hadn't happened. I still don't know whether Raya ever told Mama about it, whether Batanya knew, but I suspect that Raya had brought him at Batanya's request.

Finally the peeling, complications, and scarlet fever were gone, and I was released from the hospital. They wouldn't let me keep any of the toys, books, or the doll. I was glad that I wasn't taking the doll home, because she was evidence of my betrayal, or payment for it. On the way home Batanya told me I would be living with her for a while, since Nura and Egorka had gone to Moscow, to keep him from catching the disease (naturally, and as usual, he didn't get it). When I was back to normal, I would be going to Moscow too. She also said I wouldn't be attending school for the time being.

It was wonderful at home, the house unusually empty. I got up and breakfasted with Batanya, and then she left for work. I made my bed "smoothly" with great pleasure, even swept up, and then could do whatever I wanted. I read and crawled around on the map. Batanya found me Baransky's geography textbook. It was inscribed to Batanya, who was a distant relative of his through his wife, who lived in a madhouse. For a long time I had thought that a madhouse was something like our apartment when all of Papa's friends were there, because that's what Batanya called it. One time, in connection with my question about Baransky's wife, Batanya explained that I was mistaken and that our apartment wasn't a madhouse at all. Today someone who speaks Russian would say it was *normalny,* but in those days one used that word only about a person's temperature.

When I was allowed to go outside, I wandered around wintry Leningrad, going as far as the Kazan Cathedral and along the canal to "Christ" (my own name for the Christ the Savior Church of the Blood), along the Moika Canal to New Holland,* even all the way to the Maryinsky Theater. I adored twilight; in February and March it was purple and blue. That love remains. But the twilights are like that only in Leningrad. On my walks I asked the time from everyone, but few could answer precisely. They usually said, "Going on five," or "Must be around six." Few people had watches in those days.

While Batanya was at work, Tanya gave me lunch in Baba Fenya's room. This was the start of my friendship with Deda; before that we somehow didn't have the time and I rarely visited their room. In the evenings I had dinner with Batanya and then Raya usually came over. As she entered, she would say, "Aunt Tanya, may I gab with you?" She would stay a long time, often leaving after I was in bed. She mostly "gabbed" about her affair. Batanya would say, "Your affair is a complicated one; you'd be better off without it, because you are wasting your life." But she didn't scold Raya; she seemed to be commiserating with her. That's probably why Raya spent her evenings with us and didn't "gab" with Baba Fenya and Deda. After all, Fenya would often say, "He's a scoundrel, a scoundrel." That was her strongest word, and Batanya's, too.

The affair was with Georgii Alexandrovich (I think) Rzhanov. Back when we lived in a madhouse, Papa said, "Raya, finish up

*New Holland was the shipbuilding area of St. Petersburg (later Leningrad), modeled on Dutch wharves by Peter the Great.

this mess or would you like me to beat him up?" I had never seen Papa beat anyone up, but he was tall and I thought he was the strongest of anyone around us, so the threat must have been a serious one.

The affair lasted a long time, starting back when Raya was a student (she had entered the university as a teenager, at sixteen). Because Rzhanov had gone there, she moved to Leningrad from Irkutsk. He had a family and that must have been why the grandmothers considered him a scoundrel. I doubt that Raya was still in love with him during those years when she came to gab, because of the impression I got after I saw him once or twice with Raya when on a Sunday stroll we dropped by Kvissian's pastry shop (the name then of the future Nord and present-day Sever). He was tall and heavyset, with thick gray hair, and wore a suit and tie. There was something of the "formers" about him, but he wasn't one. Actually he was head of some publishing house. I didn't like the way he talked to me, with a condescending and disdainful smile, or that he spoke the same way to Raya. I could see she was afraid of him. I knew that he had been a Menshevik (also Party people, but not ours) and had lived at Baba Fenya's in her furnished rooms when he had been exiled to Irkutsk. I decided that Raya had started being afraid of him back then, when she was a little girl, but why she was still involved with him I couldn't understand.

When I was older I started going to the theater a lot. By the time I had seen the entire repertoire of the Leningrad Comedy Theater—my favorite theater then—I noticed a resemblance to Rzhanov in their leading man, Tenin, and took a dislike to him because of it. And when I first read Saltykov-Shchedrin I decided that there was something of Iudushka* in Rzhanov.

In the fall of 1937, before Matvei's arrest, he woke me up one night and sent me running to the pharmacy for ice because "Raya's very sick and we can't call the doctor." No one explained to me, but I was sure that she had had an abortion. Abortions were illegal then. Besides which, the abortion had to be kept from Baba Fenya. Later Raya had

*Iudushka (Little Judas), the epitome of hypocrisy, is a central character in Saltykov-Shchedrin's novel *The Golovyovs* (1876–1880).

other affairs, but I don't think there were any more abortions. I was very sorry that she didn't have a baby. To the end of her days, Baba Fenya kept wanting to marry Raya off and finding her suitors whom she refused to meet. She often said, "That scoundrel ruined her life." Everyone knew she meant Rzhanov, although after the war neither Raya nor any of us heard anything about him. I think that Baba Fenya was right: Raya never married because of him and her early dependence on him.

In those days Raya was tall and slender with a large mouth. She had beautiful, large, white teeth, which inspired Bronich to dub her "queen of pearls." She was very free and easy among Papa's friends, liked to tell jokes, laughed a lot, drank vodka with them (Papa never drank vodka, only wine, and Mama didn't drink at all), and bragged that she could drink straight alcohol and make hot punch, though I never saw her do that. I noticed that many of the young bachelors who visited us paid court to her. She was already working very hard in those days, though.

When she came from Irkutsk, Raya entered school at the Oncological Institute to study with the famous oncologist Nikolai Nikolayevich Petrov. After graduation she worked until she retired. Of course, there were hiatuses: since she didn't have children and her specialty, radiology, was in demand by the army, she was mobilized for all the wars, big and small. She was in Khasan in 1938, Poland and Finland in 1939, and of course, in the Great Patriotic War. She always did two or three jobs at a time and had enough energy left for fun and to give a lot of time to me, Egorka, and our cousin Natasha. And not only time. I think that between 1937 and 1941 she gave Batanya her whole paycheck from one of her jobs to help feed us. This was when Baba Fenya told any of Raya's colleagues who came to visit that my mother had abandoned us. I don't think anyone believed her, but that was their business.

After I moved to Moscow, and especially in the seventies and the years of our isolation in Gorky, I had less strength and time and then even opportunity to be with her. Yet she was hopelessly ill and needed help. I felt "guilty without fault." Raya is gone now, but the sense of guilt is not. This is one of those cases when life takes away your freedom to choose and you can't do what should be done, based on

*your earlier life. The dilemma of moral duty, which you think of more
and more as a function of your hair getting grayer and not falling
nicely but hanging limply next to suddenly sagging temples. Who owes
us? Whom do we owe? Or does no one owe anyone anything?*

Batanya now slept with me in the two rooms that were the
"nursery." Her bed was placed in the first room, and the couch
that had been there into her room. She moved so as not to leave
me alone at night, but every evening she checked or sent me to
check that her old room was locked. Locking up was the result of
our fully "communal" life. She was worried that her room might
be taken away. She said that the room had to be saved because
she wanted Matvei and his wife, Kalya, to move to Leningrad
from Vladivostok or Sretensk (I think), and she didn't know
whether she'd be able to get them a *propiska* (residence permit)
and living space. I didn't understand all this but I could tell it was
very important from the way it worried Batanya. She blamed
Papa for filling up the apartment with strangers, along with Matvei's wife, while she was at it.

That in general Batanya was not a loving mother-in-law, I
learned gradually. She was strict but fair with us grandchildren.
But her fairness disappeared when it came to her daughter-in-law
and sons-in-law. She spoke little and rather coldly to Papa, but
she seemed to respect him even though he was quite alien to her.
I don't think Lyova seemed as alien to her, but she couldn't stand
the way he was always correcting Anya. She would interrupt his
long rambling opinions, treat him harshly, and behind his back
scornfully call him "the eternal student," even though in general
she was very respectful of education. They later had a serious
conflict over money, which Lyova denied after her death, trying
to explain things to Mama. When Mama came back from the
camps, she pointedly refused to enter into discussions on fi-
nances with him, not only regarding Batanya's affairs but her own
as well.

The apartment in which Lyova, Anya, and Zorya lived in the
mid-1930s had been bought as a cooperative, the money for the
down payment having come from Batanya. Soon after, however
the house lost its cooperative status and the shares were returned.

Batanya expected Lyova to repay the money but instead he purchased a piano. She told me this once when she was very angry
with him over some trifling argument. I don't think she would
have mentioned this to me when she was calm, although after
1937 she told me many things, as though I were an adult.

She treated Kalya, her daughter-in-law, not with hostility but
with disdain, and I often felt sorry for her. She always regarded
Batanya with such fear in her eyes, addressing her as "Tatyana
Matveyevna" with such meekness whenever she talked to her. I
remember Kalya ironing the linen, her belly almost as big as she
was, and Batanya in the next room complaining loud enough for
Kalya to hear, "How can she be unable to iron linen properly?"
and making a point of blowing on the sheet, as if there were soot
from the iron, which had been heated on the stove. After a meal
together, at which Batanya had eaten well, she would say, "You
can't put a thing in your mouth. The woman doesn't cook; she
merely processes the food." And she would purse her lips in a
very Batanya way that no one else could match. As a child I
practiced in front of a mirror, but it never looked like her.

I think Matvei suffered a lot from the way Batanya treated his
wife. Kalya always stared at him with her round, loving eyes,
looking as if she were about to cry but uttering not a word. I was
always afraid she'd say, "I didn't mean it, I won't do it anymore,"
like a little kid. Kalya tried to do everything just the way Batanya
wanted. She took night courses in Russian literature, even though
I thought the subject could have been Chinese grammar for all
her feel for it. Sometimes she would tell me, an eighth-grader,
what she was learning in "Russian Literature of the Eighteenth
Century." It was as boring as our textbook. I was hard-pressed
not to laugh.

With time Batanya managed to move Matvei and Kalya to
Leningrad, and get them a *propiska,* and trade our two "nursery"
rooms and hers for two large rooms facing the street and St.
Isaac's on the third floor of our old building, the former Grand
Hotel. The doorman was gone by then, and so was the carpeting
on the stairs. The hallways, stairs, and banisters no longer shone.
I had no idea that in just a few years it would be my job to polish

them. Gradually the composition of tenants in the building shifted too. The former "Astorians" and other Party workers moved away, and there were more families living in single rooms. The building was becoming ordinary. Apartment houses like that were referred to as "with a corridor system."

In the meantime Batanya and I lived very well. Sometimes I had to do fractions and percents. She quizzed me some evenings on geography and history, and she made me read the historian Solovyov, whom I found boring. After my attempts at kindergarten and first grade I thought that I would never have to learn any more than I already knew at any school. I liked reading for pleasure and "to travel" along the map. On Sundays we no longer went to the theater but did attend the cinema. Though I enjoyed the movies, I never stopped loving the theater.

On occasion (less frequently than before), we went to visit Batanya's friends. Now instead of my black velvet dress I wore a knit suit Batanya bought at customs—a navy pleated skirt and a light blue sweater trimmed in navy at the cuffs and collar. It was beautiful. Better even than the velvet dress. And Batanya tied a bow in my hair, not with a white ribbon anymore, but with a wide one of light blue moiré.

Sometimes we had company. And then instead of soup we had *zakuski* (hors d'oeuvres). Batanya no longer made her inimitable *pirozhki* with meat or cabbage—there was no flour—but she would boil potatoes and prepare herring and something for dessert. And that pink tablecloth was brought out.

How much longer do things outlive people? Controlling myself with every ounce of willpower, but seeing poorly because it is hard to wipe tears under one's glasses, the morning of Mama's funeral before the body in its coffin was brought to the house, I was getting tablecloths from the cupboard, setting the tables for the wake. The first to fall on me was a heavy cloth with colored embroidery, much too big for today's tables, which used to belong to Baba Fenya and was given to me by Raya. Under it was the pink one! Now, after innumerable washings, it merely gave off a pink tint, and Mama's beautiful and fine mending stood out bright pink. Could I have ever imagined that my mother, a Party worker, antibourgeois and maximalist, who never allowed herself to use a tender word to Egorka or me, would be mending tablecloths, sewing dresses for me, dressing up Tanya, could turn into a "crazy" grandmother and great-grandmother, for whom her grandchildren and great-grandchildren would be the chief "light in the window," the justification for all the losses of her entire life. I couldn't even imagine that she would come to love potted flowers on the windowsill and tend them, making them grow and live.

Or that she would turn in her Party card with a certain pride and challenge.

This was not a demonstration for the sake of the Party or a settling of accounts. She had paid up in full long ago. And she didn't like to have others in her debt. It was simply that with that difficult, almost impossible step she fully gave herself to us, her warm, living love, which was higher and greater than abstract ideas and principles. She said almost before her death that in life you must simply live in a good and kind way.

15

In late March our quiet life came to an end, and I was off to Moscow. Traveling alone for the first time in my life. Batanya got me packed very substantially, even sewed me a new robe (which I was supposed to wear on the train) and new underwear, and bought so many things you would think I was going to live in Moscow alone instead of with my mother. Everything was made for me out of Batanya's old things, but I think the Torgsin store was opened by then, and she could buy some clothes there, too. During the years the store existed, Batanya brought her silverware there piece by piece to sell off. Sometimes she purchased food there. I remember only pastry and cheese (which I loved). One hundred grams (we used to say a quarter pound) just for me when I was getting over scarlet fever. "For the road," Batanya baked her *pirozhki* and wrapped apples in tissue paper. I loved the elongated, juicy *krymki* apples, not the most expensive kind. (The best were rosmarins, but I preferred the *krymki*. I haven't seen either kind in almost half a century.) Raya brought shells for the trip, large chocolates with a creamy white filling. (I haven't seen those since my childhood, either.)

Raya and Batanya saw me off. They entrusted me to the conductor and my neighbors in the compartment, which seemed excessive to me, since no doubt the train would have taken me to Moscow without them. I was planning to stay up all night at the window, instead of sleeping, as Batanya had told me. As soon as the train started and I had waved, I began chewing my pies, apples, and chocolate all at once, and looking out the window. I grew tired of sitting and decided to watch lying on my stomach. Then my neighbor woke me and by the time I got dressed we were at the station. Mama met me alone. She came into the car with a porter. Her face was rosy and happy. But as soon as I spoke, her expression changed, even though all I said was "I need to pee."

"Did you hold it in the whole trip?" She hissed at me in a half whisper. "Now you'll have to wait while we find a toilet."

She said something to the porter, and then we looked for a toilet. After I went, I wanted to tell Mama how happy I was to be there, but she looked so irritated and she kept saying, "Hurry it up. He's not going to wait for us forever."

I got huffy and thought, "I wish I'd stayed with Batanya forever and never come to Moscow." I felt sorry for myself.

How often Mama and I had these petty squabbles and even arguments that started with a dropped phrase, even a word, a trifle, like "I need to pee." Mama would say something softly, I'd get "wound up," or to the contrary, I'd say something and she (she never got "wound up") would create a whole theory about my crudeness, my lack of love for her or the children (my own!), or something else so removed from our actual relations that it was funny, though both of us were practically weeping. And later the same pattern was repeated with Tanya, maybe even more harshly because Tanya does get "wound up," like me. Is that the normal mother-daughter dynamic or is it my "Armenian character"?

At last, the porter got us into a carriage and we set off. It was a bright morning, and I had the feeling I was seeing Moscow for the first time. It didn't seem the same city I had viewed when we lived in the Marxism Courses. I didn't remember at all the time we lived in Moscow at the Novodevichy and then the Strastnoy monasteries (I wonder why they placed students in monasteries then?). Just as I didn't remember when Lenin died and friends of Mama's from the Communist University for Eastern Workers carried me all bundled up to his funeral. Afterward I got so sick it was almost fatal.

We drove along and Mama, now in a better mood, pointed things out to me. "That's Kalanchevka [Fire Tower] Square."

"Why?"

"Because the firemen are here. That's Sukharevka and the Sukharevskaya Tower."

"Why?"

"Why what?"

"Sukharevka."

"I don't know, maybe they sell *sukhari* [crackers] there," Mama said, and laughed so that I could tell she was making it up.

"There, you see, you make things up, too, you do," I said, and laughed. And she didn't argue or say that she always told the truth.

Then came a wall behind which were buildings, and I asked, "Is that the Kremlin?"

"No, Kitai Gorod [literally, China Town]."

"Why China?"

"I don't know. Ask Papa."

"Does he know?"

"I don't know. Maybe not."

Then came the Bolshoi Theater. I liked it right off because it was so big, bigger than the Maryinsky, and because it had horses on top like the arc of the Main Army Headquarters. On this trip I liked Moscow. We had turned onto a street with a church on the corner, not broad but still resembling Nevsky Prospect because it had trolleys and some of the houses were painted pale green and white. But though the Nevsky was flat, this went uphill.

"This is our street, Tverskaya, remember that, Tverskaya," Mama said. The driver stopped at the entrance covered with gray marble and with two marble columns on either side, and we entered through double doors into a large lobby.

There were mirrors and paintings on the side walls. Small tables and a few armchairs dotted the left side of the lobby and far on the right was a glassed-in office with a window, with someone inside and several people near it. In the back I could see two elevators a few steps up, with a doorman sitting to the left of the stairs. The driver set down my two suitcases and some bundles near one of the tables. Mama paid him and told me, "Your toilet cost an extra ten." She picked up a few bundles, gave one to me, and said, "Well, let's go."

"What about the things?"

"Nura will come down for them later," she said.

"Batanya told me not to lose anything. What if they're stolen?"

"No one will steal anything here," she said with a slight tone of disapproval. We walked past the doorman and up the stairs.

"Why not take the elevator?"

"It's only the second floor; walking's faster."

The stairs were covered with a red carpet like our old Grand Hotel. When we got up to the second floor I cried out, "It's so beautiful here!"

We were in a large airy lobby, which resembled the Astoria's. A lovely fireplace on the right, pretty tables, armchairs, and couches all around, and just where the hallway began stood a large dog, much bigger than life and as dark as the Bronze Horseman.

"It's even more beautiful here than at the Astoria," I said. "It's like a palace."

"It is a palace; you'll see plenty of this beauty," Mama said very angrily. I knew she was irritated at the beauty and not at me. "Whatever else there may be, there's plenty of beauty here at the Luxe," Mama went on. Our footsteps were muffled by the thick green carpet (just like grass, I thought).

"This building is called the Luxe?"

"Yes." Mama said yes the way people say no, and I understood that she didn't like the house.

Halfway down the corridor, which was at least twice as long as the one in Leningrad, we came to a large room. Nura and Egorka shouted, "She's here, she's here," and we were all happy. Then Nura brought the suitcases. We had breakfast and Nura kept running off to the kitchen for the teapot and to heat up Batanya's pies.

"Where's the kitchen?" I asked.

"Around the corner," Mama replied.

"What corner?"

"The corridor corner."

"Where are the other rooms?"

"There are no other rooms."

"What? Just one?"

"Isn't it enough for you?" Mama asked mockingly.

I didn't respond but a minute later asked my last question. "And where will I sleep?"

"Where you're sitting, on that very couch."

I didn't ask anything more and Mama hurried off to work. In the doorway, she said, "When you and Nura go out for a walk, come to my office. Everyone's been waiting to see you."

"Why?"

"They knew you when you were little. I used to work there then, too."

Mama left and while Egorka lay on the couch and the floor around me and Nura washed dishes "around the corner," I took a good look at the room. It was big and its two windows opened on the courtyard. A low building stood in the middle and there wasn't a single tree. *It's no better than the courtyard at the Astoria, and maybe there isn't even a gate to it,"* I thought.

To the left of the door was an alcove with a heavy green velvet portiere. Inside was a huge bed, a night table, and a small cupboard. Further left, closer to the window, was the couch on which I would be sleeping, the wall indented again, and there was a bed, and at an angle to it not far from the window stood our "golden bed." We called it golden because its posters and wire mesh were painted gold. This crib had been mine and then Egorka's, and later it would hold Natasha. There was a rather large table in front of "my" couch, and we had eaten at it. I noted that it was covered with oilcloth, the way things had been when we lived at the Marxism Courses, and not with a tablecloth, the way things always were at Batanya's. Two cupboards filled the right wall: one held books and the other our dishes behind glass. In the corner in front of the alcove there were three large suitcases on the floor as well as the two I had brought.

My examination of the room didn't produce any surprises for me, but it worried me. For the first time I felt my face taking on Batanya's expression. I only sensed it, because there was no mirror in the room to see myself. I had never—rather, our family had never—lived in a single room before. The smallest lodgings had been two rooms, on Kamenostrovsky. In Chita we had a whole half of Moisey Leontyevich's big house. At the Astoria we had two suites, at the Grand Hotel we had had seven rooms and then three, and at the Marxism Courses, three rooms. So one room was astonishing news to me, especially since I now shared Batanya's worries about living space.

I had never slept on a couch. I didn't even know how to make a bed on it. Ever since I was four Batanya had insisted that I make the bed "immediately, upon getting up." When I was a little older, she told me to do it "without leaving the room." I wasn't allowed to go to the toilet until I had made the bed. This room didn't have a desk, which used to be as essential as a bed in every other place we had lived.

While I was mulling all this over, Nura came in with the dishes and said, "Igorechek and Lyusenka, we'll get dressed now and go visit Ruf and for a walk." Our names sounded unfamiliar—no one ever called us Lyusenka or Igorechek, but Nura renamed us in our Luxe life in the capital. My original Armenian Lusik had long since become Luska, even though Raya, Batanya, and some of Batanya's friends sometimes called me Lucienna. In Moscow I became simply Lusia.

Later in school I saw my name written as Ludmila Alikhanova in the roll book and I told the teacher that I certainly was no Ludmila. I was Lusik, or at least Lucienna. She replied that there were no such names and that it was about time I learned that

Lusia was short for Ludmila. I persisted, and got her to write Lusia. Ludmila made me sick.

We started getting ready to go out, and in the meantime Nura told me about life here. She liked it and lived like a "lady." "No stoves, just look; we have heaters and it's always warm. No kerosene or Primus stoves—there's gas in the kitchen. Do you know what gas is?"

"No."

"Listen, no smoke, no soot, you don't have to clean the pots, you just strike a match and that's it, five minutes later the kettle's boiling. Alikhanov makes his own tea, imagine!"

I knew that Papa was a catastrophe in the kitchen when it came to the Primus or kerosene stove. Everything burned, smoked, and blew up with him. Everyone, even Batanya, preferred to make tea for him than let him near the kitchen "technology."

"My hands are like Ruf's now. Look, there's no dirty work. I don't even take out the garbage. You don't have to go all the way to the steambaths around here, either. There's a shower on the third floor; you can wash not just on Saturdays, but every day if you want. And you can do laundry in there, though there's no place to dry it. There's no attic, but at least they won't steal anything."

In Leningrad there had been an attic to which the doorman kept the key, but almost every week things got stolen. Once all our laundry was taken.

"While Alikhanov and Ruf are at work, I stretch out a line in here and dry it. And then I iron and it's done. You know how I wring laundry." Nura laughed again. She had a superstition: "If you wring things badly, you'll marry a drunk." So she wrung the laundry so well that Batanya would say, "Your hands make the sheets crackle." I never forgot Nura's words about marrying a drunk and while I still had the strength I always wrung out the wash to the last drop.

Nura showered me with details. "Downstairs is a canteen. When you don't have time to cook, you can take out a whole meal. They cook rather decently there." ("Decently" was Batanya's word, and it was spoken with Batanya's intonation.) "The girls who work as nannies are all very nice. And the women and single men—half the building is full of them—barely speak Russian. Foreigners. I like living in the Comintern; it's not like the Marxism Courses and it's even better than home." Nura called our Leningrad place home; that's where her city life started.

"What do you mean, Comintern? Mama said this building is called the Luxe."

"Of course it's the Luxe, but it's also the Comintern," she insisted. But I didn't agree with her because I knew that the Comintern was the Communist International, just as KIM was the Communist Youth International. Didn't she know the anthem: "Factories, arise, throw off your chains, father the world to the Comintern's call. Two classes are locked in mortal combat. Our slogan is the Universal Soviet Union . . ."

But I never told Nura she was saying "nonsense" (Papa's word). Whenever I got something mixed up, he would begin correcting me with "Don't talk nonsense." He didn't like "nonsense." As I looked at the shiny dark parquet floor, I tried my last argument, "What about polishing floors? You always said that linoleum was better; you just wipe it with a rag and it's clean."

"But, Lyusenka [that Lyusenka again!], every week the floor men come. And every week in the canteen there's a lecture for the technical workers on the international situation, and then there's talk, and jokes, and singing to an accordion. It's just like it was back at my home, but without the sunflower seeds. [Back at her home, meant her village.] Alikhanov gave a lecture once. It was very good and the girls all said that he was the handsomest of the lecturers."

I realized that Nura would never want to leave, that Moscow was going to become home to us and I could forget Leningrad. I'd never return, just as I never went back to Sestroretsk.

16

And so we went for a walk. We walked out past the doorman and turned left on the street, past the bakery on the ground floor of our building, the Filippovskaya. Past the house with the pharmacy on the corner. We came out on the square. There was a monument in the middle. It was very simple—a tall narrow gray pyramid with several steps leading up to it. It was called Liberty. (Now Liberty has been pushed to the back, and in its place is the statue of Yuri Dolgoruki, the founder of Moscow.) A strange metamorphosis took place for me with the square. Everything that seemed large to a child usually amazes the adult by its smallness. It was just the opposite with the square. Now it seems much larger than it did when I was a child.

There was a park behind the monument, and beyond that, Mama's workplace. It was called Institute of Marx-Engels-Lenin. All kinds of people inside gave me the usual "You've gotten so big; you've grown so much." And of course, they asked if I liked Moscow and if I was happy to have arrived. Because I was very polite and said yes, Mama seemed pleased and announced she would leave for a half hour to spoil us. In Leningrad, spoiling meant going to Kvissian's for pastry and hot chocolate.

We went to a place nearby, the second house on the left side of the square, and entered a tiny half-cellar, as narrow as a hallway. There were two small tables against the wall and at the end a man behind a counter was putting something into stemmed glass dishes. Egorka shouted, "Cream, cream." I didn't like cellars or milk or cream and couldn't understand what he was so happy about. But I kept quiet and waited. We sat down and were given dishes with a thick mound of something white inside, plums stuck on all sides. When I pulled out a plum with my hand, Mama slapped my wrist lightly. So I picked up a spoon to taste it. It was light and delicious. I ate it quickly, then looked at Mama.

"It's whipped cream. Would you like some more?" she asked.

I would! Thus on the first day of my life in Moscow (real Moscow life, not temporary) I had tasted and fallen in love for life with my favorite dessert. I later learned that my parents called this store "the last NEPman's," even though the seller, a small and skinny old man, didn't look at all like the fat NEPman* seen on posters.

I would soon become a very good friend of the store owner. He would give me whipped cream on account and Mama would pay later. The little cellar lasted until the spring of 1935, when unexpectedly the door was boarded up forever.

The evening of my first Moscow day Papa brought me a new book, which I read several times in a row. For a few months it became my favorite as well as the best medicine against homesickness. The book was called *Newspaper Sparrows*. It told about little boys who lived in the cellars and sewers beneath New York. They sold newspapers, running around the big cold city in the early mornings. They had no family—no fathers, no mothers, no grandmothers or older sisters. They helped one another. One of the boys got sick, and though they all took care of him, he died anyway. He was the best and kindest of them all, and his name was Charlie.

I read the book in one go, lying on my stomach on my couch, drowning in tears. Then I read it to Egorka. Then, for the third time, to him and Nura, and we all cried together. During this reading, however, misfortune struck. Egorka, sitting next to me on the couch, listened and played with a toy. It fell under the table. Crawling after it, he hit his chin on the table and bit off his tongue—not just bit it, but bit through it. The front third of the tongue was dangling loose and blood was gushing out. Nura

---

*NEP was the New Economic Policy initiated by Lenin (1921–1928), a return to private ownership and a free market. Businessmen taking advantage of the policy were disdainfully called NEPmen while they flourished in the 1920s, and were arrested for speculation in the 1930s.

grabbed a hankie, wet it, and pushed the tip of the tongue against the main part. "Hurry, call Mama," she shouted at me.

I called, and as soon as Nura took her hand out of his mouth to wet the hankie again, he shouted, with blood splattering in all directions, "I'm going to die, I'll die like Charlie."

Mama came to the phone at last and I shouted into the phone, "Mama, come quickly. Egorka is gushing blood. Gushing, gushing." The "gushing" must have annoyed her and her angry reply was, "What are you making up now. You always say it's gushing."

I bawled into the phone, "Mama, I'm not lying. I'm not making it up. It's true." She finally believed me and arrived very quickly.

As soon as Mama showed up, Egorka stopped screaming. She had come by car, even though her office was close, and she and Nura took Egorka away. I paced the room, weeping. I tried to clean up the blood from the table and floor, and cried and cried. I thought, "He'll die like Charlie. Egorka will die like Charlie." At last they returned—all three of them. Egorka showed me his tongue, which had two threads tied in a real knot, not a bow. Nura went down for ice cream and we both had some, because Egorka had to have cold things. Nura kept saying, "Oh, Egorka, you scared me so." And kept kissing him. The fear must have made her forget calling him Igorechek. Mama said nothing and kissed no one.

When Papa came home, Egorka was asleep already, and I heard her tell him about it. "Just think what a golden child he is. They put in stitches and he didn't cry." I felt a rebuke in her words and I got mad at her and even at Egorka. I wanted to say, "Sure, he didn't cry. You should have heard him before you got here." But I didn't. All the crying I did while they were in the hospital made me tired and I fell asleep quickly. I woke up in the night. I wasn't angry anymore. I was afraid that Egorka might die. I went over to his bed. He was asleep. Mama heard me walking around, got up, came over to me, and said gently, "Go back to sleep. He won't die."

Gradually I began exploring beyond our room at the Luxe. First of all, I went to the kitchen with Nura, where there really was gas, and I constantly "practiced" turning it on. There were many foreign women who did not speak Russian, but everyone seemed cheerful and very kind. Then I met two children who lived in a room almost opposite ours. The girl was a bit older than I, very serious, blond, thin, and pretty. Her name was Mirka; actually it was Mirella. When her mother called her, she would shout in the corridor, "Mirella," so that only the Rs and Ls sounded. Her brother was younger, more Egorka's age, but he and I became better friends. He was called Zhorka, though his real name was Giorgio. In his mother's rendition there were only Gs. I was happy to meet kids with strange names, because I used to think I was the only one in this predicament and it made me uncomfortable.

I used to play in their one room (I later learned that almost everyone lived that way in our building), which also had an alcove. But their things were more beautiful and better than ours. I especially liked their mother, who didn't go to work and was always very cheerful.

But most of all I enjoyed sitting or, as Mama put it, "hanging out" in the gorgeous lobby of our second floor. You could look at Tverskaya Street through the big windows; it was a busy thoroughfare, lively and crowded. I already knew that it was Moscow's "main" street, and I liked that. You could sit on the bronze dog and pretend it was a horse on the prairie. You could lounge in the armchairs or on the couch. It was a shame that the fireplace was never lit in that lobby. There was no place to sit by a fire, the way we did in Leningrad near the stove. I started visiting the other floors and meeting other children, but not too much.

The first day Mama asked me not to go gallivanting alone. "This isn't Leningrad, you know; even *you* could get lost here."

Nura always scared me by saying that the times were terrible— children were stolen, undressed, and boiled to make soap. I wasn't afraid of getting lost, but Nura's stories about stolen children were so richly detailed that I trembled. I ended up having an uncontrollable fear of household soap. I thought the brownish slime that covered it when it was wet was the blood of boiled children. When Nura washed my hair with the household soap because it was supposed to do a better shampooing job, I begged with tears in my eyes, "Just not with that, please!" I was too embarrassed to explain why.

But I never developed a fear of the street. And very quickly I began wandering around Moscow the way I had in Leningrad. My first excursion was a failure, not because I got lost (I walked only to Mama's office and back) but because the doorman wouldn't let me in. All strangers coming to the Luxe needed to get a pass at the office window. Children didn't need passes but the residents had to call down and say they were expecting them. The doorman had not seen me go out, so wouldn't let me in. I told him I lived there and he asked, "Which room number?" I didn't know and he said, "Go away little girl, go." He tried to push me down the stairs from the elevator.

I went outside and stood in the doorway for a long time. Then I went back to talk to the doorman again. He asked me the room number again. I still didn't know, and was about to burst into tears, when the woman behind the glass partition asked through the window (there wasn't a line just then), "What does she want?"

The doorman said, "They all keep coming around, pretending to live here."

When the woman asked me our room number, I thought I'd never reach home, but then she said, "What's your last name?"

"Alikhanova."

"I think they only have a little boy and a nanny," she said doubtfully, but added, "I'll call."

She called up and then handed me the phone. I heard Nura's voice and I said, "Nura, they're not letting me in. They say we only have a boy. Tell them we have a girl, too."

"I'll tell them, I will. I'll be right down."

A minute later Nura came running down the stairs. Then we spent a long time with the doorman, and Nura told him and the woman in the office about Leningrad and my illness and that now, thank God, I was better and had come to Moscow.

The first problem with the Luxe's pass system ended safely.

But there was an unpleasant residue from its existence during all the years we lived there. I began noticing that people who came to visit us didn't like it. Of course, my parents' friends weren't afraid of it, but Batanya's guests or Mama's ordinary relatives and Papa's relatives coming from Tiflis and Erivan (as those cities were called then) were clearly afraid. I was often embarrassed when I was older that my friends had to call from downstairs in order to see me. I always tried to meet them downstairs. In general, that system must have been a bit odd in those years, when Party members could get into even the Moscow Committee or the Central Committee offices simply by showing their Party card.

Very soon I began walking all over the city by myself, because the official walks with Nura and Egorka weren't enough for me. With Nura we usually turned right from the house, stopped at all the stores, and proceeded to the boulevard where Pushkin stood. We never called it the statue of Pushkin, but simply Pushkin, who was as alive as the children who swung on the chains forming a low fence around the statue, or the nannies who yelled (and there were many nannies then), "Stop fooling around; it's time for lunch" or something equally boring.

A walk with Nura meant that she sat down on a bench and we were supposed to run around and "don't go far." Nura talked with the other nannies and sometimes with soldiers. When she talked with the nannies it wasn't interesting. But when her soldier boyfriend came, I always tried to eavesdrop on them. She would chase me away. "Go run somewhere. Why do you hang around the grownups?" she would say in Mama's voice. "There's Igorechek swinging; you go swing with him."

"But you don't let us do that. You say we'll get dirty."

"Don't argue. What did I tell you—go away," Nura would say angrily. And the angrier she got, the more interesting the conversation was bound to be, and the more I wanted to hear it.

Sometimes I managed. She lied to him, pretending to be not our nanny but Mama's sister, who took us out for walks because she loved her nephew so much. "She means Egorka," I thought, and immediately had another thought. "Well, of course, he's the only one they love." "They" were Mama and Nura. And I imagined what would happen if I told Mama about Nura's lies. But I realized that nothing would happen except that Mama would scold me for snitching.

Nura always condescended to her soldier, as if she were a very important and smart woman and he was a fool. He kept inviting her to go to the movies some evening or on a day off, but she would answer, "I don't have time to go out evenings. I'm studying at the Worker's Courses and on days off too. I just make time to spend with the children."

"Boy, is she lying!" I was astonished. My own daily lying didn't seem so terrible anymore.

The soldier would feel bad, look at Nura with loyal eyes, and say, "Oh, why do you disdain me?"

He always used the formal *you* with her, while she never addressed him directly at all. But when she saw him coming toward us from the square, she would say, "Here he comes again," so that the other nannies would hear.

The soldier was nice, and he was embarrassed not only by Nura but by Egorka and me. He brought us sticky candies and pulled them out of his pocket with a shy smile. Nura, like an "old gentlewoman," would frown and say, "We have everything we need at home and the children will just get messy." I kept waiting for her to use Batanya's phrase, "How incredibly vile," but she never did. We liked the candies, despite the fact that "we had everything at home." He offered Nura candies, too, but she never accepted.

Once a nanny friend of Nura's said the same thing to her that the soldier did. She was wrong to disdain him; he was "independent" and Nura should be thinking about her life. The years were passing, and she'd stay a nanny all her life. Nura got angry and said, "I am thinking about it. But I'll never go back to the village for anything. I'd rather do away with myself than live in the country now." She spoke angrily, but I could hear tears in her voice, and I felt sorry for her. The way I felt sorry for Raya when she talked about Rzhanov. I understood that "the years were passing" for both Nura and Raya, but the reasons were different somehow.

Once, when I was very mad at Nura, I threatened to tell Mama about her lies to the soldier. Nura shouted at me and said, Tell, the sooner the better, because she was sick of us and she'd rather go work in a factory or construction site. "They need people everywhere, and thank God I have a passport. And then I'll go to Worker's Courses, and you'll be sorry you lost me."

I didn't understand what her passport had to do with it, but I didn't give in and said, "You won't leave us; you'd never leave Egorka."

"I will, I'll leave Egorka. I'll leave everyone if you say that again to me."

I believed her. I couldn't imagine life without Nura, especially with Batanya far away in Leningrad. I was afraid. Mama was never home. And what if she were? What could she do, when she couldn't even make cream of wheat without lumps? And what about the laundry? And the shopping? Or keeping track of the money? Or washing us? The house wouldn't be a home without Nura. And I couldn't imagine another, strange nanny in Nura's place. After Nura's threats, even her love of Egorka seemed fair—after all, he was little, and, well, I was big already.

I was very worried by the whole question of washing. I remember how Mama once went sowing seeds in the spring and as soon as she came back, the first thing she said was, "It was so filthy there, absolutely filthy."

Nura said, "Oh, Rufa, you go straight to the shower, and leave all your clothes there. I'll wash them all right away; otherwise you might shake some lice on the children."

Mama obeyed and went off to wash, without kissing us.

Whenever Nura washed my hair she always said you had to lather three times because lice liked black, and my hair was so black, like a gypsy's and they'd move in. "Gypsies are filthy with lice; it's the blackness."

I had never seen a louse, but I was terrified of them. I envied girls with light-colored hair, thinking it was a guarantee against lice. I first saw lice several years later, when I was in sixth grade. I was in the hallway with a few girls during break, and we were chatting about something. Suddenly something on the head of one of the girls, who was much shorter than I, caught my eye. Something was crawling on her reddish brown hair. I wanted to mention it. Then I saw that there were three insects, crawling across her neat part, gray and tiny, slightly shiny and rather unhurried. I realized they were lice and I cringed in horror. I couldn't say a thing to the girl.

Quite recently I told this story to a friend who had also been to school with that girl. She said, "Lice? Impossible, she was always such a goody-two-shoes."

For some reason Nura often mentioned gypsies when she washed me, insisting that I resembled one. The question of belonging to some nationality or other had not existed for me at all. Even Batanya's "Armenian character" I took extra-ethnically, I suppose. But I argued with Nura. "I'm not a gypsy," I always responded, because I thought that this somehow separated me from Mama, that it might somehow make it clear that I was not Mama's child and that she was my stepmother. But Nura's aims were purely hygienic. "If you don't wash, we'll just have to put a gypsy skirt on you and you'll go off, sweeping the floor with your hem." And she would conclude with, "Furbelows to the floor, a pound of shit under the furbelows." She used that saying for more than gypsies; it covered some of her nanny acquaintances who were too gussied up. And even some of Mama's friends.

Except for that expression, Nura did not use bad words in front of us and her speech patterns were totally "urban." However, some of her favorite expressions were clearly from the country or at least picked up before she became our nanny. I picked them up immediately and used them often, despite Mama's displeasure and Batanya's pursed lips.

I took up the furbelows line for life and saw in it a profound reflection of a person's essence that went beyond whether a woman washed or not. Sometimes even today as I look at young women with rear ends in tight skirts (or more often jeans) and their faces with makeup that's been troweled on, I want to use Nura's phrase, even though these women may be washed down there and they have no furbelows.

In my first months in Moscow I didn't go off far by myself. I quickly realized that this was not Leningrad, where you could see the Admiralty spire from everywhere and you could always get to Nevsky Prospect or the Neva River and then find your way. So I went from Pushkin to Timiryazev or from Strastnoy to Trubnaya—that was a right from our Luxe and left along Tverskaya to Okhotny Ryad and then down to Red Square. I liked Red Square, though it didn't give me aesthetic pleasure, as in Leningrad, but ideological. The Kremlin, the Mausoleum, Lenin—these names filled me with the delight of being part of it. If not me, then my parents were indelibly tied to it all. I had read *Red Devils* by this time (amazing that I don't remember the author's name). I envied those kids who had fought in the Civil War and regretted not having been born then and dying with them for the Revolution. "I could have been like them."

I usually kept quiet about my solo walks, but whenever I came back from Red Square I would tell everyone about it, adding a lie about seeing Budenny or Voroshilov himself. Apparently, right after Kirov was killed, or just before it, I had "seen Stalin himself."

Basically, I had spotted them all more than once, but not on my walks. Papa usually took us to the military parades on November 7 and May 1. If you climbed to the top of the bleachers and stood on tiptoe, leaning over the rails, you could see the leaders walking down the path toward the Mausoleum. Sometimes one of them would smile and wave. Then they'd go up the stairs on the square side to the Mausoleum balcony and everyone in the bleachers would applaud long and loud—me too, even though I found nothing special about them. I liked Gamarnik, the military commander of Moscow, on his horse much more, but no one applauded for him because that was the beginning of the parade.

Summer came. I was looking forward to the dacha. But it turned out we wouldn't have our usual dacha. Mama wasn't working at the Institute anymore but at the Moscow Committee.

That was close to the house, too. Around the corner down the alley to Dmitrovka, and there it was. All the children from the Moscow Committee were being taken to the general dacha in Barvikha, and that meant us, too. I wasn't sure whether this would be good or not, so just in case, I made a scene and insisted for several days that I had a headache and "I think, a fever." I knew very well that if I were sick, Mama would find time for me and I could even negotiate something. Nura supported my tantrums, because she was against sharing a dacha, too, afraid that we would catch cold or some other disease or even lice. But Mama paid no attention and Papa said "nonsense."

Mama also kept telling Nura that she had to go visit "her people." That meant Nura's parents and two brothers. I knew that they were "settled" or "in exile," but Mama and Nura did not employ these words in their conversations. Batanya had used them earlier. Nura apparently didn't want to go to exile and I couldn't understand why Mama was sending her there, when we'd be better off at the dacha. But Nura started packing sugar and grain, salt and matches, and that horrible household soap. Lots of soap, because Nura loved cleanliness most of all. She seemed to have forgotten about those "boiled children."

Mama took us to a meeting place where we were put in a bus and taken to Barvikha. I don't remember what it was like at all, but we didn't get sick or catch lice. I do remember a river, like the Sestra; beautiful but in a different way, it was bigger and had no pines on the shore. I almost drowned in that river. Since I didn't remember it, my story of how I almost drowned got longer and longer and by the following winter I had made up so many details for my friends and adults that I got mixed up myself.

Nura came back from "her people" before Egorka and I returned from Barvikha. When I asked her about her trip, she said nothing. But sometimes she'd bring it up herself and say a few short harsh things. I learned that her younger brother had drowned. He was a little older than I, and had been fishing in the ice, because there was no other food. He had been at it all day long, but Nura didn't tell how the accident happened. Then she said that her mother was very sick; her legs were swelling and she couldn't walk. "She just barely crawls around. And it's just horrible, Lusia, just horrible; they have nothing; you could claw the dirt with your fingers. No clothes, no food, nothing." Then she'd turn away and shut up.

Once she said, "Rufa and Alikhanov don't believe me that it's so bad and told me not to tell you, so keep quiet about it," she said severely. I saw her making up packages once or twice and going off to mail them. But she got letters only from her sister, Tanya, in Leningrad. I once asked why they didn't write to her—she must miss them—and she replied simply, "I told them not to write. It could get me into trouble. And there's no point. What can you say in those letters, anyway?"

17

The summer passed as if it hadn't happened, because there was nothing to tell about it except for my lying. We came home to find out that we had moved. On the second floor the big corner suite had been an office until the summer, and now we lived there. It had two rooms, a bathroom and toilet, and a large entryway. One of the rooms was as big as the lobby on the second floor. It had three windows. A barrier was made of bookcases. The place with one window was the room for Egorka and me, and the part with two windows was the dining room. Nura made herself a room in the entry, curtaining it off. The bathroom also had a window. And my parents' room had a standard window and a bay window. I liked it all, especially that I had a bed again and my own desk. And we had nice furniture—a green velvet couch and matching armchairs and tables and cupboards. The windows had green velvet drapes with pale green silk linings. It didn't worry me at all (nor my parents) that the furniture did not belong to us and that each piece had a small gold oval with a number attached with two nails.

The windows in the big room and the bay window faced the street. Mama's window and the bathroom window opened on the side street, Golenishchevsky. By then I had visited many of the children living at the Luxe and after our move I added it up: we had more living space than the rest. I wondered why. Then I remembered the doorman at the Grand Hotel who had said that Papa was a boss. I knew that Papa worked at the Comintern (everyone called it that and not the Executive Committee of the Comintern), but I had never been there. So I decided I had to go and see for myself whether Papa was a big boss or not.

Our first night in the new place, after Nura had put Egorka and me between clean, crisp sheets and given us our bedtime snack (we were always given an apple or a candy in bed; Papa had started the custom and even though Batanya called it "Armenian luxuries," she continued it), I heard music. It reminded me of Uncle Sanya and the restaurant at Sestroretsk, and so I liked it. Later I learned that we were sleeping right over the restaurant orchestra, which by strange coincidence was called the Astoria and was located on the first floor of the Luxe.

After the war the restaurant was renamed the Tsentralny and the Luxe became the Tsentralny Hotel. I think the name change came during the struggle against "cosmopolites." I've never been to that restaurant—under either name. I think that I ought to go now. The next time the children come, I will.

I was to sleep to that music every night of my life at the Luxe—until the summer of 1937.

18

In the fall of 1931 I went to second grade at School 27 on Bolshaya Dmitrovka. This was an era of experimentation with education. We were joined into brigades, then separated, then repeatedly tested. And apparently as a result of the catastrophic lack of space, we were constantly transferred by entire grade or part of a class from one school to another. After a half year some of our class was moved to a converted apartment on the fourth floor of a big gray building on Strastnoy Boulevard. For third grade I was back at School 27. In fourth grade it was Strastnaya Square, in the back of the Izvestiya building, and fifth grade on Nastasyinsky Alley. It was only in sixth and seventh grades that we were in a normal new school at the end of the block on Bolshaya Dmitrovka. And the school got a number—36.

I don't remember why (maybe I had been sick), but Mama brought me to school a few days after it started on September 1. She handed me over to the teacher downstairs by the coatroom. The woman led me by the hand into the classroom, set me by her desk, and said she would think about where to put me. The children looked at me, and I looked at them. I felt the way all new people feel, like a stranger—that is, I felt bad. There were no empty seats in the class. At some of the desks there were three children instead of two. I had never seen that in Leningrad. And even with my brief school experience I knew this was not good.

Unexpectedly a boy stood up at the second desk in the middle row, came over to me, took my hand, led me back to his desk, pushed me into his place and then sat next to me. The teacher said something like, "Well, that's fine, we found you a seat." Someone laughed in the back of the room. My new neighbor waved his fist in that direction. And I sensed that I wouldn't have to fight for my place in this class and that I had a protector. The fear of being the new kid was gone. My "protector" sat to my right. To my left was a funny-looking boy, skinny, with tufts of hair sticking out, stuck-out ears, and sort of bristly all over. He didn't push me away from his half of the bench but moved over so that the bench was fairly divided three ways.

During the break my right-side neighbor took an apple out of his school bag and cut it up into four pieces with his penknife, the existence of which impressed me no end. Then he gave me a piece, a piece to our benchmate, and a piece to the boy behind us. He took the last for himself. I also had an apple as well as a sandwich with cheese. I got them out and put them in front of him. He did the same thing with them. He said that cheese was good, but he preferred *brynza*. I didn't know what *brynza* was, but I decided to ask Nura for some tomorrow. By the end of the break we were very good friends. Their names were Seva Bagritsky on the right, Goga Rogachevsky on the left, and Rafka Frenkel in back. After classes while we were all shoving each other in the coatroom, a boy looked at Seva and me and said, "First comes love, then comes marriage, then comes Lusia with a baby carriage." Seva smacked him with his bookbag. The first lesson, or rather, the first break had determined the rest of my school life, my friends, my circle. In second and third grades I spent almost all my time with those three boys. I don't remember any of the other children. I've even forgotten the teacher's name.

We left school together. We parted on the corner of Golenishchevsky Alley, which led to the Luxe. I went home and the boys headed down Dmitrovka. I thought they all lived in that neighborhood. I soon learned that Goga lived in the opposite direction (in fact, in the house where our school would be transferred after winter break and which then became known as the Annex)—it's just that he always went to Seva's house after school. At home I told Nura about my new friends. A few days later I brought Seva and Goga to our house. Rafka didn't come because he had to tell his family if he was going anywhere. But he visited later.

All the way home I worried that there might be problems with the doorman and that I'd have to run for Nura to get them in. But everything worked out and the boys liked our house and Nura liked them. She fed us all, and then Goga suggested playing go-fish. We never kept cards in the house, even though in Leningrad Batanya sometimes went to a friend's house to play preference. I was mad at Goga because he didn't believe that we had no games except children's lotto and Papa's chess set. I then produced Papa's *nardy,** even though Egorka and I weren't allowed to touch them. Papa only brought them out when his Armenian friends visited. The boys were interested in the game, even though I couldn't explain all the rules.

*Nardy is a board game with dice, similar to backgammon, that is very popular in the Transcaucasus, especially among Armenians and Georgians.

Nura rescued me. She called me behind her curtain and told me she had cards which she used for telling fortunes. "Like Svetlana?"

"Sort of. Just don't tell Rufa, please."

"My Lenin word of honor," I swore.

So we settled on the floor to play cards. I didn't play for real, since I had never held a card before, but I did learn. Nura made a fourth with us, and Egorka sat on her lap. It was lots of fun and I picked the game up quickly because there's nothing much to it. I never progressed in cards. Go-fish is the only game I've mastered in all my years.

A few days later I went to Seva's house for the first time. It was apartment 9 on the sixth floor of house 2 in Kamergersky Alley. While we took off our coats in the entry, a cheerful woman came out of the kitchen. She was pleasantly surprised that there were three of us. She was used to Goga coming home with Seva, but she seemed happy that I was there. To the left was the door to Seva's room. The bed was opposite the door and by the window was a table—not a desk, but a regular table. It was covered with books and papers and there were more on the wide windowsill. There were two chairs by the table and a small shelf with books and toys on the wall. The room was narrow and a bit unusual because the door from the hallway was opposite a wall instead of a window. When Seva had been at our house he had given my fishtank a quick glance and said he would show me a real aquarium. But there wasn't one in his room. I figured he had lied: everyone lies about something; it seemed so ordinary.

Then a woman came in who I knew was Seva's Masha. After he met our Nura he said that they had a nanny named Masha. She wasn't anything like Nura—she was old, ugly, and mumbled. She put a big frying pan of potatoes on the table. Seva said that we didn't need plates, so we ate out of the pan. It turned out that all three of us had the same favorite dish—fried potatoes (it still is mine). Later the woman who had met us in the corridor brought tea. She was Seva's mother. She wasn't tall and seemed plump to me. She said she had come to meet me and that her name was Lida. But Seva said very sternly, "Lydia Gustavovna."

They argued; she said the patronymic wasn't at all necessary. Because of that argument I didn't know what to call her—I wanted to call her Lida but was afraid Seva would be angry.

For many years afterward I would alternate between Lida and Lydia Gustavovna and it was only after Seva's death that I settled on Lida. My children had the same problem with her name, and it was only after her death that she became simply Lida for them, too.

When Lida left, Seva bugged out his eyes and in a scary whisper announced he was going on reconnaissance. He left on tiptoe. I didn't know what was going on and asked Goga in a whisper. He said, "You'll see." Seva came back and commanded, "Follow me." We went into the hallway and from there into another room, to the right. The room was larger than Seva's. On the couch near the right wall sat an elderly-looking man who resembled Makhno* (whom I had read about) because he had a lot of hair that was either uncut or unkempt. He sort of scared me. He spoke in a very severe tone and said, "Here is a maiden and this is a new phenomenon, and how do we address said maiden?" He was almost in singsong by then. And even though he sounded grim, I could tell he was joking. I said, "Lusia." He grimaced as if he didn't like my name and said that was awful because with a name like that I always had to be nice (a pun on *mila* (nice), which is part of the name Ludmila). Always. I tried to explain that I wasn't a Ludmila, but he made a scary face and shouted "A nightmare!" Everyone laughed, he first, I last. And then Goga said, "First comes love, then comes marriage." The man said, "Who's getting married, you?" Goga pointed to Seva.

Then the man yelled, "Lida, Lida, come quickly, there's a wedding. Lida!"

Seva's mother came in, saw that I was practically in tears, and said, "Edya, cut out your gags."

I hadn't heard that word before, but I understood what it meant.

But Edya went right on shouting that the bride had to be

*Nestor Ivanovich Makhno (1889–1934), anarchist and nationalist leader in the Ukraine during the Civil War of 1918–1921.

weighed and measured, received and posted on a checklist, including her bow, which was "magnificent!"

Lida replied very calmly that she wasn't about to weigh me, but she would measure me. She led me to the doorframe, picked up a pencil, licked it so that her lips were stained, and marked my height. My line, next to which Lida wrote "Lusia," was between two others. A bit below mine it said "Goga," and above me was "Seva." A year later, in third grade, three new lines were placed on the doorframe, and mine was in the middle once more. The measurements were never taken again.

But I saw them again during the war when I came to visit Masha. Edya had died a long time before, Lida was in the camps at Karaganda, Seva was buried in Novgorod, Goga was also buried somewhere near Kursk. The lines were mute testimony of the time when we were all together in that room.

After the jokes (gags, as I learned), Edya told Seva, "Show her," and started getting up from behind the table that had been pulled very close to the couch on which he was seated. He was big—not tall, but big—and he was wearing thick knee-high socks. I think they were called gaiters in those days. Seva shoved me away from the door into the middle of the room, closer to the window. It was actually two huge windows with a door onto the balcony in the middle. The windowsills and shelves near the windows were filled with small and large aquariums. I stared at the miracle and Seva said proudly, "Not like your small fry." I didn't argue. First of all, there was nothing to argue about, and secondly, I wanted to go out on the balcony. Without a word about the fish, I asked Edya if I could go outside. He said with disapproval that apparently maidens have no interest in fauna and went back to his couch.

We went out and for the first time I saw Moscow from high up. The house faced Tverskaya Street. There are taller buildings in front of it now, but back then nothing blocked the view of the Kremlin (which was still without the red stars on its towers). Beyond it lay the whole city—roofs, towers, and churches. We stood on the balcony a long time, and then Goga and I went home.

At home I told them about the balcony and how beautiful Moscow looks from it, although it's not like Leningrad when you view it from St. Isaac's. I completely forgot to tell them about Seva's strange father. But a few days later when Seva, Goga, and Rafka were at our house, Mama's friend Nastya came to visit. Mama was not home yet, and Nastya, with nothing better to do, questioned the boys closely about everything, because she was nosy. After the boys left, Nastya told Mama that Seva's father was Bagritsky the poet, which was all right because he was a poet who suited the Party despite his permitting some wrong motifs. Later Nastya explained that Seva's family were decadent. But it was wrong to be friends with Goga because his father was Lvov-Rogachevsky, who was hostile to the Party in some way. I began defending my friendship and said that it was none of their business whom I saw. And Mama unexpectedly supported me and said it was my business but she didn't understand why all my friends were boys. "That's in school. At the Luxe I have girls." That was the end of the discussion that evening.

Nastya continued questioning me about Goga and Seva right up until 1937, but she never asked about Rafka. Apparently, his father didn't interest her at all.

I think this was my first rebellion against the "general Party line," which was followed firmly by Mama and her woman friends in my upbringing and condescendingly and with many deviations by Papa. And which Batanya fought fiercely. That same evening Nastya read some of Bagritsky's poems, the first time I heard them, and a few days later she brought his book. So it wasn't at Seva's house that I met Bagritsky the poet.

It was Nastya who also introduced me to Soviet poetry (the Komsomol and Communist verse) of the period. She brought books by Zharov and Bezymensky, Utkin, Alrauzen, Selvinsky, and Tikhonov. Papa didn't seem to read these poets. I never heard him mention their names or their verse. Nastya apparently liked them. She often spent the night at our house, and she usually slept in my room and recited poetry at bedtime. Some of the things she read I came to like; for instance, Utkin's long poem about red-haired Mottel and a few of his other works, and the poems of Tikhonov.

How did we study at school? It seemed as if we didn't at all, because in second grade the system grouped the children by tens allowing one representative answer for the whole group. So one worked and nine did nothing. In our group Rafka usually answered for us all. But in reading class, I did. I was recognized as reading not only fast but "with feeling." Seva teased me about the "feeling" part, dragging out the word like his father. But by then I had stopped taking offense at gags.

Seva and the others also teased me about my hair bow. And in third grade the teacher attacked my bow, with remarks about "petty bourgeois" taste. Until then I had been begging my family to cut my hair so that I could have bangs and no bow, but now I asked them to make my bow one size bigger. I wore a bow until fifth grade, when Anetka (a friend who worked with Papa and was always traveling) brought me a pack of silvery barrettes from Paris. The girls in my class envied me wildly, the way people respond to brand-name goods now. Batanya also approved, saying that my hair had stopped looking like the beard of Karl Marx. However, by the following year, metal barrettes were being sold all over Moscow.

Homework took almost no time at all, even though all four of us had terrible handwriting. Penmanship as a subject did not exist then. Arithmetic was laughably easy, and the assignments we were supposed to memorize and recite (something like history, geography, and social studies) could be learned in class. In class, we often read books we brought from home. Sometimes the teacher took away the book, but usually she returned it. I don't think we were marked for behavior and classwork until sixth (or fifth) grade. Exams—"spring trials"—appeared in fourth grade; before that, there seemed to have been no record kept of our work. The four of us were considered good students. I think that Rafka was the only one who did any work; he was a gifted boy, with a lively, all-encompassing mind, but more earthbound, I guess, than Goga or Seva. In the higher grades, where we were expected to do some work, Rafka was among the best. Seva always treated school condescendingly and carelessly; he never did any work seriously in those ten years. He hated science, but he was born reading and writing. That and his natural charm combined with the celebrity of his name helped him get tolerable grades and loads of free time. In sixth grade Seva decided he was a writer, maybe a poet, maybe a prose writer, maybe a playwright. His future was tied to the pen.

Goga was the most talented of us all. In lower grades he was always drawing, and his notebooks were filled with scribbles. Even among math problems you would find bizarre faces, fantastic machines, twisted bent trees. He began writing poetry early, much earlier than Seva. He always knew more than the rest of us both in school subjects and in areas that were remote for us— history, astronomy, politics. And yet he was terrible in grammar. In the lower grades he never got more than a two or a one on the easiest dictation. Of course, those weren't the grades we were given—those were Batanya's marks. Our grades were very bad, bad, average, good, and very good. Later they were changed to unsatisfactory, satisfactory, good, and excellent. Later, after our school years, the schools reverted to the pre-Revolutionary five-grade system, with five as the highest and one meaning failure.

I went to Seva's often after school. It became a tradition for the three of us to go either to his place or mine. Rafka rarely joined us and I never went to his house. At Seva's we usually had fried potatoes—crisp and crunchy—or sometimes pancakes. Nura always made a full meal, which Goga liked, but Seva and I preferred the potatoes at any time of any day. After eating we read and played. At Seva's the games always ended up in a fight, with pillows and other objects flying through the air, at which point Lida would come in and tell us to go play outside. Besides us, children from their building also came to Seva's room: the Kirillov sisters, Nadya and Valya, both very blond and very pretty, Shurik Arsky, and Yura Selivansky. We would all go outside with our sleds, and we would travel far, all the way to Trubnaya Square and up the boulevard, for the pleasure of sledding downhill right into the middle of the square. For most of the way the girls rode in the sleds, which the boys pulled. On the way back the first to split off was Goga, when we passed his house. Then I dropped off at the Luxe, while the "writers' building" kids went on to the end. I envied Nadya and Valya that they lived closer to Seva than I did.

Even though I was at Seva's three or four times a week, I rarely saw his father. We weren't allowed much in his room. Sometimes Seva called me in to be present when the fish were fed. Edya (which is what I called him in my mind, because I never learned his patronymic) would announce, "Our lawful bride is come," and then subject me to a cross-examination, with questions I couldn't answer. One time he tried to establish what Papa did.

"Well, he works."

"What, does he dig dirt or mend shoes?"

I was silent. I had learned from my Leningrad experience not to use "Party worker" and so I feverishly pondered how to explain what he did. Stuttering, I said, "He writes."

"Ah, a colleague," Edya said, giving the word a foreign intonation. "What—prose or does he versify?"

Just as I was about to burst into tears, Lida would rescue me, telling him to stop tormenting the child.

Edya's response was always the same, "She's not a child; she's a bride. She should know how to answer worthily."

It was these conversations that kept me from wanting to be in his room.

But sometimes other things went on in his room. Seva would say, "Let's go listen." We would slip in quietly. The room wasn't large and so it seemed to be full of people. Someone would read poetry and then Edya would criticize the poems. I never heard him praise anyone. But he criticized in the same way that he spoke to me—you couldn't tell if he was serious or joking. At any rate, I couldn't. I was astonished by the way Edya's guests read their poems—dragging them out, with sharp changes in volume, swaying, eyes shut. I didn't like it. Sometimes at his father's insistence, Seva read poetry. Just like the others. I really hated that and even wanted to leave. But once there were two men who read Bagritsky's poems in a way I liked. Later I learned that they were the actors Zhuravlev and Golubentsev. I think that was the first time I liked the poetry reading at Seva's house.

Later I was surprised at myself, because I don't like the way actors read anymore. But back then, I did. Recalling those times, I think that I was never comfortable around Seva's father. He embarrassed me somehow. But I was always happy with Lida; things were light and simple. That lightness in our relationship, which formed when I was nine, lasted for a lifetime.

After winter vacation, the seat next to Rafka became available. Goga moved back there, and the four of us had the second and third desks of the middle row in both second and third grades.

In fourth grade I was moved to the "annex" in the courtyard of the Izvestia building, Goga was sent to the school in his building, and Seva and Rafka stayed at the old school. At the beginning of the school year we saw as much of one another as before, but gradually the boys developed their own "male" games. And I was spending more time with the girls from the Luxe. We had reached the age when boys and girls stop being pals; the time for romantic interest had not yet come.

19

Uncle Sanya, Aunt Ronya, and her mother, Aunt Sonya, moved to Moscow from Chita. They lived with us at first. Papa considered this to be a period of incredible gastronomic pleasures, due to Aunt Sonya's cooking. Family legend has it that Mikoyan (who was them People's Commissar of the Food Industry) had tasted a sauce at our house made by Aunt Sonya and tried to talk her into coming to work for him as a consultant. From our place they moved to Gavrikov Alley and then to the building of the People's Commissariat of Heavy Industry on Solyanka. I was allowed to go to their place on my own. I took the trolley on Strastnaya Square. It was a turnaround point and I could always get a window seat. Then I would go all the way across town. Their room (in those days no one had a house or an apartment, only a room) had the same vases, the same screen, and the same piano as in Chita. And there was music. I felt sorry for Uncle Sanya, who was upset that I didn't have perfect pitch. But he consoled me, saying that the important thing was to love music and know how to listen. We read my first serious books aloud to each other, *Uncle Tom's Cabin* and one that I later read to my own children, *The Adventures of the Prehistoric Boy.*

Aunt Ronya was my doctor throughout my childhood and then doctor to my children. She had always been a friend of my grand-mother, then of my mother, and then of mine. None of the cataclysms in our family affected that friendship—not the purges of 1937, not Andrei moving into our house. In the last years of her life (she died in the fall of 1979) her interest in my life astonished me and the mutual liking between Andrei and her gladdened me.

Then my parents allowed me to go visit Zorya, Anya, and Lyova. Sometimes I was even sent there to bring something or tell them something, since they did not have a telephone. Zorya did not interest me much then. She was little and played more with Egorka. She was drawn to me and I began to love her later, when she was older and came to visit from Leningrad. But I liked the fact that they lived far away; it seemed almost out of town. It was a place with a lovely name—by the Humped Bridge, Prodolny Alley. The house was wooden, two-storied, old and creaky, like a little dacha. The yard also looked as if it belonged to a dacha, filled with lilac and jasmine bushes. But the best part was the way home. When the trolley crossed the Presnya and stopped at the zoo, I got out "to take a little look at the animals." Afterward, continuing home, I felt as if I had traveled far to another city or country, where the animals lived. How strange. The zoo seems so close now.

I also liked going by myself to visit Batanya's brother, Uncle Mosya, and his wife, Aunt Nadya. I'd take the "A" trolley, called the Annushka, from Strastnaya Square to get to their place. They lived on the second floor of a long three-storied house at the start of Chistoprudny Boulevard, almost directly opposite today's

Kirovskaya metro station. It wasn't an ordinary apartment; it was more like a dormitory. The windows of the very long and extraordinarily wide corridor faced the boulevard, while the windows of the rooms opened on the courtyard. They had two rooms. The bigger one served as the living room, dining room, bedroom, and even kitchen. A small hotplate stood on the table by the door, and the kettle was always boiling. The second room, small and as narrow as a pencil case, was the study. In that room, by the light of the green desk lamp (they were always green in those days, and Andrei longed to have one for our apartment), I had innumerable conversations with Uncle Mosya, always privately. Ever since then I have found I can have real communication only when I'm alone with a person; if there are a lot of people I can't manage—then it's just chatter. Our talks were amazing in their confidentiality (I felt I could tell Uncle Mosya anything) and seriousness.

They were always somber—both in the days when I used a broomstick as a horse to gallop down their long corridor and in the days years later when we talked about Mama's letters from camp, my life in the army, my little Tanya. I always felt his incredible education; I sensed that he was not like Mama, Papa, and their friends, and that he was interested in something else both in life and in being with me. The former did not dampen my spirits and the latter did not make me wary. I was always afraid that Mama, just because she was different from him, would do something that would be unpleasant for Uncle Mosya. But that never happened. On the contrary. While Mama never turned into a person like him, when she was with him she changed imperceptibly, growing closer to him. Much later I learned that when she was graduating from Gymnasium in Moscow, she lived her senior year with Uncle Mosya, and that for her he had almost as much authority as her mother. Now I realize that Uncle Mosya was the first true intellectual in my life; he had a completely different scale of values, and was a man who made others better for being around him. But I understand that only now.

In 1982, when I was still traveling from Gorky to Moscow, I saw a book in an old brown jacket, published in 1913 (?), on Mama's bookshelf—M. M. Rubinshtein's A Study in Pedagogic Psychology. *I had seen it all my life and remembered that it was inscribed by the author to my grandmother, but I had never had the desire to read it. I took it to Gorky. Now I had the "time and place." As I read it, I experienced that sense of confidentiality and seriousness that arose every time I talked with Uncle Mosya in real life. Confidentiality and seriousness toward the reader and the child, the subject of the book. The child's search for God, for kindness, his attempts to comprehend "life" and "death." Well, of course, he was an idealist, our Uncle Mosya. And it hurt so much that I had irretrievably lost the chance to talk to him about everything that was in the book.*

He outlived Stalin. But he did not live long enough to see the posthumous rehabilitation of his son and the return from the camps of his daughter-in-law, the mother of Uncle Mosya's grandchildren. He died in Moscow in the spring of 1953 and was buried in the Lutheran cemetery.

20

Every Saturday Nura went to the evening activities at the canteen next to the side entrance of the Luxe—not on Tverskaya, but on Golenishchevsky. Besides lectures they also had dances, which were attended by the military, both enlisted men and officers (or commanders, as they were known) from the military unit supervised by the Comintern Executive Committee. I always wanted to go too, but Mama was violently opposed. Actually her opposition was meaningless. I went anyway, as did several other girls from the Luxe.

Nura primped for these parties, sometimes wearing Mama's dresses (Mama let her), but she had her own, too. Unlike Mama, Nura didn't mind my going, but the rule was that I could not approach her there, and if I did, her name was Anna, not Nura, and she was not my nanny. She always had a good time, laughing loudly, singing, and dancing a lot. She was constantly being invited to dance. One of the commanders danced with her frequently, and this went on for a while. Then Nura began going out all day Sunday. Previously she had always spent her day off in her room sewing for herself and for us.

But one night after the dance she had a long conversation with Mama. She told her that the commander wanted to meet Mama, Papa, and us children. Because he had "intentions," and she had told him that she was Mama's sister. It turned out she had been lying again, as she had to the soldier from the boulevard. Mama was angry, not about Nura's lying, but about her ruining things for herself—now she would have to tell the commander the truth. Papa came home and also said that she had been wrong to lie, but he knew the commander, he was a "fine fellow," and let him come. And if Nura was afraid to, he'd tell him.

The next Sunday Nura fixed up the house, herself, and us as if it were Easter, baked pies almost as good as Batanya's (she had learned all of Batanya's recipes), made lots of other delicious food, and set the table beautifully. Her commander came. Egorka was all over him, because he adored military men then, and even expressed regret that Papa wasn't a Red commander. Everyone ate and drank soda pop and wine. There was vodka, too; Nura had bought it. But Papa said that he didn't drink vodka and Nura's suitor didn't either, only wine. Then Papa took him into his room and they stayed there a long time, while Nura wept in the kitchen. Mama cleared the table and shouted at us to go to bed immediately. But just then Papa and the man came out. They talked some more and then Nura went out with the commander.

Mama asked, "Well?"

"I think he'll marry her. I told you he was a fine fellow." Then he added, "If he doesn't marry her, he's a bastard."

I thought that everyone who wasn't married was a bastard, but I didn't ask because I was afraid Mama would start shouting "Go to bed" again.

But Papa said, "It's all so complicated with Nura. And he's getting a promotion and he's being transferred. Well, we'll see . . ." and then began singing his favorite song under his breath, "The father didn't believe the son that there was love in the world . . ."

Soon afterward the commander left, and we learned that Nura would be going too. They had "registered" their marriage and she now had a new last name. But Nura took a long time getting ready. She brought a new nanny into the house, named Dusya. Nura hissed at her like a snake and taught her in Batanya's voice to iron linens and make meat patties. For a few weeks our house was filled with Nura's angry voice and Dusya's mutterings. I think Dusya was much more afraid of Nura than Nura had ever been of Batanya. Then Nura left, weeping and embracing Egorka endlessly, and Dusya saw her off. Dusya wasn't a nanny; she was a cleaning lady. She was good. We had two after her, but no one could replace Nura. After she left we realized that we had not lost a nanny but one of the family.

Nura lived somewhere in Belorussia and later in the Ukraine. She would spend a day or two at a time in Moscow, always looking pretty and fancy—much fancier than Mama. In 1938 she was in Leningrad. She told everyone she had come to visit her sister, but actually she was there to ask Batanya to give her Egorka. She said that it would be better for him and that her husband was not only prepared to adopt him but had urged Nura to go for him. He was a big boss by then. After the war he became a general, which we learned from a letter Nura sent to me after Mama was freed. It was the first letter she wrote to me; she used to write through her sister, Tanya. Nura said that everything was fine, her husband and children were well, but she was very sick. We never heard anything else from her, and then Tanya, our main source of news, died in the siege of Leningrad.

I'm ashamed to admit it, but I don't remember anything about the rationing of those years. Apparently our living conditions were such that it didn't affect my memory—that is, the question of hunger did not come up. So I don't remember when they did away with the card system. I know about it, but it is knowledge acquired later, not from direct memory.

I do remember the food parcels. Papa's was delivered to the house, twice a month or more, but I don't know whether we paid for it. It had butter, cheese, candies, and canned goods. There were also special parcels for the holidays, with caviar, smoked and cured fish, chocolate, and also cheese and butter. You had to pick up Mama's parcels—not far away, on Petrovka. The dining room of the Moscow Party Committee was on the corner of Takhmanovsky Alley, and once a week they gave out the parcels. I often went for ours, and you had to pay. It contained butter and other items, but it was much less fancy than Papa's.

Mama never took part at all in running the household. Nura was given expense money and she made the decisions on how to spend it. Mama gave the other nannies money once a week (I think), and grew very angry when they tried to account for their expenses to her. She said she didn't understand any of it and if they were so eager to report, "Just wait for Tatyana Matveyevna—she'll be here soon and you can tell her." I remember that on one of her visits, Batanya scolded Mama and said that neither she nor Papa knew how much bread or sugar cost. She gave them a quiz. They failed.

However, Mama treated the parcels very seriously and even Nura didn't touch them without her approval. Mama began by dividing everything in the parcel into two parts—one for us, the other for Anya, Lyova, and Zorya.

At one time a third portion was taken out—for Valya, Mama's friend who had a baby but no husband. Papa used to insist, "Valya is a fool and he's a bastard." I don't know who that "bastard" was. And Mama would say, "It's not your business. She wanted a baby and she had one."

Valya was younger than Mama and I don't know where she came from, but Mama loved her. She lived in the big Mosselprom house in Gnezdnikovsky Alley. The room was tiny and not even hers; some people had let her in. When the baby was born, I'd go to her almost every day: with clothes, the parcel, or just some cooked food. Toward 1937 her life became more settled and she got a room someplace. I think her relationship with Mama faded slowly. Mama said that no one knew anything about Valya after 1937.

21

A year or two later, during the summer, when Egorka and I were away, our suite at the Luxe, number 9, was redone. They turned the big room into two—mine and the dining room. The bathroom was made into a room for Egorka and a kitchen. The tub was in the kitchen, and it was covered with plywood. The cubby for the maid was given a wall with glass at the top. Now we had four rooms, even five including the cubby. We didn't have to go "around the corner" for the kitchen. But I loved my own room best. Without Egorka. I could shut my door on everyone.

The mother of one of my friends said she wanted to see our renovations. She came with me in the daytime when all the adults except for the nanny were out and then said, "Now that's some repairs!" I couldn't tell if she approved or not. "So who is your father? Isn't four rooms a lot? He must be a big boss, eh?" I didn't know what he was or how to answer. What worried me was that maybe four rooms were too much.

The population of the Luxe was unofficially divided into Soviets and foreigners, but they were all tied to the Comintern. That woman, who had two children and a nanny, was a Soviet, and she lived in one room of the Luxe because the father of her children worked in the Comintern, but lived somewhere else, separately. That's probably why she didn't know my father. I had never liked her and so I quickly got over my discomfort.

In Leningrad children were a small part in my life. Of course I played in the yard of the Grand Hotel, brought them home, and sometimes (very rarely) visited them. But this socializing must not have been very important to me since I do not remember any of them. Close friendships began at the Luxe and in school in Moscow.

There was a Pioneer room at the Luxe—a club for children, set up not so much for ideological reasons as to keep the kids out of the hallways. Of course, I spent some time there, but it wasn't interesting. Our main life took place in the corridors and lobbies. We played hide-and-seek, cossacks and robbers, and other group games there.

The children divided into groups according to both age and class, the latter based on the parents' positions. (I think I violated both divisions.) There was also a language barrier for the foreign children, but that broke down quickly. All the children soon learned Russian, with their parents lagging behind. For instance, Mirella and Giorgio spoke Russian as well as I did, their mother spoke badly, and the father not at all. Their last name was R——.

Forty years later I spoke at a youth rally in Milan, on the horrible conditions in Soviet medicine, the rise in infant mortality, the lack of basic medications. I also said that we didn't even manufacture bottles and nipples for feeding babies. All this was recently printed in Izvestia *in an article by our "perestroika" Minister of Health, Dr. Chazov. The audience in Milan shouted that I was a fascist slandering the state, that I should meet with Italian Communists who knew that the USSR had good free medical care. I rejected the label "fascist." And as for meeting with Communists, I said that I had been friends with a young Italian as a child. We had lived in the same building, and now he was a Communist in Italy. But neither he nor any other Italian Communists had shown any desire to meet with me. I mentioned his name.*

After the meeting a middle-aged man came up to me and told me that he was researching the history of the Comintern and knew that my father had been in the Comintern. He told me that R—— had been a made-up name and that his real name was P——, and that Giorgio P—— lived in Rome and worked in an office. I called and met with Giorgio and his mother. It was not a happy reunion. Each of us had a lifetime behind us, and I felt that my "dissidence" was making it hard for them, that I was odious to them as Communists.

I have a funny memory. Giorgio was the first boy I kissed. We were hiding behind a big green armchair in our dining room. I don't know what he was thinking about, but I was worried about being found: we were playing hide-and-seek and the game was uppermost in my mind.

I had my first girlfriends at the Luxe, too: the Bulgarian Roza Iskrova and the Norwegian Magda Furboten. Her family had moved into the room we used to occupy. They never became "bosom" friends, but I liked them better than others. I also "hung out" with the girl whose mother didn't like our repairs. And with Nadya Suvorova, one of the Soviet children at the Luxe. We were later in the same class at school.

Of the boys, a close friend was Zharko Walter, Tito's nephew (Tito was also called Walter then).* Zharko lived almost without supervision at the Luxe; his uncle didn't have time for him. His mother was either in jail in Yugoslavia or already dead. I never heard anything about his father. He didn't want to live in the Comintern orphanage and they tried to get rid of him because of his behavior. At the Luxe he was quite different from the other boys. He wasn't dressed as nicely as the foreigners, or even as the Soviets. He looked messy and had wide-set eyes. When he talked to adults, he looked like an angry and slightly tormented animal and his reddish hair stuck out like barbed wire. He was a fighter and very daring. He was two grades behind me, even though he was only a few months younger. He rarely went to school, spending most of his time in the streets and especially in the infamous Bakhrushenka. This was a series of connecting back alleys and courtyards joining Bolshaya Dmitrovka, Kozitsky, and Goleni-shchevsky alleys. Everyone feared Bakhrushenka. People were supposed to have been mugged and killed there and even more horrible things were supposed to have happened in that neigh-borhood. Zharko felt at home in that dark place and had friends there who were much older. Perhaps that was because he was a pariah at the Luxe. The nannies, mothers, and grandmothers were up in arms about letting their children play with him. People didn't invite him to their rooms because he allegedly stole, and that was his smallest sin.

*Members of the Executive Committee of the Comintern (the Communist International) used various pseudonyms at different times in their underground work as Communists.

Our relationship began because coming home from school once I saw Zharko steal a loaf of French bread from a truck. We ran into each other in the courtyard. He knew that I had seen him, but he went on chewing calmly, breaking off pieces from the loaf under his arm. He gave me a threatening look, but I realized he was simply hungry, and said, "Let's go to my house." I knew that I would be fed after school and that Papa was home. He was often home then. He was sick; his ulcer was beginning, and he had spells of acute pain. I realized that if he was home, no one would dare throw anyone out. Papa knew Zharko because his uncle often came over to play chess with Papa. And so Zharko entered our house and no matter how much the nannies worried and said that he would lure me into the Bakhrushenka, he was accepted. Later Zharko borrowed my skates with boots (far from everyone had skates then), I don't know for what, they were too small for him, and never returned them. Maybe he sold them. I lied and said I lost them, so I could get another pair. There was a period when I was blindly loyal to Zharko and I liked everything about him: from his daring to his thievery and the Bakhrushenka.

Our building was undergoing construction then. On the fifth floor a board had been laid between one bay window and another. We were either the Cossacks or the robbers. Zharko ran across the board with a cry of "Follow me!" Without a second's thought, I ran after him. The rest of our party remained on the other side. I get scared just thinking about it now. I, who never forgot the woman who threw herself from St. Isaac's and the boy who fell from the window, didn't think of them then. I simply ran. Of course, even despite my memory of the fallen, I didn't develop a fear of heights—I wasn't the one who fell.

Before that Zharko had mostly used me—he would come over for a meal and maybe whatever he could filch from the coats hanging in the entry (I had seen him). But after I ran across that board, his attitude toward me changed. He began "respecting" me, and we began a friendship that gradually took on a shade of love. However, we didn't kiss, apparently because I was older than the time of my first kiss but hadn't grown up enough for real kissing. I even went into the Bakhrushenka with him, and his pals there knew me. Sometimes when I was late for school, I risked running through the area alone—to save a few minutes.

Gradually our friendship/half-love evaporated. I was more and more involved in school relationships. I was full of poetry and books, even politics, and on the way to my first love. In 1937, when everything was at its height and illuminated by the then clearly looming tragedy (it had already arrived in other families), I don't remember being with Zharko at all, even though he was still in the building. He had vanished from my life. I heard that he became a real lady-killer, which I can readily believe. He was very good-looking with a mean yet merry face and light, desperate eyes which must have become even more gorgeous. I think he was much more "enlightened" romantically than his peers. He supposedly remained his daring self during the war years. He went the Yugoslav partisan route with Tito and then became a general, I believe.

I wrote about Zharko in May 1988. In September or October I got hold of Milovan Djilas's book Tito: The Story from Inside. *It turned out I had reported a "cover story." Just as spies have covers in mystery books, this was a Comintern cover. I don't know which is better. Maybe both are worse. Djilas wrote that Zharko was Tito's son by his first marriage. The mother was a Russian woman. At the time I have been describing, she lived in the Soviet Union. Maybe in Moscow.*

And everything I had written seemed unfair—the stolen bread, my skates, the guys from Bakhrushenka. The boy was simply creating his own world, to somehow survive inside the "cover."

22

My first real friendship happened unexpectedly at the Luxe. In the third-floor lobby I saw a new girl—I don't remember where she had come from. She was shorter and smaller than I, even though she was a whole year older. Her name was Lena, Lena Krebs. She was Soviet, but not completely. She had a Soviet mother somewhere. Her father was a Jew, but somehow connected to Sweden; maybe he had been born there. Lena lived with him and her stepmother, who was called Binochka. She was Swedish. She loved Lena, and Lena loved her. When I met Lena, I felt that she would be a real friend, the first, the only, for life. I had never had a real friend before, and I didn't know the meaning of the word. I saw that she felt the same. I didn't notice the other girls run off, leaving us alone. We stood in the corner by the radiator (I can feel that radiator and its warmth to this day) and talked and talked. Then Lena got droopy and said she was tired and had to go home, but she didn't go, and we sat down on the couch. In a grownup way she told me she was very sick, she wasn't supposed to leave her room, she had something wrong with her heart, and she didn't play with children often. If I wanted to be her friend, I would have to visit her. And we went off to her room.

At first I thought Binochka was a girl—she was so skinny, and small, and fragile. Then I saw wrinkles (Mama didn't have any then) and weariness. Lena said, "Binochka, this is my best friend, Lusia; please love her, too." Binochka looked at me and said nothing. Then I said, "Lena is my first girlfriend; I've never had one before." Binochka smiled weakly and very kindly, saying nothing. But I think she liked me right away. At least, it felt that way.

The Krebses had two rooms that were not connected but rather next door to each other on the fourth floor. One was for Lena's father and Binochka, the other for Lena. When Lena was alone, Binochka spent almost all her time with her. But as soon as I arrived, Binochka always left us alone. Sometimes, not often, other girls came, too, but Lena confessed to me that they bored her.

My day changed radically once Lena came into my life. All my after-school time depended on Lena's schedule. She studied by correspondence and teachers came to her sometimes. I began doing my homework at her place, and since we were in the same grade, she always said she didn't need a teacher. We memorized things in parallel somehow, equally fast, and we didn't need much time for it. I played outside or hide-and-seek in the hallway when Lena rested or spent an hour or so with her father. That's how she called it, an hour or so. But that wasn't often. Our favorite pastime was reading together. I lay down next to her on the wide couch and we read the same book—not aloud, but to ourselves. The only sound was "Ready?" every two or three minutes, before turning the page. We rarely discussed what we were reading; it was obvious to us that we were perceiving the material in exactly the same way, with the same emotions and so on. We would burst out laughing or crying at the same moment. We hid nothing from each other. I even knew that if Binochka was crying it was because Lena's father had insulted her and Lena had had a fight with him.

Many of the adults at the Luxe liked talking to me. But I often sensed their insincerity, especially in Stella Blagoeva,* and I hated her for that. I realized that all those pats on the head and talk of "how you've grown" and "how pretty you look" were just so much sucking up to Papa. I knew they thought he was a big boss. I don't think I liked bosses by then; at any rate, I didn't want

*Stella Blagoeva (1887–1954), a member of the Comintern, later Bulgarian ambassador to the Soviet Union (1949–1954).

my father to be one. Sometimes these toadies would say, "You look so much like your father, and your brother looks like your mother." I would laugh to myself, because I thought fathers had nothing to do with it. "The mother has the baby and the baby can look only like the mother." This upset me. I worried constantly that I wasn't my mother's child; Egorka looked like her and I didn't and that meant she was my stepmother. Of course, the problem of a stepmother became less acute after I grew to know and love Lena's stepmother, Binochka. And I never said anything at all about fathers. The man with the cane, who had visited me in the hospital, was a deep secret.

Once Binochka told me I was pretty, but it was different—it wasn't intended to please my father. "Lusia, you should know that you are a beautiful girl. Many think the prettiest girl is Margit [a slightly older girl from the third floor], and some think it's one of the Brandon sisters [three Portuguese girls from the fourth floor], but Lena and I don't agree. We think you are."

Lena laughed and said, "You think it's Lusia, Binochka, but I don't. Margit's eyes are so blue, and Volya Brandon's eyes are three times the size of Lusia's."

Binochka added unexpectedly, "And you look so much like your father."

So I told Lena everything, about Papa and "that man" who was my father. She was the first person I could ever discuss it with. I think that I had managed to hide it even from myself.

When Lena was feeling better, she was allowed to walk in the corridor and sometimes to go to our rooms. What she liked doing best was looking out the window, but she couldn't see so well from the fourth floor. From the second, you could see clothing, and facial expressions, and many other details. We liked making up stories about the passersby, based on how they moved, what they were carrying, how they were talking with their friends. And naturally, we watched parades. They were much more frequent then—there must have been holidays besides May 1 and November 7. And people must have liked getting together and shouting "Long live . . ." and "Down with . . ."

And I also read poetry to Lena. She had read a lot before we met, but not poetry; they didn't even have Pushkin at home. She quickly got into poetry with me. Before Lena, I had been too embarrassed to read to anyone except Papa.

23

Everything until this point was written in the spring of 1988 in Pitsunda, where we had fled from Moscow so that Andrei could prepare his lecture for the Friedmann physics conference in Leningrad. At home, in our daily madness of important and unimportant things, meetings, and talks, it was impossible to get anything done. A certain way of life developed, when "you don't avoid work, but don't get the work done." In Pitsunda it was as if we were in a vacuum. The sea made noise below—not too loud during the day, but at night it was a powerful roar, tumbling the stones and gravel. In the complete darkness it seems that the sea is the whole universe, separated from our small insignificant life by the barely visible white foam of the surf. Every evening on the television we were told that it was warm in Moscow. But here the wind and rain were in charge, the temperature never rose above 55 degrees, and in the mornings it was as low as 40.

Andrei was at his desk writing a lot, and he radiated a feeling of concentration and peace. I perched on a stool and typed. Then our return to Moscow would always cut me off from my manuscript completely—I wouldn't even look at it until once again we were outside Moscow in a small suburban town for big physics. It was like the city of the future or, more precisely, a city of the future from the children's books of the thirties, filled with bubble trains and jet cities. Or maybe it was simply a dacha village?

The first impression came from Andrei's delighted tales of the accelerator located sixty meters underground with bearded physicists trying to capture various mu's, pi's, and charmed quarks, while smooth-shaven mathematicians calculate things on their incredible computers. Or maybe, it's the other way around—the physicists are shaven and the mathematicians bearded? But that's just the preamble. They are building an accelerator/accumulator complex. Almost the largest in the world. At a depth of 40 to 60 meters will be a ring 20 kilometers and 767 meters long. The same physicists and mathematicians will be capturing those and other quarks and something just as important for them, and according to Andrei, for everyone else. Every morning he goes off and returns to spend another hour or two telling me what's going on "there," about all the miracles which are like science fiction for me but are reality as well the essence and salt of his life. I listen attentively, even though attentiveness does not make higher matters more comprehensible for me. I think that we are both in luck, since his stories don't give me an inferiority complex and make all my other work seem unnecessary and crude prose. Everything, including cooking dinner, especially since Andrei's appetite is improving and mine is always good—should be worse, but it doesn't get worse.

The second impression, that this is a dacha area, comes from the cottages surrounded by pines, and the proximity of the river. It brings the perfume of damp grass and fog in the evenings.

Yesterday I discovered three white mushrooms. (For a comparison, I found only two in seven years in Gorky.) The first was small and neat, hiding in the grass, its light chocolate head peeking out. The second managed to hide at the very roots of a strongly leaning birch; it was big and heavy in its solidity, one side covered with last year's leaves and squashed on the side that grew up against the tree. The third belonged in a picture. Amid three birches, almost in the center of the equilateral triangle, not hidden at all, but showing off like a dancer in the middle of a circle. And a fine size—the cap like a generous cup. It was a thickish white underneath and the foot was thick and graceful at the same time. A miracle. I gasped when I saw it. How had everyone else missed it all day, and I found it toward evening. It's such a joy to hold a white mushroom that isn't bought, didn't come from the market, but is your own discovery, that had grown just for you, and is cut by your own trembling hand.

I returned to my manuscript after finding the mushrooms. Before that, something had shut down in me once we returned from the sea and I didn't feel like continuing this conversation.

Now we have gotten over the tension of the last few weeks in

Moscow, when the question of Armenia and the future of Karabakh hovered over everything. The pain has not passed, it has simply dulled a bit. It cannot pass, because injustice, no matter how you ornament it, is still nothing but injustice. You can tell yourself a hundred times over that it's like beating your head against a brick wall, but you can't accept it. And we live in Moscow, outsiders, so to speak. You'd think we could just say, "And what is Hecuba to me . . ." But I can't stay out of it.

Andrei waited a week—no, more than a week—for the promised telephone conversation with Gorbachev: from Monday until Friday, and then Monday and Tuesday. He never left the house and was shaking with inner tension. And I almost sank to theft. Of course it wasn't theft, but a horrible situation occurred.

On Saturday we went shopping. We were at the market and then stopped at a fruit-and-vegetable store. We needed juice. It was very hot, and we were always thirsty. I was in the car. Andrei came out with a bag full of bottles and told me that they had cauliflower in the store. I decided to buy some and got out of the car. Andrei called after me, "They also have very nice tomatoes."

"But I got some at the market."

"They're really nice; take a look."

I went inside. I didn't see the cauliflower and asked where it was. The clerk said, "In the next room."

I picked up a packet of tomatoes and went past the cashier's desk to the next room. The guard ran after me. I hadn't paid. She and the cashier and the people in line all started shouting at me. All together. Loud and angry. It was unimaginable. "Thief," and "She looks like an intellectual," "So old and without shame," "She's got a wide skirt to hide what she steals," "She's wearing glasses," and much more. I stood under this shower of shouts, unable to say a thing, and moreover, I couldn't find an explanation even for myself.

When they let me out of that steambath, that horror, I couldn't come to my senses for a while. Why hadn't they called the police? I don't know. After all, I had walked right past the cash register with those ill-starred tomatoes. Andrei said that I looked awful. And added, "Why didn't you explain?"

"What? That I was lost in thought, that I'm in a stupor, that I've

*got Karabakh on my mind and not tomatoes? Is that what I'm
supposed to tell them?"*

*Well, enough about today's life. In school we were taught that this
is a "lyric digression." That doesn't fit the situation because everything I'm writing is "lyrical"—both what is from the land of long ago
and what is from today.*

24

Not long after Nura's departure, Batanya introduced Emma
Davydovna into our house on one of her visits. I don't remember
her surname, but she was a Baltic German, who once upon a time
was the governess in the family of one of Batanya's patrons and
lived in Chita. Emma Davydovna was "deprived"; she didn't
work and was very needy. Apparently Batanya thought that we
had enough bread for one more and that it wouldn't hurt to have
another person looking after Egorka and me. Perhaps she hoped
that Emma Davydovna would manage to teach us German and
improve our manners and in some way be a counterweight to our
"Communist" upbringing. But the most important motive, I
think, was that Batanya wanted to assist a very good, kind, and
absolutely helpless person in that society. So Emma Davydovna
moved in with Egorka and me behind the divider of cupboards.
We loved her—she was very kind and calm: she spoke softly,
moved quietly, never refused to read aloud, and played lotto. But
nothing came of the German language study. "We won't study
a fascist language." I don't think she managed with our manners
either. But Emma Davydovna trained me to wash up twice a day
(Nura required only a steambath once a week and later, when we
lived at the Luxe, a weekly shower and shampoo "until it
squeaked"), to hold a needle in my hand, and even to sew a bit
and mend very well, so that I'm still proud of my ability to put in
an artistic bit of mending.

In the summer of forty-five I was traveling from the Belomorsky Military Okrug to Arkhangelsk. A senior officer was in the compartment. At one of the stops as he was going through the car he tore his uniform (of dark, thin fabric) and grew very upset. I decided to cheer him up. I pulled out a few threads from the lower seam and mended it so that you couldn't find the seam if you didn't know where it was. In reward I received a compliment that sounded rather dubious in those days, "Well, Lieutenant, you work like a German."

In my childhood, little girls were not dressed the way they are today. First there was an undershirt made of linen, cotton, or batiste, apparently depending on the family circumstances. On top there was a girdle which buttoned from behind and elastic bands were pinned to the sides to hold up the stockings. Later it was replaced by an elastic belt. Underpants were flannel bloomers. Knit panties didn't appear until 1935 or 1936. Emma Davydovna also added small cotton panties that she sewed herself. I wore them under my bloomers, changing them daily. None of the other girls wore them. Dusya grumbled about this innovation and called them German (almost like that officer). I got used to them and Emma Davydovna's panties lasted until the war. In the army I made them from the camouflage colored scarves used to hold up wounded arms. To this day, whenever I unpack new panties (they're so thin and pretty nowadays, especially the ones Tanya and Liza send), I think of the ones Emma Davydovna made for me or the "army" ones I made.

In the winter of 1934 the Moscow Committee set up a suburban kindergarten in Barvikha. Mama arranged for Emma Davydovna to work there. In that way Emma Davydovna gained social standing. First she lived in a dormitory. Later she got a tiny room in an old wooden house that looked like a barracks—I visited her a few times. The children lived at the school all the time but they could come home on weekends and holidays. Mama sent Egorka there, and he was allowed home rather often. Sometimes Mama went to pick him up, but more often Emma Davydovna brought him on her days off. Egorka lived there until it was time to go to school. Then Emma Davydovna visited us more rarely—she didn't like Moscow. I think she was happy to be surrounded by children, and that at last she had a position and independence in a world that was alien to her.

In June 1937, after Papa's arrest, Emma Davydovna visited us one last time, terrified. She was saying something about her passport, how there was no indication that she had lived at the Luxe and therefore that she had worked with us. Mama wasn't with the Moscow Committee by then; she was studying at the Industrial Academy. Emma Davydovna hoped that everyone had forgotten that Mama had gotten her the job and she was sort of asking Mama's permission not to visit us anymore. Her fear must have been in conflict with her profound decency. Mama, who was still in shock over Papa's disappearance, agreed with her, although I could see that she didn't really follow the conversation; it was all slipping past her. Emma Davydovna left, looking around in confusion, without kissing Egorka or me, or even saying a word to us. We never saw her again.

About two years later Anya ran into her on the street. Emma Davydovna still lived in Barvikha but worked in a different kindergarten, probably thinking that it would be quieter in a less privileged place and in one where no one knew about her connection with us. So the storm of 1937 passed her by. But the war was still ahead, and I doubt she could have avoided the fate of everyone who had "German" in the nationality line of their passports.

Almost at the same time that Emma Davydovna appeared in our house, Evdokia Ivanovna starting coming every day except holidays, and always when our parents were out. As far as I understood it, Emma Davydovna's presence did not annoy them. She was that kind of a person. Evdokia Ivanovna, however, was a bit "unbearable"—in her strange hat, perhaps of the last century, which she never removed, and her fingerless gloves—odd-mannered, and pathetic. She was the widow of Moisey Rubinshtein, Batanya's cousin. He had been a famous musician—first violin, I believe at the Bolshoi Theater—and he died in the late 1920s. She was from an ancient noble line. Her family broke off relations with her for marrying a Jew. I don't know whether they had remained in Russia or had emigrated. After her husband's death, she was very poor, almost impoverished. Batanya always tried to help her out.

My grandmother brought her into our house under the guise of having her lunch with us, and teach us French and manners. The French and manners were a flop, but for two hard and hungry winters, even in Moscow, Evdokia Ivanovna came to us every day—she lived nearby, in Leontievsky Alley. Sometimes she took Egor for walks, but usually she talked about the past, while Emma Davydovna listened politely and Dusya (our maid then) and I, avidly. She ate lunch with us, that is, with Egorka, Emma Davydovna, Dusya, and me. Egorka and I, sensing her poverty, felt sorry for her. Emma Davydovna mended her dresses and stockings, and Dusya said, "Bring your laundry. I'll wash it while I'm at it anyway." I don't think that Evdokia Ivanovna knew how to do anything, even how to live. But she did know how to love.

Her memories were filled with love for her late husband, perhaps overly poetic and sentimental, but not tearful. There were also recollections of music: where and what was played, how the audience reacted to a new composition, what was written later in the newspapers. Which concerts she had heard at the conservatory or in Paris. Which operas and ballets were put on at the Bolshoi or in Milan. She often sang to us from symphonies or operas. And this was all mixed up with memories or theater talk and the dresses that were in fashion then. She would give detailed descriptions of the dress she wore on any occasion. A blush would appear on her cheeks—just like the one when I saw Dusya packing a piece of bread or something for her to take home. Dusya didn't like me to see it. Tears would come to Evdokia Ivanovna's blue eyes. On those occasions I believed Batanya, who said that once upon a time Evdokia Ivanovna had been "very, very pretty." Mama called her Dunka behind her back (we heard it sometimes) and I didn't like it.

In 1935 Evdokia Ivanovna's daily visits ended. Apparently life became less difficult for her. She came only when Batanya visited from Leningrad.

After the war, Victor Rubinshtein, the youngest son of Batanya's brother Uncle Mosya, took care of Evdokia Ivanovna. She died in the midfifties. I don't know where she was buried, perhaps beside her husband's grave. He was buried in Novodevichy Cemetery, in the section where many of the Bolshoi's artists rest. Evdokia Ivanovna designed his monument herself—a tall ancient-looking white urn, over half a person's height (it might have been something from her past), on a white stone pedestal with a musical staff and two notes on it, "mi" and "fa"—which made up her pet name for her husband, Mifa.

At the end of the summer of 1934 we also got Zinka, the younger sister of Kalya, the wife of Mama's brother, Matvei. She had come from Sretensk and of course it was Batanya who moved her in with us. Kalya and Zinka were daughters of a priest and in those days (and later too) that made it much harder to get an education. Zinka hoped to go to medical school. Apparently Batanya decided it should be done step by step. The first step was the Worker's Courses. A job was arranged for Zinka and then she entered the Worker's Courses, right into the second year. I think that with her education she could have gone directly to the medical institute, but it was easier to get in with a degree from the Worker's Courses. It must have been simple for her. At any rate, I don't remember her working hard. Her job didn't seem to exhaust her either.

She was sturdy, thick-lipped, round-faced, and merry. She set her blond hair on paper rollers every night—I had never seen that before—and the resulting curls made her very pretty. But she was severe with any hint of courtship from men. Dusya would say, "Zinka won't lower herself; she's not that kind, not like Ruf Grigoryevna's Valya." Nura called Mama Rufa, but Dusya always used her full name and patronymic.

On the one hand, Zinka was an adult and used Mama's pass for the theaters almost every evening (I got the privilege only a year or two after that), but on the other hand, she helped me pour water over the neighbors' balcony—we got out there through the window—and ice skate there. Zinka joined the Komsomol at the Worker's Courses, and everyone congratulated her, although I sensed even then that she did it out of practical considerations and not because the Komsomol and the "world revolution" concerned her. In November 1934 Zinka marched in the parade under the banner of the "Peers of October"—she was seventeen, as old as the Revolution. God, how I envied her!

The following spring she moved to Leningrad, was admitted to the institute, and graduated just before the war. *I graduated from the same institute later. Then she worked in Vladivostok and China. After the war she returned to Leningrad. She joined the Party, but I think that was just as flimsy as joining the Komsomol. She didn't marry but had a son she brought up, even though I had always thought her a person with a genius for adapting to society, someone who would lead a conventional life. She was incredibly loyal to her family—her older sister, Kalya, and her daughter, Natasha, my cousin. She rarely visited us in Moscow once Mama returned from the camps. And after Andrei joined our family, never. She died in Leningrad in 1988.*

To finish up with Batanya's protégés, I will tell you about Nyutochka. I don't know her full name. She was somewhere between Batanya and Mama in age, and I remember her from Chita. She was related somehow to Moisey Leontyevich and lived as part of the family in his big house in Chita. After Moisey Leontyevich left for France, she showed up in Leningrad. Batanya actively helped her get documents to move abroad, wrote applications, and went to various offices with her. Once I overheard a conversation between Mama and Batanya. Mama said, "Why does Nyutochka need to go abroad? What will she do there?"

"What is she going to do here? Wait for you to finish her off?"

"Come on, Mother, what for?" My mother challenged the accusation.

Batanya replied with unusual severity, "You'll find an excuse what for, you certainly will; if not now, then later, but find one you will."

I listened to the conversation and sided against Batanya.

Everyone loved Nyutochka: the maids, and my parents' friends, and Papa—back from the Chita days. And like Mama, I couldn't imagine why she would be "finished off." She wasn't a "former," or an "old gentlewoman," or a "NEPwoman," or a "capitalist," or a "white guard." That all those people were subject to being eliminated didn't seem strange or unfair to me then.

Nyutochka left and we got letters from her in the early years. She was the one who told Batanya about Moisey Leontyevich's death. The letter came in an envelope with a black band. Batanya shut herself up in her room and when she came out her eyes were red. She told us that Moisey Leontyevich had died. I don't remember my reaction to her words. But that evening, when I saw the letter on her night table, I decided to rip it up: no letter—no one dead. I had ripped it in half when Batanya walked in. She grabbed both halves out of my hands, waved them in front of my face, and shouted that I was forbidden to come into her room, that I was a heartless child who loved no one. That wasn't true. I loved her very much and at that moment I also pitied her. And I loved Moisey Leontyevich. Later there were no more letters from Nyutochka, or from any other of Batanya's relatives.

And in 1961, when Mama's cousin Matvei visited from France, we learned that Nyutochka had been finished off—not by us (oh, sometimes it's hard to write "we" about the times, the people, the country, after all, it wasn't me, not me) but by the Germans. They got her for the simplest reason—she was Jewish. She was deported from a small town outside Paris, where she had lived with a close woman friend all those years, and all traces of her were lost.

Batanya had always lived and behaved as if the life of society on the large scale did not concern her. Her circle, her friends, relatives, children, and grandchildren. While she had the strength and her soul had not grown chilled by the loss of her son and daughter, the fear for her grandchildren, she had her work, books, the theater, and music. And it was all outside politics, without any expression ever of her attitude toward what was going on around her. Just the occasional angry words at Mama, as if she were the creature who bore responsibility for everything that Batanya didn't like. But there was the intervention in the fate of Tanya (Nura's sister), and Nutochka, and Emma Davydovna, and Evdokia Ivanovna, and Zinka, and perhaps others I do not know about. Actually, that did show her position, and it was very active—help someone, save someone. And with that her

Elena Bonner with her mother (left) and a friend. Leningrad, Dec. 4, 1927.

Brother and sister Matvei and Ruth Bonner. Chita, 1925.

Elena Bonner with her brother, Egorushka (Igor Alikhanov, 1926–1976). Sestroretsk, June 1928.

Ruth Bonner's sister Anna with her husband, Lev Mordukhovich, and their daughter Zorya. Moscow, 1929.

Tatyana Bonner with her grandchildren.
Left to right: *Zorya, Elena, Egorka.*
Moscow, 1929.

Tatyana Bonner.
Yessentuki, 1930.

Alexander Rubinshtein.
Moscow, 1933.

Left to right: *Alexander*
Rubinshtein; his wife, Elvira
Papadicheva; her mother,
Sofia (Aunt Sonya) Feigin;
Elvira's adopted daughter
Alla. Chita, 1931.

Lidia Suok (Bagritskaya) at sixteen. Odessa, 1914.

Right: *Seva (Vsevolod) Bagritsky (1922–1942), at left, with his friend Goga (Georgii) Rogachevsky (1922–1943). Moscow, 1932.*

Eduard Bagritsky. Moscow, early 1930s.

Fanya Rensh and Lyova Alin. Moscow, 1934.

Lusya Chernina (1922–1942). Killed at Stalingrad. Moscow, 1937.

Sick Child, *by Edvard Munch.* Author's caption: *"In Luks they did not use to take pictures, and I had no photo of Lena Krebs. I thought I'd forgotten her face. But in the summer of 1988 Andrei and I went to the Munch Museum in Oslo, and I recognized Lena in this girl."*

Egor (Igor) Alikhanov.
Moscow, 1935.

Seva Bagritsky.
Moscow, 1934.

Elena Bonner.
Moscow, July 1934.

external restraint, straightness, and even severity in dealing with the people around her.

That's how I perceived my grandmother when I was a child—I saw only the externals, even though I loved her and respected her more than anyone else in the world. It never occurred to me (or to anyone else who knew her, probably) that she was kind! And now it turns out that it was all kindness. Goodness. That's why she went to my parents' friends to get signatures and documents for her protégés, finding them a place in a well-fed family where they would survive. And why she spoke harshly, and sometimes cruelly, to my mother.

Probably in 1935, Batanya shut the door to Mama's room and told her that she had received a manuscript from her niece Lily in France. Lily was a Communist and was asking help in getting her book published in the USSR. Mama refused immediately, saying that she wouldn't even look at the manuscript and didn't want to know any Lily. She was confused and, I think, frightened by the request.

"Tell me, how did you get it? Who gave it to you?"

"That has nothing to do with you. Nothing at all." And she added, "Let me remind you that before that revolution of yours no decent person would ask such a question."

Whenever Batanya used phrases like "Let me remind you" or "Let me tell you" it was a sign of her highest degree of anger. I cringed in fear at the door where I was eavesdropping, waiting for Batanya to storm out of Mama's room, but she went on, "And I, with your permission, will talk about it with your husband myself."

With those words, without waiting for Mama's response, I dashed into my room. Batanya came in a minute later. She looked at me as if she knew I had been eavesdropping, but she said nothing. I don't know if Batanya brought up Lily's book with Papa.

The book, reminiscences of a childhood in Siberia and her conversion to communism, Lily had published later in France. In 1968 I brought the book back from Paris, in French. Alas, this cousin of mine did not know Russian.

25

On the second floor of the Luxe to the left of the main lobby was the so-called Little Red Corner. "Some little corner," I thought the first time I looked in. It was big and high-ceilinged, a full two stories high, perhaps a restaurant or even a concert hall previously. On the right was a wall separating the room from the corridor; on the left, white slender columns. I thought they were just like those in the Hall of Columns. Behind them all along the length of the room was a wide space and then four enormous venetian windows. They opened on the courtyard and were almost always covered with light beige curtains. A grand piano and chairs stood between the windows. In the room proper were rows of chairs, a low stage, and a long table covered in red baize. The Little Red Corner was used for meetings and movies. When Dimitrov, Tanev, and Popov came after the Reichstag Fire trial at Leipzig, the children in our building and many other "strangers" met with them and made them "honorary Pioneers" with speeches and red ties.

Sen Katayama's* funeral was in that hall. We had known him well. Short and with a smile for all the children, he strolled the corridor with a cane, his feet scraping the floor. He often cooked for himself in the common kitchen around the corner and stirred with chopsticks, not a spoon.

For his funeral, the stage was covered with baskets of flowers. Behind the columns were military musicians who played for several hours, and there were many people. The entire child population of the building was there, too. I think that there was yet another funeral for him after the one at the Luxe and his body lay in state somewhere else, but maybe I'm wrong.

*Sen Katayama (1859–1933), Japanese Communist, member of the Executive Committee of the Comintern.

That evening Mama and Papa were home. Egorka looked at one and then the other and said dreamily at dinner, "I wish Papa would die." Their faces fell. Papa asked in bewilderment, "What do you mean?" and then, to cover up his confusion, added, "For a joke, you mean?"

"No, for real. If Mama dies, there probably won't be any music. But if you do, it will be as good as Sen Katayama's."

Papa laughed a little too loudly. It wasn't a laughing matter. For a long time now, I had sensed that Papa was a "boss," and it often made me feel uncomfortable, and even bad. And now, it turned out, Egorka realized it too, and he let our parents know it in his own way.

In the Little Red Corner about one year later, when party leader "Uncle Postyshev gave back the merry holiday of the tree to Soviet children," we had a New Year's party. Some of the chairs were put behind the columns and a tree was set up. I don't remember whether or not we were given presents. That must also be a sign of the sated life of the Luxe children—not remembering if there was a holiday package of sweets.

And in that room they conducted the purges—I don't remember when, but I'm sure it wasn't the winter that I ate a piece of metal and I had the operation, in January 1934, but before that. The purging took place in the evenings right after the adults finished work and went on a rather long time—maybe two weeks, maybe a month. The first few days it was interesting and many of the children hid behind the drapes of the Little Red Corner, to be part of it. But after just a few days most of the kids got sick and tired of it. I lasted the longest. Probably, it was my love of eavesdropping and spying. They purged only the Soviet Cominterners, but all of them: the ones in the apparat, and the members of the Executive Committee, and the ones who worked in the dining room, and the motor pool, and the commandant's office (that is, for the superintendent of the building). His name was Brant. He seemed to love our family, especially Egorka and me. Of course, once Papa was arrested, the love died, and after that Brant was arrested too.

This is how the purging went. Several people sat at the table on stage. They called on someone who stood at the side of the stage but still in front of them and replied to questions facing the audience, with his side to the table. The questions came from the table and from the audience. And before the questions the person spoke about himself. Sometimes at length, sometimes briefly. You could see that they were nervous and some spoke very badly. There were a lot of words like "I mean" and "So to say," and coughing—they were like schoolchildren who had not learned their lessons. Everyone used the familiar "you" with everyone else and of course only surnames, and when people were called out, they were referred to as Comrade So-and-so. Some were asked a lot of questions, others very little: about Winston Churchill, about the opposition within the Party, about China and industrialization and Stalin's six conditions for restructuring the economy. I knew them better than many of the adults because there was an electric news wire on top of the Izvestia building—an innovation then. And even the ragamuffins in Bakhrushenka sang about Stalin's conditions.

They asked about people's wives and sometimes about their children. It turned out that some people beat their wives and drank a lot of vodka. Batanya would have said that decent people don't ask such questions. Sometimes the one being purged said that he wouldn't beat his wife anymore or drink anymore. And a lot of them said about their work that they "wouldn't do it anymore" and that "they understood everything." Then it resembled being called into the teacher's room: the teacher sits, you stand, he scolds you, the other teachers smile nastily, and you quickly say, "I understand," "I won't," "of course, I was wrong," but you don't mean it, or just want to get out of there to join the other kids at recess. But these people were more nervous than you were with the teacher. Some of them were practically crying. It was unpleasant watching them. Each purge took a long time; some evenings they did three people, sometimes only one.

I went a few evenings in a row, but then I stopped. I'd look in as I walked past and see that the purges were still on and I'd keep going. Once I saw my father on the stage. I got behind the curtain and made an opening to see better.

Papa was on the spot where they all stood when they were being purged. Tall, very handsome and elegant, he also seemed overheated. He kept tugging at his military shirt, pulling it out in back or down. He needed Batanya. She always said, "Stop fidgeting; stand quietly."

In those years Papa wore boots, navy blue jodhpurs, and a blue field shirt with a belt—that was in winter. In summer he wore shoes, trousers, and a collarless shirt with side buttons (sometimes he had on white trousers with white shoes), often with his jacket tossed over his shoulders. He didn't have a "proper" (Batanya's word) suit or even a tie until 1935 or 1936. He didn't know how to knot a tie and never did learn. Mama did it for him.

Apparently, I was very late. Papa wasn't talking about himself, he was being asked about Leningrad and Zinoviev. Papa explained that he had had a fight with him and had returned to Leningrad with Kirov. Then someone at the table said that Papa had written something incorrect in Leningrad. Papa immediately agreed and said he hadn't understood right away. Another man at the table mentioned a name and said that Papa had insulted that man and had been crude and that he had to correct himself. Papa agreed again. Then someone in the audience said that Papa should tell about his first wife because she was not of proletarian background, even though Alikhanov himself was. I was stunned by the question, since I didn't know of any other wife besides Mama. Papa was also surprised, but in a different way. He suddenly got red. And angry. I thought he was going to curse, but he said nothing.

The woman at the table (the only woman there) said, "Well, Comrade Alikhanov, why are you silent when the comrades ask you a question? You must answer. We need to listen too, in order to know."

What do they need to know? I wondered, waiting for Papa to say that he never had a first wife, that there was only Mama. Of course, Mama's background wasn't so good, I thought. Batanya was like a "former." But he said he had had a first wife, that they had worked together in Armenia and Moscow and Leningrad. In Leningrad she "died tragically"—run over by a trolley. She was an "unblemished Bolshevik" and her background wasn't proletarian, but good even so—"the working intelligentsia," and she was in the "working intelligentsia" until the Revolution, because she was a teacher, and after the Revolution she always did Party work. He gave her name and surname. I remember her name—Sato. I thought that I remembered her surname, but I forgot it. It was Armenian. They didn't ask Papa anything else. They must have been pleased that she was from the working intelligentsia and a Party worker, and unblemished, and that she had died. Or maybe I was pleased that she had died and that there was no first wife, but only Mama and us. Papa was going down the steps when someone from the audience called out, "What about children?" Papa seemed surprised, stopped on the steps from the stage, and asked stupidly, "What children?" Then, after a pause, he said, "You all know my children, a daughter and a son. I have no other children."

I didn't go to the purges anymore. It was very unpleasant—watching and listening to a group of adults being examined and behaving that way. Papa too. I thought about his first wife, Sato, a lot and wanted to learn more about her and see her photograph. I wanted to ask some of the Armenian women who were my parents' friends: Manya Kasparova, Farik Asmarova, Sirush Akopyan, or Asya Papyan. Why only the women, I don't know. But I didn't have the nerve.

I finally asked in 1956. I was visiting Mama in Moscow with newborn Alyosha and six-year-old Tanya for part of my maternity leave. Sirush Akopyan came to visit. The three of us sat up late— Mama, Sirush, and I—in the kitchen, reminiscing and talking. I recalled that purge, telling them what I remembered, and then asked about Sato. Sirush had known her well; they had been friends. Mama knew about her but had never seen her. A few days later Sirush brought a photograph—four young women against a landscape, the typical backdrop for old photographs: mountains, trees, sky, or sea. All unsmiling, severe, very beautiful Armenian girls. Sato was a bit shorter and plumper than the others, maybe a bit older, a bit more severe.

And that evening I learned that Papa had lied about his children at the purge. He had a daughter (perhaps still does) by a woman in Leningrad. She was older than I by a year or two. Her name was Inna, Inessa. Before her arrest Mama regularly sent money to Inessa's mother. Papa didn't want to do it himself for some reason. I later asked Mama if we should try to find Inna. But Mama said that Papa hadn't wanted it, even though she couldn't or wouldn't explain why not. I thought there must have been something unpleasant for Papa in his relationship with that woman. And he wanted to forget about her.

As I review my life with Papa, I think I caught him lying only twice—once when he said that he had no other children. And in 1937, when he said to Mama, "We have to find out what's going on; they're not going to arrest you and me." He knew that it would come to him, and, therefore, to Mama, too. But maybe he was just trying to console Mama, and he didn't lie to himself?

26

At the very start of 1934, I got sick—horribly, almost mortally sick. I had been at a birthday party for the daughter of a friend of Mama's. I think the last name was Gorshenin (but I'm not sure). Her father was one of Mama's crowd from the Komsomol Central Committee. They lived somewhere around Kalanchevka. I had gone there before by myself on the trolley from Strastnaya Square. It was a birthday and not an evening party. Around two o'clock we—the five children—were given a festive meal. The dessert was canned peaches. A big metal can was opened in front of us, and I don't think I had ever seen one before. Each child got a large peach, two halves, and several spoons of the thick and aromatic light-colored syrup. It was incredibly delicious. Then we played various "quiet" and "not quiet" games. Around five o'clock I started for home, as Emma Davydovna had demanded. But also because I was feeling rather nauseated and I was tired of the games and the children, who were not my usual group of friends. It was getting dark, and Gorshenin walked me to the stop and put me on the trolley.

I felt sicker on the trolley and developed a stomachache. At first it wasn't bad, then it grew almost unbearable. By the time I reached the last stop, I could barely get off. I forced myself to walk to the house, up to the second floor, and to our door. I passed out and later woke up in my bed. Papa was next to me, in his undershirt, wrapped in a blanket, with the ties of his underpants dangling around his ankles. He was very sick himself then—it was the winter that his ulcer acted up, and he had been in the hospital a long time, while they decided whether or not to operate. They released him without surgery. Emma Davydovna stood next to him, and she said that they should call Mama. Papa said to call Aunt Ronya. I groaned so loudly, sometimes crying out in pain, that I must have scared them, especially Papa, into calling both.

Aunt Ronya came with Uncle Sanya. She said we needed a surgeon immediately and he appeared quite quickly. He said that I had to be operated on instantly, and kept poking my stomach and making me scream. Papa disagreed loudly, saying it was nonsense to operate on a child just like that. It was probably only that the girl had had too much to eat at the party. But Mama had shown up by then and she told him not to interfere and if Aunt Ronya agreed then it wasn't up to him to decide whether I should have surgery, especially since he was afraid of surgery and that's why he was so sick. Despite my own pain, I noted that there was something after all that even Papa was afraid of. I was terrified by the hospital (I remembered my scarlet fever, when at least I had Raya) and the operation. Everyone was making noise. Musya Luskina showed up from somewhere (perhaps she had come with Mama?). I kept falling into some black hole and resurfacing. I remember that they carried me down the corridor right on my mattress. Aunt Ronya walked alongside me, patting me on the head; Uncle Sanya held one end of the mattress—to the left of my face—and he seemed very tall.

The next thing I recall is the hospital corridor, and I was on a stretcher. The pain wasn't so bad, just a heavy pressure on my stomach or in it. The light was unbearably white and horrible. Mama and Musya were nearby. Musya kept crying, which made it scarier. I was afraid that Mama would leave and then it would be absolutely horrible. The Party Congress was going to start any day and she had to register the delegates.

So I said, "Give me your Party ticket."

"Why?" Mama asked.

"So you don't leave."

"I won't leave."

"No, give it to me."

Mama silently felt in the inner pocket of her jacket, took her Party card out, and gave it to me. I'm sure she wanted to calm me down, but it scared me even more. I thought that if she could give up her card that easily, I was dying. Musya kept bawling and from time to time Mama would say quietly and angrily, "Stop it. Or leave." Just the way she talked to me when I wept, "pretending to be an orphan," and demanding something from Mama. I had no idea how scared Mama was. She stood there looking very ordinary. I later learned that the doctor who had received me and was supposed to operate had looked at the weeping Musya and calm Mama and had taken Mama aside. He said that he didn't dare talk to the girl's mother, since the situation was almost hopeless and he didn't know whether he should operate or not. Mama said, "I'm the mother. Operate."

Once after my scarlet fever Raya said we were lucky it came out the way it did; after all, the result could have been lethal. I understood that the word meant something horrible. But I liked the word and started using it. In Russian *letalny* sounded as if it came from the word *letat,* to fly. So I had lethal butterflies and dragonflies, lethal flies and beetles, lethal mice or bats, and even mosquitoes. But for some reason, I never had lethal birds; they simply flew.

Now under those unbearable hospital lights the word floated out of my memory, in Raya's voice, "The result could be lethal." But Mama was holding my hand; her Party card was under my pillow. "She didn't leave; she won't leave," I thought, and looked at her face. It was severe, precise, unbearably beautiful and white, like the statue of Psyche in the lobby of the Hermitage.

Mama's face was just as seemingly calm on June 19, 1976, when I told her that Egorka had died. In her tiny room in Zhukovka, I tried not to look at her, and yet I saw every wrinkle on her thin, exhausted, and always beautiful face. It was like stone and white. For a few seconds (or perhaps it was for a long time, I don't know) she shut her eyes. Then she opened them and looking right at me, but peering into something far away, beyond me, probably her whole life, she said, "It's not fair. Not fair." As if everything else in her past—Papa's disappearance, the arrest and death of her only brother, her seventeen years in the camps and in exile—as if all that had been fair.

They were putting the mask on me and someone said, "Breathe! Breathe and count!" And I started counting, "One lethal butterfly, two lethal butterflies, three . . ."

I know only what they told me about the hours of surgery and the first days afterward. I have no memory, because in a sense I was not there. The peaches were to blame: a thin sliver of the badly opened can had ended up in my bowl, and I swallowed it. It tore open my intestine, some upper section of it, and the perforation led to peritonitis. It was only much later that I realized that in those days, without sulfa drugs, streptomycin, and antibiotics, this was likely to be fatal. But several fortunate circumstances combined for me: it happened in the city and not off in some dacha in the country; Aunt Ronya suspected the worst right away; Mama agreed without hesitation to the hospital and the surgery; and the doctor on duty at Basmannaya Hospital was the young intern Zhorov, around twenty-seven years old. His name would appear later in all surgery textbooks as the founder of Soviet anesthesiology.

He made me live with the same stubbornness as Mama. He operated two more times, because there were pockets of necrosis in the intestine. I lay with an unsewn abdomen, lightly covered with napkins. On one side I had a carbolic acid solution dripping into my abdominal cavity. On the other side was a jar into which a catheter drained the carbolic acid, taking with it everything bad that was in my abdomen. And all the time I was surrounded by a nauseating, heavy odor of rotten cabbage. In that odor I fell into unconsciousness and returned from it. And fell again. It was like being on a swing. I understood that sometimes I was and sometimes I wasn't. The least movement, a breath, the gluing and ungluing of the napkins, were unbearable. I wanted not to be. When I "was," I saw Mama and often, almost always, Dr. Zhorov was with her. I felt sorry for them. When I "wasn't," Mama kept trying to bring me back. There were dolls and mice, white kewpies and black cherubs, and other toys. I was indifferent to them as if with every hour of my illness I was growing out of toys.

Once, with Zhorov's permission, Mama brought a girl to see me, maybe they thought that would be a powerful medicine. Mirella's voice brought me out of my unconsciousness, "What, is she dead?" I opened my eyes and saw my friend Mirella at the foot of the bed. She seemed to be in a frame, a bust portrait: the bottom of the frame was the bed's footboard, the top the strip of the yellow wall where the white begins and blends into the ceiling. She reached out for the footboard, as if trying to leave the picture, but didn't touch it, didn't come out; instead she quickly brought her hand inside the white lab coat slung over her shoulders. I could see something pink and clean, her blouse probably. And her light hair, darker than the wall, shone with a reflection of something clean. And I was covered with the stench, sweet, thick, rotten—my smell. I shut my eyes, but I wasn't losing consciousness; I shut them on purpose. I heard the desire for my death in her question—it would have been more interesting; I saw fastidiousness in her hand moving away. Probably I was wrong, probably that didn't happen. But I had never been very close to Mirella in the first place, and certainly not afterward, even though outwardly I treated her like all the other girls. Many years later, when I learned that Mirella had become a doctor, I was astonished to find that my memory of her visit to the hospital in January 1934 was so strong.

1961. March—wet, windy, Leningrad weather.

Alyosha is in a small, four-bed, hospital room, to the right of the door, closer to the window. The light falls on his pale, bluish, elongated face. This is our fourth day in the hospital—rheumocarditis, severe myocarditis. I had just sent Valya out of the room. Vanya's sister Valya is a skillful doctor. She examined Alyosha and wept so that her tears fell on Alyosha's bare chest. Alyosha said nothing. I recalled the weeping Musya, my fear of dying back then in the Basmannaya Hospital, and I practically pushed Valya out the door. Then I sat on Alyosha's bed and began talking, something about Winnie the Pooh, *which I was reading to Alyosha then. Alyosha said nothing and stared right at me. At me, into me, beyond me. Then quietly, with just his lips, he said, "I'm going to die? Yes?"*

I said, "No." I had no other words except that "No." But it was the truth for me, too. "No." The fact that I howled like a she-wolf in the stairwell of the Filatov Leningrad Children's Hospital had nothing to do with that "No." Much later after those first horrible hospital days for Alyosha I kept thinking that a child knows about death, and how does it appear, that fear, and when does it pass. I had been on the brink of death at the age of ten. But Alyosha was only four!

Even though the carbolic acid was still dripping into me and all kinds of vile stuff was pouring out, Zhorov's face was not so anxious when he unglued and glued my stomach three or four times a day. Through my stink of rotten cabbage I began to smell the cooling odor of collodion and the fresh air coming through the window. I was getting better and Mama began spending her nights at home. Every time she left Mama asked what I wanted. I didn't want anything. I was tired and wanted to rest. But once I said, "I want a reticule."

Mama was surprised and asked, as if she had heard wrong, "What?"

I explained that I had wanted one a long time, always, and not a children's purse, but a real reticule. A day or two later Aunt Ronya came with a small purse, the size of a half page, out of soft light gray leather trimmed in dark gray. It was a "real adult one," very pretty and probably expensive. It was my only purse all through my youth. The next one came after the war, from an American gift package.

Then Lyova Alin came to see me. He kept regretting that we had read about Mowgli last year with Egorka, because the hospi-

tal was a fine place to read books like that. He called us bandar-
logs after Mowgli, and said, "Well, bandarlog, you really scared
us! Of course, everyone has the right to be sick a little, but not like
this. Don't ever repeat this or I'll defriend you and unacquaint
myself with you." And he laughed and shook his round, shaved
head. That was one of his words. He'd argue with Papa over
chess and say, "It's not a question of my positions (he was always
in the opposition, but I don't know which faction), but of the fact
that he (I didn't know who) is a scoundrel, and I'm going to
unacquaint myself with him."

Papa would argue, and laugh, and say, "You can't unacquaint
yourself with everyone."

"Can and must," Lyova would shout.

"You and your opposition and your unacquainting will bring
you to the end."

"I'm there already, but you can't change my mind," Lyova
replied.

Then one or the other would say "check" and then "mate." It
was usually Papa; he was a better player. Lyova really did get to
the end: he was kicked out of the Party. I think he was the only
"oppositioner" among my parents' friends and he was the first to
be arrested among them. This must have been 1935 or early
1936.

*When I lay wounded in the hospital in Sverdlovsk during the war,
I did not know that Anya, her husband, and their daughter, Zorya,
were evacuated there. But later Batanya gave me their address. In
February or March 1942 I was back in Sverdlovsk with the hospital
train and I looked them up. I had three or four hours free and I spent
most of the time buying them food which was available without
coupons and which I could get without standing in line because I was
in the army. They told me that Fanya and Lyova—who had been
released in early 1941—lived nearby and had been working in some
factory. Lyova had left the factory, having persuaded the military
office that he should be allowed to join the army, and was in training.
Zorya went to get them. They showed up when it was time for me to
return to duty. I gave Fanya a quick hello and goodbye. But Lyova
took me back.*

We had a long ride on the trolley, and then walked another three kilometers along the tracks to my train. It was the first time I had seen Lyova in five or six years. He had aged terribly; no longer the athletic man of my childhood, he seemed ill. Where had the strongest (after Papa), merriest, and kindest of Egorka's and my older friends gone? I felt sorry for him, as if I were the adult and he an injured child. Was he the one who had taught us how to play billiards and volleyball (and soccer to Egorka), how to swim, and to read good books? I wanted to ask him about those years, about prison and the camps. Yet I didn't want to wound him with the questions and he didn't bring it up himself.

But when he asked about my mother, he said twice, "Write to your mother, bandarlog. Write to your mother." He was repeating what Batanya wrote in her postcards to me. Every one of them said, "Write to Mama."

Lyova and I reached my train and we went inside to my compartment. He said it was very nice. I put together some canned goods, soap, and shag tobacco. I never ate my extra rations, I always saved them "in case" and to send to Mama. Then we said goodbye by the car in the narrow space between two trains. Light fell from the neighboring train, harshly illuminating everything: the worn collar on his old coat, which had once been karakul; the shabbiness of his old shaggy fur hat, left over from "those days." With every cell, I sensed that he was old and sick and that he shouldn't go to the front, but I knew it was necessary for him since he was back from the "camp" world.

The other train jerked and slowly pulled out. It was quiet and the snow gave off a soft light. He said, "You've grown into a good bandarlog, a good one."

We kissed and I saw his eyes up close. They were filled with tears. As he walked between the black threads of the tracks, he looked back and waved. And then, only forward. And away from me. He grew smaller and smaller. I stood and cried, leaning against the car, against "my" home. I sensed Lyova's hopelessness and that there would be no returning for him. And his dark figure, already tiny, was him, and Papa, and Matvei, and everyone who had gone off. Before, and then, and later. I never saw Lyova again.

. . .

In the late summer of 1942, I was in Sverdlovsk again and went to see Anya. She was surrounded by suitcases and bundles, leaving for the train station in a half hour, to return to Moscow. Fanya came to see her off. I went with them to the station, there were no cars, of course. We dragged everything ourselves to the trolley and then to the platform. Taking a train was very difficult in those days. Having a ticket guaranteed nothing—you still might not get on. I pushed my way onto the train—in military uniform and with ferocity that came when there were obstacles to overcome—found an empty compartment, closed the door, and then dragged all the things and the women themselves through the window (windows opened in those days).

With difficulty I made my way through the car to the exit (I used the door this time), and Fanya and I, without waiting for the train to take off—that might take hours—went to the station square. Fanya told me that Lyova had died two weeks after reaching the front, even though he had gotten a humane position, as mailman. She showed me the death notice: "He died the death of the brave . . ." Fanya wept. I felt sorry for her, but I was calm and not at all shocked. I had known it would be like this. I remember from the notice that he was younger than Mama—born in 1902. They were all so young, the oppositioners and the rest. And so naïve!

Much later I understood that the naïveté and even the kindness of many coexisted quite smoothly (not in Lyova, the eternal oppositioner) with cruelty, if not personal then ideological. But then, in the second year of the war, it hadn't occurred to me yet. Today, suddenly, (suddenly? or was it over time?) a question came to me: was Lyova Russian or Jewish? And was Alin his real name or a pseudonym? And I don't even know his patronymic.

Somewhere in late 1943 Fanya returned to Moscow. She had lost her room. She stayed with friends and then rented a little corner. She lived in poverty, half starved. After the war Eleanor Roosevelt came to the USSR. Her assistant and interpreter was a friend from Fanya's youth, Nila Magidova, who had married an American doctor working in Moscow. Nila found Fanya and saw her a few times while Nila was in Moscow. Just before they left, I believe on the way to the airport, the whole Roosevelt contingent stopped in front of the shanty where Fanya rented a room. Nila unloaded two big suitcases—her entire wardrobe—and left it for Fanya. She also gave her some money and her fur coat. Then she flew off to America. Fanya had turned from Cinderella into a princess, and Nila Magidova was her fairy godmother. That's how the fairy tale goes. Here's what happened in our story.

Fanya was arrested. She was accused of espionage for the U.S. Her connection was Magidova and Eleanor herself. So there! The investigation was rough. Fanya was beaten viciously; all her teeth were knocked out. Her sentence began when Mama's ended. She was given twenty-five years. She was in the Temnikovsky and Potmensky camps. She got out after the Twentieth Congress in 1956.

Lyova brought two books to the hospital for me: *Animal Heroes* by E. J. Seton and *The Story of the Great Plan* by Ilyin (or maybe Ilyina, I don't remember; I haven't seen that book since I was a child). He said the first book was marvelous, and he would read it to me right then and there. The second, he said, I had to read myself and read closely, because while not everything in it was absolutely right, I had to know it. Mama who was there, going through my night table, said "Lyovka, don't confuse her. It's a very good book." They always called each other Lyovka and Rufka. Like children. But Lyova told Mama that she might think so, but he didn't. Everyone thinks for himself. And he told me that I had to think for myself. He repeated it several times.

Mama was silent, but I could see she didn't agree. I could tell they weren't talking about the book he had brought me, but about something else. I read the book. It was about the five-year plan and how well things go when there is a plan. And also how badly things go for capitalists, especially when they burn wheat, pour away milk, and destroy things they have too much of. I read the book with interest, but I couldn't decide what to think about it. I didn't discuss it with Lyova. And he didn't ask when he came to see me again. But everything that I know about the five-year plans and crises comes from that book. I never troubled myself the rest of my life to think about those things except when I had to cram for an exam at school.

Well, the time came—and it was long in coming—and I was released from the hospital. I was cured. Well, not completely. Three operations under chloroform—the first one very long—had left a trace. I had developed myocarditis.

27

Well, if I had myocarditis, I had myocarditis. It seemed that I had grown accustomed to being ill. So, when Mama said that I wouldn't be going to my regular school but to a forest school for children recuperating from illness, I didn't get upset. I merely asked if they had books there. Mama said they had a library. It sounded tempting, even though I had never been in a library. Mama took me there in a car, a Comintern car, not a personal one.

The personal car with Isakov the chauffeur appeared a year or eighteen months later. Then I told Papa that some of the kids were taken to school in a car. And that I wanted to go to school by car, too. Papa looked at me thoughtfully for a long time. I was expecting him to say, all right. He picked up my hand, tucked my thumb between my index and middle fingers, and then lifted my hand up to my eyes. I was about to be mortally offended. But Papa smiled and said, "It's not me giving you the finger; it's your hand. And stop talking nonsense." I never brought up being driven to school again.

The trip lasted a long time. Along the way I suddenly had the thought that Mama was taking me away somewhere and then wouldn't come back for me. I had no basis for such thoughts. On the contrary: all the long weeks in the hospital and afterward, Mama treated me as if I were made of glass, as did everyone else in the house. But I was made wary by the fact that we hadn't packed any of my things for the "forest school." No dresses, no underwear. Just what I was wearing. At last, in a whisper so that the chauffeur wouldn't hear (we didn't say "driver" in those days, only "chauffeur"), I asked Mama about my things. She said, "Everything's supplied by the Party." Like the furniture and curtains and so on at home—everything with a metal number on it. I was used to that. I calmed down.

We passed a railroad station called Tuchkovo and soon drove up a wide alley with tall snow-covered trees on both sides. The forest was dark beyond them. And in front was a house—not a house, but a real palace, yellow with white columns. We got out of the car and Mama asked, "Isn't it beautiful?"

"Yes. Like Leningrad."

I don't remember Mama turning me over. I do remember living there. We all looked alike. The girls had short hair with bangs and light blue flannel dresses; the boys wore suits of the same cloth, with round heads almost shaved. Fifty or sixty children of all ages. We ate, played, and studied in that big house. The lessons were unusual—five or six children to the group. Some sat at desks, while others played or went to the library. Often the teacher excused those who already knew the material. I was almost always excused from arithmetic and when others had to read aloud. But never excused from penmanship class. Everyone free from lessons could play outside before lunch anywhere on the property, which was called an estate.

There was a deep dark forest. I think that this was the first time I had been in the country in winter. It was the first time I made my way among trees and bushes with my felt boots sinking into deep snow, shuddering when snow fell on me from branches, inhaling that special scent of frozen pine, chewing the resin the girls taught me to dig out from under the bark. One time I lay down on the snow and came to love it, looking up at the blinding blue winter sky through the fir branches. From the sky would come a resounding, melodic, bell-like peal. The lunch gong. I lay in the snow until it stopped sounding and then ran to the house so as not to be late. I hated being scolded.

I enjoyed lunch because after it came nap-time, which I learned to love in the forest school. Some might find that strange. But it was special, not like in other children's institutions, with which I had a wide experience by then. We slept outdoors, under a long canopy, on wooden cots. They brought out thick cotton-stuffed sleeping bags from the house and bundled us up in them fully dressed, in our coats and boots. You'd think it would be uncomfortable, and that you'd never fall asleep. But once they finished bundling us up and everyone quieted down, you could hear the forest. The trunks creaked, the branches rustled, a bird would cry out. Then it grew completely quiet so that the clouds could be heard as you watched them move from beneath the canopy. Gradually they began to turn pink. Pink clouds. As in Sestroretsk. Long ago. You could never capture the moment when you fell asleep. I wanted to stop right on that border. I thought that you could balance on it, as if on a log, between sleep and waking. And then they were rousing us. Blue twilight, the children's faces strangely transformed by the light, and the beckoning lamps in the windows of our palace. The worst was afternoon snack, when we had to drink milk. Then there was another lesson and then free time, and sometimes free time right away because the others had "reading."

I would spend that period at the library. You couldn't take books out, but you could dig around and read everything in there. They had a lot of "ancient" books. One cupboard was completely filled with the Brockhaus and Efron Encyclopedic Dictionary. That became my reading matter during the time I was in the forest school. On the way to the library, I'd sit on the windowsill of the ballroom, where the lights weren't on in the evening. Beyond the window things looked mysterious at night. Scary. It was dark. And you could make up stories about what was out there. In the daytime it was a "clean field." Why did I name the landscape that was visible through the tall, paned windows that way? It was a low broad slope leading to the frozen lake. A path had been trampled along the ice, leading at an angle to the right, to the small village on the other side of the river. Sometimes people walked on it. Very slowly. There was nothing else on the other side. Just the white expanse somewhere very far away, somehow twirling and turning into the sky. "Clean field."

We didn't sleep in the main house, but in two dachas (one for the girls, one for the boys) at the end of the estate, about a kilometer away. We led a different life there, our medical treatment life. In the morning, while we were still in bed, we had our temperature taken. Then barefoot, throwing off our nighties, completely naked, we ran out onto the cold glass veranda, and got into a zinc-plated tub. A bucket of icy water was dumped on us and with a weak cry, each victim of toughening flew into the room where a nurse's aide rubbed her red with a towel. The first day I almost died of fright standing in line for the procedure and watching it through the glass door. But I soon came to love it, and I squealed out of custom—like the rest. After the rubdown, we dressed quickly and happily. The doctor examined some, while the others went to the nurse to get medicine. Then we went outside. The morning was only beginning, and almost before our eyes, in the fifteen or twenty minutes it took to walk to the main building, the gray dawn turned to day. Before breakfast at the big house we were all given cod liver oil, which we chased with a thin slice of black bread and salt. It was tasty.

In the evening, walking back to the dacha, I would see the dark starry sky was above it, with the moon invariably there too. Even though I know now that the moon can't always be in the sky. The snow crunched under our felt boots. And the air was so light! They took our temperature again before bedtime. The nurse would take the thermometer, smile, and say, "Normal. Good night." And after a brief whispering session in our large bedroom, bathed in warm, not scary darkness, we fell asleep.

Then one day my temperature read high. I was wrapped in a blanket and carried on a sled to a small building between the dacha and the main house. The isolation ward. And the next day came a new word, diphtheria. A round of injections, endless compresses, and disgusting warm drinks began. Then, maybe after many days, maybe the next day, Mama appeared and began dressing me. She spoke joyfully, but her face was sad and I felt guilty, as I had so many times when I was sick. But I hadn't done anything bad. I hadn't even eaten snow. Mama put on my coat, wrapped my feet in a blanket, as if I were a baby. Papa came in.

He didn't even kiss me; he just smiled. Took me out to the car and set me on the back seat. Then they spoke with the doctor on the porch of the isolation ward. I watched the trees outside, their branches swaying as if in reproach, and I repeated Mama's words to myself, "Lord, when will all these endless diseases stop?" We drove a long time. It was snowing and I thought we would never get out of the gray gloom, that the city would never come. I fell asleep.

And there was a new hospital. Long empty days in a small glass cubby. No books, no toys. No Raya, as when I had scarlet fever. No Mama, as after the operation. A sick boy was in the glass cubby to my left. There were more cubbies beyond him. To the right were a sink, a table, and a nurse always busy there. Nothing hurt and I was bored. Bored. Bored. Bored. Earlier in Leningrad, when I hung around with nothing to do and whined that I was bored, Batanya would raise her eyebrows in indignation and say, "Shall I have the regimental band come in?" I wasn't too sure what that meant, but I knew that I couldn't be bored, or at least, say that I was bored. But here there wasn't even anyone to complain to.

In the fall of 1987 Andrei and I were returning to Moscow from Borovsk and stopped by the road for a rest. I looked at the map. I saw Tuchkovo. I wanted to see the yellow "palace"—was it really so big? The river, the slope, the "clean field." So we went to reconnoiter. We found Tuchkovo, but there was nothing besides the name—a standard hamlet, no forest at all. A slope covered with ticky-tacky cooperative houses. The river was left, but there was no "clean field" beyond it—all built up. And we couldn't find even the foundation of the estate house.

When I came home after the forest school and the hospital, Mama said that in those months "we lost Uncle Sanya." He had caught typhus at a congress of kolkhoz workers and died. She hadn't told me, afraid of my reaction. I cried at night, when no one saw me, for a long time. I felt sorry for him, for Aunt Ronya, for myself. The word "death" outraged me, an inner protest of my entire being, and I felt nothing but sadness and fear. It was an abstract death somehow. I hadn't seen it and I could pretend that Uncle Sanya had gone away; I could even write letters in my head to him. Which I did at first.

A few days after that I met Seva on the street and we walked around, to Strastnaya and to Pushkin. We shared an ice cream, as we didn't have enough money for two. He asked me in great detail about the hospital and the forest school. We came to my building and he said that he would visit me with Goga soon. At home I told them I had met Seva and that now he wasn't any taller than me. Mama asked, "Well, how is he?"

I was surprised by her question; after all, I had just told her he had grown but not a lot. Mama said, "Didn't you know that Bagritsky died?" I didn't know. How could I? She didn't tell me when I was in the hospital, and at the forest school no one spoke about life outside. Even if there had been a world revolution, we'd never have heard about it. The forest, naptime, warm milk, cold baths, medicine, cod liver oil, the thermometer, "Girls, bedtime," "Girls, roll over on your right side," "Girls, wake up."

I felt guilty about Seva—we had merely walked and eaten ice cream. I felt I had to do something, immediately, so I went to Seva's. I worried about how it would be when I got there, when I saw him and Lida. I rang the bell and trembled on their doorstep. Masha opened the door and said, "Our lawful bride is here." Seva came running out of his room and Lida emerged from Edya's. She delighted in how I had grown, laughed, and said, "But you're still wearing a bow in your hair," and went back to the room where I could hear guests' voices. When I walked into Seva's room, he asked me rather hostilely why I had come. Mumbling, I said that I hadn't known that Edya was dead (it was the first time I called him that), but Seva wouldn't let me finish. He asked, "Do you want me to walk you home again?" And we went outside. But Seva did not tell me about how his father had died, how he had seen him the night before at the hospital, and about the funeral, until the night of August 4, 1937.

We had met during the last days of exams. The summer was ahead. And I quickly forgot about the awkwardness of my visit with Seva.

28

While in the hospital and right after, I grew a lot, reaching almost my present height, yet there had been a period when I was short and round, to the extent that someone in third grade had called me *flyushka* (a small bun). I wasn't too aware of my heart condition, but the doctors were, and I spent almost no time in school that year. I showed up during the exam period—newly introduced that year, it was called the trials.

I didn't fall behind in class. I was still living off what I had learned from Batanya, and was amazed that there were people who couldn't handle percents and fractions. What I remember most from the end of the school year is a trifle, but since I recall it so well, maybe it wasn't a trifle. I got my first love note. It was from a boy whose last name was Yurovitsky, and he was tall and handsome. He got good grades, but he wrote, "Lusia, I luve you." Maybe it was the excitement, but the note insulted me. Not by its bad spelling; no, I don't know why. But that sense of insult was reinforced by a physical insult.

A group of girls were playing ball in the yard behind the Izvestia building. But it wasn't a real ball, just a bladder, the inner chamber, filled with air. All the wealthier girls showed off in white canvas shoes with a rubber sole and blue trim. Me too. Several older boys, fifteen or sixteen, ran past us. One of them caught me from behind, grabbing my breasts, and ran on, shouting, "Wow, she's got real globes already." The girls laughed, but I was furious with humiliation, embarrassment, and disgust. There was nothing sexual in what I felt, only disgust. I ran home to shower, and changed all my clothes. But I could still feel the dirt from the stranger's hands on me.

In 1968 I was walking down a long empty underpass in the Paris metro and felt someone caressing my rear end. I turned sharply and

*without even getting a look at the man's face, slapped him hard. He
gasped and ran off. When I got to Ruf's apartment on the rue Boileau,
I tore off all my clothes and took a shower. When I told Masha and
Lyonya about the episode, they laughed very hard but also warned me
that my "admirer" could have done much worse. Lyonya said, "He
could tell you were a foreigner because a Frenchwoman would have
merely smiled." I couldn't tell what there was more of in his state-
ment—admiration or disapproval.*

I passed the trials very easily. Then I was sent to Pioneer camp,
and for the first time, to Papa's Comintern camp. Before that I
had always been to children's organizations connected with the
Moscow Party—that is, with Mama.

In Pushkino, in a fir forest, on the banks of the Moskva River,
the camp was a small one for only fifty or sixty children. We lived
in a big three-story house with attics and lots of large verandas.
The verandas were the bedrooms—each held ten to fifteen
beds—segregated for boys and for girls.

Three of us—Lena Krebs, another girl whom I don't remember at all, and I—roomed on the first floor almost completely
away from regular camp life: the line-ups, the hikes, the swimming, and so on. As heart patients, we were kept apart. The third
girl lived her own life, but Lena and I were together most of the
time. Sometimes I joined the general activities and went swimming, which I was allowed to do while the other two weren't. In
the evenings I went to the campfire. We sang there, but more
often there was dancing to a record player. I never danced,
though I wanted to, but I did listen to the girls gossip about who
was in love with whom and what was happening (mostly love
stories) where the girls were in charge. It was a very homey
camp—a continuation of our courtyard or our Luxe hallways
with the same "popular" kids. For some reason the girls from my
circle at the Luxe weren't at camp—at least I don't remember
Magda Furboten, or Roza Iskrova, or Mirella, being there.

Lena and I lived mostly with our books. Two or three times a
week Lena's stepmother, Binochka, brought a pile of books for
us. And we spent hours wandering in the woods not far from the

dacha, lying on our backs and watching the clouds. I taught Lena to gaze until the clouds got pink. Or on our stomachs, we would stare at a ladybug, an ant, or some other small creature. Usually, when we were in bed, I would pass on gossip to Lena that I had heard at the campfire about what was going on "in the verandas," who was climbing through the window to meet whom, and so on. We spent the whole day practically silent, concentrating and yet in full accord, together. The regime was so free that even reveille was not required and the food was often brought to our room. Heart patients. Lena and the other girl were seriously ill. I was more along for the ride, since my condition was gradually improving. I think that if I had insisted, I could have lived with everyone and like everyone. But I didn't. I liked being free of everyone else. Also, as later on, I liked being free of gym. It was only after 1937 that I felt I absolutely had to be healthy, strong, able to swim, run, dance, and hit.

The person in charge of this children's—or rather, teenage—band was a young woman named Lusia Venikas. All the kids called her either Lusia or just Venikas. Of medium height, with short hair, not beautiful but somehow very attractive, and dressed like the rest of us in dark bloomers and blouse with Pioneer tie, she didn't seem too different from the rest of the campers. There were counselors, too, but I don't remember them. I don't think that Lusia and the counselors had much of an idea what to do with us. Many of the kids—those whose parents were the leaders of the Polish, Italian, Austrian, Spanish, and other Communist parties, members of the Central Committee or the Executive Committee of the Comintern, or something else—were deeply infected with a sense of their own greatness, uniqueness, the psychology of heirs; they had transferred their parents' official grandeur to themselves. To some degree they felt they themselves were leaders and bosses. With very few exceptions, these children never became leaders, but they retained the sense of specialness, even though fate dealt them a terrible hand. Willful and capricious, they easily became the "leaders" in this unstructured camp, where some of the campers were the children of the technical and other service officials of the Comintern. Probably Lusia Venikas herself was influenced by these little leaders with big names.

The camp lived a noisy life, to all appearances merrily, with kids constantly late for breakfast or lunch, skipping exercises or nap-time, but never missing swimming, campfire, or dances. Sometimes someone oppressed or humiliated someone else—not too often, but painfully. And sometimes someone cried. And someone else was pleased to have his way. Lusia never refused anyone—she let people go into town or to the station, begging them to "be back for dinner." She allowed them to go because she knew that they'd probably go anyway. And she permitted parents, especially famous ones, to visit anytime. She was just glad that no one got lost or drowned. And everyone ate well. The food was excellent, maybe even too much so, with *zakuski,* desserts, and fruit. Of course, that didn't stop all the veranda dwellers from taking back some bread from dinner to eat in bed and to throw at one another.

The summer before, in 1934, I had been at a completely different camp, run by the OGPU (the secret police). I don't know what it had to do with the Moscow Committee or why Mama sent me there. Maybe it was because the OGPU head, Yezhov, was a friend of hers, as were the Berman brothers, also OGPU officials.

This camp was a few kilometers from the Otdykh Station. We were brought there by bus—about three hundred children between the ages of ten and fourteen. The buses stopped beside a huge treeless field surrounded by barbed wire, beyond which was forest on all sides. The children marched past a young soldier through a wooden gate that opened inward, and we were all led to a shed. The girls and boys were separated, one group going through the left door, the other through the right. We were told to undress and each girl was handed panties, undershirt, a khaki blouse and shorts, and a straw hat, also khaki-colored. All we had left of our own were our socks and sandals. Everyone had a large embroidered number over the pocket, from one to ten. We were told that these were unit numbers, by age. The youngest children were in 10, 9, and 8. There were four middle groups, and the oldest were in 3, 2, and 1. I was in 10. When we were all dressed— in an astonishingly brief time—we were shown a large canopy in the middle of the field and told that we had to be there when the bugle sounded, but in the meantime we could walk around and explore our camp. Total strangers, resembling one another in our uniforms, we little ones stood huddled by the shed and watched the older kids come out. At the bugle we ran in a bunch to the canopy. This was the first time I understood the sensation of not knowing anything and not being able to do anything by myself. I was running like everyone else. And I would do everything like everyone else.

Under the canopy were long tables and benches, and on the tables were mugs, spoons, and bowls. Each table had a banner with a number. There were counselors, dressed in shirts like us, but the girls had skirts and the boys wore long trousers. There was a girl and a boy for each table. They seated us. It was all fast and wordless. Women in white brought a big pot of soup and bread to each table. The counselors served. Then there was a main course and then pudding. It was all very tasty. The counselors asked who wanted more and told us we could eat as much as we desired at the table, but we couldn't take anything away. Then they said that the camp leader would explain everything, and that we had to sit quietly. Three or four military men came in under the canopy. One of them, the camp leader, announced that we were battalions, that our detachment numbers were the numbers of our platoons, that the first three platoons made up the first company, the next four, the second, and we were the third. Each platoon would have its own two tents—for boys and for girls, with a commanding counselor. We would go by platoon to every- thing—swimming, campfires, and play-time. Anyone who went AWOL from the camp would be sent back to town, and it would be unpleasant for his parents; you could go about in underwear only when the counselor allowed, and for meals and evening roll call you had to be in uniform and never late. He said that there were no parents' days, but we would have a movie once a week, we would be taught how to swim, and the first platoon would also shoot and ride horseback. Our commanders would tell us the rest. He said, "Pioneers! Be prepared!" Everyone shouted, "Always prepared!" Our counselors took us to our tents.

Several large and tall army tents stood at three ends of the field. There was also a place for roll call and a flagpole and campfire spot for each platoon, with logs for seats. No shade anywhere. The tents had wooden floors and twelve or more iron beds. There was a night table for every two beds. The door to the tent was open and so were the windows, one opposite the door and two on each wall. It was very clean inside and around the tent. No one went AWOL, no one was late, and probably no one got sick. As we left our meals a duty guard checked our hands and sometimes patted our pockets to make sure we weren't bringing out bread, cookies, or candy.

We were taken on hikes and taught to swim. In the evenings we sat around the campfire and sang. Sometimes the counselors woke us up at night for a drill. We had to dress quickly and line up by platoon and then march with a song somewhere or run. And then we would get a mug of milk and a piece of aromatic black bread, which tasted delicious. It was warm sleeping in the tent, and the grass was redolent at night. I didn't read a single book because we were always doing something together. I slept like the dead at nap-time. I was never late for roll call or dining hall. I was not particularly happy or particularly sad. I didn't argue with anyone and didn't become friends with anyone. I don't remember a single name or a child or a counselor. And if someone were to ask how I had spent the summer, I would say, I don't know. I did learn to swim. That was my answer, in fact. This had been my first army experience, the OGPU Pioneer camp.

Well, of course, the children's institution run by Lusia Venikas was nothing like that.

Once, toward the end of summer, she called me in from nap-time. She said that a man was waiting for me in the garden and

that I could go into town with him until evening. She looked
bewildered but I don't know why. I knew he was my father, the
"real one," as our first nanny, Tonya, used to call him. I wasn't
pleased that he had come. I was sure that Lusia would tell everyone that Alikhanov wasn't "real." Actually, I was wrong there. I
didn't want to go anywhere with him, but I went out into the
garden. I squirmed when he tried to kiss me. I ran to tell Lena that
"he" was here. And left with "him."

We went to Farik Asmarova's house. She was a friend of my
parents, and all her friends, including me, called her "Akhchi,"
which is Armenian for "maiden." Not that she was one. She had
a daughter my age, Lyalya. Mama always wanted Lyalya and me
to be friends, but it never worked out, even though we played in
winter, and she often brought me to a church not far from their
house, on the corner across from the conservatory. She taught
me, under cover of kissing the icons, in the dark recesses of the
church to bite off the beads of the ornaments. I wasn't very good
at it, because I was afraid and maybe because my teeth weren't
as sharp as hers. She did it fast and almost imperceptibly, even
to me, though I watched closely. We used the beads later to make
jewelry for ourselves and our dolls.

This time Lyalya wasn't home—she must have been in camp.
Akhchi received me as if I were a real guest. From her conversation with "him" I understood that Mama didn't know anything
about his visit and that he was planning to take me back with
him—I didn't understand where. But I didn't like any of it. As I
had that time in the hospital long ago, when I had scarlet fever
and he brought me a doll, I felt like a traitor and scolded myself
for going with him. I was already thinking about how to escape
from Akhchi's unusually gentle voice, from his embarrassment
and persistence, from the snowy tablecloth set with Akhchi's
delicious dishes, for which she was famous.

The doorbell rang. She went to get it and returned with Papa;
or rather, Papa came in and she followed, abashed. Papa did not
say hello, or even look at me. He was practically shouting at
"him" and at Akhchi. At Akhchi, "You fool, you're a mother. Just
imagine if your scoundrel was stealing Lyalya and your friends

helped?" At him, "Until the girl grows up she will live with Ruf, with Ruf and me. That's it. That's final."

Then he stopped shouting. He took a piece of pie from the table, still standing, and said very calmly, "If you want to see the child, come to the house, you're welcome. Gertselia Andreyevna ["his" mother] comes and stays. We're always glad to see her. Gertselia Andreyevna is a fine woman." Then Papa turned to me, "Come on." He didn't ask if I wanted to go. He didn't ask what I thought, as if I might not think about it at all. He left the room and I followed. On the way home (it was nearby; Akhchi lived in Brusovsky Alley), we were silent. Just as we walked down our long hallway, Papa said, "If that Venikas hadn't called, I guess I'd have had to go all the way to Baku to fetch you. Or would you have run off? And found your own way home, eh?" Papa understood everything. I hadn't said a word.

When we came in, Mama flew out at us and began shouting at me, how had I dared leave the camp, but Papa didn't let her finish. "Rufa-*djan*, it's not the girl's fault. Enough, I have work to do." And he left.

Mama was silent. To say something, I asked, "Should I go back to camp?"

Mama replied sadly, "As you like. You can go to camp or you can go to the dacha in Ilyinka. Batanya is there with Anya and Zorya. Egorka is in Barvikha. I have to leave, I have a harvest."

Mama always had sowing in the spring and harvest in the fall. I didn't feel like going back to camp. I thought that everyone was unhappy now—Mama, and Papa, and I—that it was my fault, even though it was really Lusia Venikas's fault, and I didn't want to see her.

"I'll go to Batanya's, but all my things are at camp."

"They'll bring your things later. Don't you have any others?" Mama didn't know what I had and what I didn't. That was Nura's job, or Emma Davydovna's, or Dusya's, or Batanya's. I had more things.

"Then go; here's some money." Mama handed me money, much more than I needed to get to Ilyinka.

"It's too much."

"That's all right."

I packed, and went to Mama's room to tell her I was going. She was getting ready to go to the harvest. I was very hungry, but she looked so upset and distracted that I said nothing. She kissed me; I kissed her. And I left. I stopped on the fourth floor to see Binochka and told her I wouldn't be going back to camp. I was worried about Lena there without me. Binochka said not to worry, the evenings were getting damp, summer was ending, and she would bring Lena back to the city tomorrow. Then she asked, "Are you hungry?"

"Yes."

Binochka gave me a bun and milk.

And I left. I took the trolley to Kazansky Station and then the train. There were no commuter trains. I sat on the steps on the platform between cars until the conductor chased me away after Kraskov Station. Everything would be fine and fun. But I'll never forget that day which wasn't fine or fun. The day of our third meeting.

There was a fourth and last meeting. In the spring of 1943 the medical train stopped in Leningrad, and I went home. A neighbor told me there was a letter for me, just the other day, from the front. She didn't take it but asked the mail carrier to save it for me, since I showed up from time to time. I ran to the post office. A burst of hope—maybe Seva was alive; maybe it was from him. I'd had this hope a few times before and many times afterward. At the post office, the old one on Pochtamskaya Street, now Soyuz Svyazi Street (it used to look so big to me, that post office), they found my letter quickly. Getting an old letter that someone had saved—that happened several times to me—was a special feature of Leningrad in the war years. It wasn't from Seva. Instead, from "him." It was abstractly gentle. Not surprising, since I was basically an abstract daughter. He wrote that he had been wounded, that he was in a hospital in Moscow, and dreamed of seeing me.

Try to reject him, try to return to that childhood feeling, perhaps an accurate feeling, of your treachery. The war, your pain and others', losses, wounds, Mama's letters from the camps. Batanya was gone. Papa was somewhere—or maybe he was also gone? And here "he" was—your father, wounded.

A month later, on a hot, windy, and very dusty day (the dust hung in the air and the sand raised by the wind gritted in your teeth), we unloaded almost seven hundred heavily and lightly wounded soldiers at the Yaroslav Station. I learned from the lieutenants who were aides of the station's military aides that we would stay on the tracks until morning. I went to pick up my friend Inka, and we went to the hospital. Somewhere far beyond Danilovskaya. At the door the guard would let me see only the chief physician. She permitted a meeting, even though she said they were stricter here than in other hospitals because their wounded were unusual, nervous, with head wounds. I knew what that meant. She said, "They're all in the garden now. Go."

I went out to Inka and said, "How will we find him? I'm not sure I'll recognize him."

We walked down several paths, looking around, and suddenly Inka grabbed my arm. "Lusia, look, there he is," she whispered, and pointed to a man sitting on a bench opposite a small flowerbed with dusty flowers.

I whispered back, "How do you know?"

"He looks just like you, but with a mustache."

The man looked up when he heard us whispering. He suddenly stood up and started walking toward us, limping. I remembered seeing him with a cane, limping, and with a mustache—back in Chita, the very first time.

Later I sat with him on that bench and Inka walked in the garden. We talked. Rather he talked. He asked questions, and he tried to answer his own questions. I learned that he was planning to return to Baku after the hospital. He was finished with the army. He had a wife (or a woman who was close to him) who was a dentist, and he told me his mother had died. But I already knew about Gertselia Andreyevna's death.

At the end of the previous winter our train had been in Baku, and I had tried to look her up. I got her address from information. Her former neighbors told me she had died of dysentery just a few weeks before I had arrived. They asked me who I was. I said just a friend. I couldn't tell them she was my grandmother. Batanya had been my grandmother. Just as Papa was my only father. And then, a fine granddaughter I'd be if I had to learn of her death from the neighbors. I felt guilty again. You can't just tell everyone everything, just to determine who was guilty of what and when. And if they're guilty of anything at all.

But now he spoke about himself, about how bad he felt, how well the doctors treated him, how proud he was that I was in the army, that after the war we had to be together. I listened, I tried to understand, I tried to sympathize. I tried. Of course, I had grown up and had moved away from my childish absolute rejection. Of course, I had grown kinder to everyone, not just him. But he was a stranger, a stranger, a stranger! Like wheels in my mind, the word rolled over and over—stranger! I said that I had to hurry to my train; we were leaving that night. I lied. We said goodbye—in a good way, gently, calmly. As if he really were my father and I were his daughter, as if it were really possible that we would be together someday. I don't know if he sensed that "as if." He must have. I left. Inka was waiting for me near the gate. We went past the duty soldier, who wore no epaulets—a former soldier. He said, "So quickly, girls?" I was surprised. I felt I had spent a long time with "him."

I never saw him again. I wrote him a few disgustingly formal letters. I got a few formal postcards back. After the war, when Mama returned, he wrote that his wife had died, that he was sick, and felt very lonely. I said to Mama, "Should we bring him here? Or at least, should I go visit him?" Half-joking, half-seriously, I added, "Then I'll have a Mama and a Papa." It was the first time I used "Papa" for him.

Mama bristled. "Him or me." She was completely serious, and wouldn't talk to me for several days. And I thought to myself, She's such an extremist; it's so immature.

And then our wan correspondence dribbled to an end. Is he alive? Or not? If he died, then when? Where? I don't know.

29

That fall Lena got sick. She had been ill all along, of course. But we used to walk in the corridor; she would visit me; we did our homework together and read a lot together. We had spent the summer in the "cardiac" room, we had walked in the woods and tumbled in the grass. Now she couldn't leave her room and almost never got out of bed, and she didn't have lessons anymore. When I visited and we talked, she coughed a lot and got out of breath. So, basically, I did the talking and she listened. But she still knew what was happening in the children's world of the Luxe, at our house, and at school. Now we read separately, but the same books. And our interests and attitudes were still the same. We began reading Zinger's *Entertaining Botany* and Fersman's *Entertaining Mineralogy*. Perelman's *Entertaining Physics* and *Entertaining Mathematics* I read later (I think I have the titles right). I did the various experiments described in the books. I usually tried at home first, and if they worked, I repeated them at Lena's. I liked making circular cuts in branches and waiting for the white roots to appear and then at the wrong time, not in spring, for the tiny leaves.

I particularly loved growing crystals. I would get a packet of alum salts at the pharmacy on the corner of Sovetskaya Square, make a saturated solution, and suspend a thread with a bead tied to the end to weight it into the jar from a stick balanced over the jar's mouth. I prepared several jars at a time and sometimes I added watercolors to the mixture to make colored crystals—that was my invention. I placed some of the jars on Lena's window ledge. I also put the rooting branches in little jars of water on her ledge. But when I came to visit, I would find them on her bedside table. Lena assured me that she could watch the crystals grow and the roots and leaves come out. I tried to observe it too, but I couldn't see them grow "right before your eyes." Lena said I couldn't see it because I didn't have the time—I was always running around or doing something, while she was in bed and had the time. I didn't know whether she was mocking me or not, but I didn't take offense. Actually, I began to feel she was becoming wiser than me, that she knew something that I didn't and probably wouldn't ever know.

At home, we had never had a dog or a cat. Except for the shaggy gray cat in the communal apartment in Leningrad that lived in the kitchen by the stove and sometimes wandered in the hallway. In Moscow I had fish and a series of goldfinches, bull-finches, and even sparrows. At the dacha in summer I would release my birds and then get new ones in winter. Egorka had a turtle, a hedgehog, and hamsters. I would buy daphnids and mosquito grubs and hemp seeds at the pet store. Our maids sometimes complained of the mess, especially in Egorka's room.

I would bring Lena a hedgehog or a hamster or a turtle. We called it "turtle comes to visit." Sometimes I carried a birdcage or the fishtank. The tank, which wasn't large, occasionally spent the night. This was a game, too, and then Lena and I would play out a scene (she would be the fish and I the owner, or vice versa) on the topic of how did you sleep and what were the owners like here.

Once when my fish were sleeping over at Lena's, I dropped by after school to bring them home and feed them—I had the mosquito grubs. But both their rooms were locked. That was strange, because even when Binochka wasn't home, Lena's room was never secured. I would knock and always hear her "come in." Where could they have gone? The doctors always made house calls and they hadn't taken her anywhere in a long time. That evening I went to the Krebs' house again, but only Lena's father was home. He came out of his room when I knocked at Lena's door and told me that she was in the hospital with pneumonia. I said that my fish were in her room, pointing at Lena's door, which he unlocked.

Everything was out of place. Lena's bed wasn't made and her clothes and books were scattered all over it. There were things on the floor. As I was carrying the fishtank past Lena's table, I saw two jars with crystals and a bottle with a branch that already had leaves. I put the tank down on the floor in the corridor and went back for the jars and bottle, to bring them home, too. I was never to be in that room again, but I had no way of knowing that. I was simply taking the things—the branch needed its water changed. And I would watch the crystals grow, as I explained to Lena's father, and he agreed with me and offered to help. I told him I would take the elevator down twice. It wasn't difficult. I asked him when Binochka would return. Tomorrow, he said, because she would spend tonight at the hospital.

"Then she's really bad?"

"No, no, not very," he replied.

The next day I saw Binochka looking even smaller, even thinner, even wearier than usual. But she smiled at me and said she hoped to bring me to visit Lena at the hospital in a few days. The following evening, when I knocked at Binochka's room and came in, there were several people present besides her and her husband. Binochka jumped up from the couch, came toward me, and said, "Lena's gone."

"What do you mean?" I didn't understand at first, because it sounded like what parents say when you come calling for a friend and the child's not at home. Binochka kept repeating, "Lusia, dear, she's gone. Forever."

Now I understood: Lena had died. And I went back toward the door, back to the corridor, to the time and place before I knew, before I had heard. Binochka came out with me, shut the door, hugged me, and we stood in the corridor, in each other's arms, silently. Then I started to cry and Binochka said something about Lena not being long for this world anyway, and then she cried like me.

She told me to go home because tomorrow would be a hard day; Lena would be buried. I couldn't go home, I went to the third floor lobby, where Lena and I had met, where we'd become friends for life, standing in the corner by the radiator. I put out the light, because the hallway light was enough for the people getting out of the elevator. I stood there with my face against the radiator and when I got tired, I crouched. I cried and then I'd stop, think, and remember, or just sit without thinking or remembering. I spent a long time there before I went home. It was late, and Egorka was asleep. He had come back with Emma Davydovna from Barvikha. Emma Davydovna and Mama were in the dining room. Mama started the usual "Where were you wandering around so late?" but when she saw my face, she asked, "What's the matter with you?"

"With me, nothing, but Lena . . ." I couldn't go on, but Mama understood and spoke, as if she were about to cry herself. "Died. It can't be, she can't be dead."

"It can. I thought that it couldn't, that it only happened to old people like Katayama."

As I spoke I realized that I didn't feel like crying. I wanted to curse and hit someone, but I didn't know whom. I was angry. Not at Mama, not at Emma Davydovna, not at anyone. Mama said she would find out about the funeral and went out.

I sat in silence. Emma Davydovna gave me some food and a cup of tea. I started eating. I was very hungry, incredibly so, and angry. Mama came back and said that the funeral was tomorrow, that we had to get flowers, and that I didn't have to go to school. She asked me if I would get the flowers or should she. I said I'd do it myself but I didn't know where. Mama said there was a florist across from the telegraph office. I remembered passing it a thousand times, but I hadn't paid attention, since I'd never had to buy flowers. I went to bed. As soon as I got under the covers my anger passed. I started crying again. I said I'd never have anyone to read with or laugh with or whisper and gossip with, or read poetry, and grow crystals, and talk about what was most secret, and everything else in the world. I didn't know whom I felt sorry for—Lena or myself.

Mama came in. She sat on my bed and caressed my head and told me that I was very fortunate to have had such a good friend and that I would have many other good friends, and that I shouldn't cry, and she talked about Lena. I hadn't known that Mama loved her so much. Mama's love for Lena calmed me down. But why did she say I would have many other friends—I wouldn't I couldn't have many; you could only have one best friend. "Well, it will be one then, but you will have one," Mama said.

In the morning I went for flowers and spent a long time picking through various bouquets. I didn't like any of them. They were all asters and chrysanthemums. I settled on blue and white ones. But as I walked home with the wrapped bouquet I thought how sad that it wasn't summer, when I could have gathered daisies and bluebells and small carnations, the flowers we used to put on our night table in our "cardiac" room. At home I unwrapped the flowers and when Emma Davydovna suggested they were beautiful I almost said something nasty to her—I hated them so much by then. I collected all the budding branches Egorka and I had and added them to the bouquet. Then I took all the crystals on threads from all the jars and fastened them to the flowers. And I went to the Little Red Corner.

No one was there. The chairs had been removed and a table covered in white stood in the middle of the room. I went back home and sat quietly until Mirella Rossi came. She said, "Come on. They've brought Lena Krebs." She probably had good intentions, but I got mad again. I told her to go by herself—I would get there without her. I was afraid. Then Mama came home from work and without taking off her coat she said, "Come on, Lusia, it's time." And we went together. I had my flowers and branches, and Mama also had flowers—chrysanthemums, beautiful pink ones.

There were a few adults and almost all the Luxe kids in the room. Everyone was quiet and silent. A very small coffin stood on the table and lots of flowers were around it and in it. I couldn't make out Lena's face from the door, but I saw Binochka, Lena's father, and a woman I later learned was Lena's mother. Mama and I came closer and someone took our flowers and laid them near where Lena's feet should be. Binochka walked along the length of the little coffin, took the branches out of my bouquet and put them near Lena's hands or into her hands, I couldn't tell. Then she untied the crystals and placed them near Lena's hands, where they sparkled like diamonds. When Binochka saw me, she took me by the hand and led me to the woman who was Lena's mother. She patted me on the head and embraced me and pushed me toward the coffin, toward Lena's face—it was her face and yet it wasn't. Binochka stood opposite and kept caressing Lena's forehead. I reached out to touch her too. The forehead was as cool as the columns in that room. It wasn't her; it wasn't Lena. I was cold and trembling, but I didn't want to cry. I wanted to leave. I remembered how I had crouched in the dark by the radiator last night—there was more of Lena there than here. Someone played the piano. I think someone spoke; I don't remember. Then they removed the coffin from the room. I stood by the door and saw Lena's hair and her face in profile. I didn't go down the stairs behind the coffin. I wasn't taken to the interment at the cemetery. I don't think any of the children went.

After everyone left the room and the lights were put out, I went back, picked up a few pine branches from the floor, and took them to the third floor. I shut off the light, put the branches in the space between the wall and the radiator, as if into a vase, and smelled them, and cried, and said goodbye to Lena, my first, my only and best friend. But Mama turned out to be right—I did have another only and best friend. But she wasn't my first one.

In 1937, on my first day at school in Leningrad, after class a girl came over to me, small and thin, with curly hair and light eyes. She said she had a textbook that I didn't have. She reminded me of Lena—but not with her voice or her face. I don't know what it was. "If you come to my house, I'll give it to you. If you don't, I'll bring it tomorrow." That was our whole first conversation. I didn't feel like going. I didn't feel like doing anything then. It was a strange city, a strange house, a strange school—everything was strange to me, and I was like a piece of rock shattered by an earthquake. I went. Our friendship began, suddenly and forever, like the first one, on the way to her house. It lasted until the day of her death, in the fall of 1980. Inka, Regina Etinger. She was with me all my "adult" life. Whether we were near or apart, nothing mattered. I had three years of friendship with Lena. I had forty-three with Inka.

The third best-and-only friendship was very fleeting and sometimes I even think maybe I imagined it. We met at some party in early summer 1941. We had tea and pie baked by one of the girls, argued a bit, read poetry, danced, and then went for a walk. The two of us separated from the others. Her name was Bella Manevich. I don't remember what we talked about. Nothing. We walked for a long time. We lost our group somewhere on the embankment. We spent a long time saying goodbye on the corner of Nevsky and Gogol and planned to meet on Sunday. We never saw each other again. Sunday the war was on.

In the 1950s and 1960s I spotted her name in the credits of Leningrad movies, first frequently then less so. Once I asked a friend who worked as an editor at Lenfilm about her. Yes, she was alive, yes, she was an artist, a very talented one. Yes, it was the same Bella Manevich. Why didn't we seek each other out? Didn't we trust ourselves? Our friendship? Strange! I missed out on a third friendship. But I'm grateful to life for two. Some people live a whole lifetime without one.

30

During almost all of 1934 our house was filled with the thought that Papa would be working for Sergei Mironovich Kirov again, and that we would move back to Leningrad. I was happy because I loved Leningrad, our long apartment like a railroad platform, I loved living with Batanya, despite her strictness. I had noticed that Papa didn't seem to like his Comintern friends and that he had his own friends, from outside the office. The Comintern people came over in the evenings, and they played chess, too, but it wasn't the same. I thought Papa simply didn't like being a boss here and he wanted to move to the regional committee. Mama sometimes said she hated Leningrad and wouldn't move, but everyone realized that she wasn't serious. Papa would laugh and use his favorite word, "nonsense." At first we thought we would move in the spring, then by fall, and that I would start school on September 1 in Leningrad. But the autumn passed, winter began, and we were still in Moscow. There was just talk and Papa kept saying that everything would be decided any day now, that he had talked with Sergei Mironovich several times. I think Papa saw him once and spoke by phone twice.

One evening I had a slight temperature and it was decided I would stay home from school the next day. I read in bed and no one told me to put out the light. Especially since Batanya, who had come for a week from Leningrad, was out visiting. Papa was in his bed with a hot-water bottle—he had a stomachache—also reading. And Mama, with her hair loose and wet, had just emerged from the bath and was making tea and walking around with her robe unbuttoned. Our new nanny, Olga Andreyevna was asleep by now and Mama took care of the kitchen. Mama called Papa to come eat. I wanted to sit with them, so I got up. Just then the telephone rang. There was nothing unusual about that—people called until midnight, and even later. The telephone was in the dining room and I could hear all the conversations.

(Later we got a second phone, which was in Papa's room and which I was not allowed to use, because it was "direct," and I didn't know the number. Sometimes young women from KIM (Communist Youth International) came to use it when Papa was out. They always closed the door when they talked. I listened one time when they phoned Nikolai Ivanovich Bukharin and made a date, and then they giggled for a long time. Later my girlfriends and I tried that trick too, but not from Papa's phone (I was afraid of it). We never called adults, but boys or young men from KIM, who didn't live at the Luxe but across Tverskaya Street in the Soyuznaya Hotel. We always set the rendezvous by the pharmacy which we could see well from the bay window in Mama's room, and we could watch some young man hanging around for a long time, looking at all the passing women. It was fun at first, but then I found it stupid. So one day, in sixth grade, I told my friends that I wouldn't let them use the phone anymore.)

This time Mama answered the phone. It was Matvei from Leningrad. Right after her "hello" I could tell she wasn't pleased to hear from him as she usually was, and she kept saying anxious things like, "impossible," "horrible, horrible," "Are you sure?"

She called Papa in a hollow, almost soundless voice. "Gevork, it's Matvei, it's . . ." She didn't say what it was, but after she handed the receiver to Papa she sank into an armchair, held her face in her two palms so that it was round, turned to Papa, and did not move. I don't remember what Papa said. I think he only listened to Matvei on the other end. Then Papa sat down at his usual seat at the table, where his tea glass was waiting in its holder. He set it aside and held his face just like Mama was doing; he sat and said nothing. I wanted to ask what had happened, but seeing them sitting and staring at each other, I didn't dare.

Batanya got home then. I could hear her taking off her coat. She came in and immediately asked, "What happened?"

Mama said, "Matvei called. It's . . ." Again, she didn't say what it was. Batanya practically screamed, "What happened to him?"

Papa answered. "Kirov has been killed." He said "Kirov" and not "Sergei Mironovich" or just "Mironych" as he usually did. Batanya sat down. They were all stunned. Me too. And I wondered why Matvei had called instead of one of Papa's friends. After all, he wasn't even in the Party; how would he know something so horrible before everyone else. Batanya seemed to answer my question. "Did he hear it from Mayorka?"

Mama nodded. I remembered that Matvei's best friend ever since high school had been Maior Litvin (or maybe Meier), whom everyone called Mayorka, even me. Mayorka had a brother who was a big boss in the Leningrad OGPU. I think I knew him too, but I don't remember. Actually, Mama, Matvei, and Raya had childhood friends who later became OGPU—Boris and Matvey Berman. One of them was the chief of the Cheka in Irkutsk after the Revolution and they called him the "bloody boy" there. He had courted Raya once. Batanya brought that up to Raya during an argument to reproach her.

The first to break the silence was Batanya. She said she would go to Leningrad tomorrow and needed a ticket. Mama wondered what the incident had to do with Batanya. But Batanya was in our room already, and I could hear her pulling the suitcase out from under the bed and opening the trunk. She was packing, which was very typical of her. Whatever happened, she at once took action. Papa also got up from the table—no one had had any tea or food—and started calling. Then he got dressed and went out. He looked dark and hunched-over—maybe because of his stomachache? The phone rang constantly. Mama answered, usually in monosyllables. People from the Luxe dropped by, silent or whispering. An hour later, or maybe three hours—time was behaving strangely and I couldn't tell how much of it had passed—Papa returned. Right after him came Vanya Anchishkin and also Manya Kasarova with Alyosha Stolyarov.

That Vanya was there was understandable. He and his family had moved back a long time before from his political section located somewhere in the Central Chernozem Oblast (which no longer exists). I remember when he returned with his wife because they had a little son whom they unwrapped on our dining room table and showed to everyone. Now he and Musya and the baby and Musya's older son, Vilen, lived in the Government House. Vilen wasn't an Anchishkin; his last name was Mashinsky, and he was a bit older than I, slightly pouty and slightly scared. I didn't pal around with him, even though it was interesting being with him because he read good books and we talked about them. I could tell that he didn't like Vanya and that Vanya didn't like him. That was strange, because I always saw Vanya as a merry, successful man, especially after his return to Moscow. Even though I didn't consider him kind, like Lyova Alin, Bronich, or Styopa Korshunov, I didn't think him a bad man, either. Later I became warier of him, because in sixth or more likely seventh grade, the way he looked at me made me uncomfortable. There was something unpleasant and slimy about it, the way strange men on the street looked at my friend Elka, who was tall, full-busted, very pretty, and grown-up-looking.

But I don't understand where Manya and Alyosha came from that evening. I think they lived in Mariupol then, where Manya was the Party organizer at the Aovstal factory. Perhaps they were in Moscow on a business trip? Or maybe I'm confused and they hadn't left for Mariupol yet?

I was falling asleep at the table, but since no one was shooing me away, I stayed. I don't remember what they talked about. I think they were mostly silent, like Mama and Papa at the very beginning.

I later witnessed that kind of silent sitting many times, in a house where someone had died. But this night my parents and their visitors weren't only saddened, they seemed extinguished somehow . . . haunted. A cloud of smoke floated over the table. Only one lamp, over the telephone, was lit. Mama had not turned on the overhead light, a large old-fashioned candelabrum, when she'd called Papa to eat, though in retrospect it seems simply that no one thought to turn it on. They looked like conspirators to me. I suppose I wouldn't have been surprised if there had been a knock on the door and tsarist gendarmes had entered to arrest them. Batanya came in and I was shocked that no one, not even Alyosha, stood up when she greeted them. She was in a bathrobe, but by now had regained her usual calm and she said, "Get to bed immediately." That was for me, of course, not them. I don't know when they all left.

In the morning no one was home, not even Batanya, only Olga Andreyevna, our maid, who fed me, took my temperature (it was normal), and went out to do the marketing, telling me to stay in bed. But I got dressed and went down to the concierge—for the newspapers. The mail and newspapers were always left there. Only Papa's special mail was delivered by messenger right to our room, number 9. He would knock and hand over the package or packages and say, "For Alikhanov." No one was allowed to touch that mail, even Mama, and we would put it on his desk without opening it. Later I began violating that ban and in the busy Spanish Civil War days I managed to read everything after Papa did and sometimes before him, carefully opening the packages with a razor blade. And then regluing them. Papa never once noticed.

We always got a lot of newspapers—from Moscow, Leningrad, and in foreign languages. I read everything I could find about Kirov and looked at the big photos in all the papers. I don't remember what my feelings were. I think I was still stunned by what had happened the night before, and I thought about why they were all so upset; after all, it wasn't as if he were their father or mother. Of course, they all loved him, and I did too, because I remembered him patting me on the head on Krasnye Zori Street, and how he gave me candy and took me in his car. But I recalled that even when their friend Sergei Kalantarov died in the Astoria (they always said later that he was one of the best), they weren't that upset. Everyone was disturbed, even Batanya. Had she loved Sergei Mironovich so much, too? It was strange.

Batanya started reading the papers too. Then she said that there was nothing in the papers, even though I thought there was a lot. She called Uncle Mosya and Anya, told them she had a ticket for that evening, and that they should come see her off. It somehow went without saying that neither Mama nor Papa would be seeing her off, nor I—I had a cold. After Batanya finished with them, I gathered up the papers, took out glue, scissors, and a nice drawing album that I had received in November, and started cutting out everything written about Kirov as well as his photographs. I had never made such an album before. I don't know where I got the idea. I sat on the floor in the dining room, surrounded by a mountain of cut-up newspapers. The floor was sticky with glue, and so was I. Either I had bad glue, or I kept getting sidetracked and dripping it all over.

When Mama and Papa came home, they looked gray, wet, and cold, as if they had been somewhere else and not at their jobs. They paid no attention to me. Mama walked around me and everything else on the floor. Papa simply stepped over me. A few minutes later he asked where the newspapers were and then he saw what I was doing. And he screamed at me as he never had. He never screamed at people at home. Even when he argued with his friends, he didn't raise his voice, although he argued frequently. And here he shouted, "Why are you poking around in things that aren't your business?" and "You just can't get away from her!" and "Why are you never in your own room?"

I was so bewildered that I didn't have time to take offense, and just as suddenly as he had started, he calmed down, and said, "All right, give me your notebook." I gave it to him and said, "It's an album," and started to cry.

"Come on! What's the matter! It's too late now!" He went on.

"The next time you do this, write on the bottom which newspaper you cut it out of and the date of the newspaper, and then everything will be correct."

Then he read everything I had in there, and Mama said, "What are you reading it all for again. It's the fifth time, and you won't find anything new in it."

We ate lunch in silence. Mama asked Batanya if she had a ticket and repeated that she didn't understand why Batanya had to rush off. The phone rang constantly and various people— mostly from the Comintern—started coming over that evening. Uncle Mosya and Anya arrived to pick up Batanya. My fever went up. But I sat up late that evening, into the night, at the table with the adults. And the other evenings too.

The next day, Agasi and I think Bronich and someone else came to visit, but none of them brought any presents. I don't remember how many days later it was that I gathered from the conversation that Mama knew Nikolayev, Kirov's assassin. Knew him (or was it his wife?). Now, when I start recalling those days, I'm amazed that I never asked her how closely she knew him or whether I had just misunderstood.

The day came when people went to say goodbye to Kirov—it was called "access to the body." That morning Mama went to the Moscow Committee and then returned quickly and said that you couldn't get through Dmitrovka Street at all; it was just like it had been when Lenin died, and just as cold. She was going to the Hall of Columns.

I had been there once, secretly, when there was "access to the body," when Menzhinsky* died. I saw a big line on Dmitrovka, almost to Kozintsky Alley. I had heard that Menzhinsky was dead but I didn't know about the "access" and I asked an older girl what the line was for. I stood in line for two hours or so, before I reached the Hall of Columns. We got up the stairs and it was quiet there and you could hear shuffling feet, and when we were inside the room, the music started up. Everyone walked slowly

---

*Vyacheslav Rudolfovich Menzhinsky (1874–1934) succeeded Felix Dzerzhinsky as head of OGPU (the Unified State Political Directorate), known originally as the Cheka and now as the KGB.

past the mountains of flowers, which had a very heavy perfume. On top of this mountain was a coffin, which I could barely see. I certainly couldn't see who was inside. I didn't like that, and the waiting in line had been boring. And the Hall of Columns didn't resemble the one I liked so much at matinees, when it was full of light and color. So I didn't ask Mama to take me with her to see Kirov, but I thought if she asked me, I'd have to go. I had loved him. But Mama didn't ask me.

I have never since been in the Hall of Columns for a funeral.

I spent the next few days doing my clippings about the funeral and the articles saying that "we will not forgive" Kirov's death. I don't know how long it lasted. I think my memory stretched the time from the evening when we learned of the killing to when things returned to normal for a very long time. Although actually, life never resumed its familiar old course again.

31

I finished writing this chapter in the evening. And all night I seemed to be watching a movie someone insisted on running in my head. With freeze frames: pale faces, sunken eyes, someone's hand shaking ash from a cigarette. And the lamp over the table in smoke or fog. What were they foreseeing? Those faithful Leninists, Stalinists, and Kirovites? No, I have to change the order—Leninists, Kirovites, Stalinists. My people were Kirovites. But did that change anything at all in their work, their lives, their fate? In their past and their future?

Now I ask the questions. From the sidelines. From another world. But didn't they understand, didn't they have a sense of foreboding? All the men who visited us on those hectic Kirov nights were killed.

No, not all. One survived.

After 1937 I didn't see Vanya Anchishkin for a long time. But when I returned in September 1945 from visiting Mama in the camps, I decided to drop in on the family for some reason. I had learned that they were still living in the Government House from a woman who also lived there and to whom I delivered a letter from Mama's fellow inmate. She told me that Vanya had left Musya and the family and had married someone else during the war, when he was in the army. Actually, I went to see Musya, because even though I hadn't seen her all those years, I knew from Anya, Mama's sister, that she always asked about us and even sent clothing and money to us in Leningrad through Anya.

I came without calling ahead. Vilen looked distracted, indifferent to my appearance, and generally even more shy than when he was a child. The younger boy was a lively and personable teenager. Skinny, tall (like Vanya), and resembling him. But he had not a trace of Vanya's wolfishness—now I knew what I hadn't liked about Vanya when I was growing up. Everything about the younger boy was illuminated by Musya's very Jewish good looks, especially the eyes. Musya was rather taken aback but pleased. She had been cooking in the kitchen when I arrived. She looked as if she had aged more than Mama had in eight years in the camps. She took me to the kitchen; maybe because she didn't want to interrupt her work, but it seemed to me that she wanted to protect her sons from my stories.

She told me with embarrassment that Vanya had "left her," but that he was just about to come over to see his son, that he was there often. She talked about his new wife, who was a doctor and had been at the front with him. She asked in great detail about Mama, and Egorka, and my life over the years, and she sobbed frequently and sometimes sat on a stool and wept. Even though she was always a weeper (I reminded her of how she had bawled in the hospital before my operation), I sensed her unfeigned sympathy and interest.

Sometimes you remember incredible trifles that have nothing to do with the main point. Musya was making cabbage soup and after she removed the scum from the broth, she put in a few pieces of onion skin, thoroughly rinsed. When I asked why, she said it kept the broth from being gray; it made it golden. I've been doing that ever since.

Vanya arrived. I think he was a colonel. He still flexed his deep voice and his muscles, and seemed unchanged, not even older. Since I was in uniform he jokingly took on the tone of superior officer while still acknowledging my femaleness—a typical army manner that I detested. The only thing he asked about Mama was "Is she well?" and nodded in satisfaction at my positive response. He didn't ask about Egorka at all. He was too busy with clichés, such as, he had always known I'd turn into a "first-class dame" and he wasn't wrong, and that someone like me should have married a general in the army, and since I hadn't wasn't I silly? He laughed at his own jokes. We sat down to eat. The boys were silent. Musya rushed between kitchen and table, bringing plates and food.

I had a strong sense of the shabbiness of the apartment, which hadn't struck me when I came in—it was ordinary postwar shabbiness. But compared to Vanya's flourishing state I felt it sharply, even jealously. And I reconsidered the Vanya of the past. His success and his joy after the political-section days suddenly floated up in my memory, in a different light, and I even thought: "How did he manage to avoid the fate of all the rest in 1937?" But I chased it away. And I don't accept it now, either. After all, some people had to survive, didn't they? I left almost immediately after dinner. And I never saw Vanya again.

But I saw Musya many times after Mama came back. For a while she was director of a movie house near the Kursk Station and we went there often. And sometimes she dropped by to see Mama.

One day after winter vacation I asked Papa when we would be moving to Leningrad. He looked at me in surprise, as if he didn't understand the question. Then he remembered and said, "Us? Probably never." Seeing that I was sad he added, "Too bad you didn't mention it earlier. We could have gone during vacation." But we'd take care of it in the summer—the vacation was even longer then. He seemed to refuse to understand that I was asking not about a trip but about going there for good.

I'm amazed how much I wanted to live in Leningrad. Two and a half years later, moving there because my mother and my father had been arrested, I came to hate the city with a passion. At that time being there was like being in exile, in a place where circumstances kept me against my will. It was only after I got out of the army that I forgave the city for the sadness and orphaned feelings before the war. In 1945 I became a Leningrader again, not by residence permit but in my heart.

32

In the fall of 1934 I entered fifth grade, in another new school, rather far from home, in Nastasyinsky Alley. New teachers, new classmates, new illnesses. The only good thing (which I didn't know then) was that these would be the last illnesses of my childhood. I remember nothing about fifth grade, only the term child psychologist. For some reason I was very good at moving objects quickly, solving puzzles, drawing circles and squares— doing all the tests our school psychologist gave. He never used the word "test," so I don't know what they were called. For this "talent" I was often excused from class and shown to commissions and sometimes taken to competitions where children from various schools were given the same tasks. You had to do it faster and more accurately than the rest. We were observed by our psychologists, each of whom wanted the child from his own school to win. When I often did, my coach was very loud in his pleasure and praise. Middle-aged, wearing glasses, tall but not straight—rather crooked actually—he always had a cold. He spoke gently with children, but you got the impression that it did not come easily to him. I thought his work at school superfluous and I treated him almost without respect.

That year my illnesses were not grave but I thought they were disgusting. I picked up a cold early in the fall and ended up with a middle-ear infection which with brief hiatuses lasted all winter. Sometimes the pain was unbearable. They punctured it twice. And even considered trepanation, but didn't do it.

In the spring I had to catch up with the class and prepare for exams. Batanya found a teacher who tutored in all subjects, and she came to us twice a week. She gave me assignments and made me go over material. She was annoyed by my messy Russian notebook. One day she said that it was unacceptable to give to teachers for my exam, and I would have to rewrite it. This was a long and decidedly boring job which took several days. When I finished, I was sick with boredom. Emma Davydovna praised me, saying I could do anything I wanted when I set my mind to it. Why did her dear sweet voice and her praise set me off? I jumped up from my chair, grabbed that ill-fated notebook, and, shouting nasty things about Emma Davydovna, teachers, lessons, and the whole world, I tore it up.

Then I ran to the corridor, to the corner of the third-floor lobby (my corner with Lena) and decided I'd be better off dead. Never had an illness, a catastrophe, sorrow over Lena's death or Uncle Sanya's brought on this thought—I wanted to die. I had never thought about death unless life brought me in contact with it. I never thought that it existed. And here it was—some silly, meaningless notebook that made me cry about my life and my death. By evening it had passed. I sat down to rewrite the declensions and conjugations. Nominative, genitive, dative . . . I, you, he . . . I rewrote the notebook. Well, badly, I don't know. But I had been an ignoramus in grammar before and with this teacher and these notebooks I made my breakthrough, even managed orthography. I took the exams while everyone else was in school. And I got "very good" on them all.

33

In the spring of 1935 I did go to Leningrad. Batanya, Motya, and Kalya with their little girl, Natasha, born in January, had moved from our former big apartment that opened on the courtyard to two large connecting rooms on the same floor. It was like a separate apartment with its own entry. Actually they had two entries, but Batanya turned one into a storeroom. The rooms were connecting but not isolated. I thought that Batanya had done that on purpose. She had to go through Motya's and Kalya's room to get to her own. Maybe it was a way of reminding them that she was the one who got them to Leningrad and found them living space. She had exchanged her old apartment, where she had three small rooms, for these two big rooms with beautiful Venetian windows onto the street (no longer Malaya Morskaya but Gogol Street) and onto St. Isaac's. There had been fireplaces in those rooms and they were converted to lovely tiled stoves. The mantelpieces remained. There was a lot of light and a shining parquet floor of intricate design. Later, when I lived with Batanya and even later alone in one of those rooms, I came to appreciate not only the beauty of the parquet floor, but its labor-intensiveness if you have a desire to keep it shiny.

On this trip to Leningrad I enjoyed playing with little Natasha, who was the apple of her parent's eyes, because they had had twin daughters in Vladivostok, who died—one right after birth, the other after two or three months. Kalya showed me photographs of her dead children, and it was horrible.

In the evenings Raya came to visit or Batanya and I went out to visit, and I made the acquaintance once again of almost-forgotten Lyalya and Shura Ruvinshtein and Andrei and Seryozha Prokhorov (both sets of twins, the only ones I knew then), with the nieces of Irina Semyonovna, and with other relatives and friends of Batanya's. In the daytime, for the ten or twelve days I spent in Leningrad, I spent several hours in the Hermitage and went to the Russian museum twice. I don't know what in the museums attracted me. No one sent me; no one suggested it. Of course, I remembered being taken to them by Batanya, but that's not why I wanted to go. Maybe it was *Myths of Ancient Greece,* which Lena and I had read together and which I reread several times alone over the winter; maybe it was *The Iliad* and *The Odyssey;* maybe it was just the age when beauty attracts.

Whatever the reason, I wanted to go to the museums. In all the time we lived in Moscow I had been to the Tretyakov Gallery only once and the visit hadn't aroused any particular emotions. I had never been to the Pushkin, which they called the Museum of Fine Arts then. And I hadn't been to any exhibitions. It's hard for me to separate the feelings the Hermitage elicited from me then from the later perceptions I had in subsequent visits, particularly in ninth grade when I attended the weekly lectures for schoolchildren. But to this day the word Hermitage brings on trembling that comes with being near something that I may not understand fully but that I need. Even though my knowledge or even my comprehension may have increased, these emotions are still those of a twelve-year-old girl. Emotionally I get nothing new from the Hermitage—I gained it all then. I think I was very lucky to be able to go alone to the museum for the first time at the right moment.

The Leningrad days flew by quickly; once we went to the country near Luga, to a village called Mrotkino. It was on the shore of a big lake, spread out along the lake line, all the houses the same, with the forest starting right behind their gardens. The forest was dry, evergreen, with a lot of strawberries, and later with blueberries and whortleberries. I had never seen or eaten whortleberries before and I couldn't get over how large and delicious the berries were, how profusely they grew on the bushes, and how easy they were to pick.

We—that is, Aunt Lyuba and Vadya, Nusya, Batanya, and I (plus Uncle Monya, Lyuba's husband, on the weekends)—lived in a big house on the edge of the village and the forest was not only behind our garden but came right up to the house on one side. There was a big table and two hammocks amid the pines, and we had long tea-drinking sessions in the evenings, after which the adults went off and the kids stayed outside there alone. Our next-door neighbors were Elena Evseyevna (everyone called her Lenochka) and Viktor Ivanovich Prokhorov with their twins, Andrei and Seryozha, and Lenochka's sister with her husband and their grown-up daughter, Olya. There were no small children in our group at all. Vadya was nine, and I considered myself a grownup at twelve, Nusya, Seryozha, and Andrei were fifteen or even sixteen, and Olya was over twenty. I used to get furious with Nusya (I simply hated her) when we were still chatting around the table after the adults had left and she would say in her pretend kind voice, "Lusia, bedtime for you."

Some evenings we went to the center of the village, where there was an accordion player and dancing for the young villagers and dacha residents—there were many of the latter. The village girls often invited Andrei and Seryozha to dance, and then our boys walked their partners home. Nusya would be furious because everyone knew they weren't walking them home. They were kissing, and she was in love with Andrei and was jealous. I gloated and thought it was her just punishment for sending me off to bed all the time. When we didn't go to the village, Nusya went off into the woods to kiss with Andrei. I also thought that I was in love with Seryozha, but I didn't want to kiss.

We usually spent the mornings on the lakeshore and after lunch we'd go into the woods in a big group, adults and children, to pick berries. These excursions were a lot of fun: with hide-and-seek, scaring one another, joking, and howling. Aunt Lyuba really liked joking. This was the first time I had spent so much time with her and I loved her for being kind and merry, and so little, round, and rosy. That's when I came to love her. I also liked Viktor Ivanovich Prokhorov. He talked very interestingly about all kinds of technical things, about how to orient yourself in the woods so as not to get lost, and about the stars. Most of all I liked the way he was in love with his Lenochka, just like a boy who doesn't know how to hide his love or may not even want to. Looking at Viktor Ivanovich I understood that being in love was a good thing and there was no need to hide anything. He got up early in the morning and when everyone else was just getting ready for breakfast he would bring Lenochka a bouquet, not large but beautifully selected—every morning without fail. I imagined later how difficult it was for him when he was arrested and didn't see Lenochka for a long time and how he missed her. And I couldn't think what he was arrested for, after all; not for being an engineer and wearing pince-nez.

Whenever anyone went into town or was expected, everyone went to the station down the dry, sandy, and slightly dusty road, which first went through the woods and then across a big field.

In the middle of the summer we saw Batanya off. She returned a few days later and said that while we had been at the dacha Papa had had an operation on his ulcer and that everything was fine now, although it had been bad, and now we could go back to Moscow. I didn't want to leave Mrotkino but I missed home.

At home we were met by Mama, who was very cheerful because Papa was out of the hospital and in a sanatorium by then. I was sent off to our dacha right away, where waiting for me were our maid Olga Andreyevna, back from vacation—she had gone to visit her family in Kursk or Orel—and Egorka, who had been brought from Barvikha, because he would be going to school for the first time that fall.

34

In the spring Dusya had gone to work on the subway construction and so we got a new maid, not a young girl like the others, but a middle-aged woman named Olga Andreyevna. We certainly didn't dare use the informal "you" or any other chummy manners with her. She treated me very well; I think she even came to love me. She always told everyone that I had a "radiant character." I have never heard anyone before or since describe me that way. In those days I didn't walk, I skipped and danced around. Everyone scolded me for it. But Olga Andreyevna said, "Let her dance while the dancing's good." She used my parents' name and patronymic, and they treated her with almost the same piety reserved for Batanya. When Batanya visited us from Leningrad she was very pleased to see "a decent person in the house" and "absolute order." Olga Andreyevna hired a laundress to wash and iron, sometimes a seamstress to sew bed linens and children's clothes, and the official Luxe floor polishers now appeared weekly instead of once or twice a month. Egorka, who had been living in Barvikha and came home for holidays, left her indifferent. She was the first nanny and housekeeper who didn't "adore" him.

I did less racing around the hallways, because I liked listening to her stories about the time before the Revolution, which she told in the evenings as she sewed or mended.

Olga Andreyevna had been married, but was widowed early. She had worked over twenty years in the home of Count Sheremetyev, first as fine seamstress, then as head of linens, and eventually was promoted to being in charge of the maids, the linens, and the food stores. She was hired help but the years of living in the Sheremetyev house made her a "former" too, as if she were part Sheremetyev herself.

She told us about the family's holidays and daily life, about their dishes and linens as if the dishes and linens were animate. Which porcelain and which silverware were better for which day. What kinds of laces there are for bed linens and for clothing. She talked about the count and countess and the "old count" (there was no "old countess"). But most of all, about the Sheremetyev daughters. She called them "girls" and she must have loved them dearly.

There were three or four of them. Judging from Olga Andreyevna's stories, they had a very hard life, even though they were countesses. They had to get up at six and wash with cold (with pieces of ice!) water. They had to dress immediately and do their hair neatly. Prayers. And then to the classroom until nine. Without breakfast—on an empty stomach. Then they went to greet the count and countess. And only then could they have breakfast—tea and a bun, a small bun. Sometimes they breakfasted with their parents, but more frequently, alone in their room. And then more lessons. Three foreign languages. Then Russian, history, math, and other subjects. Then sewing, embroidery, music, and dance. At two they took a walk—an hour of walking in every kind of weather—rain, blizzard. At four, lunch with their parents if they were lunching at home or just with their governesses. And then more lessons until eight. Then they could read a bit, and then dinner alone, without the adults, or visiting someone's home. Bedtime at eleven, or at ten when they were small. Not earlier, not later. At lunch they could eat as much as they wanted, but the countess and the governesses insisted that they eat very little, because being slim and graceful was most important.

Almost in tears, Olga Andreyevna told us that they were "her martyrs," spending almost twelve hours a day in the classroom. There were no lessons on Sunday, but they had to get up at five and be at church by six, and then they had horseback riding lessons. And they were always hungry. And kind! "The girls were very kind to everyone in the household." Those words were the start of all of Olga Andreyevna's stories about them. They also had to find time to teach the children of the staff of the Sheremetyev house a language or tutor them in another subject. This became a duty when they reached ten. They also had to create handmade presents for the count, countess, and the "old count."

If the girls argued and someone cried for some reason, the tears had to be hidden, the face quickly washed, and they had to pretend that nothing had happened. Because moods were not allowed. They had to be even-tempered, calm, almost merry, but not too much so. This was often difficult for the girls. But the count and countess grew angry if their daughters had "moods." No one else was permitted to be moody either. No one. Olga Andreyevna said that the girls would sneak to her room, where she would give them a piece of bread and butter. "God forbid that the count or countess find out." She also sometimes secretly helped them finish up their embroidery or knitting if they were falling behind.

She was very sorry that she hadn't had time to marry off the oldest daughter. The girl had started "going out," which meant no more lessons and her "own rooms"—a bedroom and a study and small living room—and her own maid and hairdresser. Before that, the girls did everything for themselves—making the beds and cleaning the nursery and classrooms, and everything had to sparkle, because the count came upstairs to check almost every day. The girls lived on the third floor, as did the governesses and Olga Andreyevna. Even higher were the other servants. But once the girls started going out, they would move to the second floor, as the oldest one already had.

Talking about the girls, Olga Andreyevna managed to criticize my parents in passing. She said that I wasn't being brought up at all. "No education, none," "Not even languages," and "How can a girl be brought up without music lessons?" I felt that I didn't need languages; after all, I wasn't a count's daughter. But in response to the question of music—which I did want to study and had even asked Mama for lessons—I used Mama's reply, that I had no ear. Olga Andreyevna countered that this was just an excuse, that one of her girls didn't have an ear, either. She may have been right. And now I truly regret the languages, that my parents followed the idea then current that what was taught in the schools was enough. In the larger view, Olga Andreyevna was right. And here I am, "no education, no, not even languages."

I thought that I knew everything about the girls from Olga Andreyevna's stories, and I understood her love for them completely. I would have been glad to love them myself, but I felt that I shouldn't—they were "count's daughters" after all. That was a barrier to love—not imposed by anyone but me.

I was supposed to love and did love the "Red Devils." A Russian brother and sister and their friend, a Chinese boy. They galloped off on horseback, did scouting for the "reds," ran away from the "whites," shot and killed people. I loved them more than the heroes of Mayne Reid and Cooper. Also there were the "newspaper sparrows" and the Norwegian girl Goi Dalbaack. Then I fell in love with Pavka Korchagin. Mama brought me the manuscript to read. I don't know where she got it. It was the first manuscript I ever read. The first *samizdat*. Later, in about two years, the book was published and I reread it. It seemed shorter. Then I came to love Arkady Gaidar's heroes and of course, Chapayev himself, hero of the Civil War—after the movie. The book had seemed boring. I never read about Pavlik Morozov. I don't know how I missed the books about him, but I haven't seen one to this day. In sixth grade I found Roald Amundsen and Captain Scott. One I loved for winning and the other for his great loss. Perhaps I hadn't selected the books; it's just that they were published then. It was also then that I fell in love forever with Till Eulenspiegel.

35

At that time I would secretly read Charskaya and Verbitskaya.* For the sake of those books I developed a friendship with a girl who was about two years older but in our class. Her name was Lyolya T. She lived with her mother at the very beginning of Kuznetsky Bridge, in the building opposite the photograph of Paolo, in the home of a famous Bolshoi Theater singer. The apartment was huge, dark with heavy drapes, curtains, and carpets, and furnished with large, heavy, and dark furniture. You had to walk through three or four big rooms and a hallway. At the end was the kitchen and opposite it a small room where Lyolya lived with her mother. The room was almost impassable, with its enormous amount of furniture: two beds, a cupboard, a chest, a round table, armchairs, ottomans, and more. One corner was covered with icons. Not just the corner but the two whole walls that met in the corner, so that there were icons over the beds and almost right up to the ceiling over the cupboard. Once, in a whisper, I asked her if she believed in God, and she replied with a nod. Then she took off her red tie, unbuttoned her blouse, and showed me a small gold cross. She didn't wear it around her neck, but had the chain wrapped around her slip strap. At school Lyolya was a Pioneer, at one time even the class monitor, even though her grades were on the average side, and she was "like everyone else." Her mother never spoke to me or when I was around. When I said hello, she replied with a nod, not looking at me—a thin woman of medium height, in something dark.

*Lidia Charskaya, who wrote romantic tales about Georgian princesses, and Anastasiya Verbitskaya, who wrote feminist literature, were both from the gentry and considered too bourgeois for young Communists.

Near the door to their room in the hallway was a large cupboard; not a bookcase, but it held books. I would rummage in there, pick out a book, and leave. The whole visit (right after school) took only a few minutes, during which she, her mother, and I spoke not a word. Then I'd say goodbye. Lyolya would see me noiselessly to the door. I would noiselessly slip out onto the broad and rather dark staircase. The whole thing—my arrival, the rummaging in the books, the question about God, the silence of Lyolya's mother, the absence of the apartment owner—felt mysterious and secret. A secret that Lyolya entrusted with me for some reason. I didn't know any other girls who visited her or who borrowed books from her. I knew that Mama would have practically killed me if she'd seen what I was reading. But I liked Charskaya's heroines, especially Princess Nina Dzhavakha. It was as interesting reading about them as listening to Olga Andreyevna's stories about the count's daughters. I sometimes tried on Nina Dzhavakha as an image for myself, because when I looked in the mirror I thought I saw a resemblance.

Once in Lyolya's cupboard I found Danilowski's *Marie-Magdalene*. As usual, when I went out, I shoved it deep in my desk drawer. When I came home, Mama met me, waving the book in front of my face, and shouting, "Tell me instantly where you got this garbage. Who gave you this book?? Can't I finally know who you spend your time with? Where did you get it?"

Should I tell? Give away the secret? Give away Lyolya? The singer and his apartment? The gold cross? I said nothing. Mama repeated her questions, getting angrier. I still said nothing. Suddenly she started hitting me on the cheeks. Not a single slap (which I'd had from her two or three times before), but several times on both cheeks, hard. Then she turned and vanished into her room with the book. And I bawled into my pillow. I was ashamed that she had screamed that way and, of course, my face hurt. But I was crying because I didn't know what to do. How would I return the book?

In the morning, when my parents had left for work and Olga Andreyevna was out shopping, I decided to look for it in Mama's room. I went through all the bookshelves and behind the books.

There were books perpendicular to the ones lined up in the front of the shelves. Then I checked her dress closet. Then the drawers of her desk. We never locked anything in the house. Except for the bottom drawer of Papa's desk. I knew that and I knew that that was where he kept a gun—I didn't know what kind or where he got it. They had started locking that drawer back in Leningrad. A horrible tragedy had taken place there.

One of the three sons of Villi Brodsky—the one whose name I had confused with "Trotsky"—a boy who was a year younger than I (he was six then), found his father's pistol and began playing with it. His cousin Lusya Krelstein came in. The Brodskys, Krelsteins, and some other friends lived in a commune on the Fontanka embankment in a big apartment. Lusya was a big boy, around fourteen, tall, handsome, and kind. All the little kids loved him. Lusya saw the gun and shouted, "Put it down," to the boy, but the little one, playing, aimed at him and, playing, pulled the trigger. Lusya was killed instantly. The boy was sent to his grandmother in Siberia and later died at the front. But all the adults and children were stunned by Lusya's death. And from the conversation of the adults I realized that we had a "weapon" too and learned where it was kept. I was terrified of it, as if I knew the old proverb "Guns shoot by themselves." I had never wanted to look in that drawer. But this time I did.

The key was nowhere to be found, so I took a pair of scissors and worked on the lock until it opened. On top lay the book Mama had taken away from me. Under it were pages covered in Papa's handwriting. I lifted out the book. But I also wanted to see the "weapon," so I put the pages on the floor. Now, having done my share at the typewriter, I can judge that it was a large manuscript, an entire book. Beneath it was a wooden container about fifty centimeters in length. There were two leather straps on the side. Without taking it out of the drawer, I undid the straps and raised the lid. Inside was something dark and shining, like a small rifle, but wider and more solid. I didn't know what it was called but I didn't like looking at it. I shut the lid and fastened the straps. I felt calmer. Next to it was a small worn leather holster. I took it out of the drawer and with trembling hands removed out a pistol (as I know now). I hefted it in my hands and put it back, in the holster and in the drawer. In the back there were three cardboard boxes; they looked like cookie cartons but without pictures on the lid. I took one out, amazed by its weight. I put it on the floor and opened it. Inside were bullets. They lay in even rows, shiny, very pretty, and very scary, scarier than the "weapon" itself.

I put them away, shut the drawer, and gasped in horror. The front was all scratched up around the lock, in places the wood was chipped. It was very obvious even from a distance—from the doorway. I covered the scratches and chips with brown water-color. It was less obvious, but shameful somehow, like an erased place in your notebook: no matter how hard you try, you can still tell. I was very sad that things had worked out this way, so I didn't go to school. I pretended to go. Instead, after I ate, I went up to the fourth-floor hallway, where I read *Marie-Magdalene.* I read it even though it wasn't interesting; I didn't even like it. And when school was out I went to Lyolya's house. I waited for her to come home from school and I returned the book to her. And then, as if I were coming from school myself, I went home.

Late that evening, when I was going to bed, Mama called me into her room and pointing at the desk drawer told Papa that I was reading whatever the hell I wanted and to make things worse I was also a thief.

"Well, maybe now you'll tell me where you got that book?" she added.

I said nothing. Everyone was quiet.

Then Papa said "Rufa-*djan,* she's not a thief." And to me he said, "Go to sleep, Akhchik." I did without even trying to over-hear what they were saying without me.

I looked into Papa's desk drawer only one more time—auto-matically, the day after the search and his arrest. It was half open, like all the other drawers. The "weapon" and the manuscript were gone. But Mama's beige shoes, which later became my best, were inside.

.   .   .

Today, as I type these lines, that is, over half a century since that day, I was struck by the thought that I might have been different and my whole life might have been different if I had only told Mama about Lyolya instead of protecting her secret.

In December 1937 I was taken for interrogation at the Leningrad Big House three times, with three or four days in between. One night, after they had played the "Internationale" on the radio—Batanya allowed me to listen to the radio until midnight, in bed with earphones, while she read in bed—the doorbell rang. Batanya and I began pulling on our robes. Kalya in the next room jumped up too. We had been expecting them to come for her any day—after all, she was the still-not-arrested wife of an arrested man. Natasha woke up and started crying. I went to the baby, and Kalya and Batanya to the door. I carried Natasha in my arms. One man, in military uniform, came in. He looked at Batanya, Kalya, and me, and said to me, "Let's go." He didn't show any papers and we didn't ask for any; we just stood there, stunned, bewildered. Then he said, "Get dressed quickly."

I gave Natasha to Kalya, and she held her close and headed for their room, while I went to ours on spongy, weak legs. Batanya followed, while the man stayed in the entry. Egorka was asleep. I dressed in silence but couldn't get my feet in my stockings; Batanya whispered to herself and hurriedly got out new warm socks, new mittens, her down shawl, new stockings, a shirt, underwear, undershirts, and put them all on the table. I dressed, and as I put my felt boots on, Batanya said quietly, but in almost her usual voice, "Put on heavy pantaloons. And galoshes over your boots." Then I took my coat and my knit cap with the pompon from the closet, but Batanya silently took away the cap. "Wear my shawl." I folded it in half clumsily. Batanya took it from me, folded it into a triangle, and handed it to me. I put it on somehow. And my coat. Batanya got her traveling bag from the closet, shook out its contents, and stuffed in the things she had prepared for me. Then she handed me some money— five thirty-ruble notes. I was going to stick them in the bag, but she said, "Put it in your bra." Then she said, "Well," and sat down. So did I. Then she stood up. I followed her lead mechanically. She hugged me. I had been shaking from the start and couldn't stop. I thought that she was shaking too. But maybe it was my own trembling I felt in her. She pushed me away slightly. We kissed or, rather, I pressed my lips to her cheek. She said, "Watch . . ." and didn't finish the sentence. I looked at Egorka's bed. It hurt to look at him; he never did wake up. We went out to the entry, and Kalya was there with Natasha in her arms. I looked back at Batanya once more, but she didn't move, just looked at me severely. The military man was in the hallway. I went to the stairs, and he followed. A car was waiting downstairs; we got in, both in the back. No words were spoken. In silence we drove along Liteiny and stopped at the side entrance, not the main door on the prospect. We went through the lobby, up the stairs, down the corridor. He walked behind me, nudging me forward, left, right. I noticed nothing except the harsh lighting, maybe it just seemed that way after the dark street and the fear, the horror, that was nestling somewhere in my chest, my stomach, everywhere. The man opened a door and we entered a small room. There were file cabinets and I think chairs along one wall and an ordinary desk with its side against the other. At the desk was a man, an ordinary, nonmilitary man. The one who had brought me gave me a shove toward the desk and left. I stood there. The man at the desk began speaking very calmly. I don't remember his words; I forgot them immediately. But it was something about how I'd quickly tell him everything right away, because it was late and I needed to go to bed. He kept repeating "quickly" in a calm way and began asking me who came to visit us in Moscow at the Luxe, who came rarely, who came often, with whom Papa played chess and with whom he played billiards.

I said nothing. He started naming people from the Comintern, as if to prompt or remind me, but I remembered only two—Ercoli and Chernomordik—because the others must not have been as familiar. Then he began persistently and repeatedly naming names I had known all my life, as well as I knew my own name: Styopa Korshunov, Bronich, Voskanyan, Mandalyan, Shura Breitman, and Alyosha Stolyarov. He didn't use their given names, just the surnames, and he looked down at a paper on his desk. He seemed to be reading the list. I said nothing. He repeated all his questions and gradually focused only on Alyosha and Shura. He asked when they had been to our house together. He mentioned a day, one of the holidays, in either

November or May. I said nothing. Suddenly he jumped up from the desk and, standing by the opposite wall (he was short when he stood up, shorter than I was), he began shouting.

I shifted the bag from one hand to the other, then held it in both hands in front of me. I stopped trembling. I was unbearably hot. Everything was tight on me: felt boots, coat, and the shawl bunched up under it. I felt sweat rolling along my neck and between my breasts and the money pricking my skin. And I said, "I don't know anything. I'm little." Then he came close to me and waving his piece of paper in front of my face, screamed, "Little, little, you've grown enough, you idiot, idiot, idiot!" He repeated "idiot" a few more times, more calmly, sitting back down. Then he burrowed in his papers without looking at me, a rather long time. Then he said, "You're not talking, but if we had our talk quickly, it would be better for your mommy and daddy."

While he had been sitting silently at his desk, I hadn't felt any emotions for him, not even anger. I was tired of standing, and the bag weighed down my arms, even though it wasn't heavy. But when he said "mommy" and "daddy" I exploded inside and was ready to attack him, beat him with the bag, scratch and bite. But the first military man returned and said, "Let's go." We went along the corridor. I wondered "where" and even more I thought, I wish they'd hurry it up. I was suddenly very sleepy. We went downstairs and through a small lobby. We reached the door. The man said, "Go." I pushed the door and came out in the street. I was confused. I had expected something else. That I would stay there?

I crossed the street immediately. I looked at the door, and then around me. The city was alien, dark, piercingly windy, so windy that the wet hair on my neck under the shawl and my underwear became icy. Which way should I go home? There were three routes: along Liteiny and Nevsky, along Shpalernaya, along the Neva. I chose the Neva River. I crossed Liteiny quietly, almost on tiptoe. It was completely empty—like a long, vacant, terrible corridor. Looking around stealthily, like a thief, I reached the embankment, and when I turned an even stronger gust of wind practically knocked me off my feet. I took a few steps, looking around. And then I ran. I was still afraid, but then my fear left me and I ran and ran. It was slippery, and I fell once or twice. Then I ran along the sidewalk. At Mars Field I turned onto Khalturin and only there did I slow down to a walk. The city was deserted—no policemen, no janitors, no ordinary people—and silent: only my footsteps and the wind. I heard a low rumble of a car engine behind me. Its headlights were at the end of the street. I got scared again, and ran. At the bridge over Liza's Canal (what is its real name?), I looked back. The car had stopped in the middle of the street. Was it at the house where the Otsups used to live, where I went to the play group I had hated? Was it for them?

Batanya must have been waiting; she opened the door as soon as I rang. She looked calm, but I could tell she had not dared hope that I would return. Kalya also got up when I rang the bell. I told them everything, even though there wasn't anything to tell. I wasn't sleepy. I felt agitated and happy somehow. Why? Batanya said in her usual voice, "You're not going to school today. [It was already today.] Go to bed."

Batanya looked at the clock; it was after three. So it had taken only three hours. It had felt like an eternity.

36

A personal dacha came into our lives in the spring of 1935. Though it didn't belong to us, it was leased to Papa "permanently." It came rather late. Other children whose parents were the same rank as Papa, in my estimation, already had dachas. Perhaps my parents didn't want to take on the responsibility of a dacha and preferred to send us to various camps and kindergartens. However, Egorka was about to enter school and his life in Barvikha was coming to an end. And I didn't like camp too much. I doubt these considerations were significant. It's just that the dacha was built and assigned for "his position," and resisting could have been perceived as "debasement out of pride." Neither Mama nor Papa ever lived there, though they did visit on their

days off and Mama stayed overnight a few times. I don't think
Papa ever did. The usual residents (in the summers of 1935 and
1936) were a maid and Egorka, and I stayed between camp and
trips. Lyova and Zorya spent a month both summers, and Batanya came from Leningrad for part of the summer. Sometimes
Mama's friends "dropped off" their kids for a while. Thus, another Zorya, not my cousin but the daughter of one of the Ber-
mans in the OCPU, lived with us for a short time. She stunned
me by not wearing panties under her dress and said that it felt
nice. She kept trying to get me to follow her example, but I didn't.
The very thought of going around without my underwear was
unpleasant. I think that's why I took a dislike to her and don't
remember anything else about her.

The dacha was situated rather far from the Ilyinskaya Station,
almost halfway to the next. It wasn't fenced in, but the long fence
of the Comintern Pioneer camp extended along the right side. On
the left and behind, right up to the house, was the forest. When
we first arrived there in the spring—just to see the place, before
moving in—the house was redolent with wood shavings and resin
that oozed golden from the paneled walls. It sparkled with new-
ness and made me want to smile at its incompleteness. It was
supposed to have two stories. But the real staircase wasn't ready
yet, and there was a temporary one. And there were planed
boards piled on top. They were going to panel the big room. But
that never was completed. (Maybe it was finished after us?) I
liked sitting with a book or with my thoughts in that attic, especially at dusk, despite the mosquitoes. There was an incredible
number of them in Ilyinka, maybe because of the proximity of the
woods.

At first sight of the dacha, outside, I got a terrific desire to plant
flowers, lots of flowers. I had no idea how much labor that would
entail. I went out there several days after school was over to dig
up the earth and plant seedlings. I would come back from my
agricultural labors falling down with exhaustion, my hands
rubbed raw so that a translucent liquid kept seeping from my
palms. I would have dropped the whole thing after the first day
if not for fear of being laughed at for digging up the dirt and then

doing nothing else. As a result I achieved a rather large bed of a strange triangular shape. I planted several dozen sets of phlox and tobacco root and small pinks called Chabot, I think, around the edges. When I came back from Leningrad, my triangle was white with the phlox and tobacco, and the pinks, short and touchingly tiny, were a colorful edging. I don't know what influenced my selection of plants, someone may have advised me, but it was beautiful. Ever since I have loved carnations, and tobacco, and phlox with its weak and vulnerably delicate scent.

I was free to decide how to spend the second half of the summer. I was registered in the Comintern Pioneer camp beyond the fence, but I was given permission to sleep at home in the dacha and either lunch with everyone at camp or go home. I could wander around all day as I wished. At home, they thought I was in camp, at camp they thought I was at home. I spent most of the time alone in the woods. I was not fond of family outings.

The forest beyond the dacha was endless—I never did reach the edge. By the house it was pine, dark and eerie, then came firs with almost no underbrush, and there, amid the golden gleaming trunks, you could see the bright green bushes of raspberries or the thin trunks of birches, flying up into the sky. I didn't look for mushrooms or berries, I just walked and walked. It seems that my main pleasure was in the movement, in its lack of purpose—just walking. And looking. The forest gradually turned into a swamp which I never crossed. The mosquitoes were vicious there. I followed the edge of the swamp toward the railroad and then walked by the tracks through the village of Otdykh, at the end of which was the dacha cooperative for the society of former political prisoners.

Zina Bronshtein, Mama's aunt, lived there. Long long ago she had been sentenced to death for her assassination attempt on the governor general of Kiev. Relatives got a doctored birth certificate at the synagogue reducing her age by two years. Her death sentence was commuted to life at hard labor. Zina never asked if I had been allowed to walk that far alone, what I was doing, reading, what my grades were, how I felt, whether I was hungry. She seemed to know about everyone forever, that everyone had the right to do as she wanted. And that it would always be something good. Everyone read only good things. Everyone studied and worked well. Everyone felt well. And was always hungry.

Mama said that Zina was writing a book about the old days, her hard labor, and her friends. Of course, it was a shame that they hadn't been Bolsheviks but SRs (Social Revolutionaries). But I never saw her writing or doing any household chores. Just feeding someone. Or reading. When I arrived, she set aside her book and led me from the open veranda to the kitchen. She took her book with her. She set food before me and picked up her book. And began reading from it out loud. She was convinced that I would be interested, and I was. When I finished breakfast (lunch? snack?), Zina would tear herself away from the book, smiling—not in general, but at me—and say, "Well, go play outside, Ruf" (or Anya or Etka, Mama's sister or youngest aunt). Then she'd correct herself, "Pfui, I mean Lusia." And she'd laugh.

I would go farther. Farther usually meant the lake in Kratov. There was no place closer for swimming. Sometimes I met the children from the political prisoner dachas there, like Shura Konstantinova, Mama's cousin, the daughter of Etka, who died very young. I adored Shura from afar; she had the beauty of an almost-grown woman. But she made me tongue-tied, so I didn't like meeting her or swimming with her. After she died in the war in a partisan unit, I felt guilty about having avoided her.

The Gastev boys were my most frequent companions at the lake. There were three of them. I disliked Petya, the serious and almost grownup one, but not enough to be uncomfortable around him. He later died at the front. The middle one, Lyaska, was a bit older than me and throughout my childhood and teenage years I confidently assumed that he was in love with me; perhaps he had been. He was arrested in 1941 and I met him again only in 1960—we had our own lives and the meeting didn't really work out. He now writes serious books about art. When I read them, I feel the former Lyaska in them in a strange and vague way. The youngest was Yurka. He was very little then, a year younger than Egorka. Now he's living abroad.

In the summer of 1938, a "strange orphan"* by then, I sometimes visited the Gastevs at their dacha. We slept in the garden. Petya and Lyaska reposed under the pines, with me a few meters away from them under an apple tree as big as a tent. Yurka would whine in the evenings, "I want to sleep with Lusia." The older boys snickered. And everyone got scolded by their grandmother—who was in charge at their house, just as in ours. Their father, the poet Alexei Gastev, was arrested in the fall of 1938.

Then, tired, I would come back. Past the swamp, through the firs, and then through the dark pine forest, with the daytime noises gone. Then the bugle call. In the forest it doesn't translate into "pick up your spoon, pick up your fork." It sounds pure, beautiful, mysterious. Calling me not to the dining hall but somewhere far away, and wonderful. I could see the dacha, not all of it, but the lamp on the veranda and Olga Andreyevna setting the table. I could crawl through the hole in the fence to the camp and into dinner with the others and then sit around the campfire. I could go home, eat, and then sit in the corner of the couch with a book. Or I could wander along the ballast of the railroad, inhaling the warm, special, burnt, and tasty railroad smell. Or to the station, where they sold ice cream. No one could tell me what to do. Freedom!

37

Once again I wonder, why does it happen that an event, not particularly noteworthy, not even an event, just a day, hour, instant, is remembered forever, becoming part of your existence, your biography?

I go somewhere from our medical train and then have to catch up with it. It is a cold winter night, either in Nyandoma or Muduga, for our train went everywhere to pick up the wounded. The gloomy

---

*Ilya Ehrenburg called the children whose parents were lost in 1937 (and the years "before" and "after") "strange orphans."

station hall, stinking of war and disaster. Yearning for some sleep, not sitting up on that bench, but with my legs stretched out. To stretch my legs! I fall asleep and wake up almost supine: my legs are on the bench and my head on someone's lap. A stranger, a middle-aged (in those days anyone over thirty was old) and weary captain smiled sadly at me and said, "Got a rest?" Why do I remember that station forsaken by God and all others, and my sore legs, and that man's face?

The summer of 1943 somewhere beyond Syzranya, not far from the Volga. The step of the railroad car, the click-clack of the wheels, my eyes narrowing in the sunshine, my own hair tickling behind my ears and my neck. Feeling happy with the motion and everything and everyone around me. And that smell of uniqueness. But now it's bitter with the engine smoke, and sweet with the warm grasses and steppe dust.

Late afternoon in Baghdad in 1959 or 1960, when I am a doctor with the World Health Organization. The sky is light, a bit gray, with a weak yellowish tinge—sunset, even though there is no sunset. The clumsy and exotic silhouettes of palm trees against the sky. Car horns sound in the distance, muffled by the rose- and oleander-scented air. I feel saddened by the piercing realization of this moment's uniqueness, its irretrievability. Nothing had happened, but it remains with me and in me.

Leningrad, Dvortsovy Bridge. Above me is the blinding blue sky, and blinking white ice floes are traveling down the river. The sparkle above me and below me on the river comes to me often in my dreams. Once again, this isn't an event, it is nothing—just a memory. But this time it has the smell of ice.

August was hot, stifling, with frequent showers and thunderstorms. I've always loved thunder and rain, noisy, pouring summer rainstorms. Two from that summer I will never forget.

One overtook me on the way home. I hadn't noticed it get dark. The absolute silence in the forest deafened me. And then came a flash of lightning and a thunderclap—at the same time, right over me. The rain gushed. I ran down the path alongside the road through the forest. It was dark ahead, but just to the side of the road and behind me there was light. I stopped and looked back. In the air, under the streaming rain floated a sphere—a bit bigger than the ball with which we played *lapta,* but much smaller than a volleyball. It was white with a bluish tinge. It didn't seem to be going fast, but when I started running again, it passed me and glowed up ahead. I wasn't frightened, even though I guessed that this was a lightning ball, about which I had read. The forest road curved up ahead, and my path crossed it. I hadn't reached the intersection when there was a loud, crackling noise, and the ball fell apart into sparks like a Roman candle. I could see the tree it had struck and I went over to it. At the height of my outstretched hand, the trunk was smoking with a black scorch mark that gave off the aroma of heated resin. I touched its edge with my wet hand. It was hot.

The rain stopped as suddenly as it had started, everything cleared up, birds sang, and the forest rustled happily, as if it had been afraid of that flying, glowing ball. Now there was nothing to be afraid of, and I was filled with joy. My memory of that storm is always accompanied by the tarry, smoky, wet smell of the lightning-struck tree. Later, thinking about the storm, I felt it was like a person's life—you just fly in space and then explode, leaving nothing but sparks for an instant. And it's over! Sometimes I think I had understood that even then, but I didn't know how to put it into words.

A few days later I went into Moscow for some books and to have a bath. I was sitting on Mama's windowsill drying my hair in the sunshine. I was already concerned about my hair looking good but I didn't set it with paper, the way Aunt Zina used to, but made finger waves when it was still damp. A sudden rainshower caught me in this activity, so strong that from my vantage point I could see the water surging onto the sidewalk from the gutter spouts, forming turbulent streams. The street emptied.

I stuck my hand out the window and it was soaked instantly. I felt a desire to jump into that rain as if it were a shower bath. Just as I was, barefoot. I ran down the hallway, past the stunned doorman, past the people huddled under our awning, out into the elements, under that rain, right into the street. And up Tverskaya Street. I hurried along the middle of the main street to the beginning of the boulevard and stopped under one of the four Pushkin

Square streetlamps. Pushkin stood there wet and gleaming. Torrents of rain poured down his cape, making a separate noise from the general sound of the rain. Torrents poured down from me too and suddenly I began pulling off my dress, and stood there in T-shirt and panties. They weren't panties actually, but bloomers, navy sateen, with elastic at the waist and hips. All the girls wore them in camp and in kindergartens outside town. I wore them constantly at the dacha, but in town you were expected to have a robe or dress. Back then we had dresses with a smooth yoke, a rounded neckline, a gathered skirt starting under the bust, and puffed sleeves. For some reason, they were called "Tatyankas."* When I was little I loved that name and had all my variations on it, "Tatyanochka, "Tatyanushka."

I raised my arms up high with the wet dress in my hands and waved it like a banner at Pushkin. His head was bowed reproachfully, but he gave me a condescending smile. I dashed across Strastnaya to Dmitrovka, which would soon be named after Pushkin. And along it toward Stoleshnikova. I felt as one with the rain. The drops that trickled down my face and landed in my mouth were sweet—honest, I'm not making it up—they were sweet, honeyed. When I reached the Svoboda the rain stopped as abruptly as it had started, but water continued spurting from the rain gutters. The street went back to being ordinary—with cars and reanimated trolleys. With people. I felt uncomfortable not wearing my dress. I noticed that my T-shirt was almost shamefully clinging to my newly formed breasts and that the dark skin around my nipples was showing through the fabric. The joy that had poured into me with the rain began to vanish. I walked up from Stoleshnikova to our Luxe, trying to stay close to the buildings, so that people wouldn't stare. The doorman sniffed in disapproval and said I should be ashamed of myself running around half naked in the city; I was too big for that. At home, changing into dry clothes, I burst into tears. I sensed I had lost something necessary, important, that I could never get back again. Like the green pitcher I had lost so long ago. Like my beloved Lena.

*Possibly named after the Empire-style dresses worn by Tatyana, the young heroine of Puskin's *Eugene Onegin*.

That evening I returned to the dacha, and I felt unusually lonely. Both when I was in the train and that evening on the veranda where I sat up late with a book that I didn't read, staring out at the dark trees and the dark starry August sky.

In the morning stomach pains woke me up (I was always worried by stomachaches after my operation) and I ran to the bathroom. But it still hurt. Since it was very early, I went back to bed and suddenly felt something dripping out of me. I got up and saw blood pouring down my legs. There was blood on my night-gown and on the sheet. I was terrified. I remember looking at Egorka and being glad that he was asleep. Why scare him? I went back to bed, pulled the covers up to my chin, and called Olga Andreyevna. I told her she had to call Mama immediately, be-cause I was sick. I refused to answer her questions and only said I must be having complications post surgery. Olga Andreyevna felt my forehead, which seemed hot to her, and then said I was very pale, and went off to call my mother. The phone was nearby, at the Comintern Pioneer camp over the fence.

Mama came about two hours later, and I lay in bed without stirring, terrified by the feeling that something was flowing out of me and too afraid to throw back the blanket to look. When Mama stood by the bed, Olga Andreyevna and Egorka were with her. I asked her to stay with me alone. I told her I was probably going to die because the blood was coming out from me and I showed her my legs and sheets. Mama, who had been upset until then, sank onto Egorka's bed and started laughing. I couldn't under-stand. At first I thought she was sobbing and then that she had lost her mind. I had read somewhere that madmen laugh when normal people cry. I tried to console her, I said, "Don't, don't, you'll still have Egorka, don't cry."

Mama calmed down and said that everything was fine, I was healthy, and could get up, but I had to put something into my panties so that I could walk around. Her explanation didn't ex-plain anything, though she did calm me down. But I didn't want to get up because the things I was wearing were dirty and sticky and I felt filthy and repulsive.

Mama went into the next room without shutting the door. I

heard her tell Olga Andreyevna that I had my "menses." The word was unfamiliar, but at the same time I had the feeling that I'd heard or read it somewhere. In any case, I remembered it immediately. Olga Andreyevna scolded Mama. She said that it never occurred to her that "the child was not prepared" and that "her girls" were always prepared, that the Sheremetyevs' house physician had "a serious talk" with them and that it was unforgivable of Mama not to have done it and if she couldn't then Olga Andreyevna would explain everything to me herself. Then Olga Andreyevna brought a basin, water, and clean underwear and told me to wash up and put the strips of cloth that she had folded into long pads into my panties. I did as she told me but I still felt disgusted with myself and I was ashamed to come out of the room. I didn't know what to do with the dirty water and the dirty linens. So I stood in the middle of the room, clean and dressed now, but disgusted with myself.

Olga Andreyevna came back. She said that Mama and Egorka had gone to the market by the station and that she had to talk to me. She spoke a long time: I was almost grownup and had to remember always that "a man's touch" would lead to my having a baby. She repeated "touch" several times and I asked what to do in the trolley or train when everyone's rushing. She said I was being extremely silly and that I would understand with time what kind of touching she meant, but for now I should remember the date and every month around that date I should be prepared for my "menses," that is, put on heavy panties and get the bandages ready, and she would make a special belt for me. She also said that I had to wash my own panties and wear the bandages so that the bed linens did not get soiled because that was slovenly. Even the Sheremetyev girls had to wash their own panties, and not the maids, Olga Andreyevna finished sternly.

My feeling of disgust left me after her talk. If even the "girls" had these "menses," then I was all right. It was only the confusion about "touching" that remained.

I remembered the date, but in September it happened five days early. I felt that "it" had started in our last class, and when I rose from my seat I could see a wet spot on the bench. After the bell

I asked two friends, Luba and Polya, to bring me my coat. "Did you stain?" they asked casually, as if it were an ordinary occurrence, and I realized that they knew all about it. After they brought me my coat, I decided to ask them about touching. The conversation was long and unpleasant. I was glad that we had it outside on the way home, in twilight—we were on the second shift—and I couldn't see their faces very well. I learned that in order for a baby to be born, three things must coincide—night, lying in bed, and love. In that order: night, bed, love. And the baby can resemble either the mother or the father.

I still can't believe that I was well-read, had spent a lot of time with girls my age and older, had lived for several months in the forest school and in Pioneer camp, and didn't know that sooner or later girls undergo physiological maturity. But the fact remains—I was a sassy, clever, not stupid, and sociable girl and yet in that sense and at that time I really was less prepared than my peers.

38

We had started the 1935 school year in a new building. A three-story, roomy new building. It seemed the top of the line for a school in those days. Now those buildings (the prototype hasn't changed at all) are everywhere. Every town and village has a school like that (if it has a school). Egorka went to the school too, in first grade. All the children I had ever gone to school with ended up there. Seva, Goga, and Rafka. But in different classes. There were several sixth grades. In one was Nadya Suvorova, a girl from the Luxe. Her friend was Elka Dolenko. I became friendly with them, at first simply because we walked home together. Then we began doing homework with each other. Nadya was a good student, but Elka was just the opposite. I was closer to Nadya, but I lacked her neatness and penmanship even though in the "verbal" subjects (geography, history, botany) my grades were higher.

No one in our house liked Elka much, and I couldn't understand why. Later I realized that she was much older than the other girls. She was tall and well-developed, very pretty, flashy. Adult men always noticed her even when they regarded her entourage—us—as small fry. She liked to brag about her mysterious acquaintances, parties, and presents. I never knew whether she was lying or not. One time she was in the hospital, and the girls whispered that some boy in the courtyard of their building on Stankevich Street had stabbed her. Elka never told me about it until two years later at the steam baths when, laughing, she showed me the scar on her hip, high up where the leg becomes the buttock.

"So, it really happened?"

"What did you think?"

I thought it was all stories. Elka had a lovely low voice; she sang Ukrainian and contemporary songs at home and in school, at the school assemblies and matinees. The sixth and seventh grades didn't have evening concerts because we were considered too young. Her family had a grand piano. She took music lessons in the lower grades, but she neglected her music, and her work. She almost never read books and considered poetry silly. I put up with pressure from Mama, Batanya, and even Papa about her, but I didn't give in. I loved her. For her beauty, her voice, her maturity, mystery, cheerfulness, and kindness. I loved her!

I liked Shura, a boy in my new class, and decided I was in love. I'd been hearing so much about love from the other girls. Long ago, watching Lenochka and Viktor Ivanovich Prokhorov and their love I had decided that love should not be hidden, because it was so good. Beautiful! And let everyone know! When we were driving to Kuntsevo (I was in front with the chauffeur Isakov and Mama, with Papa and Egorka in the back), I told them I was in love. Egorka immediately said, "Stupid." Isakov snorted. Papa asked, "Well, and what do you do?"

"Nothing."

"When you start kissing, then tell us, but as long as you're not doing anything, you don't have to tell."

Mama said nothing and I couldn't figure out if she was angry or not. But I didn't want to continue the conversation.

A few days later I told Elka about my "love." She asked which boy it was. I pointed him out to her; we went back into the classroom, since he had remained at his desk in the back of the room and didn't come out for recess. Elka said he wasn't bad. And then asked, "Does he have a desk mate?"

"No."

"Then move next to him."

At the next lesson that's just what I did, eliciting shocked looks and disapproving whispers from half the girls. The following day I was in the seat first thing in the morning. The girls were talking about me behind my back. I heard "boy-crazy." I could see that my presence was a burden to him and I was thinking about moving away again, but I didn't have time.

Six or seven girls from my class jumped me when I came out of school alone. They knocked me down and hit me with their schoolbags, shouting that I shouldn't sit with Shura, since they were all in love with him, too, except they "didn't force themselves on him" like me.

Just then Seva, Goga, and Rafka came out of school and pulled the girls off me. The boys dusted me off. I wiped my face wet with rain, and maybe tears. We took our old route home. Along the way, Seva said, "What were they beating you for?"

"I don't know." I was ashamed. I didn't really feel any love for Shura, but I did realize that without these three something was missing at school for me.

At Golenishchevsky Alley Rafka went on his way, but Seva told Goga that they had to see me home, in case the girls were watching and would attack again. I invited them in and they came upstairs. Olga Andreyevna called me into the kitchen and asked what to serve my guests, and I requested fried potatoes or pancakes. The pancakes, piled high, appeared quickly. Then Goga proposed a game of cards.

Seva said that he'd rather read Mayakovsky, and Goga made a face. But Seva replied, "Not the poetry, but 'How to Make Poems.' " He took a book out of his bag, waved it in front of us, and began reading excerpts: "Where Nita Jo lives," "My mama Lyamina," and others like them. We laughed. Especially over the suitcase. We were just studying "Knowing Oleg" then. After the boys left I pulled Mayakovsky down from Papa's bookcase and read "How to Make Poems." In the morning, getting ready for school I was so happy you'd think it was the start of a holiday.

During my crush on Shura, Elka met him. She flirted with him slightly and made him fall in love with her, I think for all the prewar years. She told me she visited his house and knew his family. I didn't. We were in different crowds. After I moved to Leningrad, I ran into him sometimes on my frequent visits back to Moscow in that crowded area delineated by Okhotny Ryad and the boulevard, Gorky Street, Pushkin Square, and Petrovka, where all my classmates lived. A few friendly words. "So long." "So long."

The last time I saw him was in the winter of 1942, during the victory salutes for Stalingrad. I was in Moscow for a few hours, and I wanted to run down the boulevards from the center to Chistye Profy, to visit Zorya and Anya and Lyova. We bumped into each other on Pushkin Square, and the encounter was very warm. Wartime! He accompanied me and while we walked the sky burst into a rainbow of fireworks, sounding like spring thunder. He had just returned from the army, alive and unwounded, demobilized for stomach ulcers. He was planning to enter medical school. Many years later I met his wife, Lusia. She's a doctor, an obstetrician-gynecologist. We worked together. And she took care of my Tanya when she was pregnant and gave birth to our Anechka under her supervision. Lusya and I planned to get together at home for many years, but never did. I haven't seen Shura since that winter.

The next day I moved away from Shura to the second row, where there was a free seat. Nothing strange about that—I just wanted to sit closer to the front. And it didn't matter where I sat; it didn't matter that it happened I was next to a boy again. His name was Kostya, and he lived on Gorky Street next door to the Luxe. Sometimes we met in the morning and walked to school.

He was one of the smallest in the class and his best friend was the tallest, Zhenya, whom we used to call, "Mister-reach-that-birdie-for-me."

They both read the newspapers and we always discussed the political news. I got to like the papers gradually, after the album I made when Kirov was killed. They were "active" Pioneers like me. Seva had scorn for this side of my life, but since we were in different classes and therefore in different detachments, "politics" didn't affect our relationship. I often did the political news in class and made up newsletters. One of the boys (Kostya or Zhenya) was a good artist and always did the design. At one time I was a group leader and then chairman of the detachment. Zhenya had the same position before or after me. They were good kids, but I know nothing of what happened to them after seventh grade. Changing my seat beside Shura to the one next to Kostya returned me, if not to their good graces, at least to normal relations with the girls. My two new friends did not elicit great interest in them then.

It was The Year of Pushkin. Along with the state revival of Pushkin we could also read Zhukovksy and Lermontov. Not only "On a Poet's Death," but his exciting love lyrics. Goga went to school with Baratsky. Seva was reading Karolina Pavlova and Annensky. Even though we had a volume of Esenin at home, I copied some of his works into my beloved notebook. I've lost so much, but not that. The three of us began our mornings with a discussion of the latest chapter from Veresayev's book *Pushkin in Life*. Installments were printed every day in *Izvestia*.

School now had a literary circle. There were four sixth-graders—the three of us and Volodya Sappak. But the boys felt like full-fledged members and read their first poems there. I was just a support person. In the circle I began my friendship with the ninth-graders Mika Obukhovsky, Borya Barinov, Lyaska Gastev, and Igor Rossinsky. Igor was Seva's cousin. But I had never been friends with him before that year.

When I came home from my bout with scarlet fever in Leningrad, Raya gave me a book called *Three Fat Men*. The author's name seemed strange to them—Olesha. Everyone pronounced it like the first name "Alyosha." I will remember the illustrations all my life. The girl's name in the book sounded like an cuckoo's cry—Suok. But I've just learned that Suok was the maiden name of Lida Bagritsky and Igor's mother, Olga, whom everyone called Olya. And the writer Yuri Karlovich Olesha was Seva's uncle and Igor's stepfather. Igor and Seva were on friendly terms with him, but I soon saw that Igor's relationship was complicated, with many pros and cons. All of Igor's relationships were complicated. And who could have had simple relations with Olesha? I was afraid and shy of Olesha the first few times I met him and I think that he was embarrassed around me as he was with all teenage girls.

Igor worshipped his mother and said she was a "marvelous lady." Both boys felt that Olya was a "real" artist. In the spring of 1936 Olga Gustavovna asked me to sit for her; she wanted to do my portrait. This was the period when I was in love with her: "I want a hairdo like Olya's," "a ring like Olya's," "a hat like Olya's." Of course, I kept all those "wants" to myself. I knew that Seva would laugh at me. And Mama would jump to the conclusion that I had become a "golden youth." That's how she described all my friends from the writer's apartment building by the Art Theater. Igor saw how I felt about his mother, and maybe that's why he made me his confidant. He entrusted me with his deepest secrets and felt I was the only one he could talk to. He said that he liked Seva but didn't trust him completely because "everyone loves Seva too much."

Igor was musical, studied music intensely, and considered himself a composer. He tried to write essays on music and read them in our circle, but they were unintelligible. The kids made fun of him. He was very vulnerable and took jokes very hard. He was hopelessly in love all through his youth with a girl from his class named Lyolya. I didn't like her. She spoke in crude street slang and had an unpleasant habit of giggling and covering her mouth with her hand, along with an unremarkable face (at any rate, I don't remember a thing about it), and fabulously long silvery braids. It was those braids that made her Igor's Lorelei, and he turned pale and then red whenever she passed by, giggling. I sometimes thought he might pass out when she was near. And I was afraid she would wound him irreparably with her laughter. Igor bought tickets to the conservatory and swore to Seva and me that he would invite her, but it always ended with me going instead. Seva was bored by music then. Whenever Igor invited him, he said, "Let Lusia console you."

Igor's father, Misha Rossinsky (which is what Igor and I called him), lived near Leningrad Prospect. The boys and I sometimes visited him. He was a large bon vivant with a fast patter and the Jewish jokes typical of Odessa. He fed us tasty treats and persuaded the boys to drink wine, for which I would scold them later on the street. Seva would reply something like, "Oh boy, you're like your Batanya. I'm really scared!"

The boys liked going to Misha's because he gave them pocket money, but then they stopped for a while. When I asked why, Igor, blushing and stuttering, told me that Olya thought that Igor should get over his lovesickness and have Misha invite the boys over. Misha also brought in some girls (Igor said "professionals"), and then he left. The boys joked with the girls, danced and drank, and then realized that they were there for "experience," got scared, sobered up, and left. Igor was very upset that his mother was capable of taking part in "such banality" (also his words).

Igor was very sensitive about things other than love. About everything. Unlike Seva, he was not apolitical. He read the newspapers and sought the truth; he got into arguments at Komsomol meetings. The trials and arrests of 1936 and 1937 were unbearable for him, even though neither his mother nor his stepfather were arrested.

He said that you can't live if everyone around you is an enemy and practically shouted at me that you can't live if everyone around you believes it and you (that was me) don't. What right do you have not to believe? And then he'd weep.

In August 1937 he visited the NKVD office (now the KGB office) at 24 Kuznetsky. We all went there to find out about our parents. And never learned anything. He asked the man on duty to arrest him because he had "thoughts inappropriate for a Komsomol member."

The man didn't arrest him but called his mother. She took Igor home. A few weeks later, on the night of September 15, Igor jumped out of a sixth-floor window of his room. He fell on the sidewalk of the Moscow Art Theater, right where now there is a flower stand in summer and where before women used to sell flowers from pails. The stems were always wet. Igor used to buy me small bouquets. And say something about his undying love for Lyolya. Blond, light-eyed, tall, and handsome.

Besides the literary circle I also belonged to the club led by the physics teacher Nikolai Semyonovich, who told us interesting things, did experiments, and let us solder tree ornaments, wire for radio in the classrooms, and do other projects that gave us the satisfaction of accomplishment. I wonder if this club didn't start me on my love of fixing lamps at home and so on?

Seva got the idea of putting on a production of Pushkin's *Gypsies* for the New Year's program at school. He selected the actors. Volodya Sappak was the old gypsy; I was Zemfira. He was both Aleko and the producer-director. But I don't remember who played the young gypsy. One day Seva distributed the parts. The next day we knew them by heart; actually, almost everyone had known them before. And then the rehearsals started. One day. Two. Three. All the actors but me were superb, or at least gifted. I was hopelessly bad. Seva tore out his hair, practically lay down on the floor and shouted that he had never suspected I was so stupid and couldn't even take two steps and lift my arm in a special way, that I wasn't human, I was a doll, a stupid doll. Then he stopped shouting, stopped the rehearsal, and we went home. All the way home he kept asking me if I would be hurt if he found another Zemfira, because I would make the show a flop and he couldn't stand a flop. I told him I wouldn't be hurt. He kept asking over and over. I couldn't persuade him that I didn't like playing a part; I hated it, that's why I couldn't do it, and that the only reason I agreed was because he had decided I would be Zemfira. I don't know whether he believed me. I always thought he couldn't accept that someone might not enjoy acting.

The next day a new Zemfira was found, who resembled a real gypsy only with her dark hair. An ugly girl named Tanya. She turned out to be gifted. Sometimes after rehearsal Seva even said, "A talent!" I thought he was a little bit in love with that talent. I took on props, costumes, curtains, and so on (as I would so many times later). I liked it so much that I didn't have time to fret over Seva's love. I never tried acting again.

40

Because of after-school projects and Seva's house I was rarely home and lost contact with the Luxe gang. And our home was changing too. Mama no longer worked at the Moscow Committee; she was studying at the Stalin Industrial Academy, planning to become a construction engineer.

I thought that strange. It was that very year when, thanks to my Pioneer experiences, I decided to work in the Party. When I told my parents, my mother pointed out skeptically that I had no organizational skills. Papa laughed and said that he thought I did. He had seen me walking down Golenishchevsky Alley with a large group of boys. And he thought I had organized them rather well. A real "street girl."

"How could you, Gevork!" my mother chided him.

He replied that for Siberians like my mother "street" was a bad term. In Tiflis the street was a warm place. And all he meant by "street girl" was a young woman who walks down the street and the whole neighborhood is dying to trail after her or at least watch her go. I was flattered that he used "young woman" instead of "girl," and I liked his explanation.

Mama's classmates came to visit, and to study. They didn't seem as interesting or colorful as her friends in Leningrad and in our early years in Moscow. Actually, they were more classmates than friends. They all had trouble with their studies and Mama helped them. But I had the feeling that they bored her as much as they did me.

Her real friends came over less frequently, and when they did, they no longer looked insouciant, determined, and joyfully strong. Had they aged? Only Agasi was as noisy as usual and maintained his custom of sending ahead a crate of fruit as a signal that he had left Erevan and was in Moscow, coming to see us in the evening. Styopa Korshunov was still cheerful when he visited. He had finally married and kept talking about his wife, so we all knew he was madly in love. In general my parents didn't approve of showing or talking about love.

Other visitors, like Bronich from Nikolayev, Shura Breitman from Odessa, and all the rest from Leningrad, were sad about the general situation. And I was surprised that now instead of sitting around the dining room table and having a tea party or drinking wine, they went into Papa's room for long, quiet talks.

I noticed that Alyosha Stolyarov and Manya Kasparova were particularly subdued and that she kept looking at Papa sorrowfully. I knew that Manya adored Papa, that she thought the moon and sun set on him. When we were little, Egorka and I spent the night at their place on Sivtsev Vrazhek. I was still puttering in the kitchen but Egorka was in bed and he kept whining about "for bed." Manya didn't understand and clucked around him like a hen. He pretended to be crying. I came in and explained to Manya and Alyosha that we needed something "for bed," whatever they had, an apple or a candy or even a cracker. Manya started saying that it wasn't hygienic and who had trained us in such a bad habit? I said, "Who? Your Alikhanov, that's who." She shut up, and Alyosha laughed and said that even little children could see how she adored her Gevork. Manya couldn't argue with that, and she went to find us our bedtime snack.

God, memory is such an amazing thing! Yesterday I was writing about the friends of Mama and Papa. Then in the tub I thought some more about it. Why had Manya and Alyosha looked more depressed than the others the last two years? Especially Manya? Why had her eyes been so sad? And I remembered Manya's brother, Ivan Kasparov, had been secretary of the Leningrad City Party Committee. He was arrested right after Kirov's death. And that explained it all. It's just that 1937 came into their family earlier than for most.

And that started me off on memories of Ivan Kasparov's family.

I don't remember him much. But I recall his wife, Genya, his mother, Tatyana Sergeyevna, and his daughter Tanya, a large, vivid, and beautiful girl. After 1937 I would visit them in Leningrad and Tanya and I were pals, if not friends. I brought her to our school dances a few times, and all the boys fell in love with her for the evening. The fate of their family was typical of the people who were caught by the sword of justice in the early thirties. In camp Ivan returned to his pre-Party profession. He was a doctor by education. He survived, and returned. Genya was also a doctor. She wasn't arrested and worked in one of the Leningrad maternity homes. In 1937 and 1938, the usual sentence was ten years without right of correspondence, which actually meant execution for the husband, and for the wife eight years, or if she were very lucky, five years, as a member of the family of a traitor to the homeland—the "ladies' charge."

In the late twenties or early thirties Vanya (Ivan) worked in Moscow. They lived in the Government House, and Papa brought us there once when Mama was sick and our nanny was in a stew. Tanya and I went for a walk and we were entrusted with Egorka, who was a bit over three years old. We went on the embankment where several barges with sand and lumber were moored by the wharf. A finger dock led to one. The workmen, who were completing one of the wings of this building-city, were not on the embankment. The day was warm, and the church domes glittered. We decided to play in the sand. We dragged Egorka down the planks to the barge and fooled around in the sand for about an hour and a half. Then we went back on shore. I saw that the barge, swaying gently, was moving away from the moor. And in the sand, so clean and yellow, was Egorka, rolled up and asleep. It was impossible to get back to him on the barge. I was terrified. I screamed. That woke Egorka up, and he walked over to the edge and waved, pleased with his first boat trip. I shouted for him to step back and ran along the shore parallel with the barge and screamed like crazy.

Tanya wasn't frightened at first and treated it as a game. She hopped and laughed. My screaming, mixed with crying, made her understand. She started shouting too—either at Egorka or for help. At last men working on the road heard us and came running. They hooked the barge and pulled it over to the shore—the embankment was not stone then—and they removed Egorka from his first "ship." I grabbed him and hauled him by his tummy, since I couldn't pick him up, back to the Kasparovs. Then I called Papa to come get us quickly. I hated myself and blamed myself for leaving Egorka on the barge.

I had forgotten my own brother! It wasn't Tanya's fault, but I didn't feel like staying at her house. I visited many a time more with Papa—they were his friends. But the memory of that incident somehow complicated my relationship with Tanya.

After her return from camp, Mama saw Vanya and Genya in a cafe. They were afraid to meet at our house or theirs. Mama had come in secretly from Luga to Leningrad and Vanya from some other place. A few days later a policeman ordered Vanya to leave Leningrad for the place where he was registered. Genya blamed Mama for this. Did she think Mama had denounced him? It was ridiculous, and Mama was mortally offended.

And then they got mad at me. Tanya had married a doctor right before the war or in its early years, and he worked in a rural area. Someone told me she had a cow and garden. The postwar years were lean. And I said that if I weren't preparing for entrance exams to the institute, I'd like to have a garden myself. This was relayed to the Kasparovs as if I had mocked the garden and was stuck up because I was getting a higher education and that Tanya was mired in that life because she didn't. More ridiculousness. But we never again saw Manya Kasparova, Papa's closest friend.

Manya's husband, Alyosha, was a model for me. He was of medium build, slim and elegant, wise and kind, and a very restrained man. He made me lists of books I should read, and he often lent me volumes from his own library. When I returned them, he always found time to talk about what I had read. These were not formal talks, unorthodox from the point of view of their Party crowd, deeper than with Papa's other friends. Perhaps not as heartfelt as with Lyova Alin, but more serious. Of course, by then I was two or three years older than when Lyova Alin was arrested. Before the war I often spoke of Alyosha with Tanya Kasparova. I felt she was jealous of my friendship with him.

And now I have a son named Alyosha. And Tanya Kasparova's son is also Alyosha, but he's ten years older.

Besides the friends I considered "real," Papa's co-workers came to visit. Ercoli, Walter, many Poles, Chernomordik, Blagoeva, and other Bulgarians, and Ibarruri. We often had a very handsome Palestinian whose name I don't remember. I thought he flirted mildly with Mama. Sometimes the Indonesian from suite 8 and his Russian wife dropped by. Actually she was Jewish, but at the Luxe all the Soviets were called Russian. She was one of the few Luxe wives my mother related to. Their small daughter Sunarka, a charming mix of European and Asian, spent whole days in our apartment.

Sunarka lived to our right. On the left, in suite 10, were the Ercoli family:* husband, wife, and son, Aldo. Aldo wasn't very friendly and rarely appeared in the hallway. I don't think he was friends with anyone from the building, and I don't really remember anything about him. His mother was friendly and cheerful, a very nice woman with gray hair and a youthful rosy face. She spoke Russian badly yet was the first to laugh at her mistakes. When Ercoli came to see Papa, they usually spoke French. If they used Russian, he talked slowly, pronouncing the words carefully. Apparently he didn't play chess. I don't recall him playing with Papa (Papa guided all those who played right to the small table where the board was always set up). Sometimes Ercoli visited me rather than Papa. He was studying Russian with a tutor and he needed my assistance with his homework. I helped him and other adults at the Luxe with their Russian. Sometimes I even helped Papa, and was very proud. Naturally, I knew that Ercoli was one of the leaders of the Italian Communist Party. But I thought a leader should be different. Taller. More heated. Maybe even more passionate. He should speak in a fiery manner, not so calmly. I often caught myself thinking that Lenin wasn't much of a leader as I pictured one. Neither was Stalin. I wanted Spartacus,

*Ercoli was the Comintern pseudonym of Palmiro Togliatti (1893–1964), Italian Communist, member of the Executive Committee of the Comintern, 1935–1943.

I guess. And when I met Germanetto in the halls (I read his book, *A Barber's Notes,** at about the same time that I read Giovagnoli's novel†), stooped, limping, and carrying a cane, I would worry that things were bad with leaders. Not with their ideas, God forbid. Just their looks. I wanted a handsome leader. Not Ercoli. And there was his punctiliousness with lessons, as if he feared his teacher. I didn't learn his real name—Palmiro Togliatti—and the fate of his family (he divorced that gray-haired, rosy woman) until the 1950s.

Misha Chernomordik, Papa's deputy (his title was deputy deputy personnel head), was a stocky, dark-haired, smart man. His complexion corresponded to his surname (which meant "Black-face"). He was dark, almost brownish. Egorka used to think Chernomordik was his nickname. His behavior at home with Papa always looked like a continuation of the office routine. Endless papers and discussions. I think it was Papa who brought Misha into the Comintern. They (the Party adults) used the expression "brought with him," when a person taking a new job brought with him people he had known earlier. Chernomordik's wife, Olga Dmitrenko, to me seemed very stern and even mean. Lida, Misha's daughter from his first marriage, sometimes stayed with them. I thought Olga treated her cruelly—like a real stepmother. I wasn't friendly with Lida, but I sometimes pretended to be, because of Olga. To "show" that stepmother. My attitude toward Olga changed, later, when she lived with Mama. I had to mature in order to understand Olga's vulnerability and touchiness and to see that she was a kind person at heart.

Our dacha near Ilyinskaya Station had two halves. If you faced it, we lived on the right side, and Misha Chernomordik's family lived on the left. Olga's mother (everyone called her grandmother), their year-old son, Yura, and Olga's niece, Nelka, lived with them. We had Zorya. She and Nelka were the same age and they both fought over the right to play nursemaid to Yura, who

---

*The memoirs of Giovanni Germanetto (1885–1959), *A Barber's Notes,* were first published in Russian in the USSR (1930) and only later in Italian with a foreword by Togliatti. †Raffaello Giovagnoli (1838–1915) is the author of *Spartacus* (1874, translated into Russian in 1880).

was a picture-perfect baby—chubby, rosy, blond, and constantly babbling.

Later that child joined the ranks of the "strange orphans" of 1937. After the arrest of his parents, he was adopted by Nelka's mother and her husband, a professional army man. The boy got a new surname, a new patronymic, and I think even a new birthplace. In the war his "father" became a general and abandoned the family. Yura followed in his footsteps, graduating from the Suvorov Military Academy and then officer's school. He spent his vacations with his "mother." There he sometimes encountered her friend, or relative, who came from faraway Kazakhstan and gazed at him with love and longing. The woman stirred no emotions in him. And his memory did not dredge up images from early childhood that would have helped him recognize his mother.

Olga, after eight years in the camps, worked in a geological expedition and worried that her very existence might spoil her son's life. So, even though it was 1956, she took no steps toward rehabilitation. Our mother finally persuaded her through letters to quit her job and come to Moscow. She was rehabilitated very quickly (as was Misha Chernomordik posthumously), and she lived with Mama while waiting for her own room. It was already spring 1957. I came from Leningrad with Tanya and Alyosha. It was time to wean Alyosha and I couldn't do it alone. But I could leave the children with Mama and Olga— they could manage together.

Just then Yura was coming from the Far East to Leningrad for his leave, and his "mother" wrote to him to stay with us. He was very young, thin, not tall, and well put together, very taciturn and shy. He wasn't used to us—our whole way of life with lots of people, friends, crowding, and Alyosha crawling all over the place.

Olga's sister had thought a lot of telling Yura about his real father, but Olga had been categorically against it before she was rehabilitated. She still had doubts. My mother sometimes felt he had to be told, and sometimes not. I was the only one categorically for it. Egorka, who had just gotten out of the army and coached boxers at the Luzhniki Stadium, then under construction, counseled, "Don't butt in; they'll figure it out without us."

Egorka did tell us that Yura, who was more open with him than with us, wanted to leave the army and go to school. Khrushchev was cutting back the armed forces then, so his plan was quite realistic. While Yura was away, we finally decided to tell him. The job fell to me.

We stood in Mama's dark room by the window. We could see the outline of buildings, lit windows, the headlights of cars on the bridge. In a steady voice, without emotion (Tanya called it my "physician's voice" when she was little) I told Yura his own story. It was hard. Yura made a point of not looking at me and said nothing throughout my tale, which was long and filled with difficult pauses. Through his silence, when he nervously struck a match to light a cigarette I could see how his hand was trembling. I could see his reflection in the mirror. I didn't look at him directly, but I sensed his amazement. That strange woman was his mother. And his surname was Chernomordik. And he was a Jew, on his father's side. And he had another sister, not Nelka.

To finish up my story about Yura (I call stories about such children, and I have several of them, "children's stories"), I don't know anything about his life today. We used to be in frequent communication. He graduated from the geology institute, then worked in the USSR and abroad. He had a family. Olga became a grandmother. But once Andrei came into our home, they disappeared from our lives. Yes, all of Mama's old girlfriends vanished. The old saying "Once bitten, twice shy" was true. They really were scared. By the end of Mama's life the only ones who remained were Fanya, Annet, and two or three Polish "old Bolsheviks" who had gone through our camps.

41

When Stella Blagoeva, as she was known in Moscow, came to visit, her sweet voice and her toadying manner made me want to throw up. I think Mama and Papa felt the same way, but they controlled themselves. I was rude.

Theoretically I should have adored Dolores Ibarruri, La Pasionara. Just like all the newspapers! However, I didn't like her in our house. She paid no attention to anyone but Papa—not Mama, not us. I don't think she even said hello to Egorka or me. She was big and seemingly dark on purpose. She laughed loudly and spoke loudly. Her voice didn't simply carry from Papa's room, it seemed to fill the house. She brought presents. Egorka got shorts that were too dressy for Soviet life. I was given a snowy knit T-shirt which was my favorite for a long time. Spanish hats and badges with a raised fist and her slogan NO PASARAN. Not long before his arrest, she gave Papa a handsome wool knit shirt, bright blue, almost cornflower in color. I don't remember Papa wearing it. But Mama wore it in bed, huddled against the wall, several days after Papa's arrest. And when she turned her pale face to me, the shirt made it purplish, almost lifeless. Mama wore it constantly afterward, and ended up in the camp in it. And she returned in it, by then mended over and over. In 1935 and early 1936, I thought that there was something between Papa and Dolores, something intimate, and I tried to catch them. My interest passed, but the mistrust has remained.

At one time Boris Ponomaryov came constantly to our house.* Mama brought him into Papa's life. According to Mama, she asked Papa to give him a job in the Comintern, because "the fellow is literate and smart and is hanging around the Moscow Committee with nothing to do." Ponomaryov had just graduated from the Institute of Red Professors or something like it and had met Mama when she worked at the Moscow Committee. We all called him Borya at home. Dusya, our maid then, used to say, "Well then, everyone's had lunch, but Borya's still running around somewhere."

I have a vague memory, not even a memory but a shadow of one, that I somehow connected Ponomaryov with the baby that Mama's protégé Valya had. I know nothing to support this childish feeling. And I don't myself remember Ponomaryov being at our house. He doesn't seem to have made much of an impression

---

*Boris Nikolayevich Ponomaryov, born 1905, Soviet statesman and Party figure, worked for the Comintern from 1937 to 1943.

on me. Of course, had I known ahead of time that he would become the man who replaced almost the entire Comintern single-handed and would be the leader of the world workers and Communist movement, I wouldn't have made that mistake. What I have recounted here is more the effect of Mama's recollections than mine.

Dmitri Zakharovich Manuilsky visited us several times. I knew, of course, that he was one of the "main" Cominterners. Perhaps the most important one, even though George Dimitrov was considered the boss.

I was bursting with curiosity, more than my usual amount. Dmitri Zakharovich looked like both Taras Bulba and Puss in Boots in some sly variant. He was always very friendly and joked with us and with Mama if she happened to be home. But I never got a good look at him. Usually when Papa had company, tea with sandwiches, cookies, and Papa's favorite poundcake, Gold Label, was set in the dining room. And no one objected to Egorka and me hanging around in the dining room or even participating in the adult tea. But when Dmitri Zakharovich came, Papa asked for tea to be served in his room. I didn't dare bother them there. I sometimes made up excuses to go in, that I urgently needed money for a notebook or permission to go outside. I think Papa knew what I was up to, but said nothing. On these reconnaissance trips I noticed that Dmitri Zakharovich did not like to drink tea sitting down; he preferred to stand in the bay window and look out. He did it with such concentration that I wanted to look out the window myself, to see what he was watching. When he left, he never forgot to chat with us for a minute or two. I noticed that Papa—who usually didn't bother telling Mama who had dropped by, since she came home late when most of the guests had gone—always mentioned Dmitri Zakharovich's visits. I thought it was because Manuilsky was such an important man.

His last visit was two or three days before Papa's arrest. He joked with me as he left, asking me about my exams and how I was doing in school. He said that I was growing up a beauty, that it was clear now. Mama came home right after his departure, and Papa, moving chess pieces on the small table in the dining room, said that Manuilsky had just left. Mama asked anxiously, "Why did he come?"

"I don't know; no apparent reason. Just to drop by."

I keep thinking that Manuilsky knew that Papa was about to be arrested. Perhaps he even sanctioned it. But, God, we think and imagine so many things.

42

In sixth grade I returned to Seva's house after almost two years. I was older, and unconsciously I now treated Seva differently. I had a heightened interest in everything about him. Lida accepted me both as a girl she had known for a very long time and as a near-adult. So much so that she always presented me to her guests. Often when Seva's only company was his cousin Igor and me, we were invited to Edya's (now Lida's) room to have tea or dinner. I think it was only then that I saw Lida's sisters, Olga (Olya) Gustavovna (Igor's mother) and the youngest of the three, Serafima (Sima) Gustavovna. Like Lida, they insisted I call them by their first names, informally. It wasn't hard with them, and I did just that. Olya visited Lida less frequently than she did Sima, even though she lived in the same building, usually just dropping by for a few minutes. Sima was there almost every day and all day. Her husband, Vladimir Ivanovich Narbut, a round-headed, unsmiling, one-armed man, was usually with her. His empty sleeve was tucked into his jacket pocket—he had been wounded in the civil war. I trusted him. He was the only one of Lida's steady guests that Seva (and I, of course) called by name and patronymic.

I was a bit afraid of Olya's husband, Yuri Olesha, who was always huffy and seemed to burrow into you with his unkind eyes. Seva called him simply Yura, but I didn't call him anything. I had already read *Three Fat Men, Envy,* and his stories. I liked the

writer Olesha very much in *Three Fat Men,* and I didn't understand him in the others. I thought that instead of writing the truth,
he was pretending. This adolescent attitude remained, along with
my fear of Olesha the man, for many years. And it passed only
when I read his posthumous book, *Not a Day Without a Line.*

Igor Postupalsky was often at Lida's. Everyone called him just
Igor and I never heard his patronymic. Lida's room was littered
with paper and the typewriter banged away. There the one-
volume collection was put together, and then the almanac *Eduard
Bagritsky,* and his collected works were in preparation.

The room was always full of fun. Masha would be cooking in
the kitchen. Festive Lida flitted from the kitchen to the main
room, Sima set the table, and the dishes were unusually beautiful,
like a birthday party every day. Sometimes I easily fit into this
happy mood, but sometimes it frightened me, put me off. I hadn't
forgotten how shy Edya's jokes had made me feel. Now I knew
him, Bagritsky the poet, from cover to cover. He had become my
favorite Soviet poet. Despite the fact that he was Seva's father,
though that played a part too.

I was astonished at how quickly his room had become Lida's
and filled up with papers—even though they were his. And all
those people. Even if they were relatives, like Sima. Or friends. I
didn't like Igor Postupalsky. He thought nothing of dropping into
Seva's room, as if he were a boy who lived on the same floor, a
pal. That's the way Seva treated him (at least to all appearances),
like a pal. Sometimes I sensed a degree of condescension, as if
Seva were the adult and Igor the teenager.

I tried to avoid even the slightest conversation with him; I was
afraid I might be rude. I was jealous of Lida on Bagritsky's
account and on Seva's. Where did she get that expensive karakul
coat? Or the fancy dishes, white and blue? Why was she constantly wearing beautiful crepe de chine dresses now? Why did
Seva always have money? Why now?

I had no idea that Bagritsky's work was to be widely published
after his death. I felt angry that it all happened without him. I was
even irritated over the record player that appeared in Lida's
room. The sound of fox-trots and tangos reached Seva's room

too. Or Kozin singing the treacly song about "let's shake hands and set off on a distant path for many years." He would also set off on that path himself.

A few years later we would often dance in the square inner courtyard to music from that record player. We would dance to anything, even "Kakhovka." Misha Svetlov,* walking past, would grimace and beg piteously, "Please, anything but that, please!"

School, clubs, poetry—all that continued. We stopped the pillow fights in Seva's room. The boys and one of the Kirillov sisters read their poetry and attacked one another's works viciously, almost the way the older group had once done in Bagritsky's room long ago. Goga and I were always drawing contour maps. For some reason we had a lot of them in sixth grade—in geography and in history. I did it well and got my "good." Goga accomplished it brilliantly and quickly, so that while I struggled with mine, he did his and Seva's. They both got "very good." Goga deserved his, and Seva got his for sitting on his bed and reading Selvinsky (he was in his Selvinsky period) and exclaiming every five minutes, "This is genius! Listen to this!"

Sometimes we went sledding with other kids on Trubnaya Square, the way we had in third grade. But more frequently we went to the Dynamo skating rink on Petrovka. Seva taught me to skate, but I remained a beginner all my life. Almost all the kids from our school went to the rink, which was small. I remember it nestled between buildings, a simple waltz floating overhead and slow snowflakes falling onto it in rhythm. We left in a big crowd, almost the whole class, and instead of heading home, we went past the Bolshoi Theater, down Manezhnaya, and turned onto the embankment. There was a bakery on the corner. Seva—who had the most money and could pay for everyone—bought candies of layered chocolate called Esmeraldas. Then we walked through Red Square, and finally went our separate ways. I don't remember just the two of us walking in sixth grade.

Spring came and the school year ended unnoticed. We spent

*Mikhail Arkadyevich Svetlov (1903–1964), called the "poet of the Komsomol." His "Song of Kakhovka" (1935) was one of the most popular songs in the USSR for years.

Gevork Alikhanov. Moscow, 1935.

Elena Bonner with her grandmother and brother. Leningrad, autumn 1937.

Elka Dolenko.
Oct. 16, 1937.

Regina Etinger
shortly before she died.
Leningrad, 1982.

Elena. Leningrad, November 1937.

The ninth grade of School No. 14. Leningrad,
1938–39. In the third row, second from right,
is Elena Bonner; in the second row at far
right, Inka (Regina) Etinger.

Tatyana Bonner with her grandchildren Natasha Bonner and Igor Alikhanov. Leningrad, 1938 or 1939.

Raisa Bonner (Rainka), Elena Bonner's aunt, with her daughter Tanya. Gorky, 1954.

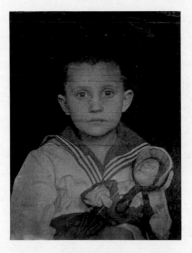

Natasha Bonner, Elena's cousin, after evacuation from besieged Leningrad. Novosibirsk, 1944.

Seva Bagritsky. Moscow, 1937.

Igor Alikhanov. Leningrad, April 28, 1938.

Seva Bagritsky. Moscow, 1938.

Elena Bonner.
Leningrad, 1940.

Elena Bonner.
Leningrad, 1949.

Officers and noncoms of military-
medical train No. *122*. End of *1942*.
Elena Bonner is at center in the first
row. In the second row: second from
left, train commander Vladimir
Dorfman; third from left, political
officer Pavlov.

Seva Bagritsky. Moscow, October
1941. On February 26, 1942, he
was killed on the Volkhov front,
near the village of Myasnoi Bor.

Ruth Bonner with her son, Igor Alikhanov. Leningrad, February 1946. The first photo of Ruth taken after her return from the camps.

Elena Bonner. Moscow, 1940.

Ruth Bonner (1900–1987) with her great-granddaughter Sasha (Alexandra). Newton, Mass., summer 1984.

Tatyana Bonner (1879–1942). Chita, 1916.

Elena Bonner with her first grandson, Motya (Matvei). Moscow, March 1974.

a lot of time walking around the city, traveling to Neskychny in a big group. Everyone passed exams comfortably. I did very well, with just one "good" in Russian and the rest "very good." I always did better on finals than in my course work. And I considered exam period to be almost a holiday, both at school and in college. At home, my successes were received calmly. Papa said something nice and Mama didn't seem to notice. That hurt a bit.

Before leaving for summer, the boys made plans for a fishing trip. Seva said in all seriousness that he had decided to take me with him. He decided? What about Mama? Of course she wouldn't let me go. Overnight! Not at home! In all-boy company! What things she said. Seva and Igor Rossinsky were the sons of writers, "golden youth"; Mika Obukhovsky and Borya Barinov were too adult; and Goga was a nihilist in a dirty sweater with a dirty neck, the son of that Lvov-Rogachevsky, who thought he could have his own opinion on everything. I didn't pay attention to the adult boys; I didn't even understand what was wrong with that. I took offense at "golden youth." But I was furious on Goga's behalf. I shouted that his sweater wasn't dirty, and that Goga wasn't dirtier than the others, that it wasn't his fault they were poor just because his father was missing and he goes every week with his mother to sell books. And that she wasn't a Communist but a fool and a bourgeois fool at that.

Here Batanya interrupted. She had come from Leningrad "to find a little peace at the dacha." She scolded me, told me, "vile thing," to apologize immediately to my mother. And without a pause she advised Mama that Seva and Goga were "very decent boys." She would let me go with them. And she moved on to reminiscences of picnics and overnights in the hills near Chita, where she had always let Mama and Anya go. Mama disappeared into her room—the issue was settled. Batanya told me to take a sweater, breeches, an extra pair of socks, and a second pair of sandals. Any other time I would have complained, but I obeyed without a murmur. Then she told the Nun to bake *pirozhki* for me to take, lots of them, and some other food.

The Nun was our new housekeeper, a recent replacement for Olga Andreyevna, who had left forever, to either Kursk or Orel, where her sick sister had her "own house." The Nun was a friend of Olga Andreyevna from her former life and became a maid because her convent was shut down. Mama wasn't too eager to take her, but Batanya insisted. Egorka and I called her the Nun behind her back. We got so used to it that now I don't remember her real name. She was the most aloof housekeeper I ever knew. She did everything. Fed everyone. Everything shone. But we never heard her voice. She never told Egorka or me what to do. From Saturday evening (we had already switched back to the regular week by then after all the different attempts at five-, six-, and ten-day weeks) until early Monday morning she would disappear. She didn't sit at the table, not with the adults, not even with Egorka and me. In fact she never sat in the rooms, only in the kitchen or in her cubby. She never invited me in there. Every evening, whether Mama was home or not, she put a sheet of paper on the dining room table with her account of expenses and the change. Egorka and I always avoided that money, even though we didn't mind picking up the change Papa took out of his trousers at night, simply telling him we had it.

I also remember the Nun because in the summer at the dacha she washed the floors every day and then sprinkled them with fresh-cut grass. It gave the house an incredible scent, especially at night. And in early summer, one day the house was filled with birch branches with small leaves, still sticky and a tender yellowish green. I asked her what for, overjoyed by the pleasure of it. Quietly, almost in a whisper, she told me about the Feast of the Trinity and the sacrament that accompanied it. I think that was my first conversation on "religious themes," and practically my only conversation with her.

Her cooking was delicious and abundant and she enjoyed it. The dishes had unusual names: *klops,* convent *kasha,* fish monastery-style, *rastegai, paskha, kulich.* And we had a Lenten day, Friday, but no one complained. Everyone liked her Lenten fare as much as the other meals. I think I learned the word from her. Before that I knew the word "Lenten" only in the context of cooking oil. (Vegetable oil is used instead of butter during Lent.)

. . .

We had to leave very early for fishing. The clock on the street
showed almost five when I got out to Sovetskaya Square by the
pharmacy. The meeting place throughout my childhood. The
boys weren't there. The sky was turning pink with light, barely
noticeable clouds. They were pink. I had seen many sunsets, but
this was my first dawn. The first in my life! It looked like a sunset,
but the colors were more subdued—softer, I guess. And the sky
and the earth were calm, smooth, tranquil. Andante, not allegro.

The clean empty street, the pink illumination of the Moscow
City Council building, the rosiness of infancy on everything—the
sky reflected in the earth, to the earth looking at the sky. The
coolness made a light shiver run over my body, like ripples on
water. I was happy with anticipation and also that no one had
arrived yet and that I was alone. A special state of separateness
from everyone and everything. Childhood, when the world is you
and the rest slides past. Youth, shyness, anticipation. Like standing at water's edge, testing it with your toe. Go in? Or not?
Probably old age brings that separateness back, as light as a pink
cloud that is overhead right now. But the anticipation will be
gone.

When I saw the boys appear on the corner of Moscow Art
Theater Alley, I ran toward them. I felt like a cloud. And I was
flying!

We went to the train station on the trolley because the metro,
brand-new that year, didn't run that early. Then we ate in the
suburban train, spreading the Nun's *pirozhki* on the seat. Delicious! We were going to Podolnechnaya Station, where Goga
knew someone. There we were given a boat. And we had to sleep
in a shed in the hay. We had everything: boat, and fish, and fish
soup, and last year's faintly aromatic hay in the shed, right on the
shore of the lake, which seemed endless to me. It was different,
not like a dacha, even though dachas had forests and water and
fields. The boys fished in the morning and slept in the afternoon.
And we had a fire at night. The first campfire that wasn't a

Pioneer one. To this day the memory of it flashes before me whenever I start a fire.

We went back that evening. Weary. I napped, resting my head on Seva's shoulder. I dozed and heard what the boys and the old man sitting by the window opposite were saying. He asked Seva, "Your sister?" He meant me.

Seva said, "Yes."

"You look alike. Brothers and sisters always look alike."

An eternity would pass. I would be having coffee and cake with Tanya at the Writers' Union cafe. Zyama Paperny would come over and join us. And suddenly, thoughtfully, he would say, "Listen. She looks like Seva, you know. And like Bagritsky."

Seva left to spend the summer with a friend of his father's, Commander of the Army Mitya Shmit, who was in charge of an army somewhere in the Ukraine. Before he left he kept bragging that he would "hunt" and do some real fishing, not like Goga's Podolnechkini. With Mitya Shmit himself. With his heroic past, "from Zhitomir to the Balta." And his future. He was just like a little kid. I had seen Shmit at their house a few times and I didn't notice anything particularly heroic about him besides his insignia. Especially since we had our own army-commander visitor— Tolmachev, Mama's friend. But I didn't like him, because I thought that Mama liked him and she flirted with him.

Papa brought me arrangements for Artek, the All-Union Pioneer camp—for hero children who picked cotton, caught spies, and raised horses for Marshal Budenny's cavalry. I wasn't a hero, but Papa said I "almost deserved it," for my good grades on exams and more importantly for not being sick once all year. I told him I would never be sick again.

"How do you know?" wondered Papa.

But I knew, even though I couldn't explain it. I felt it inside. The anticipation of the trip, the Crimea, the sea, was so engrossing that I didn't feel any jealousy when I learned that Mama was taking Egorka to the Crimea in July to the Central Committee Sanatorium Melas. I even thought it was fair—since I was going to the Crimea, Egorka should be taken too. And the best part was that I never again felt jealous toward Mama over her "golden child," who never did get sick.

Artek was everything it should have been. Sunny, the air scented by sea and oleander. Excursions, trips to meet famous Bolsheviks vacationing in Suuk-Su, swimming, horseback riding, boating. I learned to row and to ride a horse a bit. Whenever I mounted, I had to overcome fear. In the evenings we had a big campfire, dancing (I danced with boys for the first time), and songs. I wandered by the sea alone, I climbed Au-Dag, collecting minerals and then trying to classify them by comparing them with the specimens at the camp museum. I collected herbs.

We did have heroes in our detachment. A girl from Belorussia who had caught a spy (I'm so sorry I forgot her name; I think it was Luchko). There was a boy who raised horses, named Barazbi Khamgokov, from Kabardino-Balkaria. I had a crush on him. He had a medal, which he attached to everything he wore, even his T-shirt. I often wondered what happened to him later.

I had a pleasant time. But two misfortunes occurred that I handled badly, sometimes grieving for days at a time, unable to overcome my misery and sorrow.

Maxim Gorky died. The counselors told us and the whole camp held a funeral meeting. Why did I take it as a personal loss? I had read his trilogy by then, his stories, I knew *The Maiden and Death* by heart (I wasn't aware what Stalin had said about it), and I knew *Makar Chudra* by heart too. He was a writer I loved.

And a few days after that, in the reading room, I learned of the death of Agasi Khandzhyan. I cried out at the unexpected news, and the other children looked at me. I left the reading room immediately. Why didn't I want anyone else to witness my grief and my sudden fear? I walked up and down the distant and empty paths of the camp's park. I didn't understand—what had happened to Agasi? He had been in Moscow recently—the same as usual, merry and healthy. And why was I afraid?

I decided to call home the next day. It was easy at Artek. You bought a coupon at the post office and went to the camp director's office to use his phone. I called home but there was no one there. Then I phoned Papa at work. He was surprised to hear from me but when I started to mention what I had read in the paper, he interrupted me and said I should rest well, not get sick, and that they all loved me, that I shouldn't miss them, and that I should wear my dress every night, that it was very becoming. I had a new dress, of yellow viscose with a red belt—I called it silk.

It was a silly, ridiculous call. Papa never talked like that, especially when I was phoning long distance. Instead of calming me down, the call made me more upset. I was as scared as I had been after Kirov's murder. But now I was older and it was all the more serious for me. Anxiously, but still participating in the merry Artek life, I waited for my return to Moscow.

The Moscow kids were leaving camp in their own train car. As we went through Melitopol, we were seized by the desire to buy fruit. I succumbed to the general excitement and bought a bucket of cherries, because Papa's favorite jam was cherry with the pits (mine too), and a bucket of pears, spending my remaining money to the last kopeck. The cherries were in the bucket, but I tied up the pears in my *sharovary* (wide trousers). At the Moscow Station I didn't see my parents among the ones greeting the campers. I knew Mama was in the Crimea but somebody was to meet me. The counselors had told us that everyone had been informed.

All the other children and their parents left, and I was alone on the platform. The bucket of soggy cherries stood at my feet with my knapsack and the bundle of pears was leaving a wet spot on the ground. I tried to walk, dragging all of that; it was heavy. I was hurt—I did this for them, and what about them? They couldn't even meet me. The platform seemed endlessly long, since we had been in the next-to-last car. I moved along slowly and felt small, unneeded, and abandoned. And dirty from the trip and from my sticky gifts of the south. I decided I would throw them into the first garbage can I saw and would never, ever again buy fruit to bring home when I went south. The rubbish bin was far away, at the head of the platform, and I kept my eye on it as I inched along.

I didn't notice a smiling Papa run up to me. He was very pleased that he hadn't missed me. My anger vanished. He picked up the cherries and pears. We walked to the car where Isakov was waiting and drove home in style. No one was there, because Batanya was in Essentuki, Mama and Egorka in the Crimea, the Nun on vacation. Papa said that Mama wanted me to go to the Comintern camp for the rest of the summer. But now he had to hurry back to work, and we'd discuss everything in the evening. He gave me money to buy some food.

This must have been my first time alone all day in the apartment and I suddenly felt like the lady of the house. It was a pleasant, calm feeling. I picked through the pears, throwing out the rotten ones, and then I tackled the cherries. There were an awful lot. I poured off half and ran to Seva's, but neither he nor Lida were in town. He was still visiting Mitya Shmit, and Lida was vacationing in Odessa. There was only Masha, who was happy to see the cherries and said she would make jam straight away. I asked her to make some for us and went home for the rest. Then I shopped, cleaned house, washed up, and returned to get the jam.

I realized there was a lot of time in a day and I could get a lot done. When Papa came home, I had the table set and I had made fried potatoes and pancakes (with fresh jam for them). I had learned to produce both dishes at Seva's house. The two other things I could cook were cream of wheat (Papa's only food when his ulcer was acting up) and fried eggs. He was delighted by the table. Later, after he tasted the jam, he said it was as good as Batanya's or Sofia Matveyevna's, the mother of Aunt Ronya.

"Did you do it all yourself?" he asked, dipping another pancake into the jam.

"Yes!" Was I ashamed to lie about the jam? Not a bit, I don't think.

After dinner I asked Papa not to send me to camp. "Please. I've never spent a summer in Moscow. And I'll feed you."

Papa, already engrossed in his chess, said, "We'll see," to my whining. And we never returned to the question.

My days were completely free, and I was alone. None of my friends was around. For the first time I didn't feel like reading. All I wanted was to keep walking through stifling Moscow, smelling of dust and flowers, to travel far on the trolley and then walk back toward the house, peering into alleys, courtyards, and churches. I felt as if I were seeing Moscow anew, except for my school and the center of the city. Maybe it was my first time there.

I stumbled into the Zamoskvorechye district, not where the Government House and the Udarnik movie theater were, but the side streets and alleys between Pyatnitskaya and Ordynka. I discovered Petroverigsky and the Menshikov tower, in the alley behind Kropotkinskaya Street. All these places were connected by the Annushka, the A trolley line, which I liked because it wasn't crowded in the daytime. I could ride for a long time by the windows, leaning out and sometimes even touching the trees that the trolley passed.

This feeling of a new city and connecting with it on a profound level recurred for me in Baghdad and Florence. Me. And the city. Alone. Revealing itself only to me. A gift for me.

Once I found the Museum of Fine Arts, now the Pushkin. I had come up from the embankment and was headed for home when I stumbled upon it. After my first visit I went there every day, as if it were my job. Papa and I would have breakfast, and then he went to work. I walked to the museum. In the last days of summer I'd drive with him to the Comintern and then I was close to the museum. The days passed.

In the evenings if Papa didn't have company, we went out on sprees. I'd put on my yellow dress, attach a flower to my hair with my barrette, and Papa would call me Carmen. And we'd go to the Aragvi for dinner or to the restaurant on the corner of Strastnaya, which I can't remember now. Until then I had only eaten in bakeries or cafes with my parents, and only in the daytime. So these were my first "adult" times out. As I dressed, I thought of Olga Andreyevna's stories about the Sheremetyev girls and told myself that I had started coming out, too.

Papa had never had so much time for me before. This was the only way to talk, just the two of us. We read poetry to each other, for I realized that he didn't have many people to read to. And we talked about a lot of things. Even about the world revolution and that "we'd have to wait a bit with it." And about Hitler and *Mein Kampf,* which I hadn't read.

I kept waiting for Papa to bring up Agasi, but he didn't. So one day I asked. Papa shrank back, lit a cigarette, and then said it would be better not to talk about it. For the first time I began to realize that he wasn't a cheerful person. Maybe a happy one, because he loved Mama. And us, I guess. He was the typical Armenian father, permissive with his children. But not cheerful. And not all that successful, powerful, and strong, beloved by others. There could be people who disliked him a lot.

I put this all together and into words only later, after Papa was gone. During the long nights I suffered because I couldn't picture him in prison. How was he? What was he thinking? How were they executing him? How were people shot in general? I thought I knew everything about Mama: that it was hard for her, that she worried for Papa, and us, and Batanya. And I felt that because I knew, my knowledge helped her in some way. But I didn't know about Papa and I couldn't help him. Even in my thoughts.

That month, that hot urban August, was a gift from the gods because I spent it with Papa.

By the end of the month my dinners out with Papa ended, because he ran out of money. I started cooking cream of wheat for breakfast, stirring it so that there wouldn't be any lumps. We dined on fried potatoes and sausage, and I learned to my amazement that Papa didn't like potatoes. I couldn't understand such a thing—not liking potatoes! Sometimes we went to people's houses for dinner. The Kasparovs, or Musya Luskina and Vanya, and even once to Farik Asmarova's—the Akhchi, at whose house Papa found me when the "other one" tried to kidnap me. I was reluctant to go, but Papa said, "Nonsense. Akhchi is a good comrade. I've known her all my life. Forget about that. She's the best cook in Moscow, better even than the Armenians at the Aragvi."

Then the Nun reappeared and started washing, cleaning house, and feeding us. I don't know with what funds, probably her own. That had happened with many of our housekeepers. Of course, they were repaid, but they might have fed us anyway.

Mama and Egorka returned and we went to meet them. Papa reached up and helped Egorka down from the train and then

Mama. She squealed and kicked her legs. I was struck by the brown beauty of her legs. Their faces were like dark chocolate, like mulattoes. I had never tanned like that. The four of us walked down the platform. And I felt that my parents were just the way they had been in Leningrad. Happy. Young. Beautiful.

Batanya came back the next day. She had a talk with the Nun and then scolded my parents for always being short of money, for being "completely irresponsible." I didn't like her discussing that with the Nun, even though money wasn't a problem for me. When I asked for money for the movies, notebooks, books, or a ribbon, I always got it. Papa usually gave me more than I needed. Of course, when I asked for a bicycle, Mama said we had no money.

But I got the bicycle anyway. It was a birthday present that year, in 1937, from Bronich. Papa and Mama said I was lucky that Bronich was in Moscow for a meeting with Sergo Ordzhonikidze. Right on my birthday. Then they laughed at him for being as rich as Henry Ford and told him it was time to marry. I was astonished that they couldn't see he had been in love with Mama all along and had never married because of that. I loved him even more for loving Papa, too. But I was wrong; Bronich married soon afterward. However, he didn't have time to bring his wife to meet us, and they were arrested before Papa.

43

Our family's life style must have been very high for those days. We always had food. After 1930 or 1931 we had the special packages from work, so that there was enough food for the people Mama and Batanya helped. We always had a housekeeper. But then Mama was almost never home, and she didn't have regular days off until the last few years. When she worked at the Moscow Committee, the meetings, conferences, Party sessions, sowing and harvesting periods came one after the other, and I sometimes didn't see her for weeks at a time. I left notes for her in the dining room if I needed anything, because she left when I was asleep and returned after I went to bed. We had a Party dacha in which everything belonged to the Party, just like our furniture in the apartment. Before that, we rented a dacha or the children were sent to a privileged children's institution. Mama and Papa went south to the sea for a vacation every year at some Party resort. When they were sick, they were treated at the Kremlin hospital, while Egorka and I were doctored by Aunt Ronya. We bought books, but we never purchased a single chair. We used pitiful, cafeteria-style plates and cups and glasses. And aluminum knives and forks. Batanya, holding a teaspoon in her hand, said disdainfully, "I should bring my own!" And I thought, *Why don't you take your silver from the trunk and give it to us?*

Sometimes a seamstress came to the house. She made bed linens and even quilted blankets (Mama liked good bed linens, and I inherited that preference from her). She sewed for Egorka and me: flannel shirts; skirts and trousers usually cut from old clothing from Batanya's inexhaustible trunk. Mama always wore a skirt and blouse. The need to purchase something new became a problem that was solved by a compromise involving the trunk. Out of it came a piece of cloth for Egorka's suit, then Mama had a coat made from cloth that had been in there since the Revolution.

GORT appeared in those years. I don't remember what the initials stood for, but it was a store for senior officials. You needed a pass to get in—it was located in the Government House. GORT-A was on the second floor and GORT-B on the first. A was supposed to be a class better. We first had a pass for B, then we moved up a floor, but I didn't notice any difference. In the first few months of GORT, Olga Andreyevna and I bought six stainless-steel forks, knives, and spoons. Stainless steel was something new, and I thought it beautiful. Having flatware meant major progress in Mama's household. Batanya approved and said Mama wouldn't have stooped to this before.

Later Mama bought me a fall coat. I hated that purchase at the time, and also later, when Mama was arrested. It was a boyish coat, dark gray, very heavy, and of unbearably rough fabric. So rough that it rubbed me until I bled around the neck and wrists. I hated it for that and because it made me a clumsy, boxlike monster. And I wanted so much to have a colorful, light, girl's coat. Mama cut me off with her "No money," which was true. But I also knew of her constant attempts to make me ugly, because she thought it would protect me from something. Papa frowned when he saw my new coat. I overheard him say something to Mama and she replied that "the times of Lusia's bows are over, and the later she starts dressing up, the better."

But Batanya rebelled and scolded Mama in front of me, "Why make the girl homely; it's better to know that you're not ugly than not to know it."

Soon after, Batanya took me to the Torgsin store where they sold clothing. I had been there with her many times to the food Torgsin, more often in Leningrad than in Moscow. They were located in the former (and present) Eliseyev stores. Every time she bought me an almond pastry. Round, fresh-baked, aromatic. Just one, just for me—it cost five kopecks. Her favorite granddaughter.

The "clothing Torgsin" had everything and Batanya started buying all kinds of things. I watched her almost in horror, because I was sure no amount of money could pay for all that. She purchased two leather coats, for Mama and Anya, and cloth for suits for them, and knit sweaters for herself and them, and some other fabric. Then she said it was my turn, and she began trying wonderful things on me. She bought me a beige knit suit and a dark red knit blouse, and another one just like it, but green, for Zorya. I asked why Zorya got only a blouse. "She's too little for such expensive things," Batanya replied in her usual strict way. The answer also meant that I was big enough.

The suit and blouse became my "dress-up" outfit for all the prewar years. And I wore them for two years after the war at the institute. As I mended them in the evenings, I thought of Emma Davydovna. Later Mama unraveled them and knit dresses for one-year-old Tanya. The leather coat also had a long life: Mama left for prison in it and came back in it from the camps. And I also wore it in my first few years at the institute. Buy expensive clothes!

When we left the store, loaded with packages, I asked Batanya where she had gotten so much money. She said she had foolishly brought almost all her silverware to sell at Torgsin and now it was closing down forever. She couldn't forgive herself for such short-sightedness, because "silver was more dependable" than all these rags. I didn't understand what "dependable" had to do with it. And she also said that it was over; she wouldn't be able to dress her grown children anymore. Of the fabric Batanya bought then, Mama had a lovely dressy dress made for New Year's 1937 and I got a pale blue blouse which the Nun embroidered in cross-stitch.

That ended Mama's clothing acquisition for many years. And mine. I arrived in Leningrad in my wool coat, and I didn't get a winter one until the following year. Zina (my aunt Kalya's sister) had a new one made and gave me her old one, which I loved. After my "iron" coat, it seemed wonderfully warm and as light as a feather. But my parents never had much money or even a hint of savings.

44

Seva returned at the end of August and called. I got so excited hearing his voice that he asked me what was wrong. I put on my yellow dress. I really wanted to put a flower in my hair, the way I did when I went out with Papa, but I felt embarrassed. We met by the pharmacy and were both bewildered by happiness and something else that had not been between us before. I asked him how Mitya Shmit was, and the hunting and fishing, but Seva didn't seem to hear me. He suggested going to school. "Why?"

He said we had to.

On the way he praised my homeroom teacher, Alexandra Vasilyevna, who taught math. She really was nice. Besides her and Nikolai Semyonovich, the physics teacher, we had no memorable instructors. Near the school Seva suddenly told me to wait outside because he had to do something that was none of my business. I was a bit miffed. He came back quickly very happy. He said he had seen Alexandra Vasilyevna and that she asked if the "collegium of advocates" had returned yet. That was her name for me because I was always coming to her on behalf of others in trouble. Sometimes I did it because I wanted to; sometimes I was asked by the troublemaker. They thought I was a teacher's pet, and I might have been. I had noticed that she treated me warmly and that it had nothing to do with my parents. There were plenty of children in school with parents more important than mine.

Before I went to school in Leningrad I didn't really care if my teachers noticed me. But once I became a "strange orphan," I began to appreciate those who showed even a drop of concern for me. That's why I loved our history teacher, Manus Moiseyevich Nudelman. Of course, it was also because his were the most interesting lessons I had ever had. I also liked and respected our principal, Klavdia Vasilyevna Alekseyevna, even though she taught the most useless subject of them all, "The Constitution of the USSR and Social Sciences." In 1938 they introduced a fee for middle-school education—400 rubles a year. I worked as a cleaning woman part time and made 120 rubles a month, but I still couldn't afford to pay the tuition. I went to see Klavdia Vasilyevna with my resignation—I was planning to go to night school. They began those schools to replace the workers schools. Klavdia Vasilyevna took the piece of paper from me, read it, got up from her desk, shut the door to her office, and said quietly, "Do you really think I'd take money from you for your education? Go!"

In order to be exempted from the fee I had to submit an application that was reviewed by the council and with Komsorg, or the Komsomol organizer. Now people seem to forget that in 1936 every school had one. It was an adult, a Communist Komsomol, who kept an eye on the political and moral state of the students and teachers. The job was done away with shortly before the war, but in those years, that person terrified everyone in the school—as the obvious representative of the

NKVD. *Anyway, I didn't apply. Then who paid for me? I think it was Klavdia Vasilyevna herself.*

Then we went for a walk and Seva said I had a surprise waiting at school, but he wouldn't tell me what. As we were saying goodbye at the column of our marble entry and talking about something else, he said, "We'll be sharing a desk again. As we did in third grade."

"How do you know?"

"I asked Alexandra Vasilyevna to transfer me to your class."

"Did you tell her why?"

"Yes."

"What did you say?"

"What's the difference? It's done."

"What about Goga?"

Seva replied sadly, "I couldn't do anything for Goga. He's going to be at school far away, on Kalyaevskaya. They've got new districts for schools now. Alexandra Vasilyevna wanted to keep him, but it didn't work because the Komsorg was against it."

Once again I sensed that "they" (though I couldn't tell you who "they" were) were unfair to Goga. But my "they" were related to Batanya's pronouns—"they," "their," "your"—that she used when she was angry about Mama, Papa, and their Party friends.

A strange school year began. I awoke every morning into a fresh holiday, which never ended and was interrupted only by sleep.

Washing, dressing, breakfast flew by like lightning. Then I hurried, knowing that on the corner of Gorky and Golenish-chevsky Seva would be waiting. And if not on that corner then on Golenishchevsky and Pushkinskaya. We flew at each other. And then the day was like a whirlwind: next to each other at our desk, homework together at his house or mine, then going out with the rest of the gang and together, poetry, clubs, books, together, together, together. Then night—fall asleep, wake up—an instant. And then another day like the one before. When I visited Aunt Ronya, Anya, and Uncle Mosya, I sometimes was with Batanya and sometimes without, but I always was accompanied by Seva. And I went to his relatives with him. And to the theater, the movies, the skating rink. I thought that I saw nothing and heard nothing but him. I sat in class and only felt him next to me. Yet I remembered every word the teacher said. Or dictation. The teacher's voice seemed to be coming from another world, but I'd make no mistakes. A miracle! And I had time for everything. Read. Memorize the poetry heard that day. Get a "very good" in my favorite subject. Listen to Elka's and Nadya's secrets (we were in the same class now). Help Roza Iskrova with her Russian homework. "Please," "thank you," "goodbye." I'm polite. I never blew up. I never yelled at Egorka. I was kind. Everyone was kind. Everyone smiled at me. At home. At Seva's. On the street. In school. The coat lady at school smiled at me. And the saleswoman at Filoppovskaya bakery. And the doorman at the Luxe.

When I went to Seva's house after the summer, Lida laughed and said she had to get up on tiptoe to kiss me. I had to stop growing, she said, or I'd be taller than Seva. During the day Narbut, Khardzhiev, Postupalsky, and someone else worked in her room. Sima was constantly there. In the evenings there were so many guests that it was cramped. People had tea not only at the table, but by the nightstand, under the mirror, and on the windowsills.

But we didn't have time for the grownups. Seva's room was overcrowded too. We were planning a journal, and had heated arguments over the title first and then selection of the contents. The submissions to our editorial board quickly got too heavy. I can't remember everyone who showed up in those months—to argue, to write, to edit. When Lida's typewriter was free, she let me use it, and I would try to type with one finger. My mess made Lida gasp and if she had a moment free from her guests and her work, she typed for us. We called the journal *Sputnik,* or *Companion.* There were two editors, Vsevolod Bagritsky (Seva's formal name) and Mark Obukhovsky. I was their assistant, and Seva joked that I was the Noncreative Assistant. That was the truth, because I was the only one who didn't write, didn't even attempt to write. We had many authors: Goga Rogachevsky wrote heroic-romantic poetry. I'm so sorry I forgot it all! There's one quatrain that remains: "I'd rather live briefly but burn brightly, to melt the pole and ice and warm them up." I considered Goga a mature, real, great (and many other adjectives) poet.

When Goga read his poetry, head thrown back, his neck as thin as a baby's, the room grew still. We didn't listen to anyone else as attentively as we did to Goga. I thought that Seva was a little jealous. But he read poetry—his own and others'—better than Goga. Now I preferred how authors read and considered actors' reading to be trite.

Goga gradually spent less time with us because his new school was far away. He studied hard, had a part-time job, and fell in love. For good. For his whole short life. She was a girl from his new school, very attractive, red-haired, with a rosy face and green eyes, triumphantly beautiful. Her name was triumphant, too: Viktoria. About two years later we went swimming at the reservoir. I was lying on the sand and shielding my eyes with my hand looking at Viktoria, who had just come out of the water. She was like a statue that had been dipped in molten gold. Her golden red hair flowed down over her shoulders, and the glow continued on the golden fuzz of her arms, back, and legs. All the boys on shore snapped to attention and stared at her. Our Goga was among them, tall and skinny, with his touchingly ungrownup neck. "I'd rather live briefly . . ." And it was brief: twenty-year-old tank captain Georgii Rogachevsky died near Kursk. I didn't hear anything more about Viktoria when I was young.

There was a lot of poetry in our journal. Mika Obukhovsky published a poem on the Fall of Man. Seva had to decide whether or not to put my initials on the dedication to a poem. I've forgotten one word of it, and for that reason Lida and I did not include it in the posthumous book of his poems we edited. It was the first poem ever dedicated to me, and I thought it very serious, even tragic verse. Seva asked me whether or not to use my initials. I said no. But I was sorry that there was no dedication and was hurt that he left the decision up to me. The hurt passed quickly, however.

Lyaska Gastev wrote about art, and Igor Rossinsky about

music. Something like political articles were turned out by Mirya Valentei. Borya Barinov produced humorous short stories, in the style of Zoshchenko.* Volodya Sappak was already writing about the theater. There were other authors, all boys. The only girl we had was Valya Kirillova. Her poem was rather invigorating in the Communist Komsomol vein.

When the poet Kirillov and his wife were arrested, Valya and Nadya were sent to an orphanage. I know nothing else about them.

Our circulation was five copies, and there were two issues. I have a copy of the first in my attic. I keep scolding myself for not getting it out. Where are the other copies? Who has them? Did they survive?

Sometimes in our evening walk around the Kremlin we had passionate political discussions. A trial was under way, and the General Procurator's speeches were published in the press. Seva did not read the papers and avoided these talks. He said nothing, but walked, whistled, quoted poetry, and asked us to guess the author. We all would switch to poetry. I never could understand whether he really wasn't interested in what was going on around us or if he simply didn't want to discuss it. And I noticed that I no longer had a desire to read the papers, listen to political news, or open Papa's packages. It wounded me, destroyed the joyous festive feeling of flight which which I woke up in the mornings and hurried off to see Seva.

---

*Mikhail Mikhailovich Zoshchenko, (1895–1958), writer of short stories imbued with a skeptical and ironical tone. In 1946 Andrei Zhdanov, Stalin's culture commissar, attacked Zoshchenko, the poet Anna Akhmatova, and the composer Dmitri Shostakovich, as part of a crackdown on the arts.

45

The Executive Committee of the Comintern had a small vacation house a few kilometers from Kuntsevo on the banks of the Setun River. Executives and their families spent their time off there. The children usually had their winter and spring vacations there, too. There were no teachers or supervisors for the children. There was a charge for room and board, but I don't know how much. Everything was "of the highest quality." The house was reserved for the "highest echelon of power" of the Comintern. The families of my friends from the Luxe were never there, so I guess they didn't belong to the Comintern "establishment."

The teenagers fell in love and (especially the girls) told secrets for hours. The boys hung around in the billiard room, when the adults weren't there. I didn't have any friends, but I loved the place. In the spring it looked like Sestroretsk, especially the Setun, which flowed very near the house at the foot of the hill. Even though it was much smaller than the Sestra, its winding bed and its banks covered with bushes (so many bird cherries!) constantly attracted me. And Kuntsevo was my favorite place in winter. I could spend half the day, returning late either for lunch or for dinner, wandering alone, delighting in the beauty and my love for everything that revealed itself to my eyes. My memories of Kuntsevo—not the house, but the place, the forest, the river, the foothills and valleys—are among my best.

We usually set out for Kuntsevo by car in order to arrive by Saturday dinnertime and return to Moscow after dinner on Sunday.

But in seventh grade I refused to go there. Mama insisted, and we had horrible fights over it. One time when I insisted on staying home, she locked me in the apartment. I discovered a way out—

through the window of my room to the balcony and then via apartment 8 to the hallway.

I felt like a pariah among the girls in Kuntsevo. To myself I called them show-offs and stuck-up. I don't know why I didn't get along with them. Perhaps because they were older, more like young ladies, probably. I couldn't make contact with them, and it was unpleasant for me.

That year our crowd was planning a New Year's Eve party, a grownup one, with everyone chipping in. We decided on my apartment, because we had the most room. The discussions and plans, the collecting of money, the shopping list started weeks ahead of time. I was the least knowledgeable of all the girls, and they elbowed me aside. My job was to find out how many plates, forks, cups, and shotglasses we had. The shotglasses worried me. My parents drank nothing but dry wine. The girls assured me that there would be very little wine and just one bottle of champagne.

I worried whether I should mention the wine to Mama, but decided not to tell her ahead of time. When I asked for permission, she agreed right away. Of course, she said. She always preferred to have people come to our house than have me go out. But she frowned when I said we were chipping in. She suggested that the Nun bake *pirozhki* and dessert. And we could have a cake and chocolates. And we could get something from Oriental Sweets, our favorite store. But I begged. I said that the kids wanted to contribute, and that they'd go to someone else's house if we didn't let them. Mama agreed. I don't know why I wanted that party so much.

Just before New Year's I visited Seva. He hadn't been at school and I dropped in without calling. He was grim, and didn't listen to my chatter. When I asked him why he hadn't been in school, he said he had overslept. Lida's room was quiet, and I asked where everyone was. He said that Lida had gone to the Postupalsky house, and Sima was home.

"What about Vladimir Ivanovich?" I wondered about her husband, Narbut.

"Vladimir Ivanovich was arrested." He added, "Incidentally, so's Igor."

"Which Igor?"

"Why are you so stupid? Not my cousin. Postupalsky."

"Then why did you say incidentally?"

"Because Mama decided not to tell me." He made a face and said, "I eavesdropped." And then, "Actually, we should say 'among others,' instead of 'incidentally.'"

That became our code word for arrest—so-and-so among others. Later, when the time came for letters, that's how we put it.

The fun ended at Seva's house. From the plump, merry, and well-dressed young woman that Lida had resembled in the last few years, she instantly turned into Seva's serious mother. Sima came every day. They had tea together, without inviting us. The manuscripts that had been all over the place were gone, and the clatter that came from Lida's room was no longer the typewriter, but the sewing machine. I think she sewed to soothe herself. *The way, many years later, Mama would pick up her knitting as soon as something bad happened when Andrei lived with us.*

Every night at the Luxe bands of soldiers made arrests and we could hear their loud, masterful steps. The faces of the residents reflected doom. Papa's too. The father of my friend from the fifth floor, Lusya Chernina, was arrested. I tried to console her. I told her it happened to everyone. And she said, "Not at your house." I answered with a convinced "It will." Hiding my wild secret hope that maybe, just maybe, it wouldn't. Lusya Chernina's mother later shared a room with my mother in the lower floor of the Luxe's outbuilding in the courtyard, which was called the "NEPman" building, to which the families of arrested men were "exiled" from the main building—temporarily, until the wives were arrested. Mama was taken a few days before Lusya Chernina's mother. They later met at the Akmolinsky Camp for Wives of Traitors of the Homeland, the acronym of which, ALZHIR, sounded like Algiers.

Almost every day Seva gave me news about neighbors and friends. Among others, the father of Yura Selivansky. Among others, the father of Sofa Bespalova. Among others, the stepfather of Lena Berzin. Among others, the prince. That's what he called Prince Svyatopolk-Mirsky, who was often at Lida's.

I replied in kind. Among others, the mother of Elka. Among others, the father of Nadya Suvorova. Among others, the father of Margit Krayevskaya. Among others, Tanev. Among others, Popov. Among others . . . Among others . . . It was like a game. And we were so scared. And then somehow we'd get over the fear.

Almost every evening we used Mama's Moscow Committee pass to go to the theater. The Meyerhold. The Chamber. The Vakhtangov. The Moscow Art. The Korsh. My hair looked so good. I secretly borrowed my mother's dark blue, almost-black dress with the white round collar. Seva described it in the poem he had dedicated to me. And I'd be flying again. The familiar corner by the pharmacy. The skating rink. Poetry.

Winter vacation began, and Egorka was sent to Kuntsevo. I begged Mama to let me stay in Moscow. We compromised on a week in town and a week "in the air." On the thirtieth of December I decorated the tree. The Nun baked her amazing *mazurki,* like meringues. No one else knew how to make them. She told me they used to bake them at the convent for feast days. Their aroma filled the house. I waited to be called for dinner, but Mama and Papa were shut up in their room and didn't emerge. The Nun set the table and went to bed. I called my parents, but they didn't come out right away. Both were downcast and pale. I couldn't tell if they were tired, upset, or sick, because we ate in silence. I asked if they liked the tree and Papa said that all trees are beautiful before the party. I couldn't tell if that was praise for my work or not.

He got up, went over to the tree, sniffed it, and said that in Tiflis when he was little, his sisters did a tree for Christmas. Mama asked me to clear the table. She said, almost apologetically, "I'm just not up to it." I thought, "She's sick. For New Year's. What a shame." I took the dishes to the kitchen and went to their room. Papa was at his desk tossing the dice from his *nardy*. Sitting and tossing. Mama, fully dressed, lay on the bed.

"Are you sick?"

"No."

But I had already guessed that she wasn't. I tried desperately to figure out who had been arrested. Who? And for the first time I knew that our turn was coming, inexorably and soon.

Mama said, "Go to bed. You have a holiday tomorrow." And the fact that she had left the holiday for me alone simply confirmed that it was coming.

I lay down and fell asleep immediately. It must have been a reaction to my anxiety. I awoke just as suddenly. I could hear a popular tango that Seva liked coming from the restaurant downstairs. That meant it was before two, when the band stopped, although just before the holiday they might have played later. It was dark in the dining room, but there were voices in my parents' room. I went to the door. And I could hear my mother blow her nose. Then she spoke, crying. I had never seen her cry. She kept repeating "all my life" and sobbing. "All my life," and a sob. Papa replied softly, but I couldn't make out his words.

Suddenly she shouted, "I've known Styopa all my life. Do you know what that means? I've known him three times longer than you. Understand? Do you understand?"

Then only sobs. And a creak and slippers shuffling on the floor—Papa had gotten out of bed. I jumped away from the door, afraid he was coming out. But he began pacing the room—five steps to the window, five to the bed, like a pendulum. He struck a match.

Mama began speaking again, "Tell me, do you believe it? Do you believe this nightmare?" She had stopped crying. "Do you believe that Agasi . . . Do you believe that Pavel, that Shurka . . . Do you believe that they . . . ?" She didn't complete her sentences, but it was clear. Then she spoke calmly and softly and said, "I know that you can't believe it."

Papa replied in a strange, pleading voice, "But, Rufa-*djan,* how can I not believe?" After a pause, he went on. "They're not arresting you and me, after all."

"What?" Mama was either laughing or crying. "We'll get ours! And soon!"

Mama reminds me of Batanya, I thought. *But Papa, how can he?*

I couldn't stand by their door anymore. My feet were like ice and I was shivering so hard I was afraid they'd hear my teeth chattering.

I crawled under my blanket, but the shivering didn't stop. I shut my eyes and pictured Styopa Korshunov's happy face, his curly hair, flaxen like a village boy's. When he visited us, Mama and he behaved like children: Rufka and Styopa. They kept reminiscing about the time they'd stolen carrots from the Chinese gardens and tried to swim across the Chitinka River with them. How they were diving and Styopa got into a whirlpool and how he was saved by Mama's Uncle Mosya Bronshtein, young then, and who had died on the ice of Kronstadt, putting down the sailor's rebellion. He taught his nephews and their friends, including Styopa, a "stylish" swimming stroke. Mama was an excellent swimmer. When my parents went on their annual vacation on the Black Sea, Papa joked that they'd get to play their favorite roles. Mama could be a fish and he, a mountain goat. He loved the mountains.

I don't remember my parents' attitude toward the families of their friends who were arrested before Papa, or who was arrested when. They seemed to go all at once. Earlier it had been only Lyova Alin and Styopa Korshunov. But that night Mama had named Pavel Bronich and Shura Breitman. After Lyova's arrest his wife, Fanya, came to us often. Mama seemed unusually kind and attentive to her. Styopa Korshunov had been secretary of the Irkutsk Oblast Party Committee, and Mama was very worried about his wife and newborn child. But she was arrested soon after, and we had no further information about them.

46

The next morning I got up late. Papa was having tea in the dining room, appearing gray and grim. I looked at him and he turned his head sadly, as if he'd been able to see me standing by their door the night before. Mama was gone, but Papa didn't go to the office—he worked in his room. My girlfriends came over with food for the party, so much that we filled up both windowsills— and they were very wide. Papa said it was wrong not to have any fruit, so he gave me some money and told me to buy apples and tangerines. I was glad for an excuse to call Seva and go to the store with him. When we got back, Mama had come home for lunch. Seva declined to join us, and so I saw him to the stairs. On the right-hand side of the corridor, there was a big reddish brown seal on the third door from the lobby. A weight hung from a tiny string embedded in the wax. Seva stared at me. "The people who lived here became among others last night," I replied to his unspoken question.

Those seals that jumped into your eyes appeared on many doors on every floor of our building over the winter of 1936–37, and especially in the spring of 1937. The seals were broken in a few days. Under the supervision of Commandant Brant, two or three suitcases and bundles of books were removed. The furniture and things that had the Comintern tags were cleaned. The floor polishers showed up, and in a few days a smiling Brant welcomed the new tenant and helped him with his things or called a porter. And right away, that same evening one of the kids would knock at the door and ask the standard question posed by all Muscovite children: "Do you have stamps?" The one who got there first would tell the other collectors to keep away.

The change in residents in our building kept pace with the arrests so that the population remained about the same. And the taking away of people became an ordinary, commonplace event. Quietly, at night, in the first half. So that the steps, cries, and occasional weeping were heard before three. I know of only one incident when the scenario was violated. Sometime in April or early May, I heard shots from upstairs. I didn't realized at first what it was, but it took place at night, long after the restaurant music had stopped. The shots excited me and made me happy. I realized that for many nights I had been waiting and waiting for something unusual to happen. I looked out of the window but saw nothing. I wanted to creep out into the hallway, but when I opened the door to the dining room I saw Papa. A white figure in the predawn dusk—he was in his underwear, standing and smoking. Without taking the cigarette out of his mouth, inhaling quickly, the tip flaring and almost vanishing as he puffed.

"Is that shooting?" I said, even though there was no need to ask. I was sure.

Papa didn't answer my question. He said, "Go to bed." He sat down in the armchair and lit a second cigarette with his first.

In the morning I learned in the communal kitchen from the kids and nannies that a German Communist named Eisenberg (I think I have his name right) from the third or fourth floor had done the shooting. He had killed two NKVD men and wounded another and himself. (Or had they shot him?) I didn't know the man. I may have seen him in the hallway, but I couldn't picture him. I asked the kids and tried to question some nannies from the upper floors. No one wanted to talk to me about him, but he became a hero for me.

This was a break, a chasm in my consciousness. I couldn't connect the thought that he was a hero, that everyone should shoot when they come for him, with my conviction that our country was the best, and that the whole world needed the Revolution. With the conviction that "we will build a better world."

I was sure that if they came for Papa he would shoot too. Definitely. But I chased that thought away with my ever-weakening hope that they wouldn't come for him. *And even today I am still convinced that if they had arrested Papa at home and not at his office, he would have shot at someone. Why am I so certain? The childish silly faith that your father is the strongest and bravest man in the world? Just as your mother is the most beautiful and kind? I don't know. But I'm sure he would not have gone quietly.*

At lunch Papa unexpectedly asked, "Well, you can't live without Seva, right?" I felt myself blush and looked down at my plate.

"Fine," Papa said. "And how about him?"

I gathered up all my strength and said, "Him too!"

And Papa said in Armenian, *"Sirta vorkanot shusha e chi sokhana."* He translated, " 'The heart is like glass: if you break it, you can't repair it.' "

Mama said, "Gevork . . ." I looked at her, waiting for her to start the usual, "Don't talk like that in front of the child." But she smiled and looked at me, then at Papa. There were tears in her eyes.

I put on my new blouse for the party. Our unsmiling Nun was pleased by the way it fit me and with her embroidery, which was lovely, astonishingly symmetrical, and in delicate colors. And I looked good in light blue, although I was a bit embarrassed by its transparency. The guests came early, and by eight o'clock the two rooms we were allotted—mine and the dining room—were crowded, and everyone wanted to sit down at the table. Elka's voice was lost in the noise. She insisted that you can't start a New Year's party before eleven, but it had begun already. A record was spinning on Lida's record player, and people were dancing. Some kids in my room were playing flirt—it was the first time I had seen the game and I was about to pick up the cards myself. But one of the girls asked me to get a large platter, so I went to the kitchen. I looked into Egorka's room, and Mama was on his bed in her new red dress. It didn't become her at all. Papa, looking official in a suit and tie, was sitting next to her, patting her shoulder, and trying to persuade her to go out. I think they were expected at the Mikoyans'. Mama, almost weeping, asked him to go alone. "I can't, I can't," she repeated piteously. "I'll stay with the children. We can't leave them here alone."

"Of course we can; they're not children. And nothing will happen to them from two bottles of Napareuli wine and a bottle of champagne. We can leave our Akhchik alone. I understand

these things better than you, Rufa-*djan*. And she's not alone; she
has her Romeo. Right, Juliet?"

He turned to me. Horrors. I had read *Othello* before going to
see Ostuzhev play the part at the Maly Theater. But I hadn't read
any other Shakespeare. But I nodded. Another lie!

But Seva, Mika, and Igor hadn't arrived yet, and I was beginning to worry about them. I wanted to call, but I didn't want to
call. I was mad at them for spoiling the party.

Papa persuaded Mama to go to the Mikoyans'. Before leaving
they stopped in the dining room and Mama wished us all a happy
new year, and we wished them luck. In the entry Mama kissed
me. I was sorry to see her so pale and skinny, with red swollen
eyes. She didn't even seem pretty.

Seva still hadn't come. I called and Masha said he had left
three hours ago. I was worried. Seva, Mika, and Igor finally
showed up a few minutes before twelve, as we were opening
the champagne. Everyone was shouting, clinking glasses with
their friends and across the table. I wanted to join my glass
with Seva's, but he was looking the other way. I had two or
three sips of champagne—it tickled and tasted good. When I
stood up my head spun, but it went away quickly. People were
throwing tangerine peels, bread crusts, and streamers across
the table. They landed in the potato salad and the herring.
Both were made with onion and the smell nauseated me. Seva
was far away and wouldn't look at me, and neither would
Mika. Igor was in the corner gazing out the window.

The guests pushed the table back against the wall—I thought
they wanted to dance. But they took the record player to my room
and danced in the dark. Some people went into Mama's room,
and when I looked I saw a couple on the couch in the bay window
and one on the bed hugging. They started playing spin the bottle
in the dining room, a game that Seva joined in with great enthusi-
asm. He went out into the entry to kiss more frequently than the
others. And most frequently with Elka.

I went to Egorka's room and stood with my head pressed
against the window. Then I went to the kitchen to wash out the
disgusting herring plates with cold tap water. Igor came in, and

I asked him where they had been. He told me he'd never go anywhere with Mika again. They had gone to visit some older girls. One was named Tamara. Mika wanted the same thing that Igor's father, Misha Rossinsky, had desired earlier when he left him and Seva with those "professional" girls. Igor started to leave as soon as he understood what was up, but Mika locked himself in the other room with one of the girls. And Seva wouldn't leave without him. In fact he didn't want to go at all; Igor had to force him. Igor was almost weeping as he told me. So was I.

Then the guests started bringing in platters of food to the kitchen. There was an awful lot left; Mama had been right. The Nun's *pirozhki* and the sweets were what got eaten the most. And Papa was right also—all the apples and tangerines were gone. The kids wanted to go for a walk, then changed their minds, and couples filed to not only my parents room, but Egorka's and mine. Then everyone left at about the same time. Mika played the fool, threw his coat over his head, and kissed my hand. I didn't like it. Seva stood around in the entry and left with the rest. The party was over. It had never been one for me.

I put on my robe and started sweeping up the peels, streamers, and squashed food. I wanted to get it done before my parents came home. And the Nun. I was ashamed to have them see the place looking like this. When the rooms were clean and aired and the onion smell was gone, I tackled the kitchen. I remembered we had forgotten to light the candles. I lit them and turned off the overhead light. It was fresh and quiet and the flames danced. The tree gave off a snowy forest smell again. The phone rang. In a strange and deep voice Seva said, "Happy New Year." I was quiet, pleased but still a bit angry. Then he said, "Mama kisses you." And added, "So do I." He hung up. We had never kissed. Not in words, not in action. They were strange words. I thought about them and ran my hand over a candle flame, not painfully.

My parents came home. Mama asked, "How was your party?"

"Good, good, really good." At that moment it was true, because I had forgotten everything that had happened before Seva's phone call.

In the winter of 1939 Seva and I walked past the Luxe. He looked up at our former windows and asked if I remembered that party. I said, "And how." Then he told me he written some doggerel about that night. All I remember is "The girl took Mika, undraped him and raped him." I reminded him that he had another poem about that night. I read the one about "Let me kiss you, I said to Tamara. And she agreed. It was a dream."

"Really? Are you sure that I wrote it and that it was about that night?" Seva asked.

"I am!"

After the new year Mama sent me to Kuntsevo. I walked alone a lot and joined the others in the living room only in the evenings. It was the same crowd as usual. There was a new boy with beautiful green eyes that looked like a cat's. I don't remember his name, but I liked him, so much so that I played dominoes with him, a game I hated. One day after lunch he disappeared. That evening a girl said that his father had been arrested in the night and he had returned to town. It was the same here: someone joined the "among others."

But it was good in the forest. I walked on skis or on foot, sinking into the deep snow, getting it packed into my felt boots. Egorka and I shared the room we always had when we were in Kuntsevo with our parents, but then we had to sleep on couches. Now I could luxuriate in the unusually wide bed and read until dawn if I wanted to. In the evening Egorka would threaten to tell Mama that I read all night. Then he'd fall asleep. And I enjoyed myself with my book.

On the last Saturday of vacation Mama and Papa came. And on Sunday Seva and Elka arrived on skis. I had been inviting them since last year to visit Kuntsevo. Not together of course. And it turned out that we couldn't bring them into the dining room. All that sparkling silver, the starched napkins, the *zakuski,* and the waitresses in little caps were not for my friends. We were told it was our own fault, that you have to pay for your guests ahead of time in Moscow. When Papa returned to the room after his negotiations he looked as if he had a toothache. It's a good thing Egorka was with Seva and Elka in the living room then.

We went to lunch without them. Mama gathered up the

zakuski, bread, mineral water, and fruit from our table and took them to our room, so my friends didn't go hungry. But I was disgusted by that incident, and I think Mama was too. It was after the incident that she stopped insisting I go with them every Saturday. And Mama began begging off from the luxurious weekends. Without Papa she must have felt like an outsider. And even with him. I had the feeling that they never did become "Soviet aristocrats."

Papa went away somewhere and returned only in late March. I never got a straight answer as to where he had been. It was either to lecture in Minsk or "none of your business." Egorka and I, although removed from Comintern business because of our age, nevertheless knew there were many situations in which the only answer Mama could give was "none of your business." Privately, I decided that Papa had been to Spain, which made it interesting. And better. I thought that the trip made it impossible for Papa to become an "among others." But perhaps I made up Spain completely. Mama always denied he had gone there.

47

Seva did not return to school after vacation because he fell ill. A triple dose—German measles, chicken pox, and measles. Mama decided I should not visit him, but Aunt Ronya lifted the ban, saying I'd had all the childhood diseases, that I couldn't get them myself, and I couldn't bring the infection back to Egorka. I started going every day, and we were together until evening.

Winter. Early 1937. On the way home from school I ran past people in front of the building of the Procuracy USSR. It used to be the Moscow Party Committee building, where Mama had worked. I used to pass the doorman and skip to her room or to "the favorite of Moscow laborers and metropolitan workers," Lazar Moiseyevich Kaganovich, to get pencils and paper from him for my classmates. Now a trial was being held in that building. Demonstrators outside were demanding the death sentence for the enemies of the people. It's not that I was opposed, but I didn't like these shouting, agitated people and their parading around. It was upsetting and made me tremble inside, as at exam time. Or before surgery. Was it fear? Maybe because among the defendants was the father of Yura P., a boy I knew slightly. They called him "cornflower" for his very blue eyes, and that embarrassed him. I was embarrassed too (maybe that I knew him) as I made my way through the crowd to the other side of the street. It used to be called Bolshaya Dmitrovka and now it was Pushkin Street. I turned onto Moscow Art Theater Alley, the new name for Seva's Kamergersky Street.

Masha opened the door and went to the kitchen. While I took off my coat, Rayechka, the wife of the writer Mark Kolosov, peeked out into the hallway. There were four rooms in the apartment—two belonged to the Bagritskys and two to the Kolosov family. Later they would have three. After Lida was arrested, Kolosov took over Seva's room. Rayechka was round, pregnant. When last winter the newspapers were full of the law to ban abortion, Seva said that Rayechka would invariably be pregnant now. I remember her always pregnant and always peeking out at the sound of the doorbell.

Seva was in bed with his triple illness. His face and hands were covered with spots, which were smeared with a white salve and the purple of gentian violet. He was cranky sometimes and Lida asked me what to make for him and then suggested that I feed him. He ate better that way.

Seva realized this. He liked it, and it got to the point where he wouldn't let Masha dust or clear dishes. "Let Lusia," he would say. Lida had been medicating his spots, but then Seva demanded that I do it. We agreed that I would do him above the waist, then leave and let Lida finish. There was both playfulness and something serious about all this.

While Seva slept in the daytime, I went to Lida's room. Her sisters, Olya and Sima, were often there. Gradually I stopped feeling like a girl visiting their son and nephew and came to feel like their friend: the difference in our ages didn't matter. Our relationship has lasted to this day. It was due primarily to Lida that this happened when I was only fourteen. She was the one who accepted me that way. My relationship with her was deep, familial, and frank. It was at first tied to Seva and later to our common grief and memory of him. With Olya my friendship developed from my early crush on her. I had wanted to be just like her, with the same hairdo, the same dresses, and to laugh, walk, and be angry just like her. This childish need to be like Olya, however, passed with the years.

48

Before his illness, Seva and I never talked about our feelings. Did I ever think about that? I don't know. Probably, but I was shy. No one ever recalled my childhood title, "our lawful bride," except Masha—not Seva, not Lida, not her sisters. Seva was getting up now, but lay on the bed dressed—a semi-invalid. I sat at the table by the window and did my homework, while he read a book on the bed. Then he said, "Put out the light."

I asked if his eyes were hurting again, the way they had at the height of his illness. He said no.

"Then why?"

"I want you to."

I got up and turned off the light. He asked me to sit on the bed. I sat facing the window, feeling Seva's feet at my back. The cross of the window sash was visible in the dark. There must have been a moon. When my eyes adjusted, it didn't seem so dark in the room.

"Do you love me?" Seva asked.

I said nothing.

Then he said, "I love you."

"I love you, too," I said. And I thought, *What now? What should I do?*

Just then the door opened and Lida asked, "Why sit around in twilight? May I turn on the light?"

"Yes," Seva said.

The light hurt my eyes. I squinted and didn't see Seva's face but I could feel mine turning unbearably red. Then I looked at him and at Lida. Seva, jokingly, said, "Love and marriage . . . Why are you blushing?" That was intended for me. And to Lida, "Lusia is my fiancée."

Lida smiled and said, "Some news. I've known that for many years."

I felt I could breathe again. I had been short of air. My color went back to normal. Everything was normal. And easy. No discomfort.

From that evening on we talked about love. Funny. Silly. In detail. We talked about where to live. Here, in his room. When it would happen. Seva said after final exams in tenth grade. How many children? Seva said three. Two boys and a girl. The first boy would be called Edya.

"What about the second son and the girl?"

"That's up to you."

I walked home in the light snow, skipping. And thinking, "Artur and Agatha, no, Pavlik and Polinka, no. All right, the boy would be Seryozha and the girl Lena." Then I changed my mind—I'd leave Lena but still think about the boy. There was time.

I saved Seva's seat at our school desk while he was out sick. For a time Elka sat with me. I warned her that it was only until Seva returned and then she'd have to go back to Nadya Suvorova. She left and Igor Shiryaev joined me, and in fact I liked him. But I told him that everyone knew Seva was near-sighted and that he had to sit in the first row. "So only until Seva comes back, and in fact, you'd better change now." Igor left.

At last Seva returned. I hadn't noticed how much he had grown at home, but now he was much taller than me, even though I was one of the tallest girls in the class.

My birthday was coming and Mama asked whom I was planning to invite to my party. With feigned horror she added,

"You're not going to have a whole crowd, the way you did for New Year's?"

I reassured her that I didn't want another party like that. Mama gave me ice skates. She said she hoped I wouldn't lose these. That meant she remembered the ones I said I lost when Zharko didn't return them. She gave me Papa's present, a small black pen with a green permanent nib made by Parker. A present like that in those years! It was the first Parker I ever saw, the first permanent pen in my life, in our class. It did turn out to be permanent. It hasn't worked in a long time, but it is one of my chief treasures.

I had my party. The boys were Seva, Mika, Igor, Goga, and Liska. They all had books for me. And Seva gave me a bouquet of gillyflowers, which caused me to blush. So did he. The girls had different presents—a cup, embroidery threads and hoops, an elephant figurine, a vase, an album. There were girls from school, Elka and Nadya, and from the Luxe, Roza Iskrova, Magda Furboten, and Lusya Chernina.

Lusya told me that she really liked Igor, and I wanted them to spend more time together. Maybe then Igor would forget about Lyolya, who didn't love him at all. Once, while Seva was sick, I sent Lusya in my stead to a concert with Igor, and he didn't get angry. So I had hope. I wanted everybody to love somebody and everyone to be happy. And I was glad that Egorka as usual followed Seva around and gazed at him adoringly.

After dinner we listened to Leshchenko's songs on records Igor had brought. I could tell that Mama didn't approve, because Leshchenko was considered almost counterrevolutionary. And I was grateful that she said nothing. Then we went for a walk, on our usual circuitous route. But at the bridge Seva held me back and when the others went around the Kremlin and turned onto the embankment, we ran over the bridge, down to Lebyazhy Alley, and then on the boulevard past the museum.

It was our first time alone at night. A different walk. Different words. And my hand stayed in his hand in his pocket the whole time. We stood that way for a while by my front door and then I went upstairs. My room smelled of gillyflowers, and the scent made me dizzy. Or maybe it wasn't the scent.

We went skating, as we had the year before. Not to Petrovka, where all the kids went, but to Gorky Park. It was wonderful there. We could skate in the rink, or slide on the walks along the river. The music from the rink gradually faded. The streetlamps were reflected like lilies of the valley in the gleaming ice. And then we could skate back to the strains of a waltz. I once told Seva that this park had been built and run by Mama's friend Betti Glan. Seva laughed and said, "Thank you, Betti-petti-metti." Why was that so funny?

We usually walked home along the Ring Road, where there were still trees. I would break off twigs to grow leaves, as I had when Lena was alive. I set up bottles in my room and in Seva's. It was almost mine, too. I don't remember how I studied in those months, but every day I absorbed new poetry. And everything that I memorized then I remember now, while much of what I learned later is gone. Seva had a new poet every day, Blok, Kuzmin, Gumilyov, Khodasevich, Balmont, Sologub, all the Symbolists, Annensky, Karolina Pavlova, Akhmatova, the anthology *Reader-Declaimer*. And basically it was "Tikhonov, Selvinsky, Pasternak." It's not that I forgot Pushkin, but I lived that winter and spring on other poets.

49

And spring, boisterous spring, came upon us. March vacation. *Dame aux camelias* at the Meyerhold Theater. Seva called before the theater. Excited me. I said, "By the pharmacy, as usual," and hung up. Papa looked at me closely and thoughtfully and said, as if talking to himself over the chessboard, "Looks like it's really Romeo and Juliet."

April 1—back to school and practical jokes. It was so warm that I took off my elastic stockings (I had silk ones, but I saved them for the theater) and went to school in socks. Maybe the climate was different in Moscow then. Or is it just my age?

Seva's birthday was approaching, and I worried about what to get him. I wanted my present to be with him forever, to last forever. Mama promised to think about it. Later she asked, "Do you like Papa's Caucasian belt?"

"Of course. And I'm used to it."

As far back as I could remember, Papa had always worn that belt with its unusual buckle and the silver dangling ornaments over his navy blue uniform. Papa put on a suit only for special occasions and then he tucked the dangles into the belt loops.

"It's practically eternal," Mama said. "I gave it to Gevork before Egorka was born."

"Was it expensive?"

"Not very. But we have to ask someone to bring it to Moscow."

A few days later Mama unwrapped a package before me. There were two black belts with silver ornaments. They may have been less fancy than Papa's, but I liked them better.

"Who's the second one for?"

"Papa. The eternity of belts comes to an end. I'll give this one to Gevork for his birthday."

"When's Papa's birthday?"

"In September."

"Why don't we ever celebrate it?"

"Because his father died that day."

I decided I would give Papa a present that year, but it wasn't to be. He was already gone by September.

On Seva's birthday, April 19, I was in Kuntsevo. A greenhouse there served two rest homes—for the Comintern and the Central Committee. You could buy flowers year round, both bouquets and potted plants. I purchased a pot with three tall purple hyacinths. Mama let me go to Moscow alone, even though it was Saturday and they were staying overnight. It turned out to be our last trip to Kuntsevo. We didn't go during the May holidays. Later Batanya, the Nun, and Egorka went to the dacha. I didn't say goodbye to Kuntsevo, but I remember the slope to the bridge, the whimsically twisting river with overgrown banks, and the dark forest in the distance. And the discomfort in dealing with the residents of the rest homes—from young to old.

Carrying the flowerpot I approached the intersection of Gorky Street and Moscow Art Theater Street and saw Seva race out of his driveway on a bicycle. Bent low over the wheel, he flew into Telegrafny Alley. Whizzing by. Unreal. Like a vision. I was terrified for him, even as I was amazed by the beauty of the vision. The flutter of Seva's blue shirt, the whirl of the spokes, the speed. I stopped, frightened by the new, powerful and agitated feeling that filled my heart. I think that I truly fell in love with Seva at the precise second that fear stabbed me.

Lida opened the door. She was dressed up, and Sima was wearing a light blue blouse.

"Where did Seva go?" I asked anxiously.

"To Oriental Sweets. He claims that you can't live without them."

"She can't live without Seva," Igor said, looking out from the living room. Olya's very loud and penetrating laughter came from the room. And then Yuri Karlovich's voice, "That's not funny. It's very serious." Yuri Karlovich looked so unhappy that I lost my desire to laugh. But he was like that often. I sometimes wondered how Olya managed to laugh so much around him. He repeated, "Especially with the flowers. Very serious."

Everyone was happy at dinner. No. At dinner everyone tried to be happy. But Lida gave herself away with her sunken eyes and her smile, in which the eyes had no part. Sima's eyes were red and swollen. But no one mentioned anyone who had become one of the "among others." Conversation stopped when we heard the elevator and the door slamming. Then we would all resume talking. At once. Loudly. Or did it just seem loud? We were waiting in Lida's room, the way we did at the Luxe at night. The way everyone did everywhere. But the time for us hadn't come yet.

Lida would still send Seva on a vacation to the Caucasus. Then Papa would be arrested. I would write to Seva. And he would fly home as soon as he got it. On the street outside the main entrance to our building he would give me a coral necklace that he bought with the money left over from his ticket. When Lida returned from the camps and exile to Moscow, she told me she was eternally grateful to me for that letter. Seva would not have come home without it. And they would not have seen each other before her arrest and before he went off to war.

The authorities came for Lida in early July. One day earlier she and Sima had stood in line to see some boss in the NKVD. He didn't say anything about Narbut and Postupalsky, but he did mention to Lida that she wasn't supposed to ask—she wasn't anyone to Postupalsky. Lida got hysterical and shouted some things at him. But when they came for her, she was calm. The arrest warrant had her name incorrectly as "Bagritskaya, Lidya Georgiyevna." They had been in such a hurry that they'd mixed her patronymic up with his. She refused to go with the wrong warrant. Strange as it may seem, they left her apartment. Lida vanished for three days to get her teeth fixed. (Just as in the normal course of life, people had trouble with their teeth and other matters.)

Perhaps if she had disappeared completely the NKVD would have forgotten about her. There had been situations like that— the NKVD had too much work. Lida returned on August 3, however, and the police came for her the next day. I was just about to walk home and Seva was going to escort me. We were in the hallway, and he opened the door just as the bell rang. There were three men. Polite. Calm.

Sima, Seva, and I sat on the couch while Lida packed a suitcase. One man stood in the hallway near the open door to the room (I noted that Rayechka didn't look out at all when they came and the Kolosovs were as quiet as mice in the daytime) while the other two rummaged in the cupboard, closets, and shelves, transferring all the papers to the table. One sat down and went through them. The second put them back. I don't remember if they kept a record of the search.

Lida shut her suitcase and sat down opposite us. Seva silently moved to a chair next to his mother and put his arm around her. After the search concluded, everyone went out into the hall. Lida said something to Masha, kissed Sima and me, and pressed close to Seva. She was short, just reaching his shoulder. She kissed him several times and pulled away. She said, "So sad that you're still so little." A man touched her arm, and she jerked away and walked out to the stairs. They followed. The door shut. They were gone. They had taken her away.

The Oleshas arrived right afterward. Yuri Karlovich said it was a good thing they hadn't taken Bagritsky's papers; it meant they would let Lida go soon. Sima said she had a horrible headache and that she would be arrested soon. She lay down on the cot. The Oleshas left, and so did we—to go to Seva's room. We sat in the dark on the bed, huddling, and I felt Seva trembling. But he didn't cry. Then he started talking. Not about his mother, but his father. How they took him away to the hospital. How Lida had brought Seva there once. He thought his father was getting better, but the next day Bagritsky died. Then he realized he was there to say goodbye. He said he would live in Odessa or with the Oleshas. He had to make it to sixteen and then he'd get a job. I heard his every word. But at some point I fell asleep.

He said, "Are you asleep?"

"No."

I saw light in the window. Morning. Mama didn't know where I was. We walked down the empty, dead street. Another dawn. Also pink, but very different. At the entrance we touched each other with cold lips, and Seva went back without a glance. Why did I let him return to an empty house? What was I afraid of? My tears? Mama?

Mama was at the table, clouds of smoke floating over her. She said, "Show me your panties." I didn't understand, but I picked up the hem of my dress and pulled down my panties. And stood there. A second, an eternity? I don't know. Unspilled tears, hatred, and pity consumed me. I went to bed and covered my face with the sheet. The hatred passed. I cried and then told her. "They arrested Lida." Mama lit a cigarette and replied with a question addressed into space, "God, what did they get her for?"

I never heard Mama ever use her beloved "golden youth" in reference to Seva. I sensed he had become "her own" for her that night just as I had been Lida's own for a long time. But soon Mama would become "among others," and we would grow up. Fast in some ways, slow in others.

In the early spring of 1941 I came to Moscow to apply for permission to see Mama. Seva had been married and divorced, all in one month. I learned about it from his letter—after the divorce. From the train I went to the Art Theater Alley, as usual. Masha opened the door and Rayechka looked out. In his room Seva sat on the bed, half dressed. A strange woman was finishing dressing in the middle of the room, and she instantly slipped out the door. I asked Seva, "Who's that?"

"No one!"

There were two rings with large dark stones on the table. I picked them up and threw them violently out the window.

"You idiot, how will I ever give them back?"

"Don't."

We had breakfast and discussed the best way to write my appeal. Seva had experience, having gone to visit Lida already. I took off to the Gulag office. Later that day a friend told me that Seva was having "an affair with a stunning woman, the wife of composer D."

That evening I was walking down Gorky Street and Seva was coming toward me. Pale, his light-colored coat unbuttoned. He lifted his arm in greeting and stood swaying. He opened his mouth, but said nothing. I could smell the alcohol on his breath and I recoiled. Then I walked around him and ran toward Sovetskaya Square, stopping at the corner. I was ashamed to leave him alone, and I ran back. He was at the curb, perhaps considering whether he should cross or not, and I led him home. Masha and I undressed him and put him to bed. Masha scolded me for letting him get so drunk. I told her I had nothing to do with it.

"Oh, this isn't the first time for him," she went on in a whisper. "It's time for you to come back for good. You're not a little girl anymore."

She returned to the kitchen, and I sat near Seva's bed. He was snoring. He had never snored before. I used to be able to lie next to him and sleep quietly through the night. No more! And that woman in the morning! And that stupid month-long marriage! And the alcohol!

I walked out on the balcony. We had slept here so often, the two of us or with Egorka or Seva's Igor. I was always by the wall, and Seva by the rail. Out here on the balcony he had chosen our common star—Vega. Now I no longer knew if we had been born under a common star and would be together forever. Or whether we'd have children, Edya and a girl, whose name I hadn't yet chosen. It grew cold. I quietly set the chair to keep the balcony door open, and I left to spend the night at Elka's house on Stankevich Street.

Did I betray Seva that night? A little at first, when I was on the street? And then completely, when I left? But I know I wasn't ready to do it any other way. Little? Seva always used to say, "You can't go to the Hermitage . . . to the party . . . you're too little." I guess I grew up only in the war.

My God, memory has led me so far from that evening of April 19, 1937, when we sat around the party table in Lida's room, celebrating Seva's fifteenth birthday.

> *I never gave anyone anything.*
> *I never loved after my fifteenth birthday.*
> *I stayed and lived with a half-mad old woman.*
> *I'm dressed and shod by that old sorceress.*
>
> Vsevolod Bagritsky (*1941*)

We sat through dinner and tried to be merry. Then Yuri Karlovich said he had to go somewhere. Igor also left; he was writing a sonata, or thought he was. Seva said, "Let's go," and we rode up in the elevator, not down. Then walked up two short flights of stairs, and Seva opened a door. We were in the attic, and Seva held me by the hand and led me through obstacles and lumber on our way to the skylight. He clambered out and, once on the roof he hauled me up. Below was the street, cars moving, the dark silhouette of the building under construction, where the ice cream parlor is now. We could see the Kremlin and the city, much farther than from the balcony of Lida's room. It was chilly and my head spun. But I felt no fear—I wanted to fly. I hugged Seva. He put his arms around me and nuzzled my neck. And began kissing my neck and chin on his side. Then we sat on the edge of the skylight. And kissed! For the first time! We sat for a long time, without moving, our lips pressed together, but not even kissing. We didn't have the strength to get up or to stir.

And suddenly I realized that there was something in my pocket. The belt. How silly! I'd forgotten to give him his present. I laughed, and that was a release of tension. We looked at each other, and Seva asked, "Why are you laughing?"

"I forgot the present."

"What present?" He didn't understand. I took out the belt. And we started pushing it through the belt loops on Seva's trousers. On the roof! Which was not easy, even though the roof was not steep. All the kids from Seva's building could confirm that. Many people liked being up there, but I don't know if any of them went upstairs to kiss. Pretty soon they all knew why we went there. Seva called my present a "virginity belt" and added, to embarrass me, "only until school's over." The next year he wrote a poem, "All that's left is the belt you gave me. Station. Whistle. Train leaving. Farewell, farewell, my dear." That was when I became a Leningrader again, against my will. Each time I had to go, it was like having a heart attack. Two years later, Seva wrote. "You'll marry. So will I. Alas, we'll say. A portrait in a square frame will leap upon the desk to remember youth by heart." And a few months later, "Suddenly a note on my desk today. My God! You're back, then. Nearby. I can't believe it."

It got warmer. Day and night we were drawn to the roof. Not only to kiss, but to be there. To watch the stars over the Kremlin towers. We could see everything very well. The wooden scaffolding. The cables. The workmen. Or we'd sit close together, sometimes with a textbook. I'd read aloud and Seva would pretend to listen. Or, if he was reading someone's poetry, he'd say, "Read to yourself."

"You'll have to redo your exams or be left behind. You'll have an extra year of school," I would threaten. He'd insist that he'd manage somehow.

I was in good shape with school because I was determined to get Seva and Elka through exams. I had to write some of her papers, because she not only refused to study, but didn't want the bother of distinguishing chemistry from physics. She was having stormy affairs outside of school. One day she told me she had met Stalin's son and he was in love with her.

"What about you?"

"I'm still thinking." Elka laughed, revealing under the plump lips of her small mouth one crooked tooth, which was very becoming. She had become quite adult and even I, a girl, thought she was gorgeous. She was free of adult supervision. Her mother, whom she had feared, had been arrested. And I don't think she paid any attention at all to her father. Sometimes an aunt, or the vice principal, or someone else at school would lecture her. Not from our school, but from school 25, where the "big shot" children went. Elka met them at their parties.

I was with her a few times, and she introduced me to "her" Vasya and pointed out various VIP daughters and granddaughters. Vasya, despite his inarguably impressive and even romantic surname, which worked magic with all the girls, did not stir me. I just didn't like him. And as for falling in love—neither Apollo Belvedere nor heavenly angels would have attracted me in those days. Every hour without Seva seemed like the worst of my life.

As for the "famous" girls—the two Svetlanas, the daughters of Stalin and of Molotov, and Gorky's granddaughters Dasha and Marfa—they were younger and stuck up. I don't remember the other ones Elka pointed out.

When she invited me to a dance for the May holidays at the school, I didn't go. She didn't describe the dance to me, and she didn't bring up the "great" son (as Seva called him). But a new name appeared almost immediately, Arkan (or maybe it was a nickname), who "could do anything."

"Everyone's afraid of him."

"What school does he go to?"

Elka told me I was an idiot, everyone knew him, he didn't go to school, and there was no point in talking to me at all.

My love life! School life! But there was also life at home. By then our Luxe had turned into a disaster area. Of its five hundred "suites" (they used hotel terminology) almost every third door had the horrible wax seal. The mark of Cain. Or the seal would be removed because a new tenant had appeared. Some moved in for very brief periods. No sooner would you get used to a new face than it would vanish. And another seal on the door. You had to try very hard not to see it as you walked by, otherwise you couldn't live with the light that was inside you. It would flicker and die out. You would say hello to someone in the elevator or hall. And willy-nilly, you would catch yourself thinking, *When will he be arrested?* Or even more horrible, *What if they take Papa? What if they take him tomorrow?*

When they arrested Papa we were moved immediately from our four-room apartment to a single large room facing the court-yard on the second floor. A seal appeared on our old door. It jabbed me in the eyes every time I walked by. Behind the seal were all our books except for the children's books. The superin-tendent, the one who used to feign great love for our family, allowed us to take them. Batanya's big trunk was there too, the one from which she would take out silver things to sell at Torgsin, or a piece of fabric in order to make a "decent suit" for Papa or a new skirt for me. That trunk had been sealed during the search because Mama had no key for it.

The next day Batanya and Egorka came from the dacha. Our maid had vanished, afraid of being swept up. We "moved." And we discovered that we had no money in the house. Batanya had a bit, which she needed for a ticket to Leningrad. We got a telegram that Aunt Lyuba's husband, Monya, had died. Mama didn't react to the money problem. She didn't react to anything the first few days after Papa's arrest. Batanya said she could have sold a few things from the trunk, but now it was all lost. And we could have sold the books, even though books didn't sell for much. She said "all these people" were selling their books. And then she got on her hobbyhorse, saying that "they" should have thought at least two steps ahead. A normal person should have known and been concerned about the children at least. Then she would look at Mama and abruptly stop talking.

I figured out how to get our things, but I was afraid to tell them. I went to see our neighbors in suite 8. Sunarka's father had been arrested before ours, and they were planning to move somewhere (they didn't make it, because her mother was taken a few days later and Sunarka was sent to an orphanage). Toward evening I brought Mika and Borya Barinov to the Luxe, and we spent a couple of hours hanging around the hallways. When things quieted down, we went to Sunarka's, and into our old apartment through the balcony, which extended to my room. We began bringing in books—first onto the balcony, then to Sunarka's room, and then running on tiptoe down the hallway to our room. We dragged the trunk the same way. I was afraid the boys wouldn't be able to manage it, because it was so heavy and wouldn't fit. But it did! We broke only one windowpane. I was terrified when it fell. But there were no passersby outside and no one in the building heard it.

Batanya watched the whole procedure anxiously, but not with condemnation. Mama continued to say nothing. The sweaty, tired boys were ready to leave. I took them down the backstairs and came back. Mama still said nothing. Batanya praised me and gave me a small package to take to the common rubbish bin in the communal kitchen. I asked what it was. Batanya did not reply but looked over at the trunk—it no longer had the three reddish brown seals. Just an ordinary trunk. Solid.

It lived with us in Leningrad. It came back to Moscow. It was always in Mama's room. Now it's in mine. Someone recently said that it should have been thrown out long ago. Never! First of all, it might have been part of Batanya's dowry. And secondly, it's a witness—inanimate, but a witness nevertheless.

The number of children at the Luxe did not diminish as quickly as the number of adults taken away. The families were moved into the "Nepman" building in the courtyard. After some time the mother was usually arrested, and then the child was taken to an orphanage. Or by relatives. The ones who were older—like me—usually went off on their own. Sometimes the adolescents whispered questions like, "Do you know where—— went off to?" The name was sometimes Russian, more often foreign.

I asked about Lusya Chernina, and I got her address from someone who knew someone's still-not-arrested mother. She had gone off to her aunt in Stalingrad. I corresponded with her until the war and during the first year of the war, until I received the notice that "sanitary instructor Ludmila Chernina died valorously in the battle for the freedom and independence of our homeland." In Stalingrad! Lusya's mother was in the camps with mine. I later learned that they had adopted Lusya. And she died without knowing she had been adopted.

"They defended the homeland"—they said that about her, and Seva, and Villi Brodsky's son, and Petya Gastev, and Goga Roga-chevsky. About the many, many who perished. And so did we: Yura Dushenov, me, and the many others who survived, the "strange orphans" of 1937. It was during the war that our "strangeness" ended, for most only temporarily, and for the time we became like everyone else, even though we had been "like everyone else." Our exceptionality, if any, existed before the arrests and deaths of our "ideological" and "Party" parents.

When I finished school I applied to the journalism department. I did well in my entrance exams, but at the mandate commission (they had one then) I was told I was unsuitable. I was sorry, of course, and yet I didn't really mind. I didn't think it strange. I accepted it as any other event in the order of things. And with the same examination documents I entered the Herzen Institute.

That we were "like everyone else" is evident now much more than it was before. No matter what you read, what you pick up, whom you talk to—everyone has had a close relative or friend who was "illegally repressed." I always said that there are no people in the country who were not personally involved in this "strange" process. They were in these categories: "civil war," "speculators," "prostitutes," "former," "NEPmen," "hiding gold," "Promparty," "miners," "kulaks," "nationalists," "opposition," "from occupied territory," "POWs," "cosmopolites," "doctors," "Tatars," "Germans," "Chechens," "Ingush," "Balkars," "Kalmyks," "Balts," "Leningraders," "writers," "dissidents"—I must have left someone out, workers and peasants, soldiers, sailors and professors, intellectuals and illiterate, believers and atheists, Party members and non-Party people. Everyone, absolutely everyone—black and white, red-white-and-blue, or polka dot. Everyone has people who were arrested, exiled, shot. Perhaps a father,

*perhaps a mother, perhaps a brother, in-law, friend, neighbor, uncle,
aunt, sister, brother-in-law, sister-in-law. And they all had children
(the ones who were old enough)—children! And now grandchildren.
And when I hear people say that they didn't know, say, "God, could
it really have been like that?" or, more rarely, "It couldn't have been!"
I want to shout, "Don't believe them!" It means they didn't want to
see, didn't wish to know. And most importantly, it means that their
heart never ached, they never helped with a package, a letter, compassion, a word, a smile, a look, even a thought. They're not human. And
they're not "like everyone else." We, the "strange orphans," are the
real "like everyone else."*

50

The Pioneer room at the Luxe stopped functioning, and the
corridor became deserted and quiet. No longer did hordes of
"cossacks and robbers" gallop through them. The children who
had been "resettled" from the fancy floors to the "Nepman"
building sidled through the halls. When I became "resettled," I
made a point of making a lot of noise in my low-heeled shoes and
spoke very loudly. When I ran into Stella Blagoeva, the future
Bulgarian Minister of Foreign Affairs, and saw she was trying to
pretend I wasn't there, I barked a "Hello!" at her. That prompted
her to tell me I was brazen and obnoxious. She had a good
command of Russian.

Even the children who had not been resettled were subdued.
Sometimes I had the feeling that everyone in the beautiful Luxe
was hidden away like mice. Perhaps that's why the world revolution never came?

Even our irrepressible Egorka was subdued. His hallway nickname was Tiger Cub. Of course, as he began to read, his hobbies
changed. He would gulp down a book and if it struck a chord in
him, he'd sit down to write his own. He would outline the con-

tents in a thick notebook. His pen creaked, ink splattered, he panted. He made up new crises and fates for the heroes, the way he'd have liked things to happen and not the way the author had it. Then he read "his book" to everyone who came his way, even our housekeeper, the Nun. I was amazed that Papa listened to him as he moved his chessmen in the evenings. I thought Papa was pretending. But from his comments to the "author" I could tell he was paying attention.

Egorka developed a contrariness. In the evening Mama would say once, twice, three times, "Egorka, bedtime." Then Papa would say, "That's it, Egorka-*djan.*"

And then Egorka would whine, "Ma-a-a, I'll go, but can I read to you for a half hour, all right?"

Mama always agreed, the way she later agreed to read with her grandchildren.

I think that while the family, and national, tragedy of 1937 made me a non-neurotic person, more of a survivor, it broke and spoiled something that was good in Egorka. Perhaps the main God-given gift he had.

May 1 was coming. In the newspapers, along with the May First appeals, the wrathful condemnations and calls for increased vigilance, along with the tough talk, there was an article on the coming premiere of *Anna Karenina* at the Moscow Art Theater. People talked about it at home, at school, in the communal kitchen at the Luxe. They talked about it so much, I suppose, because it was an opportunity to rest from the daily avalanche of misery in the newspapers. They shouldn't read the papers! I had become a newspaper reader in December 1934 and only discovered this truth in the middle of 1936, after Gorky's death. Don't open the papers! Not even for the Spanish Civil War. I'd hear about Spain somewhere or other, or I could glance through Papa's messengered papers.

There was so much talk about *Anna Karenina* that I began reading it quickly. I had only read Tolstoy's *Childhood, Adolescence, and Youth, War and Peace,* and *Hadji Murat.*

A memory. My Tanya was reading War and Peace. *She was fifteen or so. In the summer, in Peredelkino. Viktor Borisovich*

Shklovsky came over. He looked. And said, "What happiness to be reading War and Peace *for the first time."*

We were at the second performance, I think, on May 2. Papa had bought the tickets two or three days before. Three tickets. When Papa said the third ticket was for me, Batanya compressed her lips. Then I heard Mama trying to soothe Batanya, telling her they had ordered two tickets for her for May 5. I guess Batanya forgave us. I don't remember whom she took with her. The three of us went to the play—Mama, Papa, and I. I hadn't been to the theater with them in a long time. Or with adults, actually. Around 1935 I started going alone, beginning with the Children's Theater, which was on Teatralny Square to the side of the Bolshoi, and then to all the other theaters. This was Papa's last time at the theater. And the last for Mama for many, many years. And the last for the three of us.

Our seats were in the second or third row. Two seats from the center aisle, on stage right. I had never had such good seats. Mama's pass was for a box, but I didn't like boxes. For many years afterward, I was always in the balcony, at best in dress circle. And now I can't even remember the last time I was at the Moscow Art Theater.

It's amazing that I can recall the tiniest details about us, the theater, the audience, and very little about the play itself. I do remember the scenery and props onstage, the costumes, especially of the actresses. Papa wore a suit, so he seemed a bit of a stranger. And he was pale. After his trip he began having stomach pains again. His ulcer. Mama was wearing her red dress. She was a hundred times more beautiful and more familiar in her blouse and usual suit. I had a suit from Torgsin that Batanya bought for me. But, to use Batanya's phrase, we looked "perfectly decent."

I thought that Alla Tarasova (although beautiful) hammed it up as Anna. I didn't like Vronsky (played by Massalsky). I liked Karenin (Khmelyov) despite his big ears. I liked Betsy. Especially her dress, which was very pale pink and ethereal. During the first intermission I fell in love with the buffet and the pastries and oranges from Spain. I have this vague sense that these were my first oranges. I had eaten only tangerines before—lots of them. They were sold everywhere in those days, even in the school cafeteria for a five-kopeck piece—round and juicy and wrapped in paper. After the buffet we strolled about in the lobby. I was in a good mood and could see that Papa wasn't particularly moved by the play either. None of the adults, dressed up and impor- tant—looking about, walking and laughing all around us— seemed moved by what they had seen on the stage.

During the second intermission Mama said that Batanya had been right. "You know, Gevork, we probably shouldn't have wasted the tickets on you and Lusia. You two should go to *Adrienne Lecouvreuer* or *No Pasarán*."

"We're romantics. Though it's too late for me. But she's at just the right age. Right?" he asked me.

I didn't know what to say, because I sensed something more in his words. But I didn't know what, so I said nothing.

Gradually the play drew me in and touched me. By the time of the scene with Seryozha, I was sniffling and then bawling, so that Papa stuffed his handkerchief into my hand. The suit from Bata- nya had no pockets, so I didn't have a hankie.

After the play, I was uncomfortable, because in the love I had watched onstage there had been something I hadn't understood or liked. We walked home. It was warm, and spring was in the air. Mama asked how I had liked the play. I tried to explain my feelings. "You probably think that's love. I don't. Tell me, is that love? Is it?"

Mama said nothing. Papa replied, "It's not love. It's passion. A scary thing."

This was the last time the three of us walked together in Moscow.

The day before, May Day, had been sunny and bright, but not warm. Everyone woke early. Mama had to get to the Academy before the streets were blocked and then to the parade from there. Papa and Egorka were going to Red Square to watch the parade. At breakfast Papa said he didn't feel like going at all, and if it weren't for Egorka, he wouldn't. "Besides, my stomach hurts."

Mama replied, "You think I want to go? It's like a sharp knife for me now." Then she dressed, kissed Egorka automatically, adjusted my barrettes (they were always crooked), and left.

Papa departed with a skipping Egorka. I was last to leave, and by then a delicious aroma had already filled the kitchen. In terms of cooking, the Nun recognized church holidays and any other. I had been saddened by my parents' conversation; there was something upsetting about it that I tried to avoid in my own thoughts.

The anxiety vanished as soon as I ran out onto sunny Gorky Street. There were music blaring out of the loudspeakers, flags fluttering, and smiling people on the sidewalks. A group of teenagers with big paper poppies walked past me, laughing. I laughed too and hurried to the school. Lots of kids were in the courtyard. Everyone was dressed for summer, but even in the sunshine the cold wind gave us chills. The girls shivered and jiggled to keep warm. The boys hugged them, as if to warm them up. Seva hugged me. It was simple, even though the whole school could see. As we lined up Alexandra Vasilyevna walked past us, smiled, and said, "My little turtle doves, isn't cooing at your desk enough for you?"

Seva replied, "Of course not, Alexandra Vasilyevna."

Then our school set out. We weren't far, just ten minutes' walk from the Mausoleum. I think we were the most centrally located school in Moscow. But it still took a long time to get there, because many people attended the parades in those days. And I think that everyone, and not just the schoolchildren, had a good time. We all wanted to see the leaders on top of the Mausoleum. We knew them by sight, and that made them seem familiar, like friends or family. (Now most of the leaders are anonymous, and only one or two faces are familiar. And in a few years even those faces slip from memory. For instance, I remember Khrushchev, Brezhnev, and Andropov, but not Chernenko. And even if you showed me photographs, I wouldn't be able to identify the Politburo members from those years. Good or bad, even horrible, they passed quickly.) But then, I was thrilled at the prospect of seeing Stalin, Voroshilov, Budenny, and of course, Yezhov, who was, after all, Mama's friend. I heard that he used to have a picture of Egorka and me on his desk, when we were little Leningraders. And ever since their Odessa days, his wife had been a friend of Bagritsky's—practically family! And all the others on the Mausoleum. I was fully certain that not only I but everyone marching with me, waving flags and banners and artificial flowers, carrying heavy posters, and shouting slogans fiercely, were all thrilled to see that group of people on the right wing of the Mausoleum.

And I repeated to myself (God, what a little fool I was!), "You can't commune more closely or more purely with the great feeling [or 'word,' I don't remember) called class." And I felt sorry that while I loved Mayakovsky, Seva, marching next to me and holding my hand, did not. After all, it was said (and by Stalin!) that he "was and will remain" the greatest poet. I also felt sorry that I was revolutionary and Party-minded while my (I had been using the possessive for some time now) Seva was not.

After the parade had crossed the Moskva River, people wandered off because it was impossible to cross back until it was over. It lasted a long time, until four or five in the afternoon. Everyone wanted to walk through Red Square and see the leaders. And there were a lot of people, workers, in Moscow. After our part in the parade I usually went to Musya Luskina's house in the Government House, to have lunch and nap until I could go home. This time Seva came with me. Musya, Vanya, and Vilen were out. Their younger son, born while they were doing collectivization in the Central Chrenozyom Oblast, and the housekeeper were there. She fed us. Then we went to Vorobyov Hills, beyond the park into the woods. The trees were in bud and without leaves. If you squeezed the buds, they were sticky and aromatic. Hundreds of crocuses carpeted the ground, white islands on the still dark and damp earth. And we found a new place where it was safe to kiss. It turned out it was good in the woods, too. Not only on the roof.

51

After the May holidays we were allowed to look at the final exam questions for orals. The teachers told us that the tests would be very difficult because we were graduating from the new seven-year school program, which was equivalent to the old ten-grade system. This would be the end of mandatory schooling and those who chose to could go to work. I wrote down the questions in chemistry and physics, which seemed very easy to me, and showed them to Seva. He read them closely and said, "Never."

"What?"

"I'll never be able to answer a single one of those questions."

"What will you do?"

"Not take the exams."

"But how?"

"I'll get sick!"

I was terrified of illness, probably because I had been ill so often. But being sick was not necessary. Lida went to a doctor who gave her a note attesting that Seva had been ailing most of the winter. She took it to the school's director, and he was excused from exams. Of course, he had long talks with various teachers who told him how much he'd have to learn over the summer, and then they'd meet with him in the fall. But there wouldn't be makeup exams, just discussions. Seva said, "It doesn't matter." It turned out to be very simple to get out of exams, but I had never known. I had spent many winters being out of school sick and then taking exams in the spring, like an idiot.

So in fact Seva graduated from school much earlier than I did, with my good grades. Earlier than Nadya Suvorova, who was the best student in our group. But Lida said she would teach Seva a lesson for his laziness. She would send him for the summer to live with friends in Essentuki. Seva resisted "like a lion" at first, and then had to give in. Lida persuaded him by saying that she and Sima had to work hard for Vladimir Narbut and Igor Post-upalsky, and Seva's presence in Moscow not only distracted her but in some fashion tied her hands. What could he say to that? Of course, I didn't see how Seva could be in her way. I thought it would be better if he didn't go. Essentuki was so far away. Separation.

And Igor had changed so much lately. He no longer pursued his music, school, and books. He told Olya he was still young and he wanted to repeat the year. He simply stopped going to school. He spent days lying on his bed and reading nothing but the newspapers. It was horrible.

One late spring evening I told Seva we should try to get Igor to go out with us. Seva had some money and we decided to splurge at the ice cream parlor. "And then let's go to the Hermitage garden. All the girls have been there, and I never have."

"We won't go to the Hermitage. You're too young," Seva said with great severity.

"Why?"

"When you grow up, you'll learn."

I didn't understand why he was so strict. For the next two years Seva still thought I was too young.

It took a lot of persuading to convince Igor. I said this would be a farewell evening since Seva was leaving the next day.

"So let him make his farewells to you. He doesn't need to with me. And anyway, I'll die soon, and then you can have a farewell evening," he said out of the blue.

Seva called him a fool and we left without Igor. Neither Olya nor Yuri Karlovich was home. They had a housekeeper, but I didn't see her.

We sat in an ice cream parlor and had ice cream with a cookie stuck in the scoops. Then we took a walk around the Kremlin. There were lots of people out, dressed for the coming summer, and that lent a festive air to the street. I told Seva I felt sorry for Igor lying there under a mound of newspapers. Seva got angry and said that his "cousin is fooling himself, thinking he's a Komsomol who needs nothing but newspapers, which could drive anyone crazy."

We walked back in a sad mood. Seva must have been pretending to be angry with Igor, because he felt sorry for him, too. Then we sat on the roof and kissed. Seva told me he was flying out the next day, but this was the first I heard of it. That must have have been Lida's most effective argument. Flying! None of our friends had been in a plane yet. Not even Papa, I don't think. Mama once had a ride over Moscow with her friend, the famous pilot Kokkinaki.

52

Exams started. I think we had six, but they were no harder than usual. I got a Good for exposition, and then Very Good's in everything else. Three days later, I received a letter from Seva which he had posted as soon as he got to Essentuki. Letters came every day, and I picked each one up at our pass bureau. Ran up two steps at a time, dashed into my room, shut the door tightly, and then read it. I wrote a daily letter, too. I saw that even though separation was awful, letters were some compensation. And I was learning something new about my Seva.

The last exam was on May 27, at one o'clock. In the morning, after Mama left, Papa and I had breakfast together. He wrote something, rummaged in his desk drawer, and then got ready to leave. He wore his light suit and white Russian shirt with a small embroidered pattern around the neck and down the off-center placket. He looked into my room, smiled, and said, "Well, Carmen-Juliet, good luck! Would you happen to know where I can get a couple of clean handkerchiefs?"

I laughed at his mistake in Russian cases and then gave him two handkerchiefs—he liked one on each side of his jacket. His stomach doesn't hurt today, I thought.

He repeated, "Well, good luck!" and left—young, handsome, so good-looking.

I went to school, without hurrying. There was lots of time before one, and I could hammer some answers into Elka. We always took exams in the same half of the class. I was in group B, she was in D. I answered my questions easily and got my "Very Good." Then I had to wait an hour and a half, as usual, for the rest to finish.

Alexandra Vasilyevna listed those who would have to take makeup tests, then said that since we had finished a seven-year course, we would get diplomas of graduation and not simply certificates of grade completion. They would be handed out on June 1 to all seventh-graders. And we had to come with our parents, since these were important documents. There was a contradiction in her speech. On the one hand, we were children and couldn't be trusted with the diplomas; on the other, we were entitled to diplomas; which made us adults. Then she wished us a happy summer.

We all rushed out into the yard and planned where to go next—the movies, a walk, or a boat ride. I lied, saying I was expected at home. I wanted to get Seva's letter, and write an answer. Also I had recently started a diary and I wanted to write in it.

As I got my letter from the pass office, I noticed that the girl didn't smile. Usually the girls on duty always joked about my letters; everyone knew about my love. But I ran upstairs, not caring about her mood.

I pulled at our door, but it was locked. "Why didn't she give me the key as well," I thought, and started to run back down. But the door creaked behind me, and the Nun peered out into the hallway. Wondering why the door was locked when she was home, I went in. And . . . and I came down to earth. A soldier was with the Nun and I could see another one through the open door of the dining room. He was at Papa's chess table. The Nun said nothing, but I didn't need an explanation. It was clear. It was our turn, that's all . . . But who? Papa or Mama?

I went to the dining room and past the unmoving soldier into

Mama's room. One man was writing at Papa's desk, another was looking out the bay window, a third was rummaging through the books. Mama sat on the bed that was along the left wall. Straight, but leaning forward. Probably there's no other way to sit on a bed comfortably. Her arms were bent at the elbow and her fists were pressed against her shoulders. She seemed to be pulling an invisible shawl around herself. Her hair was unkempt and therefore curlier than usual. And her face . . . her face . . . I couldn't look at it. It hurt. I wanted to scream. She was pale, whiter than the sheet that showed under the lifted corner of the blanket. She was wearing the bright blue man's shirt that Dolores had given Papa and it cast blue reflections on her white face. *Why does she have on a wool shirt when it's so hot?* I thought irrelevantly. I took a step toward her, but tripped over books on the floor and was forced to look down. When I raised my eyes, Mama's gaze stopped me. It was like a wall. An order. I couldn't disobey. She stared at me a long time. *She's saying goodbye,* I thought. *And she's afraid I'll start crying. Because then she will too.* I stopped thinking. And then Mama spoke calmly, although her voice was a bit louder than normal, the way someone sounds when she is trying to speak clearly. "Go to your room." It was probably to keep me from saying anything or doing anything, most importantly from rushing to her and embracing her. She looked away.

I walked to my room, past the still-seated soldier, and shut the door. I felt the letter in my hand. One of the men opened my door, and our eyes met. His were empty and without any color. White. I had read about "white eyes" but now I was seeing them. I shut my door, but he opened it again silently and our eyes met again. He wasn't tall, but exactly my height. I sat down on the chair near my desk and did not move. Mama's look at me was, in farewell. That meant it was she. That was better than Papa, because Papa would save her. No. No one could save anyone. Otherwise they would have saved their friends. Then it would be better if it were Papa. No. I exploded with all these thought fragments. And I shouted silently to each: "No. No. No." The man got up from the table and went to the entry. Quickly, through the round neckline of my Tatyanka dress, I stuffed Seva's letter into my bra.

The man came back, and I gloated. I felt I had tricked him. Did he think I'd read Seva's letter under his white eyes? I don't know how long I sat there. A long time. Then I felt hungry. And I needed to go to the toilet . . . It was strange, my whole soul or heart, whatever, ached so much and yet . . .

I was afraid to get up. Those white eyes. I talked myself into it for a few minutes, and then stood up. I went to the toilet and then washed my face, my hands, my neck. I could feel Seva's letter in my bra and that gave me courage. As if he were here, too. I remembered Papa's "Romeo" and almost wept. But I controlled myself. The man from the entry watched me in silence as I walked to the kitchen. The Nun was there. Her hands were clasped tight on her lap and her face was lowered. "Is she praying?" I thought when she looked up and gave me a strange stare. I asked her for some tea, which she poured. She got out bread, butter, cheese, and cold meat patties. I ate quickly, and I asked her to make sandwiches and fresh, good tea for Mama. "Please, like for Papa!" The Nun shuddered at the word and looked at me in fright.

She made tea and sandwiches with cheese and meat patties. *Cold meat patties are a favorite in three generations of our family: my parents, Egorka and I, and Tanya and Alyosha and even Tanya's husband, as if he were of our blood. I don't know about my daughter-in-law, Liza. And I don't know the tastes of my grandchildren, either—a bad grandmother. In name only!*

I took out a glass in a holder. It was on top of a hanging cupboard in the kitchen—the only place for keeping dishes, since we didn't have many. I put it before the Nun. She whispered in fright, "But it belongs to Gevork Sarkisovich." She filled it with tea. Holding the tea in one hand and a plate in the other, I went past the one in the entry, not even calling him a man in my mind, past the seated white-eyed one in the dining room, and into Mama's room, where I saw that there was no place to put the food. The main one was at the desk. I don't know why I was so sure that he was in charge. The desk in the bay window, which was considered Mama's, was piled with books and papers and so was the little table by the bed. The round black table was the children's table for Mama and her sister, Anya, and brother, Motya. Later it belonged to Egorka and me. When Egorka went to school, Mama took it back.

I returned to the dining room, put everything down on the table, and went to the kitchen for a stool. I set it down in front of Mama. Walking past those motionless statues in the entry and dining room—one seated, one standing—was unpleasant, even scary. I overcame my fear, but when I took the glass back up in my hand, I could hear the spoon rattling in it. Mama hadn't moved. She looked at me and reached out, and I thought she wanted me. But she put her palm down on the glass, as if to warm herself. Then she gently caressed the glass holder. I thought I was going to cry. Mama must have felt it too, because with her other hand she gave me a nudge and said, "Lusia-djan, go to your room."

I knew she was afraid of my tears. Or maybe her own? She never called me that name. I realized that she simply wanted to use Papa's word. I went to my room even though I was dying to sit next to her, to hold her, and to cry.

White eyes watched me. I sat, but it was hard to control my agitation and fear of sitting down. So I would get up, take a few steps around the room, and then sit down again. I wanted to fling myself on the bed and cry, my face in the pillow. Or beat my fists against the wall and scream. But while that one was watching? I sat down again. I heard steps. The main one came into the dining room, Mama followed, and last came the one who had rummaged in the books.

"They're going to take her away!" I rushed to Mama. Once again she stopped me with a look and said, "May they go into your room?"

God, why is she asking . . . I thought when the man in charge walked into my room, followed by the one who had been behind Mama. He immediately went to the shelves by the wall to the left of the door, bent over and ran his fingers over the spines of the books without taking them out. He pulled out the Mayakovsky and shook papers out of it onto the desk—I had been writing, checking if I had memorized the line breaks.

The leader sat at the desk. It was small, with two drawers, one narrow the other wider, but both rather deep, so that I was already bumping my knees on them. He pulled out the drawers with both hands and dug through them simultaneously. There were boxes of paints, notebooks, a pencilcase, and a thin packet of letters from Seva held by a pink rubberband. He hooked it with his index finger and it slipped off. I found that very painful. Then he pulled out a blue notebook from the bottom—my diary. Impulsively I lunged at him and took it away. "It's my diary. My diary. You can't have it." He extended his arm, and stared at me with his face, but not his eyes. He was my height. *Why are they all so short?* I thought. All our relatives and friends were tall. And there weren't many short people in the Comintern halls either. His face contorted in anger or in a smile—I couldn't tell—and he said, "I don't want it." He turned, looking around the room. I looked with him, and I had the feeling that it was no longer my room.

There wasn't much to see. Bookshelves. A window. A half meter from the window, my desk. A chair. Another chair by the wall. Beyond the chair, Batanya's trunk covered with a bedspread. Games on top of it. My old baby doll. A sack containing lotto, which no one played without Emma Davydovna. And a stack of quilted blankets, piled one on top of the other—the way they do it in Armenian houses. Red. Green. Blue. Behind the trunk a small chest, which is still with me today, on my balcony. I use it to hold flowerpots in the summer. My underwear was in the chest. On top of it was Batanya's alarm clock with the melody that lives in old alarm clocks. Above the chest a medicine chest with a mirror. It held my underpants, two of my first three bras, cotton, hairpins, and so on. On top of it was my first bottle of perfume, a present from Mama's cousin Raya, when she had come to Moscow for a conference of oncologists. It was called My Dreams. Raya said it reminded her of L'Origan de Coty. And Mama had grumbled that I was too young for perfume. My bed was along the perpendicular wall. It was covered with a pique blanket—starched and snowy, like all our linen under the Nun's care. At the foot of the bed, a small black child's chair. Like the table by Mama's bed, it came from her childhood. And along the wall opposite the trunk, a couch. An ordinary mattress on legs, covered like the trunk with a bedspread. Under the couch were two empty suitcases.

Looking around my room behind the leader, I realized I had loved it. I thought about it in the past tense. Without pain. It had passed. The room was in the past. Over!

The man in charge lifted the edge of the bedspread and revealed three locks on the trunk. The center lock had a rather large key and when Batanya turned it, there was a pleasant but loud ringing noise, like the front door bell. The side locks were opened by a flat funny-shaped key.

"The keys?" he asked, turning to Mama.

"It's my mother's trunk. She has the keys."

"Well, should we break it?" he asked nobody in particular.

The one going through my books said, "It's a pretty trunk."

"Seal it," the chief said. And he went through the blankets on the trunk. He'd pick up a blanket and toss it on the couch. Then he crouched by the chest and stuck his hand inside. Got up. Opened the cabinet. Shut it. Picked up the perfume. Opened the box. Shut it. Put it down. White Eyes came with a pitcher. It smelled like the mail. I remembered Batanya. I used to go to the post office in Leningrad with her to send parcels to someone. *God. Batanya and Egorka don't know yet. They're at the dacha.* I pressed against Mama—I wanted to look into her eyes. She patted my shoulder, but her eyes were shut. White Eyes put strings into the locks and smeared them with wax. The wax dripped onto the floor. The chief went through the bed, bending back the mattress, shifting the pillows. I watched his hands, and I thought that wherever they had been I could no longer touch. Then he took out a seal from his breast pocket and pressed it to each lock of the trunk. How I hated him at that moment! There they were now in our house—those seals. I hated him! He picked bits of wax out of his seal and blew them away.

He put the seal in his pocket and buttoned it. He told White Eyes, "Seal the bookcases, too." And he walked straight at Mama and me. We moved away from the door. As he passed, his eyeless face came close to mine again, grimaced, and said, "There, that's all, and you were afraid!" I had heard these words before and not quite understanding, I suspected there was something indecent in what he implied. I felt myself blush. Just then Mama said, "Lusia, I've arranged this with the comrades. You'll go to Anya's now."

"With whom?" I was so stunned that she had called them "comrades" that I didn't understand what she wanted. "No. I'm not going anywhere. I won't."

"Lusia, let's not argue today. Please. I'm asking you. Put on your sweater; it must be cool by now."

She gave me a look. I interpreted it to mean: I mustn't argue. I mustn't tell her in front of them that I want to be with her. That I'm afraid, that I'm afraid I'll never see her again, never see Papa again. That I want to cry and say, Mamochka, Mamochka, over and over . . .

I went to my room, took the Mayakovsky from the desk and noticed that I still had my diary in my hands. I added it to the book and in my other hand picked up my sweater from the chair. And so, I went over to my mother and offered my face, but she didn't kiss me. She raised both hands, pulling me closer with one, pushing me away with the other. Then she said, "Go," and turned me away from her. And I went. Someone shut the door behind me to the dining room. There was a soldier in the entry. The door to the kitchen was shut. "Did the Nun shut it or did they?" I wondered automatically and went out into the hall. Before I had taken another step, the lock turned in the door behind me. I don't remember whether I saw anyone in the hall-way or how I walked past the doorman.

The cold on the street brought me back to my senses. My knee was pressed against the shop window of the store where I pur-chased ribbons. I put down the book and notebook and pulled on my sweater. It didn't make me any warmer. I reached the corner of Pushkinskaya and Strastnaya, and got on the Annushka line. It must have been a quick ride; I even passed my stop, because

I suddenly saw Aunt Anya's house passing in the window. I walked through their dark courtyard, thinking, *It's always dark here,* and climbed up the stairs. The door opened immediately, as if they were expecting me. Lyova stood to the right and a bit behind him and to the left was Anya. Zorya wasn't around.

"What are you doing here?"

"Mama sent me here to spend the night."

"What's happened at your place?"

"I don't know. They're searching, Mama's there."

"Where's Alikhanov?" I noticed that instead of his usual ingratiating "Gevork" Lyova called my father "Alikhanov."

"He's not back from work."

"Stop trying to kid me! Work! Has he been arrested?"

I didn't understand what he was getting at and tried to enter the apartment. Anya said something. Lyova practically shouted at her, "Anya, damn it, you're always . . ." And he barred my way with his right arm across the doorway. Then he spoke in a loud whisper, very fast, "We can't let you in; we can't. What's the matter? Don't you understand that?" He repeated it several times, spraying me with his spittle. Anya said something. I could see her mouth moving, but I heard nothing except Lyova's whisper as loud as a shout.

I retreated from the door until my back pressed against the banister. The door slammed. I stood there, unable to comprehend what had happened to me. Then I wiped my face with my hand and started down the stairs. I hadn't reached the bottom of the flight when I heard the door opening. When I turned, Lyova was in the doorway. I was afraid he would call me back. But he said nothing and then started to close the door slowly. I shouted, "Scoundrel!" and I saw him turn white.

"Scoundrel! Scoundrel!" I screamed as I ran for the gate. And in the arch I said, "Ah, what a scoundrel!" A man walking by stopped and said, "What?" I ran on toward the Kirovskye Vorota. And I burst out laughing, out loud, uncontrollably, and something clattered inside me. I was laughing because I had been just like Batanya in word and intonation. Every time she came back from visiting her daughter Anya, she would say to Mama, "He's a scoundrel. Ah, what a scoundrel."

And Mama would try to soothe her by saying, "All right. At least he loves Anya."

And Batanya always said, "He doesn't love anyone. Except himself."

The laughter stopped as quickly as it had begun. I had to find a toilet, but the one on the boulevard was closed. It must be nighttime, I thought. I looked around, but there was no one. I squatted behind the little house, and went on toward the Kirovskye Vorota. I was frightened at being alone in the city at night. But the fear was nothing compared to my new big fright, which was growing stronger. I think I tried to deflect it with my fear of the city at night.

I reached Strastnoy Boulevard, which had been renamed Children's Park of the Sverdlovsk Region. I sat down on a bench. A couple passed, arm in arm. The man said, "What's the matter? Won't anyone take you?" The girl laughed. I thought that maybe I should go to someone's house. Aunt Ronya. Uncle Mosya. Lida. They'd let me in. But I was ashamed. What if they asked, "Why didn't you go to Anya?" And I was also ashamed, as if I were sick. Contagious. As Nura used to say about someone, "She has a bad disease. A ba-a-ad one." There was something shameful in that contagion. And in my shame.

I got tired of sitting and when I stretched I felt something jab me in my bra. It had been there all along, but I had been distracted. The letter, Seva's letter. I crossed to the sidewalk where the streetlamp was on, and tore open the envelope. Seva wrote that he had been to Pyatigorsk and had visited Lermontov's grave, that he was going to the sea. By car. That wasn't it . . . At last . . . Poetry . . . No, here it was. "Igor is lying when he says that you can't live without me. I'm the one who can't live without you. I don't want to go to the sea. I want to go home. I want to be on our roof . . . ."

My darling, my poor Seva. He doesn't know. I began to cry. I went back to the bench, and buried my face in my knees. Again

I didn't have a handkerchief. And I cried and cried. Then I began thinking: What should I do now? What will happen to Mama? Papa? Will I never see them again? Mamochka . . . Papa . . . My Alikhanov. Maybe I should get away? No, I can't leave without Seva. And what about Egorka, Batanya? I had to go home. I didn't even know if they were arrested or not. Who? Just Mama? Just Papa? Both of them? What should I do? I lifted my face and looked around. Maybe I was looking for help, advice from the trees, the dark windows of the houses.

A shimmer from the ground caught my eye. I got up and went toward it. A small gold heart lay on the ground. It might not have been gold; it could have been gold-colored. I'd never had jewelry; neither had Mama. I didn't know anything about it. That laughing floozy must have dropped it. Or some other woman. I thought the owner would return. I sat back down on my bench and held the heart on my extended palm, so if the owner walked by she would see it. I examined it; it was so touching and pretty. I may have fallen asleep, but I suddenly noticed that the sky was lighter. And it was cold. My second dawn. The first was also in late May, a year before, when we went fishing at Lake Senezh. It seemed now to have been in a different world, a different time. A different era. Later Seva and I would put it exactly that way, "Everything that happened then was before our era." Our era began with the summer of 1937.

The heart was still in my hand; its owner hadn't come. I closed my hand—the heart was mine. Later it became Tanya's. Everything passes, but things remain, even such small ones. I think it's called "material culture." I got up and headed home. As I came out on Pushkin Square, I realized that it was still early. No one was around. I got to our main entrance, and pushed the door, but it was locked. I didn't ring. I thought, what if Papa had come home? Why wake them? And then, if I come back this early, they'll know that I didn't spent the night at Anya's. I crossed the street and walked along Leontyevsky Alley. What's it called now? Then I came out on Herzen Street, turned onto the boulevard, walking slowly toward Pushkin. "Pushkin, the secret freedom . . ." How happy I was that we already knew Blok. That poetry lived inside us. That helped. I didn't feel contagious any-more, and I wasn't ashamed of anything. I felt very bitter and afraid. But not of the white-eyed and eyeless ones. I was afraid of finding out what had happened to my parents, but I had to. And I had Egorka to take care of. I had changed: my childhood had ended. On the night of May 27, 1937, on the Moscow Boulevard ring, by the statue of Pushkin.

When I approached our house a second time, the front door was open but the pass bureau was still closed. It was too early for letters, anyway. I walked by the doorman, if not skipping or running as usual, then certainly without a sense of humiliation, and I said loudly, so that the whole lobby could hear, "Hello." I thought that he nodded with a clear expression of sympathy in response to my greeting, which sounded like a shout.

Our door was shut and I knocked softly. The Nun opened it. She was dressed and her head was bound in a black scarf. That meant she was planning to go out. So early?

The Nun whispered, "Quiet, I think your mother is asleep."

"And Papa?"

She shook her head. "Your father didn't come home. I'm off to the dacha. As soon as they left, your mother said for me to bring back Tatyana Matveyevna and Igor first thing this morn-ing." Like all the nannies, she called Egorka by his formal name, Igor. A lot of other people in school and in the building called him that too. She had taken the two suitcases out from under my couch and was wiping the dust from them in the middle of the entryway.

"When did they leave?"

"Over two hours ago. Your mother kept running up and down, up and down, after they left. And then she said for me to go to the dacha early before, God forbid, they showed up there. And why did you come back so early from your aunt's? Couldn't sleep? Well, how could anyone sleep?"

She didn't wait for a reply, and I didn't have to start the day with a lie. The sense of being branded and contagious and that it was shameful had passed. But the shame of what had happened on Lyova's stairs had not.

The Nun left, and I went to the dining room. It was clean. The floor sparkled, and the net curtains stirred. The chessmen were in the same positions as the night before last. No one was allowed to move them. If Papa didn't put them away in their box, that meant he was thinking over the move. I looked at the door to Mama's room. Papa's gone! Mama's sleeping! The question of who was arrested no longer needed to be asked. But was she asleep? I opened the door without letting it creak, and met the gaze of Mama's wide open eyes. She lay on her side in that shirt and skirt, on top of the blanket. As pale as she had been last night. I don't know why, but I was sure she hadn't shut her eyes for a minute. And she managed to keep me away now, too.

She closed her eyes and asked, "Have Batanya and Egorka come?"

I realized she didn't know the time, didn't know how much time had passed.

"No."

"Then I'll just lie here a little longer. You go," she said, without opening her eyes.

I went out to my room. I picked up a blanket from the trunk and came back. Mama already had turned to the wall, staring at it. I covered her, but she said nothing. I returned to my room, went over to the bed, and put my head on the pillow. And suddenly felt I was very tired.

I was awakened by a knock on the front door. I ran to the entry and found the girl who usually helped out in the pass office downstairs. With a mound of newspapers. "If you subscribe, then pick them up on time. Too lazy to come downstairs?" she said harshly.

"And the letter?"

"No letters for you. They're writing them!" And she walked away.

No one on the Luxe staff had ever spoken to me like that. Nor anyone else. *So that's the way you're going to be?* I thought. *I'll be ruder than that; just wait.* And I learned almost immediately, surprising myself with my voice, intonation, and vocabulary. Sometimes I got scared, what's happening to me, what will Batanya say? *And one time, around 1940, when I had let someone really have it in our Leningrad communal kitchen, Batanya said, "Some people are protected by their breeding; others defend themselves through rudeness. You lack the breeding." She didn't approve, but neither did she disapprove. She was no advocate of nonresistance. And she had plenty of breeding, even too much.*

I looked in on Mama. She was still facing the wall and said only one word, "Go." Now I understood that she was afraid to talk to me. She didn't know what to say. Maybe she was looking for an explanation—not for herself, but for us. Oh, how silly she was and how sorry I felt for her. And for myself, for Egorka, for all of us. I didn't dare think about Papa, I felt so sorry for him. But most of all I pitied Mama. Silly. Silly. No explanations were necessary. What was there to explain? It happened to everyone. Well, if not everyone, then most. And the others would experience it tomorrow. No, she wanted to understand and wanted us to understand, because she was a Party member. So what if she belonged to the Party? What was she supposed to do? She couldn't become a non-Party person, could she? And there was nothing to explain. I hated them. A lot. Who? Lyova. White Eyes. Eyeless. And maybe the girl with the newspapers. My imagination didn't go any further. Even for the soldier who had been here with White Eyes and Eyeless I felt no hatred.

53

Actually, things were difficult with my hatred. The list of people gradually expanded. I began to hate the people who gave out information about prisoners on Kuznetsky Bridge, house 12. Those who accepted transfers—fifty rubles—in the windows of the prisons at Lefortovo, Matrosskaya Tishina, Krasnopresnenskaya, and Butyrki. In Leningrad, at Kresty and the Big House. The investigator who questioned me. The Komsorg who expelled me from the Komsomol.

The neighbor who lost a slip and accused me of stealing it in the communal kitchen because "everyone in their family has been arrested." With the years the list grew, but it didn't change anything. But I didn't hate the ones the newspapers had praised and then denounced, like Yagoda, Yezhov, Zorya's father, Berman, Zaporozhets, and all the ones on the endless portraits, or the ones who were defendants in the trials. I didn't feel anything toward them. Not even hatred.

I didn't feel hatred for the Germans. Of course, the ones I met were already prisoners. At a station a train carrying prisoners of war stood next to our hospital train. An emaciated German, looking like a Leningrader during the blockade, looked out of the upper window. He was asking for "brot, brot," and made signs. I gave him my rations, a piece of soap, and a pack of shag tobacco. They tried to expel me from the Komsomol for that. I didn't repent, but the girls decided to forgive me anyway. They said that I was "basically kind" and that prompted my "political mistake." And they were sure that I'd improve.

I think they didn't throw me out because our deputy political officer, Pavlov, knew that they wouldn't be able to find another senior nurse as we were approaching the front and had to take in as many as six hundred or even a thousand wounded. Especially a nurse that Murin, head of our evacuation office, called an SP (his term for a "sensible person"). After the meeting Bronka Pruman, a Jewish girl from Novograd-Volynsky, whom I had picked up at some way station and convinced the chief to take on as a hired clerk, laughed with me. She was like the German, a result of my so-called kindness. And if I were to improve, I wouldn't pick up any more strays. I had a few more. Asya Deitch, granddaughter of the Deitch who was also known as Akselrod, Zasulich, et al. Then there was Vovochka, a little boy whose mother later found him. I was so sorry to give him up. There was another young woman from the Ukraine. How could you call it kindness, when I really scolded those three strays? For some reason, they were all slow, and clumsy, and disorganized—certainly no soldiers.

Now it was Pavlov I hated. It was bad enough that he seduced girls and we had to send them home, weeping and pregnant. We collected

*our new warm fox cloths to be used for diapers, and our additional
rations. And he wouldn't even come out to say goodbye. I felt very
sorry for the short, blond Verochka Teshkova. Even more, he was the
most useless man I had ever encountered. Worse than anyone. He
appeared on the train about the same time I did, after an arm wound.
A young stud with a Party card in his pocket. None of our medical
crew—the chief of the train, the doctor, the two senior nurses, and the
pharmacists—was a Party member. And everyone except me was
twice his age. Yet he never picked up an extinguisher during a fire. He
never carried a stretcher during a bombing raid. He never stayed once
in the train with the people we couldn't remove and hide in the woods.
And he was even too lazy to read the war communiqué to the troops.
He'd have someone write it down, read it, and pass it on to a soldier
or nurse's aide to read to the wounded in the train.*

*And he snooped. Who were you, where did you come from, who
were your family? It was easier for me. I'd just tell him in a challeng-
ing way: my father is an enemy of the people, ten years without
permission to correspond. My mother is the wife of an enemy of the
people, eight years. But he hated me too. Viciously. Because the girls
and the rest of the crew liked me. He never ever signed a single citation
for me. "First let her denounce her parents." After the war he went
back to his native Yaroslavl. Now, maybe, he's leader of some veter-
ans' council. Why not, he's a Hero of the Great Patriotic War. "I hate
being patient."*

*Later I came to hate the captain from the political section. He kept
pretending to be well-disposed to me. "Your initiative, Komsorg, is of
the highest sort." "Everything in your unit is in order, lieutenant."
And one time he called me in, as if on business, and started telling me
that he wasn't interested in Komsomol work, that the war was now
moving onto enemy territory. That people would see a lot. Might
become interested. I should report to him on people's moods and so on.*

*"And the foreigners might take an interest in you [me!]. They know
everything about us. And your parents are enemies. So they might try
to recruit you. Or we'll even help them. And you'll help us. And I
think the time is coming for you to stop messing with pus and shit and
the wounded. And reading Pushkin and Blok to the girls. We'll bring
you closer to us . . . You're literate and . . ."*

*I wasn't the naive fool with dreams of the world revolution any-
more. And I had seen a lot. But I hadn't expected anyone to talk to
me like that. My God, did I let him have it. In literary Russian and
the other kind. How I hated him at that moment. I think if I'd had
a pistol, I would have shot him on the spot. He turned into a "pale-
face" while I had my say. Then he said, "All right. Not a word about
our talk. And I have to think about what to do with you. Remember
that, lieutenant, I'll think about it."*

*I told one person about the conversation, and waited. I was lucky
they didn't arrest me. Nothing happened. But it's a pity that I don't
remember that captain's name. He was a front-line hero, too. He
already had several medals on his chest. And now they may reach
down to his fly.*

*Basically, my hatred was also nonintellectual, emotional, and per-
sonal. But once I rose higher. Spring of 1942. Frosts until late May.
Our trains were filled with frostbite victims. Amputated feet and
hands. And the smell from these victims (our usual term for our
product, wounded, doesn't apply) was so strong that we got dizzy and
nauseated while bandaging them. Sometimes I raced out to the vestibule of the car so as not to throw up in the operating room. And I felt
so sorry for them, because the pain was worse with frostbite than from
wounds.*

*I was on night duty, and at some station the military commandant
sent a soldier for me. A woman in an echelon of evacuees was having
a baby. Horrors. I had never seen a birth, and didn't pay too much
attention in the textbook, either. So much for the Russian Red Cross
courses! Obstetrics for nurses in the reserves. They say that you need
to know where children come from. The rest is unnecessary. Medical
kit, iodine, gloves, cap. Everything is sterile. But what now? All I
knew was that I'd have to tie the umbilical cord. The only one I'd seen
was in a textbook. And I'd forgotten.*

*I climbed up into the car; it was dark and smoky. A lot of women
and children. It was cold and stuffy at the same time. The smell was
dirty, hungry, and unwashed. A philologist will say that those are not
adjectives that apply to smells. A woman was spread-eagled on the
lower plank bed. My first reaction was that she was shameless. That
passed. I didn't see her face at first, because it was dark in the lower*

bunk. I made out her damp dark hair, and her red wet face with dark smears. She'd scream, and when the pain eased, she'd wipe her face with her hands, and the soot would spread on her face. Her hands and face were terrible. She was covered above the waist by a quilted cotton jacket and her feet were also covered. But her spread knees and her belly were bare. And from her crotch, which was unnaturally swollen, something dark was coming out. It was only after the baby was born that I realized it had been its head. She had only two or three contractions while I was there. And that scary, unhappily red and slippery creature fell and crawled onto something gray that had been spread under the woman. Its fists were up and it screamed . . . and screamed. I was so untrained and stupid that the cry scared me instead of reassuring me. But one of the women behind me said joyfully, "Oh, what a good cry! So loud!"

I found the umbilical cord. Wearing gloves, I picked up the bandage and began tying it about ten centimeters from the baby, so as not to crush it. Someone said, "Take it lower, lower," I moved halfway down and tied it. I felt it pulse. And intuition told me, make it as tight as a tourniquet. But I couldn't untie the bandage. I took another piece and made it tight. I got the scissors and looked around. Everyone was silent. I took a deep breath and cut. The cord slipped out of the scissors, but then it crunched like a thin chicken cartilage. And blood gushed out at me and all around. I even recoiled. I forgot that you were supposed to tie the other end, leading into the woman. The blood kept coming. "How do I stop this bleeding?" I wondered feverishly. One of the women put a basin nearby. Was that what I was supposed to do? The mother kept asking, "Who is it? Well, what do I have?" I didn't understand the question. At last someone said, "It's a girl, a girl."

The mother said, "What's your name?"

"Lusia."

"Well, then, she'll be Ludmila."

I looked into her face again. Pretty, beautiful, and even made better by the dirt.

Another woman said, "Let go. I'll clean up the bride and wrap her up, or she'll catch cold. Tie up the end, go ahead." And she took napkins and cotton balls out of the sterile kit with her bare hands.

And then the afterbirth. It's a good thing it came out quickly, *because I thought it was a second baby. She was wrapped up instantly and handed to the mother, who murmured in such a quiet, intelligent voice that it astonished me, "Lusenka, my Lusenka." Like my mother when I was sick.*

The soldier who had brought me opened the door. "Sister, hurry it up. The signalman is heading for your train." I turned to the soldier and then back to the mother and child. The woman who had wrapped the baby said, "Autumn ones are no good; they almost always die. But your girl is a spring one. The ones born in spring are the hardiest."

The new mother said, "Thank you, thank you, Lusia."

I jumped down onto the hard frozen ground. Our staff car was almost opposite. I got in and shut the door. It was warm in the vestibule. Our girls didn't economize on the coal they stole from passing freights.

The train started. Slowly, and then faster, the dark cars of the echelon moved past our windows. "Thank you, Lusia." Lord, no one had called me Lusia in ages. Once I left childhood, I left my childhood name behind. Now I was Elena, Lena. And why did I suddenly burst out with Lusia in that heated freight car? Why was my heart, or my soul, or whatever it is that aches, hurting so much? I had no letters from Batanya in Leningrad. No letters from Egorka in Kazakhstan, where his school had been evacuated. He didn't write, but Katya did, the daughter of our gym teacher, who was sent out with the smaller children because she was lame. No letters from Mama.

Only one letter. And I wish it hadn't come. A letter from Mika Obukhovsky. He wrote that Seva . . . Seva was dead. When, he didn't know. Where, he didn't know. He didn't know anything, but he wrote the letter. But it was impossible.

It couldn't be, because it could not be. Seva could not be dead. Mika was lying. I had always suspected that he was in love with me. He would court Nelka or somebody, but he always . . . And now he was lying. It couldn't happen to Seva. I'd been carrying the letter around in my pocket for a week, and like an invocation, I kept repeating, hundreds, maybe thousands of times a day, like a prayer, no, no, no. The wheels said, no, no, no. But in my sleep I heard them say, gone, gone, gone. I woke up; it was no, no, no. I was losing my mind.

Through the window I saw a dark station building, some houses, also dark. Everything was so joyless. I went into the car. The staff room was made up of three compartments with the walls knocked down. A dull lamp glowed, illuminating the portrait. Mustache, thick lips that seemed made up. "Bastard! You bastard! It's all your fault. Everything. Everything." Did I say it or think it? I didn't hear my voice. But I got scared, even if it were only a thought. But it got started and I couldn't stop it. "Bastard. I hate you."

Why, on that day and at that hour, did my hostility go beyond the circle of concrete people to a symbol, to something more generalized? Just as emotionally as before, without thought, historical preparation, study of the materials of congresses and trials, without even reading the speeches to know who said what.

It's complicated! Take Lyova, the husband of Mama's sister, my uncle. He chased me away on the evening of May 27, 1937. Yet by the winter of 1937 I visited them from Leningrad as if I were coming home. His first fear and shock had passed. And my friends visited me in their house, and two-thirds of them were orphans of 1937, like me. Lyova played his violin for us, the Hungarian Dances and the czardas. And when the guests left and the dishes were washed (God forbid breaking a piece of his service!), he sat at the piano and played Rachmaninoff. In the summer of 1939 he and I went to Borovsk to rent a dacha. He would live there with Zorya and Batanya and Egorka. I already had a job, a silly position, as archivist at a factory that kept changing its name—from Communist Party of Germany to Ernest Telmann Factory. On that trip, we had to change trains and spent part of the night in Maloyaroslavets and walked around the town, reading poetry. During the war I visited them in Sverdlovsk and helped them move back to Moscow. Then there was the fight over our things which he wouldn't return. The horrible letter to Mama, when they were trying to catch her and take her away a second time. Normal relations among relatives. An argument in 1968 over the Czech invasion. Andrei moving into our house and Lyova forbidding Anya and Zorya to see us. Now Lyova is eighty-seven years old and as helpless as an infant. I feel sorry for him. And it's painful to listen to him remember one thing and toss another out of his memory for good. Everyone wants to have a "radiant path" behind him toward the end of his life.

54

Batanya, Egorka, and the Nun arrived. Batanya was even more severe than usual, but collected and businesslike. I felt calmer. But she was also nervous, and I could see it because she sometimes moved her lips soundlessly. She tossed her straw hat right on the dining room table and went straight into Mama's room, shutting the door behind her. I felt funny going over to the door to listen in front of Egorka. I might not have done it that way anyway. Egorka began whining, "What am I supposed to do?" I don't think he realized why he had been brought back from the dacha. I took down *Quentin Durward* by Walter Scott from my shelf and handed it to him. In a pedagogic mood, I had told him last month, in Mama's voice, "You're too young for it." He grabbed the book and got lost in it. Batanya spent an hour with Mama, and I didn't know what to do with myself. Then she was closeted in the kitchen with the Nun. Egorka must have tired of reading and disappeared. He went down the hall or to a friend's house. Batanya emerged from the kitchen and sent me to the store. She wasn't like Mama. She gave me a list and money—everything was clear and you couldn't forget anything. I was glad to have something to do. I wanted to act, but not in the store, of course. I didn't know what people did in this situation. Milk, butter, cheese, sausage, bread. At the store I realized that I was hungry. In the bakery I broke off a piece of the roll and ate it right there. "What a pig I am. Mama's in bed staring at the wall, Papa is gone, and I'm chewing."

I put the packages on the kitchen table. Batanya was packing something into her purse. "Feed Egorka and eat, too, and if I'm held up, put him to bed. And don't go anywhere. Understand?"

"Where's the Nun?"

"Not the Nun; you know her name. She's gone. Learn to

manage without a housekeeper." Her lips moved silently and then she said in awe, "A decent person. Amazingly decent."

Batanya left. I put on the Nun's apron and peeled potatoes. I fried them. It's a good thing I learned how to do that at Lida's house. Then I went to find Egorka, who was at Zhorka's house. He left looking stunned and quiet, but I didn't pay attention. I told him to wash his hands while I looked in on Mama. She wasn't moving and I thought she was actually asleep and not pretending. I was holding the frying pan in one hand and serving Egorka with the other when he said, "Look what those enemies of the people are like. Some of them even pretend to be fathers."

I slammed the frying pan down on the plate with a bang and shouted at him, "Just try saying that again, just try it. I don't know what I'll do to you; I'll make mincemeat out of you, I'll . . . I'll . . ." I burst out crying and ran to my room. Everything I had been keeping inside the last twenty-four hours came spilling out. A few minutes later Egorka walked in, and patted me on the head, which made me cry harder.

"Lusia, forgive me. I'm sorry, please, I didn't know."

"What, what didn't you know? That Papa isn't an enemy? How could you even think so? He's a good man. Better than all the ones who haven't been arrested."

"I won't anymore."

"What won't you, you pathetic fool?"

"I won't think that about Papa anymore."

He was so little, so skinny, with his shaved head (Mama's stupid thing about shaving his head every summer; she used to do it to me, too), standing there crying. I bawled even more, now out of pity for him, and said, "Let's go eat."

We were putting away the potatoes and sandwiches, washing them down with tea, when he asked (so persistent!), "What about the others?"

"What others?"

"The others they arrested. Are they enemies?"

"No, nobody's an enemy."

"How do you know?"

I was stumped. How did I know? But once I said so, I couldn't retreat. Especially since our friends and acquaintances—of this I was sure—weren't enemies.

"There are no enemies; it's all lies, believe me."

"Sunarka's father isn't an enemy, either?"

"Of course not."

"That's good." He was Egorka's stamp friend. And in general Egorka liked the Indonesian and Chinese Cominterners. And when Hsu Te-li came, he was beside himself with rapture.

Egorka brought the dishes out to the kitchen, and I washed them very inefficiently. I spilled boiling water on the floor when I was filling the dishpan.

Suddenly I panicked that Egorka would tell everyone that there were no enemies. I told him that we knew that there were no enemies. But he couldn't tell anyone. "And don't you talk to anyone at all."

"What do you mean, I have to be silent forever now?"

"Silly. Don't talk about the enemies. Or about politics."

"Oh! All right, I won't talk about politics."

"Go to bed."

"May I read?"

"You may." He was still in the kitchen. "What are you hanging around for?"

"Lusia, give me *Quentin Durward*. Can it be my book now? All right?"

"All right."

And that's how we would leave our father's house, because our father's house was gone. He with Scott, and I with Mayakovsky.

Epilogue

I finished this manuscript in the summer of 1989. Andrei read it in early September and said warmly, with just a tinge of envy, "You write better than I do." I replied, "You're exaggerating!" But I felt happy.

That night, as if there had been no break in our conversation, he said that now he knew them all: Batanya and Nura, my father and mother. He called my mother Ruf Grigoryevna, the way he always had. He said he could imagine her easily now—young and intransigent, but basically as he had known her. And then he said, "You were born of your grandmother, even though you had an Armenian character."

I replied that he was also his grandmother's child, and that I loved the grandmother and the Sakharov in him, but rather feared the Sofiano element in him—I thought it cold. Andrei said I was probably right, but he had never thought about it. And then he said how much he regretted that his mother had never had the opportunity to open up so fully and happily in her love for her grandchildren as mine had. And how empty our house had become without my mother. If he had known how empty it became without him! How icy it had become! Not a house, but a shelter! I didn't know either. As I lay next to him, I scolded myself for not finding the time to go through Mama's papers.

The next night (the days were always devoted to other people's affairs; it was that way when Andrei was alive, and it's the same now, without him) I sat down on the floor by Mama's desk and spread out its contents on the floor, as I had right after the forty-day anniversary of her death. Her work record book. Her pass to the clinic. A certificate from the Industrial Academy, where Mama had studied before her arrest. A certificate from the Gymnasium. In the space for "class" a naive student hand had erased "merchant" and written "bourgeoisie." A box of photos. Old and yellowed on hard cardboard. Mama's family in the middle of the last century. And new ones, of the children and grandchildren. Letters. From grandmother, from me, a thin packet of letters from the grandchildren, and an even thinner one of letters from Igor, Egorka. A separate pile from her girlfriends, all former inmates of the camps. And in a cellophane wrapper, notices of rehabilitation, for Papa and for her, with the standard formula: "rehabilitated for absence of proof of crime." And next to them, two death certificates. Igor—Egorka—senior assistant to the captain of a big Soviet freighter, had died suddenly in Bombay on June 19, 1976. And Papa's, which did not indicate where he had died. I remembered the May morning when he left the house for the last time, young and smiling. Where, how had he been arrested? His secretary told us that Papa had been called into the NKVD for a business conversation. And that was it! A telephone call crossed out a life. What happened to him beyond that line?

I shut my eyes and as I had in my childhood, when I told Egorka that the shadows running along the ceiling and walls of our dark nursery were a movie that I was showing him, I showed myself a movie about my life.

Childhood. Well off. Normal. Papa and Mama had their work, friends, the Party, love, and us, the children. I don't know in what order to put them. Was their love first? Or us? Or the Party? A happy family. A happy childhood. (A tangential thought—the critics, both left and right, would really let me have it for that happy childhood if the manuscript ever became a book. They'd bring up everything including the poster in the school lobby: "Thank you to Comrade Stalin for our happy childhood." Mama and her child-rearing methods. Papa who was in charge of personnel at the Comintern and read Blok and the banned Gumilyov. And even my grandmother in her white hat and silk coat.)

May 1937. We were moved. To a rather spacious room on the same floor. And a brick red seal appeared on our old door. Later the boys and I stole Batanya's trunk and books from there. Then Batanya went to Leningrad with Egorka (and the trunk). I wrote Seva a letter and he flew back from Essentuki. In late August just before the schoolyear began, Mama sent me to Leningrad. She was expecting to be arrested and every day of freedom was becoming more and more intolerable for her. On October 29 Matvei, Mama's brother, was arrested in Leningrad. They searched for a long time, and the gray Leningrad dawn was glimmering when they took him away. Heavy large snowflakes were falling. I stood on the windowsill and stuck my head out the open small pane within the big window. I saw Matvei look back at our windows with a bewildered smile on his face. Maybe he was holding back tears.

That evening Batanya sent me to Moscow to rent Mama a room somewhere in the outskirts and to bring her there with the help of the boys. We took a room in Maly Yaroslavets. We moved the bed, some dishes, and her huge drafting table. Mama said she would go to Leningrad with me. This was during the November holidays for the anniversary of the Revolution. She spent three days with us and then left, promising Batanya not to return to the Luxe, but to stay in Maly Yaroslavets. A while later Anya called and said that Mama wouldn't come out of her room at the Luxe and was waiting to be arrested. Batanya sent me back to Moscow. This was early December.

Mama was no longer on our floor in the main building but in a tiny room in the NEPman building, a room the size of a train compartment, with Lusya Chernina's mother. The night I arrived, Lusya's mother was arrested. They came very matter-of-factly and took her away. I went to see Seva during the day and when I returned Mama was gone. She came home an hour or so later. She said she was frozen stiff—she had been walking with Papa's friend Surik-Suren. (I knew him well, but can't remember his surname now.) She took a chocolate bar from her pocket, a thick one. I boiled water for tea and tried to persuade her to go to Maly Yaroslavets. After all, that was why I had come to Moscow—on Batanya's orders. Mama said nothing, and I knew that she wouldn't go. That she couldn't wait to be arrested, as if it were the way out of the state she had been in since Papa's arrest. We had tea, but we didn't touch the chocolate. She must have forgotten about it, and I didn't dare bring it up. Then I went to wash in the bathroom at the end of the corridor. As I was coming back, I saw two soldiers in our doorway.

I entered the room with them. Mama said in a resounding voice, "Well, that's it." She was still wearing Papa's purple-blue shirt. She quickly pulled a sweater over it and took her suitcase, packed long ago, from beneath the bed. As she threw her leather coat from Torgsin onto her shoulders, she turned to me. I was astonished by the radiance of her face and by the smile she gave me. She embraced me and kissed me several times and whispered barely audibly, "I have only you, only a daughter, no son. Never mention Egorka; they'll take him away."

She smiled and gently pushed me aside. She went out the door, and one soldier immediately followed her. The other looked around the room and then said, "Tomorrow we'll come back for your brother." He left without closing the door. The corridor was very quiet. I shut the door and saw the chocolate bar on the table. I put it in my pocket. I took the tiny case that I had brought from Leningrad. I tiptoed down the corridor to the backstairs and out into the courtyard. I never set foot in the Luxe again.

I called Seva from a telephone booth—I was afraid to go to his place. We met at the metro and went to the Leningrad railroad station. It was one a.m., and the mail train to Leningrad left at two. A ticket for an unreserved seat cost a little over sixty rubles. We kissed on the platform. When it was time, I got in and climbed up onto the third (luggage) shelf in the car and cried, nibbling on the squares of chocolate to cover the taste of my salty tears. Decades later Mama would tell me that she dreamed about that chocolate bar in prison . . .

It was December 10, 1937. Election day was on the twelfth—the first election under the new Stalin Constitution.

The words *arrest, prison, parcel, camp, exile* had become part of my life. The line at Butyrki Prison and a money transfer to Mama. A line at Lefortovo and then at Lubyanka prisons (I don't remember which of the two came first), a money transfer to Papa. You shove fifty rubles (worth only kopecks today) through the window and hold your breath, worried that they won't accept it. I didn't have a passport; you get one when you're sixteen. And I was even more worried that they weren't there anymore. And every day on the way home from school the piercing moment of hope, that Mama was home. The only other time I loved Mama as passionately as I did then was in the last months of her life.

In March 1938 they didn't accept my money for Papa and the thread connecting us—the fifty rubles—which I could almost feel with my hand, broke off forever.

A year and a half later, Mama's first letter came. The return address was ALZHIR—not a geographical location, but an acronym standing for the Akmolinsky Camp for Wives of Traitors to the Homeland. Mama's letters. "Study hard." "Help your grandmother." "Be a model Komsomol." "Take care of Egorka." Not a word about my love. Or my banishment from Moscow. Or my separation from Seva. And just before I graduated—getting harder every hour—"It would be good if you became a doctor. It's a profession that can come in handy everywhere, even in the camps." How can you answer letters like that? With a teenager's cruelty, I thought that it would be better to have no letters. I was studying hard anyway, and helping Grandmother—shopping, laundry, cleaning, washing the floors, and working as a cleaning woman in our building. But I told Batanya not to write about my job.

And I did belong to the Komsomol. When they tried to expel me because of my parents, I didn't turn in my card and fought for and got the right to keep it. I went to Moscow to the Komsomol Central Committee.

One of Mama's letters contained a note for Mikoyan, in which she asked him to save Papa, or at least learn something about him. It said that Papa had always been faithful to the Party and something else I do not remember. Mama asked Batanya to get this note to Mikoyan (she used only his first name, Anastas) personally. I was the one to go to Moscow—to their dacha in Serebryanny Bor. First I spoke with Ashkhen, his wife, who was very kind to me, perhaps excessively so. Then Anastas arrived and we had a private conversation. He said there was nothing he could do; he couldn't even find out anything. I had to trust him. And then he said that he and Ashkhen would like to have Egorka and

me live with them, to sort of adopt us. This insulted me and got
me almost as mad as had the organizer at the Komsomol meeting
who proposed that I renounce my parents, since they were traitors. I replied very harshly, almost rudely. After that meeting I did
not see him until the summer of 1954, when he summoned me
from Leningrad by government telegram so that I could learn
something about the fate of my parents.

Mama was soon allowed to have parcels sent to the camp—ten
kilograms every three months. We sent them to her friends as
well, whose addresses she gave us. They were the Polish women
from the Comintern, and Liza Drabkina and Olya Dmitrenko
(Chernomordik's widow), whose son I told twenty years later
that she was his real mother. Once Mama sent us the address of
a man named Volkov. Up to that point I had thought that only
women were in the camps. We packed inexpensive things—
bacon, shag tobacco, heavy men's underwear, sugar, and cookies.
I did the shopping. But when it came time to send a parcel to
Mama, Batanya would unlock her trunk (I don't think that she
locked it to keep us out; it's just that she had her "rules"), take
something out, and go to the second-hand store to sell it. When
she returned, she would take hunter's sausage, blue tins of caviar,
canned brisket, thin woolen underwear, expensive cigarettes, and
chocolate out of her traveling bag (the one she gave me when I
was called in for interrogation). Packing the parcels and nailing
shut the crates was my job. During the packing, my mouth wa-
tered: we had forgotten the taste of our favorite foods in those
years. Sometimes I tucked one sausage into my pocket, bending
it in half, and then fed it to Egorka without even tasting it, because
by the time I could get at it without Batanya seeing, I was feeling
guilty. In one letter Mama asked for a small mirror and tweezers.
For some reason that got me mad and the night before I sent the
parcel I plucked my eyebrows for the first time in my life. Batanya
said something I'll never forget. "Are you preparing to become
somebody's bedroom property?"

The return address on the parcels was ours, the sender's name
was mine, and the surname corresponded to the surname of the
recipient. We did this to get around the law that permitted prison-

ers to get parcels only from their relatives. I don't know how the camp authorities allowed our parcels through to Mama's friends. It was such an obvious trick.

You could mail the packages only beyond the hundred-kilometer limit around Leningrad, that was the regulation. Egorka and I could not handle more than three at once—I took two and he took one. We had to travel by trolley and then train to Tolmachevo. It was 105 kilometers outside Leningrad and the post office was right by the station. Once we turned in the parcels and shook our stiffened hands, we could lie under the pine trees by the station or walk in the woods. That was in the summertime. In the winter, by the time we finished up, it would be getting dark and cold. We'd stand on the platform, stamping our frozen feet and dreaming that the train would come soon. The trains weren't heated but they were warmed by all the people in them.

I finished school and ended up at the journalism department at university. The admissions committee didn't pass me—my parents were traitors to the homeland. But I didn't take offense. I went to the Herzen Pedagogical Institute to study Russian literature. I picked a school with evening courses—I had to work.

Then came the war, the infantry, I was wounded. After recovering I was transferred to work on a hospital train: wounded soldiers and bombing raids, bombing raids and wounded soldiers. And night after night without my only hope—to sleep through the night. But that wasn't terrible. The horror lay ahead—Seva's death, on February 26, 1942. In the village of Myasnaya near Lyuban. How did I keep from breaking then? Or perhaps I did break? After all, with him I also lost the treasure that had been entrusted to me by God or by love. And also my rosy, light world view. It came back to me only with the birth of my daughter. I had it when I wrote this book. And when Andrei died it left again, this time probably never to return.

In the summer of 1988 Andrei and I were driving to Leningrad. Between Malaya Vishera and Lyuban, there are mass graves along the right side of the road. Many of them. Innumerable. We stopped and walked among the monuments, reading the inscriptions. Soldiers and officers of the Second Strike Army. Seva's. I wandered unnoticed into the forest and without thinking about it started picking strawberry flowers for a bouquet for Andrei. The way I used to collect them for Seva and his mother. It was all jumbled up, Andrei and Seva. As I bent down for a berry, a tear fell on my hand. I came back, handing the berries to Andrei. He gave me a bouquet of blue flowers, and I saw that his eyes were damp, too.

On May 30, 1942, Batanya died in the siege of Leningrad. I felt guilty for the first time in my life. The guilt has never left me—I wasn't with her! I had thought that Defending the Homeland (it was always capitalized) was my only duty. So many years passed before I understood that we have other duties. Everyone has his own! I saved the postcards she sent to me from Leningrad during the blockade: "Write to your mother," "Take care of Egorka," "If I manage to save Natasha, I deserve a monument." She did save Natasha. Now, Batanya's youngest granddaughter is a grandmother herself.

Mama's sister, Anya, decided that we shouldn't write to her about Batanya's death. I stopped sending letters to Mama completely. But I continued the parcels to her and to my other protégés. All through the war I set aside two of the three crackers we got in our daily rations (they were flavorful when you soaked them), and I set aside sugar and all the shag tobacco. Maybe that's why I didn't start smoking in the army, because I thought the tobacco would help Mama survive.

Egorka. When the war started he was thirteen. He was evacuated from Leningrad with his boarding school. From there he was taken to the "labor front." I found him in Omsk at a huge factory—he was working as an unqualified machine tool operator. He was a tiny, wrinkled old man, dystrophic, who had miraculously survived in some hospital where he had had dysentery. The director of the factory did not want to give him up—"he was mobilized into the labor reserves." I used all the words I had learned by then and even grabbed my pistol. When I got the director to agree to his leaving, it turned out that Egorka had no clothing for going outside. The black workshirt, full of holes, that he wore without an undershirt was all he had. He slept at the factory because he could have frozen to death on the way to the dormitory—some of the kids actually had died that way. I said I would find some clothing for him at the military headquarters (it was the officers there who had turned up Egorka for me) and come back for him. He clutched at me like a baby and practically wept, "Lusia, don't leave me here." God, he didn't believe that I'd come back. I took off everything I was wearing, down to my bra. I put two army shirts and a jacket on him, wrapped his shirt around his head, put my coat onto my naked body, and we walked in the minus-forty-degree weather to the trolley, which took us to the station, where we waited for my hospital train. He became a civilian orderly on military hospital train 122. I was terrified of bombing raids—I was at one end of the train and he was at the other. I was always worried about him. The wounded men loved him, especially the ones with head injuries. The presence of a boy calmed them down somehow.

A year later he entered the Maritime School in Arkhangelsk. And a year after that he was going to be court-martialed—on a trip he and two other boys stole some fish from the hold, fried it, and ate it. They were hungry. Fortunately, my boss let me go and I reached Arkhangelsk before the trial. With the help of the political director of the school (there were some good ones) I managed to get Egorka and his friends released and sent as ordinary sailors, without rank, into the fleet.

In August 1945 I went to visit Mama—the first time I had seen her in more than seven years. Three officers were traveling with me, and one of them turned out to be the procurator of Mama's camp. He gave me permission for a two-week visit—extraordinary! He must have been embarrassed—he was a man who spent four years overseeing a women's camp in Kazakhstan while I, a young woman, was in the active army.

Mama's hair was shorn after her typhus; it was short and curly, and she seemed very pretty and merry. The joy of our meeting was mixed with a certain alienation. I later learned that I didn't have that problem only with Mama, but with everyone I went to visit. It was an inexplicable inner tension that I covered up with forced liveliness. And here there was the additional burden of being forced to lie about Batanya. Mama's sister insisted that I tell her that Batanya was blind and living with her. I obeyed (because it is difficult to tell about death). It's a good thing that Mama's campmates were all around. It was a mixed camp with free communication and fraternization within the compound. That's where I met Volkov. He wasn't a political prisoner but he helped many of the women in her barracks. That's how he ended up on her list.

In December, Mama's eight-year term ended. I don't remember why, but she was being released from the camp in February. I had polished the floor and decided to keep the New Year's tree up until she could see it. When the bell rang and I opened the door, I thought she was a beggar and I offered her some change and a piece of bread. That mistake still hurts.

Mama wasn't allowed to live in Leningrad after the camps, but with the help of my friends, young poets, I got her a job as matron at the Writers' Union Pioneer camp in Luga. She lived there in the summer and in the winter secretly in my room. I had several girlfriends sharing my room then, because they all had problems with housing. They had returned to Leningrad after having been evacuated for the duration of the war. Some of the houses were now occupied by others; some had been bombed out of existence. They greeted Mama warmly, but she was withdrawn and secretive. I could tell that she didn't share our postwar jollity and didn't approve of our way of life. Parties, dances, poets, students from the Military Medical Academy. While she managed to make contact with some of the girls, there was an impassable barrier between us. Now I understand that each of us had her own experiences. She had the death of her husband, prison, and camp. I had my own losses and, as it seemed then, a completely different life. Neither of us knew how to be open with the other, and I didn't want that. I was annoyed by the way Mama still treated me like the fourteen-year-old she had left, and her questions drove me crazy: "Where are you going?" "When will you be back?" "Where have you been gallivanting?"

I wanted to shout "Go to hell!" every time she said something to me, but I controlled myself. And I think that proximity breeds compassion. The way we felt for one of the girls who was always pilfering the few things we had. We all knew she was the one, but we didn't force her out. Where would she go? Out onto the street? Thank God, one day she stole something and disappeared from the dormitory that my room, large in the Petersburg style, with polished floors and windows onto St. Isaac's, had become.

Sometimes Egorka came around. He was in service on the Baltic and he spent leave in Leningrad. As soon as he entered the house he would whisper to me, "Tell her not to kiss me." (He never said "Mama.") And I would reply angrily, "Tell her yourself!"

I decided to get him out of the navy and went to see Admiral Stepanov. I whined about my invalid condition and helplessness and flirted openly to a disgusting degree. He released him from the navy and gave him permission to take admission exams to any naval college, but Egorka didn't have a graduation certificate from school. We mobilized my girlfriend's brother, a famous physicist. And my friend, too—she had already graduated from the Herzen Institute and had taught Russian and Russian literature in evacuation. Most important, we found a "friend" in the admissions commission of the Military Medical Academy through the daughter of the Academy's deputy director who was having an affair with one of our friends. Egorka got in, but he was expelled a few days later because he sneaked off somewhere during the obligatory two-week quarantine.

I went back to the admiral. First he said, "That's it. There's nothing I can do." But I convinced him to allow Egorka to enter the Military Physical Culture Institute, which had just opened. Egorka had been a boxer in the navy and even had some standing in the sport. The admiral gave permission, and Egorka was registered at the institute on the basis of his admissions exams to the Military Medical Academy. It no longer mattered that the exams had been fixed. Few things made me happier than getting Egorka into college. I thought that all my sisterly obligations were fulfilled. And that Mama should be grateful to me for making life so easy for her sonny boy. Boy, was I pushing it—expecting gratitude!

In those years I was in and out of hospitals constantly. They all were very concerned about my eyes and recommended that I learn Braille while I could still see. I got tired of it, just as I was sick and tired of my studies at the Herzen Pedagogical Institute. I didn't study hard. Since I wasn't really planning to be a teacher, I decided to switch to medicine. In the army I had developed a love, even a passion, for nursing. And I'm certain that my personality (at least when I was young) was that of a typical "nursie." But I wasn't about to go to a medical vocational school when I was halfway to a college degree, albeit in philology. Mama stood firm: "You're sick. You'll go blind!" That made me dig in harder and I studied for the entrance exams. I passed very well, but the medical commission turned me down. My eyes again! I made an enormous row at the office before the man in charge of admissions for all institutions of higher learning in Leningrad—there used to be a job like that. And I became a student at the First Leningrad Medical Institute.

In my third year I decided to have a baby. The doctors were against it, and Mama was with them. In the heat of an argument with her I shouted something I had not thought about before. I told her that she wanted me to live like an invalid and to spite her I would live like a healthy person. After that she wouldn't talk to me for several days. It was during that time that it occurred to me that there was some truth in what I had said.

Tanya was born, and she quieted us down immediately. But Mama kept me away from her in a funny way. It was a petty thing—she wouldn't let me bathe her. I was sincerely happy when Mama got sick and had to spend several days in bed. Tanya was almost a month old before I got to bathe her myself for the first time.

We stopped being strangers then, but minor skirmishes, and even major arguments, continued to occur. She wasn't very pleased by my first marriage. She barely put up with the father of my children and treated him unfairly, with a hint of the snobbery with which Batanya treated her sons-in-law and daughter-in-law. But it was not important in my mother's life; it was peripheral. Only the grandchildren mattered. It was amazing how much warmth and inner radiance she had preserved for them. And the grandchildren gave her great-grandchildren. Little kids say, "My mother is the best." I always want to amend that a bit to "My mother is the best grandmother."

Initially, Mama was rather reserved with Andrei. But perhaps that was just the manner she had then of appearing cool, a kind of "social" pose which disappeared toward the end of her life. But the more complicated and then the more frightening our life became, the closer Mama drew to us.

During our exile in Gorky it was astonishing how she was able to mobilize her physical and spiritual energies to visit us, to deal with the world press, to go live with her grandchildren. She spent seven years in the United States, traveled to Europe, and never stopped worrying about us. Her letters could be bitter when she complained about her loneliness. Along with her great worry for the future of her grandchildren, I could tell that she felt unneeded in their lives. I thought that was unfair toward Tanya and Alyosha. And even though she didn't come right out and ask to live with us in Gorky, her desire was evident in the context of her letters. However, I didn't dare take her into exile with us.

And then we returned to Moscow. It seemed natural for Mama to live in her own house with us, with Andrei and me. Tanya brought Mama to Moscow in June, and in December she died. We had only six months to be together.

Why had she faded so quickly? Should she not have returned? Was the separation from her grandchildren and great-grandchildren unbearable? Or maybe it's just too much to change your entire life style at the age of eighty? The questions arose after the funeral, and I will never be able to answer them. But Mama's notebook is about loneliness, just as were her letters from America to Gorky.

But I won't speak for Mama. Let her speak for herself, from her notes of August and September, 1987:

> I'm starting to adjust. I'd gotten used to living alone . . . (just as I once got used to sleeping alone). And I've found a pastime—the television. I never liked it much before. I'm reading

less—my eyes get tired and my brain and memory aren't what they were. The older children [that's Andrei and I!—E.B.] sometimes take me for a ride—that's a great amusement for me too—I love looking at the "wide world" from the car window.

They're basically happy, very busy, and closely welded to each other. They don't need anyone else around; they're happy together. The only thing that worries them is being separated (the children in the USA), and well, of course, A.D.'s children.

Sometimes I listen to good music. Greig, Beethoven, Mozart. My soul grows still and my reason weakens. It (music) had never caused such agitation before. I've stopped listening now; I'm afraid of this new anxiety. I live as if I were playing mute. . . . And yet I desperately want someone close to me, without irritation. . . . For the last few days I've been unable to give up telling myself stories. So many ruined lives will remain after me. . . . I didn't defend them with a single word, or even a memory. . . . I keep silent, I keep silent and torment myself with how things are now and they were a long time ago. Now I do nothing and, most important, I don't want to do anything. I've crawled into my solitude as if it were a black hole. I've sunk into the past and I'm perishing in it. I was pushed into it by the pure and long-suffering Igor Pyatnitsky [our friend and the son of one of the leading Comintern workers—E.B.] with his stories about the investigator who was in charge of the Comintern cases. . . . There was one notation that he had killed Comrade A. during an interrogation. I'm certain that it was Gevork. . . .

My daughter feels that seeing people (Igor Pyatnitsky) is bad for me. What a stupid doctor she is. How could I possibly learn anything from anyone that would be more horrible than my own life. . . . I feel that I am in solitary confinement.

That was Mama's last notebook. I really did argue with Igor Pyatnitsky, telling him not to talk so much about 1937, the arrests, the interrogations, the investigations, because after each visit Mama's blood pressure went up or she had heart trouble. I tried to avoid the whole topic with Mama, seeing how upset she would get. But now I think I was wrong. Nothing I could have done would have spared Mama from thinking of the past. Just as you can't protect yourself from feeling guilty toward the dead, if only because they are dead and you are alive. Mama felt guilty toward her mother because her fate ricocheted into her mother's life. I feel guilty toward my mother for my life and my happiness. Mothers and daughters! Mothers and daughters.

March 24, 1991

Index

A Note About the Author

Elena Bonner was born on February 15, 1923, in
Moscow. She volunteered for army duty in 1941 and
served at the front, where she suffered head wounds
causing near-blindness in her right eye and failing vision
in her left. In 1950 she married Ivan Vasilyevich
Semyonov, with whom she had two children. She
graduated in 1953 from the First Leningrad Medical
Institute and practiced as a district doctor, a pediatrician,
and as a foreign aid health worker in Iraq. After Stalinism
was denounced, Bonner joined the Communist Party in
1965. During the next few years, she became increasingly
involved with the political underground and in 1970, at
the trial of a fellow dissident, Bonner met Andrei D.
Sakharov, the leader of the Soviet human rights
movement and winner of the Nobel Prize for Peace in
1975. They were married in 1971. From 1980 to 1986
they lived in Gorky, the city to which Sakharov had been
exiled by the Soviet authorities. Elena Bonner's *Alone Together* (1987) is a memoir of those years. Since her husband's death in 1989, Bonner has continued as one of the
leaders of the democratic movement in the Soviet Union.

A Note on the Type

The text of this book was set in Plantin, a type face
cut in 1913 by The Monotype Corporation, London.
Though the face bears the name of the great Christopher
Plantin, who in the latter part of the sixteenth century
owned, in Antwerp, the largest printing and publishing
firm in Europe, it is a rather free adaptation of
designs by Claude Garamond (c. 1480–1561) made for
that firm. With its strong, simple lines, Plantin is a
no-nonsense face of exceptional legibility.

Composed by ComCom, a division of The Haddon
Craftsmen, Inc., Allentown, Pennsylvania
Printed and bound by Fairfield Graphics,
Fairfield, Pennsylvania
Title page photograph by Patrick J. H. Aison
Designed by Anthea Lingeman